Creation, Fall, Restoration:

A Biblical Theology of Creation

To my son, Jordan,

Remember your Creator in the days of your youth …

(ECCLESIASTES 12:1)

Creation, Fall, Restoration:
A Biblical Theology of Creation

ANDREW S. KULIKOVSKY

•

MENTOR

Copyright © Andrew S. Kulikovsky 2009

10 9 8 7 6 5 4 3 2 1

ISBN 978-1-84550-446-5

First published in 2009
in the
Mentor Imprint
by
Christian Focus Publications Ltd,
Geanies House, Fearn, Ross–shire
IV20 1TW, Scotland
www.christianfocus.com

Cover design by Paul Lewis
Printed by Bell and Bain, Ltd., Glasgow

Mixed Sources
Product group from well-managed
forests and other controlled sources
www.fsc.org Cert no. TT-COC-002769
© 1996 Forest Stewardship Council

TABLE OF CONTENTS

ABBREVIATIONS

AUSS	Andrew University Seminary Series
BAGD	W. Arndt, F.W. Gingrich, F.W. Danker, and W. Bauer, *A Greek-English Lexicon of the New Testament and Other Early Christian literature*, 2nd edition, University of Chicago Press, Chicago, 1979
BBC	Beacon Bible Commentary
BDB	F. Brown, S.R. Driver, and C.A. Briggs, *A Hebrew and English Lexicon of the Old Testament*, Clarendon Press, Oxford, 1953
BETS	*Bulletin of the Evangelical Theological Society*
BSac	*Bibliotheca Sacra*
CBQ	*Catholic Biblical Quarterly*
CRSQ	*Creation Research Society Quarterly*
CSR	*Christian Scholar's Review*
CTJ	*Calvin Theological Journal*
CT	*Christianity Today*
DBSJ	*Detroit Baptist Seminary Journal*
EBC	Expositor's Bible Commentary
EvQ	*Evangelical Quarterly*
ESV	English Standard Version
ETS	Evangelical Theological Society
GJ	*Grace Journal*
GKC	E. Kautzsch and A.E. Cowley (editors), *Gesenius' Hebrew Grammar*, 2nd edition, Clarendon Press, Oxford, 1910
GTJ	*Grace Theological Journal*
HALOT	L. Koehler and W. Baumgartner, *The Hebrew and Aramaic Lexicon of the Old Testament*, E.J. Brill, Leiden, 1994
HS	*Hebrew Studies*
Holladay	W.L. Holladay, *A Concise Hebrew and Aramaic Lexicon of the Old Testament*, Eerdmans, Grand Rapids, Michigan, 1988

IBHS Bruce K. Waltke and M. O'Connor, *Introduction to Biblical Hebrew Syntax*, Eisenbrauns, Winona Lake, Indiana, 1990

IBRIRep Interdisciplinary Biblical Research Institute Research Report

ICC International Critical Commentary

ICR Institute for Creation Research

JASA *Journal of the American Scientific Affiliation*

JBL *Journal of Biblical Literature*

JoC *Journal of Creation*

JETS *Journal of the Evangelical Theological Society*

JMT *Journal of Ministry and Theology*

JSOT *Journal for the Study of the Old Testament*

TWAT E. Jenni and C. Westermann (editors), *Theologisches Handwözum Alten Testament*, Theologischer Verlag, Zurich/Munich, 1971

Louw-Nida J.P. Louw and E.A. Nida, *Greek-English lexicon of the New Testament: Based on semantic domains*, 2nd edition, United Bible societies, New York, 1989

NAB New American Bible

NASB New American Standard Bible

NEB New English Bible

NET New English Translation

NIV New International Version

NICOT New International Commentary on the Old Testament

NICNT New International Commentary on the New Testament

NIGTC New International Greek Testament Commentary

NIDOTTE Willem A. Van Gemeren, *New International Dictionary of Old Testament Theology and Exegesis*, 5 volumes, Zondervan, Grand Rapids, Michigan, 1997

NIVAC NIV Application Commentary

NJV New Jewish Version

NPNF	Nicene and Post Nicene Fathers
NRSV	New Revised Standard Version
OTL	Old Testament Library
PC	*Philosophia Christi*
PSCF	*Perspectives on Science and the Christian Faith*
RelS	*Religious Studies*
TDOT	G.J. Botterweck and H. Ringgren (editors), *Theological Dictionary of the Old Testament*, Eerdmans, Grand Rapids, Michigan, 1990
TMC	*The Master's Current*
TMSJ	*The Master's Seminary Journal*
TS	*Theological Studies*
TWOT	R. Laird Harris, Gleason L. Archer and Bruce K. Waltke (editors), *Theological Wordbook of the Old Testament*, 2 volumes, Moody, Chicago, 1980
VT	*Vetus Testamentum*
Wallace	D.B. Wallace, *Greek Grammar Beyond the Basics*, Zondervan, Grand Rapids, Michigan, 1995
WBC	Word Biblical Commentary
WTJ	*Westminster Theological Journal*
Zerwick	Maximilian Zerwick, *Biblical Greek*, Pontifical Biblical Institute, Rome, 1963

Acknowledgments

Praise to the living God,
the Creator of the universe, and the Savior of humanity.
Without Him, I can do nothing, let alone complete this project.

Thanks to my loving wife, Debby,
who has had to share me with my books and my computer
for the last ten years.

Thanks to my parents, Mykola and Doreen,
who nurtured me spiritually as a child and
instilled in me a deep love for God and His Word.

Preface

This book is the product of five years' intensive research. The motivation to write it came from a realization that many evangelicals — from the professional biblical scholar down to the average parishioner — no longer read the early chapters of Genesis as a straightforward historical account of the creation of the universe and the formation of everything in it. Instead, evangelicals have tended to follow more liberal theologians in reinterpreting the creation narrative as either a metaphor for 'God-directed' evolution, or some kind of analogical story, or, more recently, as a 'literary framework.' Despite being the orthodox and dominant interpretation throughout church history, the straightforward historical account is now a minority view — at least among trained theologians and pastors.

I believe the main reason for this theological and hermeneutical reorientation is due to a general ignorance of either theology or science — or both! Having talked with many Christians with a scientific background, they seem to have very little grasp of the philosophy of science, and very little appreciation of the epistemic basis for both scientific knowledge and biblical revelation. In other words, they have a philosophical blind-spot: they cannot see that scientific knowledge is not the absolute truth they think it is or wish it to be. Yet many Christians — and especially those with theological training — seem completely intimidated by scientific data and the truth-claims of leading scientists. It is almost a case of 'scientists say …' equals 'God says …' and theologians, lacking the confidence to question these truth-claims, just accept them at face value. Moreover, Christians who hold to the ultimate authority and inerrancy of Scripture feel that the creation and flood accounts must be reinterpreted to fit the scientific consensus, lest their high view of Scripture be undermined by 'scientific fact.' In other words, it is their desire to save the Bible from being contradicted by scientific fact that has led them to reinterpret the early chapters of Genesis.

Those Christians who feel the need to do this, however, are rarely ever consistent. The same hermeneutic is never applied to the gospels. Like the creation account, the virgin birth, Christ's miracles, and His bodily resurrection are also scientifically impossible, yet evangelicals have no problem accepting the record of these events as straightforward historical accounts. Christians need to realize that all science is provisional. The history of science reveals that scientists are often wrong — indeed, spectacularly so! Furthermore, science is confined to revealing truth about the *natural* world. Science is, by definition, incapable of revealing truth about the *supernatural* world. Science is not the enemy of Scripture — it just complements it.

This book, however, is not just concerned with the defence of the traditional orthodox interpretation of the creation and flood accounts. It also looks at our present relationship with the created order and our role as God's stewards of His creation. This is particularly topical at present in light of the earth's increasing population and associated pollution, and the allegations of human-induced 'climate change' and its detrimental effects. Furthermore, it looks at the future of the created order and its eventual restoration at the consummation of the kingdom of God.

It should be noted that this book is first and foremost a theological and exegetical work that directly deals with the text of Scripture and presupposes that it is authoritative and inerrant in the autographs. I have chosen to leave the science to the scientists. Apart from a few passing references where relevant, it does not deal with any scientific arguments.

It should also be noted that although I am critical of many of my fellow Christians' views on these topics, it is not at all my intention to cast doubt on their salvation or their devotion to Christ. My objections are aimed at their ideas, not their persons. I have made every attempt to accurately represent their views and present their arguments in the strongest terms possible. I have read far too many works that totally misrepresent the traditional orthodox young-earth creationist position and I do not wish to commit the same error.

Finally, I would like to thank Dr Carl Wieland and Dr Jonathan Sarfati from Creation Ministries International for their encouragement and support, and Dr William Barrick from The Master's Seminary for his substantial feedback on an earlier draft of this work. Any errors, of course, are my own.

Andrew S. Kulikovksy
November 2008
Adelaide, South Australia

CHAPTER I

Why a *Biblical* Theology of Creation?

WHY a biblical theology of creation? Is such a project necessary or even warranted? Should not the task of studying the physical creation be assigned to the scientist rather than the theologian? Should not the task of the theologian be the exposition of the gospel of Jesus Christ?

The book of Genesis, in its very first chapter, states that it was God Himself who brought the world and everything in it into existence. Thus, it is not unreasonable to examine in detail what God Himself has said regarding His creation through His special revelation to mankind — the Bible.

Creation is often viewed as a peripheral doctrine — one that is not essential to the Christian faith and is only taught in a few chapters. Yet, apart from the early chapters of Genesis, the doctrine of creation is one of the major themes of the Psalms, and referred to many times by Jesus and the New Testament authors.[1] Indeed, the total number of Scriptures referring to creation is astonishing.[2] While it is true that belief in the biblical account of creation is not necessary for salvation, these Scriptures form the foundation upon which the gospel is built.

In fact, as one begins to study the Scriptures and the theology of the gospel, it becomes increasingly clear that the doctrine of creation is fundamental to Christian theology.[3] As G. Van Groningen succinctly put it, '[a] proper understanding of the beginning is crucially important for the entire Bible.'[4] Francis Schaeffer also noted the centrality and importance of a sound doctrine

---

1 e.g. Matt. 19:3–5; Mark 10:6–8; John 17:24; Rom. 1:20; 8:19–22; Eph. 1:4; Heb. 4:3; 2 Pet. 3:4–5; Rev. 3:14.

2 It should be kept in mind that the truth and importance of a doctrine does not depend on the amount of Scripture which directly affirms it. The doctrine of the Trinity, for example, can hardly be called a non-essential, yet it is only explicitly affirmed by a handful of verses.

3 Bernard Ramm, *The Christian View of Science and Scripture* (London: Paternoster, 1955), 26. This is not a new idea. The Apostles' Creed (first or second century A.D.) and the Nicene Creed (A.D. 325) both affirmed the doctrine of creation as primary. Creation was also a central element of Thomas Aquinas's *Summa Theologica* (1265–1273), and the Strasburg Reformer, Wolfgang Capito, wrote in 1539 that an understanding of creation is 'the head of divine philosophy' (cited in Douglas F. Kelly, *Creation and Change* [Fearn, Scotland, Christian Focus Publications, 1997], 16). Creation was also affirmed in the Westminster Confession of Faith (1646).

4 G. Van Groningen, 'Interpretation of Genesis' *JETS* 13/4 (Fall 1970), 218.

of creation: 'Christianity as a system does not begin with Christ as Savior, but with the infinite-personal God who created the world in the beginning and who made man significant in the flow of history.'[5] Schaeffer lamented that creation was 'the first category that many churches either failed or refused to recognize.' He continued: '... these people do not realize that they are lost evangelically. ... This lostness is answered by the existence of a Creator. So Christianity does not begin with accepting Christ as Saviour, but with In the beginning God created the heavens and the earth. ... That is the answer to the twentieth century and its lostness (the original cause of all lostness) and the answer in the death of Christ.'[6] Indeed, it is no coincidence that John's Gospel begins by echoing the opening words of Genesis: 'In the beginning ...'

Bernard Ramm also saw the importance of a sound doctrine of creation: 'The theological, the ethical, and the practical are so conjoined in the Bible with the statements about Nature or creation that it is impossible to separate them, and to impugn one is to impugn the other.'[7]

The doctrine of creation roots Christianity in history — and therefore, reality — from the very beginning. Creation must be understood as an act that caused the beginning of history, not as an act which occurred outside of it. Furthermore, the creation account not only signifies the beginning of the history of the earth and the universe, but also marks the beginning of the history of mankind.[8]

The Function of Biblical Theology

Biblical theology is that branch of exegetical theology which deals with the process of God's self-revelation in Scripture, and 'its nature and method of procedure will therefore naturally have to keep in close touch with, and so far as possible reproduce, the features of the divine work itself.' Or, as Graeme Goldsworthy explains, biblical theology 'is the theology as it is presented in the Bible within the historical process of progressive revelation.'[9] Not only are the biblical writers historical witnesses, they are also *theological witnesses* in the sense that they testify to the reality of God and His activity as it impinges on the history of mankind.[10]

Thus, biblical theology is concerned with 'how the revelation of God was understood in its time, and what the total picture is that was built up over

---

5 Francis A. Schaeffer, 'Genesis in Space and Time' in *Complete Works of Francis A. Schaeffer*, 2nd edition, 5 vols (Wheaton, Illinois, Crossway, 1985), 2:68.

6 As cited in C. Catherwood, *Five Evangelical Leaders* (Fearn, Scotland, Christian Focus Publications, 1994), 135–136.

7 Ramm, *Christian View of Science and Scripture*, 26.

8 H. Wayne House, 'Creation and Redemption: A Study of Kingdom Interplay' *JETS* 35/1 (March 1992), 6–7.

9 Graeme Goldsworthy, 'Is Biblical Theology Viable?' in R.J. Gibson (editor), *Interpreting God's Plan* (Carlisle, Paternoster, 1998), 43.

10 Gerhard Hasel, *Old Testament Theology: Basic Issues in the Current Debate*, 3rd edition (Grand Rapids, Eerdmans, 1972), 169–170.

the whole historical process.'[11] In other words, biblical theology is concerned with tracking the progressively unfolding matrix of truth revealed in history and recorded in the Scriptures.

According to Gerhardus Vos, biblical theology has four central character-istics:[12]

1. The progressive unfolding of divine revelation in a long series of acts and events in history.
2. The process of revelation is not only concomitant with history, but the 'facts of history themselves acquire a revealing significance.'
3. The process of revelation is organic such that each progression results in a more mature revelation, not a 'more perfect' one.
4. Practical adaptability.

Note also that biblical theology assumes that Scripture is inspired by God, and is a true and inerrant record of God's real and personal communication to humanity.[13] Biblical theology also assumes *sola scriptura* — that Scripture *alone* is the supreme and authoritative revelation which must shape our presuppositions.[14]

At the fifty-first annual meeting of the Evangelical Theological Society, the outgoing president, Wayne Grudem, exhorted the members to 'tell the Church what the Bible teaches us about some current problem.'[15] This work is an attempt to carry out Grudem's exhortation in relation to creation. The aim is to produce a biblical theology of creation which tells the church what the whole Bible teaches about God's creative acts in history, and tracks the progressively unfolding truth concerning creation as it is revealed in *all* the Scriptures.

Given that a biblical theology is inherently *biblical* and based purely on what God has revealed in Scripture, detailed scientific discussions of theories and observations relating to the physical creation will not be covered. Nevertheless, where appropriate, current scientific theories, inferences, and implications will be briefly pointed out and summarized.

Scripture and General Revelation

The challenge facing biblical theologians, and all students of the Bible, is the question of integrating general revelation and the conclusions of modern science into our understanding of Scripture and, in particular, our doctrine of creation. At present, the understanding of many Christian, as well as non-Christian, scientists stands in stark contrast to what the language of Scripture appears to be communicating. In response, many evangelical theologians, wishing to maintain the doctrine of biblical inerrancy, have felt compelled to

---

11 Graeme Goldsworthy, *Preaching the Whole Bible as Christian Scripture* (Leicester, IVP, 2000), 26.

12 Gerhardus Vos, *Biblical Theology* (Edinburgh, Banner of Truth, 1975), 5–8.

13 Ibid., 11–13.

14 Graeme Goldsworthy, *Preaching the Whole Bible*, 25. My emphasis.

15 Wayne Grudem, 'Do we act as if we really believe that "The Bible alone, and the Bible in its entirety, is the Word of God written"?' *JETS* 43/1 (March 2000), 6.

modify their interpretation of what the Bible teaches about creation to bring it in line with the current scientific consensus. But is this the correct approach to the problem?

Two Books of Revelation?

Many evangelical scientists and theologians attempt to resolve this question by holding to the notion that God has revealed Himself in two 'books' — general revelation and special revelation. This theory originated with Francis Bacon (1561–1626) in 1605[16] and maintains that God gave humanity two revelations of truth, each of which is fully authoritative in its own realm: special revelation (the Bible) is authoritative in all matters relating to spiritual truth, salvation, ethics, morality, and Christian living, whereas general revelation is authoritative in all matters relating to the natural world. Although these two revelations differ from each other greatly in character and scope, they cannot contradict each other, because they were given by the same self-consistent God of truth. Furthermore, the tasks of the theologian and the scientist are seen to be the interpretation of Scripture and the interpretation of nature, respectively, and each have their own specific methodology and procedures for determining the true meaning of the particular book they are studying.[17]

The basic tenet of the dual revelation theory is summarized by Bernard Ramm: 'God cannot contradict His speech in Nature by His speech in Scripture. If the Author of Nature and Scripture are the same God, then the two books of God must eventually recite the same story.'[18] In fact, Hugh Ross considers nature to be just as inspired as Scripture — a sixty-seventh book of the Bible[19] — and he appeals to Psalms 19 and 50 for scriptural support.[20] Indeed, the basic maxim for those who accept the dual revelation theory is 'all truth is God's truth.' Yet as C.L. Deinhardt comments, 'The prevalence of this maxim among Christian writers could make one think it is a quotation from Scripture, with very likely a long history of theological treatises about it and biblical exegeses supporting its use in justifying "truth" being drawn from science, nature, psychology, etc. But I have yet to find the text in the Bible.'[21]

Even on the face of it, the idea of two non-contradictory 'books' of revelation seems flawed. The fact is that these two 'books' do appear to contradict each other at numerous points. Such conflicts are nearly always resolved by simply reinterpreting the special revelation in Scripture. In other words, general

---

16 J.R. Moore, 'Geologists and Interpreters of Genesis in the Nineteenth Century' in D.C. Lindberg and R.L. Numbers (editors), *God and Nature* (Berkeley, University of California Press, 1986), 322.

17 John C. Whitcomb, 'Biblical Inerrancy and the Double Revelation Theory' *GJ* 4 (Winter 1963), 4.

18 Ramm, *Christian View of Science and Scripture*, 25.

19 Hugh N. Ross, *Creation and Time* (Colorado Springs, NavPress, 1994), 56–57.

20 Hugh N. Ross, 'General Revelation: Nature's Testament' *PC* 21/1 (Summer 1998).

21 C.L. Deinhardt, 'General Revelation as an Important Theological Consideration for Christian Counselling and Therapy' διδασκαλια (Fall 1995), 50.

revelation takes priority over special revelation, implying — at least in the minds of many interpreters — that the two are not equal. This has been demonstrated time after time in the publications of the American Scientific Affiliation (ASA). In his review article on the ASA and the Creation Research Society, William Lane Craig notes that '[t]he whole point of the double revelation theory was supposed to prove that "these two revelations must agree; if they do not appear to do so, it must be because we are misinterpreting either one or both." But the Bible always seems to come out on the short end.'[22]

David Diehi highlights the central interpretive implication of the dual revelation theory when he asserts that 'general and special revelation are equally authoritative and infallible *for the respective truths that they in fact reveal.*'[23] In other words, general revelation, through scientific study, is the final and infallible authority on matters pertaining to the natural world, whereas *the special revelation of Scripture may contain errors of fact when speaking about the structure, form, operation, and dating of the universe.*[24] Thus, the dual revelation approach implies that whenever there is an apparent conflict between the conclusions of the scientist and the interpretations of the theologian, then the theologian must re-evaluate his interpretation of the Scriptures at these points in order to bring the Bible back into harmony with science. Since the Bible is not a scientific textbook, it is not thought to speak authoritatively on issues relating to the actual form and operation of the physical world. Proponents of the dual revelation theory believe that only careful scientific study can give us detailed and authoritative answers in these areas. This is especially true for those questions relating to the origin and nature of the universe, the effects of the Edenic curse, and the reality, significance, and effect of the Genesis flood in the time of Noah. Therefore, it is not difficult to determine which 'revelation' gains the supremacy in any dual revelation theory. Science conquers all.[25]

But is such an approach really justified? To answer this question it is necessary to further explore what is actually meant by the terms 'general revelation' and 'special revelation,' as well as the nature and purpose of these two kinds of revelation.

General Revelation

The classical definition of general revelation is given by Bruce Demarest and Gordon Lewis: '[T]he disclosure of God in nature, in providential history, and

---

22 William Lane Craig, 'Evangelicals And Evolution: An Analysis Of The Debate Between The Creation Research Society And The American Scientific Affiliation' *JETS* 17/3 (Summer 1974), 141.

23 David W. Diehi, 'Evangelicalism and General Revelation: An Unfinished Agenda' *JETS* 30 (December 1987), 448. My emphasis.

24 Examples of this belief can be found in Paul H. Seely, 'The Firmament and the Water Above. Part I: The meaning of *raqiya'* in Gen. 1:6–8' *WTJ* 53/2 (1991), 227–240; Paul H. Seely, 'The Firmament and the Water Above. Part II: The meaning of "the water above the firmament" in Gen. 1:6–8' *WTJ* 54/1 (1992), 31–46; Paul H. Seely, 'The Geographical Meaning of "Earth" and "Seas" in Genesis 1:10' *WTJ* 59/2 (1997), 231–256.

25 Marvin L. Goodman, 'Non-literal Interpretations of Genesis Creation' *GJ* 14/1 (Winter 1973), 29.

in the moral law within the heart, whereby all persons at all times and places gain a rudimentary understanding of the Creator and his moral demands.'[26] Elsewhere, Demarest adds: 'General revelation, mediated through nature, conscience, and the providential ordering of history, traditionally has been understood as a universal witness to God's existence and character.'[27]

Millard Erickson offers a similar definition but, as Robert Thomas points out, he slips in an additional connotation for the meaning of 'general.'[28] Erickson understands general revelation as 'general' not only in the sense that it is universally available to everyone, but also in the sense that its *content* is general.[29]

Diehi, on the other hand, appears to have invented his own definition: 'General revelation is a revelation of God through his works of creation and providence in a natural, continuous, universal, indirect and nonpropositional mode.'[30] Furthermore, he asserts that 'the message of general revelation, while general about the character and will of God, is quite specific when it comes to matters about creation.'[31] Clearly, Diehi's and Erickson's definitions represent a significant departure from the definition of general revelation traditionally used by theologians. How, then, should general revelation be defined and what is the biblical basis for such a definition?

Firstly, in what sense is general revelation 'general'? While Erickson believes the content of the revelation is general, Diehi argues that the content of the revelation 'about creation' is quite specific, including what God has made (e.g. the heavens, firmament, rains and fruitful seasons, and similar.).[32] Yet it is difficult to see what Diehi actually means by this. The heavens, the firmament, the rains and the like are indeed quite specific things, but this only indicates that God has created many specific things that are distinct from each other. While this may provide some insight into the character and nature of the Creator, it says very little about the creation itself. Nevertheless, Diehi argues that if general revelation 'includes both knowledge of God and knowledge of creation, and if it is an objective and infallible revelation, then not only does theology have a reliable and divinely authoritative source but so does science.'[33] However, as Diehi acknowledges, such a conclusion is conditional upon showing that general revelation does indeed include 'knowledge of creation' and if so, to what extent.

---

26 Bruce A. Demarest and Gordon R. Lewis, *Integrative Theology: Knowing Ultimate Reality, the Living God*, 3 vols. (Grand Rapids, Michigan, Zondervan, 1987), 1:61.

27 Bruce A. Demarest, *General Revelation: Historical Views and Contemporary Issues* (Grand Rapids, Michigan: Zondervan, 1982), 14.

28 Robert L. Thomas, 'General Revelation and Biblical Hermeneutics' *TMSJ* 9 (Spring 1998), 6.

29 Millard J. Erickson, *Christian Theology* (Grand Rapids, Michigan, Baker, 1998), 154.

30 Diehi, 'Evangelicalism and General Revelation,' 443.

31 Ibid., 448.

32 Ibid., 449.

33 Ibid. Indeed, Diehi believes the Bible is not the only infallible source of truth (448).

Secondly, in what way is science related to general revelation? It is quite common for theologians and scientists to view science and general revelation as one and the same thing,[34] although most understand science as the study of God's general revelation in the same way that theology is the study of God's special revelation. For example, Norman Geisler declares: 'Systematic theology is as meaningful as science is, for theology is to the Bible (God's special revelation) what science is to nature (God's general revelation). Both are a systematic approach to the truths God has revealed in a nonsystematic way. In each case God has given the truths and left it for man to organize them in an orderly way.'[35]

Robert C. Newman claims that knowledge from general revelation is based on a much larger body of data than that of special revelation, and therefore provides far more detail than Scripture.[36] But Newman fails to see that data is just that — data. It is not communication and it does not speak for itself, since there are often different interpretations for the same data set. Therefore, raw, uninterpreted data cannot be revelation.

Diehi, on the other hand, considers general revelation to be 'progressive throughout the whole of human history. ... As we investigate more deeply and fully the creation of God, he progressively unveils to us its true nature and structure. ... Thus to progress in a knowledge of general revelation is to be able to better understand the significance and application of the teachings of Scripture. It is to be able to know more precisely what Scripture does and does not teach.'[37]

Diehi's application of the term 'progressive' to general revelation is curious. He appears to be drawing a parallel with the progressive nature of biblical (special) revelation which is progressive in the sense that it was revealed over an extended but *limited* period of time. Describing general revelation as progressive, however, means something quite different, since according to Diehi, general revelation continues *indefinitely*. Diehi also assumes that the knowledge gained from general revelation through scientific study is cumulative in the same way that our knowledge of God grows as we see Him progressively reveal Himself in salvation history. But this is a very naïve view of the historical progress of science, which was not at all accumulative, but rather, occurred through 'revolutions,' where many of the currently held paradigms and theories were completely overturned and replaced by new paradigms and theories.[38] In fact, if

---

34 See, for example, Ramm, *Christian View of Science and Scripture*, 23; Bruce K. Waltke, *Genesis* (Grand Rapids, Michigan, Zondervan, 2001), 77.

35 Norman L. Geisler, 'The Relation of Purpose and Meaning in Interpreting Scripture' *GTJ* 5 (Fall 1984), fn 6.

36 Robert C. Newman, 'Progressive Creationism' in J.P. Moreland and J.M. Reynolds (editors), *Three Views on Creation and Evolution* (Grand Rapids, Michigan, Zondervan, 1999), 131.

37 Diehi, 'Evangelicalism and General Revelation,' 453–454.

38 See Thomas S. Kuhn, *The Structure of Scientific Revolutions* (Chicago, University of Chicago Press, 1996). The history of science will be further discussed in chapters 2 and 3.

Diehi's conception of general revelation is accepted, then we are forced to view it as a dynamic, constantly changing source of 'knowledge.' The problem is that at many points in history, scientific knowledge has been quite wrong. But if general revelation (as Diehi conceives of it) has been wrong many times, then how can it be viewed as authoritative, let alone infallible?

Is there any warrant, then, for broadening the scope of general revelation to include scientific study? Robert Thomas answers in the negative for several reasons: (1) Knowledge of general revelation should be common to all people: 'It is not something they must seek to discover. It is not hidden truth such as the mysteries of special revelation revealed to the apostles. It is information that is common knowledge to all ... and impossible for mankind to avoid.'[39] (2) Modern science is not general revelation since most scientific knowledge is of recent origin, and only comprehensible to those with advanced training in the various scientific disciplines. (3) The subject of general revelation is God Himself (cf. Ps. 19:6; Rom. 1:19–21; Acts 14:15–17; Acts 17:24–28; Rom. 2:14–15, etc.), not the physical world.[40] (4) Humanity's invariable response to general revelation is *negative* (cf. Rom. 1:18–21). As Thomas notes: 'For human discoveries to be categorized under the heading of general revelation, those discoveries must be objects of rejection by the non-Christian world, not revelations of truth ... to suggest that discoveries of the secular Western mind are direct results of positive responses to general revelation is to contradict what Scripture says about unregenerate mankind's response to that revelation.'[41] Therefore, the notion that general revelation includes scientific data, reasoning and conclusions cannot be maintained.

Thirdly, Diehi argues that all biblical statements are 'dependent on general revelation for rational, empirical and personal meaning' and therefore, general revelation has an 'epistemological priority' over special revelation. 'It is in the logical, empirical and personal structure of creation as general revelation that we have a basis for the meaning of any proposition, Biblical or otherwise.' Indeed, the laws of logic are 'grounded in general revelation,' and without logic, no statement of Scripture is intelligible.[42] But on this point Diehi is quite mistaken. The capacity to reason is an inherent part of human nature. We are created in the image of God, and since God is a rational being, we too are rational beings. When God told Adam and Eve not to eat from the Tree of the Knowledge of Good and Evil, they understood what He meant and that death would result.[43] They did not have to turn to the scientific study of the garden to determine God's intent! Diehi goes on to argue that in order to understand Psalm 23, for example, one has to have at least a basic knowledge about sheep and the role of

---

39 Thomas, 'General Revelation and Biblical Hermeneutics,' 10.

40 Ibid., 7–9.

41 Ibid., 9–10. Of course, unbelievers *do* reject or suppress the *teleological implications* of the natural world, which is what Romans 1:18–21 teaches.

42 Diehi, 'General Revelation and Biblical Hermeneutics,' 450.

43 This is clearly indicated by Eve's response to the serpent in Gen. 3:3.

the shepherd.[44] Again, Diehi is mistaken. Such knowledge is gained by studying the relevant culture not by studying general revelation.

Finally, what do the Scriptures themselves teach about the nature and function of general revelation? Psalm 19:1–4 is often cited as supporting the concept of the 'two books' of revelation and that scientific study can reveal specific information about God and His creation:

> *The heavens declare the glory of God;*
> *the skies proclaim the work of his hands.*
> *Day after day they pour forth speech;*
> *night after night they display knowledge.*
> *There is no speech or language*
> *where their voice is not heard.*
> *Their voice goes out into all the earth,*
> *their words to the ends of the world.*[45]

Regarding verse 1, Diehi points to the phrases 'glory of God' and 'the work of his hands,' and argues that general revelation reveals not only knowledge of God Himself, but also knowledge of the things He has made.[46] Yet, Diehi fails to note the synonymous parallelism between the two halves of this verse. While each half is distinct, it also serves to reinforce the other half. The 'heavens' reveal the majesty and greatness of God, while the 'skies' (synonymous to 'heavens') reveal His incredible creative activity. Both halves focus wholly on God, not on the actual creation. The skies do not proclaim themselves; they proclaim the work of God.

In addition, the translation of verses 3–4 is not straightforward. Verse 3 simply emphasizes the fact that the heavens do not have any actual audible voice. Note that the word 'where' in verse 3 in the NIV is not in the Hebrew. The two clauses are semantically parallel: in declaring God's glory, the heavens do not employ speech or language, and they have no audible voice. Yet, verse 4 explains that, despite the lack of verbal communication, God's message in creation is broadcast throughout the earth and reaches everyone.

The Hebrew Masoretic Text of verse 4 has קָום (*qǎwwām*, 'their measuring cord') rather than קוֹלם (*qôlām*, 'their voice'). The LXX and all modern translations, however, prefer *qôlām*, since it appears that a scribe erred by dropping the lamed (ל) when copying קוֹלם, which resulted in קָום, and 'their measuring cord' does not appear to make much sense. Yet, 'voice' does not seem to fit the context any better, given that the preceding verse states that the heavens do not have any actual voice. Secondly, the principles of textual criticism suggest that the 'more difficult' reading is preferable.

How, then, should verse 4 be translated? The semantic range of *qǎw* is not completely settled. In Isaiah 28:10, קָו (*qǎw*) is synonymously parallel with צַו (*ṣǎw*, 'precept') suggesting a similar meaning. In Psalm 19:4, the Syriac Peshitta

---

44 Diehi, 'General Revelation and Biblical Hermeneutics,' 450.

45 NIV.

46 Ibid., 448.

renders it as 'their message'[47] and this appears to be the rendering that makes the most sense of the text. Thus, Psalm 19:1–4 is best rendered as:

> *The heavens declare God's glory;*
> *the sky displays his handiwork.*
> *Day after day it speaks out;*
> *night after night it reveals his greatness.*
> *There is no speech and there are no words,*
> *their voice is not heard.*
> *Yet their message goes out to the whole earth;*
> *their speech reaches the ends of the earth.*

Whether we accept *qāw* from the Hebrew Masoretic Text or *qôlām* derived from the LXX, the point of this text is that even though the creation does not audibly speak or communicate in human language, it nevertheless testifies to God's existence and His power and glory, and that this testimony is universal. Language and physical location present no barriers to 'hearing' and seeing God in creation. This is consistent with Paul's point in Romans 1:20 — no one has any excuse for not acknowledging God because creation has made His existence and power obvious to everyone.

Yet Romans 1:20 is commonly cited by advocates of the dual revelation theory as proof that general revelation includes science and reveals truth about the physical creation. Romans 1:19–20 states: 'since what may be known about God is plain to them, because God has made it plain to them. For since the creation of the world God's invisible qualities — his eternal power and divine nature — have been clearly seen, being understood from what has been made, so that men are without excuse.' Again, note that what has been revealed is knowledge *about God* — specifically 'God's invisible qualities' — not scientific facts or knowledge about the physical creation. Note also the purpose for this revelation: so that mankind cannot claim ignorance as a reason for not accepting God.

Richard Young argues that if the expressions in Romans 1:20 are interpreted in light of 'the central Creator/creation/idolatry motif that runs throughout the passage,' it is apparent that 'God's eternal power would then pertain to God's creative energy, and God's deity would pertain to the idea that the Creator, not creation, is sovereign and deserving of worship. Thus what is manifest throughout creation is simply that God is the Creator who should be worshiped.'[48] Young also notes that if τὸ γνωστὸν (*to gnōston*, v. 19) is rendered as 'what is known' it would create a tautology: what is known has been made known. Therefore it would be better to take it as a reference to that subset of knowledge that God has chosen to reveal to humanity about Himself.[49]

It should be clear then, that neither Psalm 19:1–4 nor Romans 1:19–20 offers any support for the view that general revelation encompasses specific

---

47 See entry for קַו (I) in *HALOT*.

48 Richard Alan Young, 'The Knowledge of God in Romans 1:18–23' *JETS* 43 (December 2000), 704.

49 Ibid., 704, n 38. Cf. NIV — 'what may be known about God.'

knowledge about the physical world, including modern scientific conclusions and theories. What, then, is the purpose of general revelation? Romans 1:19–20 clearly teaches that general revelation reveals to *all* humanity, past and present, that God exists, that He created the universe and everything in it, and that He is great and powerful. Thus, *the physical world is not a second book of revelation from God, but a signpost pointing to God the almighty Creator.*

In the final analysis, the double revelation theory fails to acknowledge the inherent limitations of scientific knowledge and method, especially in relation to the study of origins. John Whitcomb adds:

> The scientific method assumes without proof the universal validity of uniformity as a law of nature, by extrapolating present processes forever into the past and future; and it ignores the possible anti-theistic bias of the scientist himself as he handles the 'facts' of nature in arriving at a cosmology (a theory concerning the basic structure and character of the universe) and a cosmogony (a theory concerning the origin of the universe and its parts).[50]

The Primacy of Special Revelation
Mark Noll writes:

> The height of foolishness is to confuse the tasks of creator and creature (Rom. 1). Humans are creatures, not the creator. As such we will always be limited by our finitude from seeing the whole picture. We will always be predisposed by our fallenness to misconstrue the results of historical inquiry for our own idolatrous satisfaction. We will always be trading the advantages that come from living in the God ordained particularities of our own cultures for the blindness that comes from being unable to see what is so obvious to those who gaze upon the past from other frames of reference.[51]

In other words, it is impossible to discover the truth about creation by relying on our own knowledge, ideas, and methods, simply because we are finite and fallen human beings. Not only does our humanity prohibit us from having exhaustive knowledge, but our fallen nature also inhibits our ability to perceive, to reason, and to assess. Moreover, the object of scientific study — the natural world — is also fallen. While it still reveals the glory and greatness of God, it is, nevertheless, in 'bondage to decay' (Rom 8:20–22). The image it presents is to some extent distorted.

Nevertheless, Diehi objects to using sin or sin's curse on creation or a supposed deficiency in general revelation as an excuse for reducing general revelation to a second-rate position such that, in theology and science disputes, Scripture is taken as the only trustworthy source of truth.[52] However, not only does Diehi

---

50 Whitcomb, 'Biblical Inerrancy and the Double Revelation Theory,' 4.

51 Mark A. Noll, 'Traditional Christianity and the Possibility of Historical Knowledge' *CSR* 19/4 (June 1990), 402.

52 Diehi, 'General Revelation and biblical Hermeneutics' 448.

fail to understand the nature and purpose of general revelation, he also appears
to place far too much confidence in the ability of scientists — who are fallen
human beings with biases and agendas — to produce an accurate assessment
and come to unbiased conclusions.[53]

A much clearer picture of creation can be gleaned from the special revelation
of Scripture. The Scriptures tell the story of our creation, of our sin in Adam,
and of God's gift of salvation in Christ. The message of general revelation in the
natural world, on the other hand, is more modest. It is limited to proclaiming
that God exists, that He is the almighty and all-powerful Creator, and that
in the past, He has judged the world for their sin and rebellion.[54] Regarding
salvation, however, Wolters posits that general revelation is 'useless,' and the two
revelations are not even comparable.[55]

The Scriptures, unlike general revelation, are presented in the words of
ordinary human language. As Wolters points out, '[t]hey are plain in a way that
general revelation never is, have a "perspicuity" that is not found in the book
of nature. In a way, therefore, the Scriptures are like a verbal commentary on
the dimly perceived sign language of creation.'[56] For this reason, the special
revelation of Scripture should always take priority over both general revelation
in the natural world and the conclusions of modern science. The revelation
of Scripture is the filter through which all else should be interpreted. Indeed,
Calvin, long ago, suggested that the Scriptures are the spectacles with which to
read the book of nature and that the illumination of the Spirit is needed to give
us proper eyesight for the reading.[57] As Graeme Goldsworthy points out, 'all
reality depends upon the creative word of God.' Thus, 'the word of God must
judge the ideas of men about truth and error, not the other way round.'[58]

In addition, special revelation occurs in history and concerns historical
events, and thus reinforces the link between Christianity and factual history:

> Is not God's revelation first event, and only then knowledge? Does
> not revelation occur in history, and not first of all in ideation? Is not
> revelation the history of God's acts in time and space, and not merely
> as information[?] Information is data, facts, measures, statistics,
> knowledge? [sic] While revelation yields information, it is not consti-
> tuted by information as such but by God's disclosure of himself through
> historical events.[59]

Yet the most important and significant attribute of special revelation is that
it is the testimony of the Creator Himself regarding truth that is inherently

---

53 This will be discussed further in chapter 2.

54 The Noahic flood is an example of God's judgment in the past of human sin and rebellion. This
    is discussed in more detail in chapter 10.

55 A.M. Wolters, *Creation Regained* (Carlisle, Paternoster, 1996), 31.

56 Ibid., 33.

57 John Calvin, *Institutes*, 1.6.1.

58 Graeme Goldsworthy, *Gospel and Kingdom* (Carlisle, Paternoster, 1981). 49.

59 Thomas C. Oden, 'Response to Hugh Ross on General Revelation' *PC* 21/1 (Summer 1998).

inaccessible to human perception and inquiry. Allan MacRae summarized this point well:

> The greatest importance of revelation lies in fields in which the facts are inaccessible to the observer. No human being was present when the earth was made. No one could see the various processes that occurred, or tell from his own observation what is their purpose and ultimate destiny. The earth as it exists today can be studied, and inferences made as to its past history. Processes now going on can be observed and measured, and estimates made as to their occurrence in past times. After all this is done, much remains to be learned. How much easier it would be, if a revelation about these matters could be secured from the One who made the earth.[60]

Indeed, it is precisely for this reason that, when studying origins, more attention needs to be paid to the Scriptures — the special revelation of 'the God who is there' and who 'is not silent.'

Allowing the conclusions of modern science to determine our doctrine of creation is essentially a denial of the historic, evangelical doctrine of *sola scriptura*.[61] No longer does Scripture alone determine what the Christian church should believe. Instead, the scientific priesthood is now telling the church what to believe about creation and how the Scriptures should be interpreted to fit in with those beliefs. For many, the Bible 'is to teach us how one goes to heaven, not how the heavens go.'[62] But the central issue is not so much about the scientific accuracy of Scripture, but rather its *historical* accuracy. Does it accurately describe past events in propositional form? While all agree Scripture is not a textbook on science, those who have a high view of Scripture believe that when it does touch on areas such as science and history, it does speak truthfully and authoritatively.

---

60 Allan A. MacRae, 'The Scientific Approach to the Old Testament Part 1' *BSac* 110 (January–March 1953), 22–23.

61 It is often stated that *sola scriptura* applies only to matters of 'faith and life.' Indeed, this has become the basis for allowing science the authority in matters concerning origins (see for example chapter 7, 'Hardening of the Categories: Why Theologians Have opposed "New Knowledge"' in M. James Sawyer, *The Survivor's Guide to Theology* [Grand Rapids, Michigan, Zondervan, 2002]). However, this is another instance of revisionist historiography. As Don Carson points out ('Recent Developments in the Doctrine of Scripture' in D.A. Carson and J.D. Woodbridge [eds], *Hermeneutics, Authority and Canon* [Grand Rapids, Michigan, Baker, 1995] 14), 'Precisely because the Reformers' theological formulations were shaped by the controversies of their age, it is clear that the "faith and life" formula was meant to be an all-embracing rubric, not a limiting one. They claimed that the deposit of truth lies in the Bible, not in the church or in the magisterium of the church. Their concern, in other words, was to spell out the locus of authority in order to rebut their Roman Catholic opponents, not to restrict the range of the Bible's authority to religious life and thought, away from history and the natural world. The modern disjunction would have seemed strange to them.'

62 This saying is generally attributed to Galileo, although some attribute it to Jerome or Cardinal Baronius.

Chapter 2

Scripture, Science, and Interpretation

H ermeneutics is the formal process by which the interpreter employs certain principles and methods in order to derive the author's intended meaning. Naturally, this is foundational to all theological studies, and before a biblical theology of creation can be built, it is necessary to discuss the hermeneutical approach that will be utilized and how it will be specifically applied.

Biblical Inerrancy

Presuppositions and pre-understandings have always played a significant role in the hermeneutical process, and one such presupposition is biblical *inerrancy*. Inerrancy is a complex doctrine, but it is internally coherent, and consistent with a perfect and righteous God who has revealed Himself. Broadly speaking, the doctrine of inerrancy identifies Scripture as true and without error in all that it affirms, including its affirmations regarding history and the physical universe.[1] Article IX of *The Chicago Statement on Biblical Inerrancy* states:

> *WE AFFIRM* that inspiration, though not conferring omniscience, guaranteed true and trustworthy utterance on all matters of which the Biblical authors were moved to speak and write.

> *WE DENY* that the finitude or fallenness of these writers, by necessity or otherwise, introduced distortion or falsehood into God's Word.

Concerning the role of history and science in the interpretation of Scripture relating to creation and the flood, Article XII states:

> *WE AFFIRM* that Scripture in its entirety is inerrant, being free from all falsehood, fraud, or deceit.

> *WE DENY* that *Biblical* infallibility and inerrancy are limited to spiritual, religious, or redemptive themes, exclusive of assertions in the fields of history and science. We further deny that scientific hypotheses

---

1 For detailed expositions of inerrancy see 'The Chicago Statement on Biblical Inerrancy' *JETS* 21/4 (December 1978), 289–96; Norman L. Geisler (editor), *Inerrancy* (Grand Rapids, Michigan, Zondervan, 1980); D.A. Carson and John D. Woodbridge (editors), *Scripture and Truth*, 2nd edition (Grand Rapids, Michigan, Baker, 1992); D.A. Carson and John D. Woodbridge (editors), *Hermeneutics, Authority and Canon* (Grand Rapids, Michigan: Baker, 1995).

about earth history may properly be used to overturn the teaching of Scripture on creation and the flood.

Indeed, as Herman Bavinck noted, when Scripture touches on science it does not suddenly cease to be the word of God.[2]

Of course, a high view of Scripture is 'of little value to us if we do not enthusiastically embrace the Scripture's authority.'[3] Indeed, many scholars who claim to be evangelical have either rejected this doctrine outright, or have redefined it to allow for errors in historical and scientific references. Francis Schaeffer described the denial of biblical inerrancy as 'The Great Evangelical Disaster.' He noted that accommodating Scripture to the current scientific consensus has led many evangelicals to a weakened view of the Bible and to no longer affirm the truth of all that it teaches — not only in regard to theology and morality but also regarding science and history.[4] Why, then, have many so-called evangelical historians and theologians denied inerrancy and infallibility in relation to history and science? John D. Woodbridge suggests they believe that if the Bible is only infallible for faith and practice, then it cannot be negatively affected by evolutionary hypotheses.[5] The irony of this position is that in trying to defend inerrancy, they have essentially given it up!

But even if one affirms the superiority and inerrancy of the special revelation of Scripture in all areas, what are we to do with science? How does science affect our interpretation of specific passages and our overall theology? These are pertinent questions when constructing a biblical theology of creation.

It is often stated that the theologian is the God-appointed interpreter of Scripture, and the scientist is the God-appointed interpreter of nature. For example, Roger Forster and Paul Marston present the relationship of the Bible and theology, and the relationship of nature and science as follows:

2 Books:	Bible	Nature
Human Interpretation:	Theology	Science

The point here is that both books (the Bible and nature) are true and infallible, but their human interpretations are not.[6] In other words, interpretation occurs in both theology and science, which means there is also a possibility of making interpretive errors in both fields. Thus, denying a particular interpretation does not necessarily mean or imply that biblical inerrancy is being questioned or denied. In the same way that a scientist may wrongly interpret certain scientific

2 See E.J. Young, *Studies in Genesis One* (Grand Rapids, Michigan, Baker, 1964), 43.

3 D.A. Carson, 'Recent Developments in the Doctrine of Scripture' in D.A. Carson and John D. Woodbridge (editors), *Hermeneutics, Authority and Canon* (Grand Rapids, Michigan, Baker, 1995), 46.

4 Francis A. Schaeffer, *The Great Evangelical Disaster* (Westchester, Illinois, Crossway, 1984), 37.

5 John D. Woodbridge, 'Some Misconceptions of the Impact of the "Enlightenment" on the Doctrine of Scripture' in Carson and Woodbridge, *Hermeneutics, Authority and Canon*, 269.

6 Roger Forster and Paul Marston, *Reason, Science and Faith* (Crowborough, East Sussex, Monarch, 1999), 322.

data, the theologian may also incorrectly interpret a particular passage. However, Forster and Marston offer no solution to this problem, nor do they discuss the methodological problems and issues relating to scientific research. They simply dismiss the problems of scientific research by merely stating that there are also problems in biblical interpretation.[7] David F. Payne, on the other hand, acknowledges the primacy of biblical revelation when he states:

> [I]t must be decided what exactly the biblical teaching is before any criticism of its accuracy can be made. ... The majority of Concordists take the scientific data as their starting-point, and interpret the biblical statements to fit them. But it is essential to achieve first a sound exegesis of the latter; and then, if any rapprochement is necessary, it can be made on a firm basis. Biblical exegesis is paramount, even when the scientific challenge is under consideration.[8]

This raises the question of epistemology and the possibility of knowing. How can the interpreter know whether his exegesis is accurate or whether a particular interpretation is the correct one? Can the interpreter know anything for certain, or should all interpretations be held tentatively? Upon which criteria can such an assessment be made?

Scripture and the Problem of Interpretation

It is certainly true that different interpretations of Scripture abound, especially for those Scriptures which teach about creation. But are all interpretations valid and equally plausible, or is there only ever one correct interpretation? If there is only ever one correct interpretation, how can it be determined?

Human Language as God's Medium of Communication

The Bible is God's special revelation and its purpose is to communicate specific truth to all humanity, past, present, and future. In order to accomplish this, God employed common human language as the medium for His message. The biblical account of creation does not discuss the question of whether God can meaningfully speak to mankind or whether mankind can understand God. It is simply assumed as 'self-evident' that God and mankind could engage in meaningful linguistic communication.[9] Thus, Jack Barentsen concludes that 'God must have endowed man with adequate faculties to respond to and interact with his Creator.'[10] Indeed, 'Genesis describes God as the first language user. ... [He] instituted language as the vehicle of communication between man and himself.'[11] Similarly, Packer points out that Genesis 'shows us that human thought and speech have their counterparts and archetypes in [God].'[12]

---

7 Roger Forster and Paul Marston, *Reason and Faith* (Eastbourne, Monarch, 1989), 267.

8 David F. Payne, *Genesis One Reconsidered* (London, Tyndale, 1964). 6, 8.

9 Jack Barentsen, 'The Validity of Human Language: A Vehicle for Divine Truth' *GTJ* 9 (Spring 1988), 30–31.

10 Ibid., 31.

11 Ibid., 38.

12 J.I. Packer, 'The Adequacy of Human Language,' in Geisler, *Inerrancy*, 214.

Furthermore, God continued to employ human language as His medium of communication throughout biblical history. When God spoke directly to Moses, He used intelligible human language; when He spoke to His prophets He used intelligible human language; when Jesus taught He used intelligible human language; when He appeared to Saul, He used intelligible human language.

Nevertheless, there are many who claim that language in general, or the biblical languages in particular, are somewhat deficient in that they are unable to communicate with the same precision as modern languages. Hugh Ross, for example, argues that since biblical Hebrew has a much smaller vocabulary than English, Hebrew words can convey many *different* 'literal' meanings.[13] This is surely a very naïve view of language. Vocabulary size is irrelevant. Indeed, all languages 'are quite able to express complex, deep, or subtle ideas. Virtually anything that can be said in one language can be said in another, provided one takes enough time.'[14]

God is sovereign and He wills to be understood, and actively reveals Himself to us.[15] Human language 'offers no resistance to his purposes and cannot frustrate his desire to communicate.'[16] As E.R. Clendenen succinctly writes: 'Language works. A skillful reader will experience what a skillful communicator intended to accomplish through the agency of a text as an interface takes place between the worlds of the author, text, and reader.'[17] Indeed, everyday human experience confirms this to be so. As innate users of language, human beings readily engage in meaningful linguistic communication. Such communication is not always easy, but it is never impossible.

Propositional Revelation and Truth

God's linguistic communication to humanity as recorded in the Bible takes the form of *propositional revelation*. God supernaturally communicated His message to a chosen spokesperson in the form of explicit cognitive statements of truth, and these statements are recorded in sentences that are not internally contradictory.[18] As Carl Henry states, 'the inspired Scriptures contain a body of divinely given information actually expressed or capable of being expressed in propositions. In brief, the Bible is a propositional revelation of the unchanging truth of God.'[19] By proposition, Henry means 'a verbal statement that is either

---

13 Hugh N. Ross, *Stanley Lecture Series*, Toccoa Falls College, March 18–20, 1997.

14 Vern Sheridan Poythress, 'Adequacy of Language and Accommodation' in Earl D. Radmacher and Robert D. Preus (editors), *Hermeneutics, Inerrancy and the Bible* (Grand Rapids, Michigan, Zondervan, 1984), 360.

15 Michael Bauman, 'Between Jerusalem and the Laboratory: A Theologian Looks at Science' *JoC* 11/2 (1997), 19.

16 Poythress, 'Adequacy of Language and Accommodation,' 352.

17 E.R. Clendenen, 'Postholes, Postmodernism, and the Prophets: Toward a Textlinguistic Paradigm' in David S. Dockery (editor), *The Challenge of Postmodernism* (Wheaton, Illinois, Victor, 1995), 144.

18 C.F.H. Henry, *God, Revelation and Authority*, 6 vols (Waco, Texas, Word, 1976–1983), 3:457.

19 Ibid., 3:457.

true or false; it is a rational declaration capable of being either believed, doubted or denied,'[20] and adds that '[n]othing can be literally true but a propositional statement.'[21] Likewise, Norman Geisler notes that 'the normal and consistent New Testament usage of "truth" is of truth in the cognitive, propositional sense.'[22]

Roger Forster and Paul Marston claim that a statement can still have genuine historical content but be allegorical in form.[23] In other words, a distinction is made between historical fact and historical event. A particular historical fact may be presented in the form of a non-historical event. But on what basis can one claim that a non-historical event represents a true historical situation? Such distinctions are not only arbitrary they lack any coherence, and are surely motivated by concerns totally external to the Bible. Mcquilken and Mullen add: 'To deny the possibility of words corresponding to reality is ultimately an attack on the nature and activity of God. ... Evangelical faith is that God can communicate and indeed has communicated in words all the truth about ultimate reality he thinks it necessary for us to know.'[24]

Viewing the Bible as propositional revelation from God implies there is the possibility of verifiable facts involved. God has verbally communicated in a propositional form to humanity, not just truth about spiritual matters but also truth relating to history and science. If truth was not expressed in this way then the interpreter can never be sure of anything — even their own salvation.

In Scripture, propositional revelation most often takes the form of historical narrative.[25] Indeed, Rodney Decker points out that

> Scripture employs narrative genre deliberately, but it does so in such a way that the historical basis (event) for the narratival depiction (text) is absolutely essential. The revelation value of the Bible depends on its history value. ... Historical narrative explicitly appeals to history to verify what it teaches: names, places, events, dates etc. are cited. ... If these references are not trustworthy, it casts grave doubt over the theology being propounded in narrative fashion.[26]

---

20 Ibid., 3:456.

21 Ibid., 3:430.

22 Norman L. Geisler, 'The Concept of Truth in the Inerrancy Debate' *BSac* 137 (October–December 1980), 333.

23 Forster and Marston, *Reason and Faith*, 217. They cite John 4:38 in support, but this verse is clearly a metaphor. In commanding the disciples to reach out to the Samaritan people, Jesus employed a common saying as an illustrative metaphor. While Jesus' command relates to a real and actual situation, the individual elements of the metaphor are not referring to real and historical people, places and events. In other words, Jesus did not have a literal reaper and a literal field in mind.

24 Robertson Mcquilkin and Bradford Mullen, 'The Impact of Postmodern Thinking On Evangelical Hermeneutics' *JETS* 40/1 (March 1997), 71.

25 This does not mean that other biblical genres do not contain propositional statements, or that statements from these genres cannot be rephrased or transformed into propositional statements.

26 Rodney J. Decker, 'Realistic or Historical Narrative?' *JMT* 4/1 (Spring 2000), 59–60.

Keep in mind that true communication does not necessarily lead to exhaustive knowledge. Francis Schaeffer writes: 'It is helpful ... to distinguish between true communication and exhaustive communication. What we claim as Christians is that when all of the facts are taken into consideration, the Bible gives us true knowledge although not exhaustive knowledge.'[27] He adds: 'we can have confidence that this is true history, but that does not mean that the situation is exhaustively revealed or that all our questions are answered.'[28]

The Influence of Postmodernism

In the nineteenth century, Søren Kierkegaard, although a deeply religious and pious man, proposed that true knowledge was completely subjective, and that absolute certainty was impossible. In other words, it is not possible to express absolute truth in propositional form.[29] Thus, Kierkegaard unwittingly became the father of postmodern existentialism. It is unfortunate that this same kind of postmodern thinking has convinced many interpreters that it is virtually impossible to be certain of the meaning of a text, especially the biblical text.[30] Many believe that language 'cannot accurately communicate thought to another person's mind,' and that meaning is relative, especially in relation to the interpreter's present subjective perceptions.[31] Donald Williams notes that postmodernism 'manifests itself in literary study that ignores (or "deconstructs") traditional issues of meaning or even aesthetics. ...'[32] In effect, language and the communication process is 'deconstructed.' The usual meaning and implications of common words, grammar, expressions and idiom are rejected, along with normal interpretive procedures. Instead of being a natural and intuitive activity, linguistic communication becomes a problematic task with insurmountable hurdles. This is clearly illustrated by Mark Noll in his critique of the hermeneutics of certain conservative Christian groups. He accuses them of

> an overwhelming tendency to 'essentialism,' or the conviction that a specific formula could capture for all times and places the essence of Biblical truth for any specific issue concerning God, the human condition, or the fate of the world [and] a corresponding neglect of forces in history that shape perceptions and help define the issues that loom as most important to any particular age ...[33]

---

27 Francis A. Schaeffer, *Genesis in Space and Time*, in *The Complete Works of Francis A. Schaeffer*, 2nd edition, 5 vols. (Wheaton, Illinois, Crossway, 1985), 2:22–23.

28 Ibid., 23–24.

29 Barentsen, 'The Validity of Human Language,' 27.

30 Michael Stallard, 'Literal Interpretation: The Key to Understanding the Bible' *JMT* 4/1 (Spring 2000), 14.

31 See Mcquilkin and Mullen, 'The Impact of Postmodern Thinking,' 71.

32 Donald T. Williams, 'The Great Divide: The Church and the Post-Modernist Challenge.' Paper presented at the annual meeting of the Evangelical Theological Society (Colorado Springs, November 14, 2001), 2.

33 Mark A. Noll, *The Scandal of the Evangelical Mind* (Grand Rapids, Michigan, Eerdmans, 1994), 127.

Clearly, Noll thinks that following a systematic procedure when interpreting the Bible in order to accurately determine what God is saying to all men in all times, is somehow presumptuous and negligent. This is surely postmodernist existentialism applied to biblical interpretation!

Bernard Ramm, on the other hand, is more subtle: 'Revelation is the communication of divine truth; interpretation is the effort to understand it.'[34] Nevertheless, the implication is the same. Although God communicates inerrant truth, the interpreter may misunderstand it. Despite God revealing Himself in history as recorded in the Bible, the interpreter can never really be certain about the meaning of this revelation, and must always remain open to alternative interpretations. Unfortunately, those who hold such a view rarely apply it consistently. Their skepticism and uncertainty are almost never applied to scientific interpretations and conclusions.

In contrast to previous generations,[35] we seem to be caught in a state of biblical and theological uncertainty. As Mcquilkin and Mullen poignantly note, 'we seem to be in the process of losing any assurance of certainty about knowing and communicating objective reality. And many evangelicals are becoming at least moderate relativists.'[36] This has serious implications for biblical and theological studies. If the meaning of a text cannot be known for certain because no particular understanding can claim to be authoritative, then there is no basis for integrating it with other related texts in order to produce an overall theological statement or synthesis. In fact, the problem runs deeper still. Interpretive uncertainty essentially implies that it is meaningless to talk about the authority, infallibility and inerrancy of the Scriptures because the Scriptures do not really tell us anything — or at least anything of which we can be certain. The meaning ascribed to each text is merely a human interpretation which may or may not be correct. This, of course, means that the central pillars of Christianity, the doctrines of sin, atonement and judgment, the virgin birth, and the physical resurrection are mere interpretations that may or may not be correct. Indeed, since historic Christianity is merely a systematic framework of biblical interpretations it too may not be correct. Therefore, this view of biblical interpretation can only lead to liberalism or agnosticism.

Furthermore, arguing that interpretation is always uncertain due to the supposed limitations of language is ultimately self-defeating and incoherent, as Mcquilkin and Mullen point out:

> If we do not do interpretation on the premise that God has spoken and that he can be understood, that truth about him can be communicated accurately in words, we run the danger of ending up where postmodern thinking has taken some proponents: speaking nonsense. That is, they

---

34 Bernard Ramm, *The Christian View of Science and Scripture* (London, Paternoster, 1955), 31.

35 Luther held that it was possible to be certain about the meaning of Scripture. (Robert L. Thomas, 'General Revelation and Biblical Hermeneutics' *TMSJ* 9 (Spring 1998), 16.

36 Mcquilkin and Mullen, 'The Impact of Postmodern Thinking,' 71.

use words in an attempt to communicate their own thought about how impossible communication with words is.[37]

Is it possible, then, to be certain about the meaning of a given text? If we assume that Scripture is revelation from God, that it is the word of God, then it *must* be possible for any person, regardless of their culture, language, or historical situation, to comprehend, at least in a general sense, what Scripture is saying. If God's communication is not objectively understandable then He has essentially failed to communicate. In effect, He may as well not have spoken at all! If this is the case, then on what basis can the Bible be regarded as the word of God? What authority can it possibly have? Indeed, what is the point of having an authoritative, infallible, inerrant message if it is impossible to ascertain its meaning?

Historical-Grammatical Exegesis

The key to understanding the biblical text is to apply a hermeneutic that takes into account the historical and literary context. This can be done by employing *historical-grammatical* exegesis. This method presupposes that human beings are rational creatures capable of linguistic communication, and that linguistic communication is meaningful and objective. Historical-grammatical exegesis involves a systematic approach to analyzing in detail the historical situation, events and circumstances surrounding the text, and the semantics and syntactical relationships of the words which comprise the text. In essence, it attempts to formalize what language speakers do automatically and unconsciously whenever they read a book, watch television, or engage in conversation.

The importance of a systematic approach to interpreting Scripture cannot be underestimated. Walter Kaiser points out that

> the basic teaching of all of sacred theology is inseparably connected with the results of our hermeneutics; for what is that theology except what Scripture teaches? And the way to ascertain what Scripture teaches is to apply the rules and principles of interpretation. Therefore it is imperative that these rules be properly grounded and that their application be skillfully and faithfully applied. If the foundation itself is conjecture, imagination, or error, what more can be hoped for what is built on it?[38]

Space does not allow for a detailed exposition of the historical-grammatical method and how it is applied,[39] but two articles of the *Chicago Statement*

---

37 Ibid., 75.

38 Walter C. Kaiser, 'Legitimate Hermeneutics' in Geisler, *Inerrancy*, 119.

39 For detailed expositions of the historical-grammatical method from an evangelical perspective see 'The Chicago Statement on Biblical Hermeneutics' *JETS* 25/4 (December 1982), 397–401; Earl D. Radmacher and Robert D. Preus (editors) *Hermeneutics, Inerrancy and the Bible* (Grand Rapids, Michigan, Academie, 1984); Gordon Fee and Douglas Stuart, *How to Read the Bible for All its Worth*, 2nd edition (Grand Rapids, Michigan, Zondervan, 1993); Grant R. Osborne, *The Hermeneutical Spiral* (Downers Grove, Illinois. IVP, 1991); William M. Klein, Craig L. Blomberg and Robert L. Hubbard, *Introduction to Biblical Interpretation* (Dallas, Word, 1993).

on Biblical Hermeneutics are worth noting. Article XIV explicitly affirms the
historical basis of Scripture:

> *WE AFFIRM* that the biblical record of events, discourses and sayings,
> though presented in a variety of appropriate literary forms, corresponds
> to historical fact.

> *WE DENY* that any such event, discourse or saying reported in Scripture
> was invented by the biblical writers or by the traditions they incorpo-
> rated.

This is reinforced by Article XX, which affirms that the Bible also speaks truly
on matters relating to history, science, and the natural world:

> *WE AFFIRM* that since God is the author of all truth, all truths,
> biblical and extrabiblical, are consistent and cohere, and that the Bible
> speaks truth when it touches on matters pertaining to nature, history,
> or anything else. We further affirm that in some cases extrabiblical data
> have value for clarifying what Scripture teaches, and for prompting
> correction of faulty interpretations.

> *WE DENY* that extrabiblical views ever disprove the teaching of
> Scripture or hold priority over it.

Note also that the denial explicitly disallows the teachings of other fields,
including philosophy and the sciences, to 'trump' the teachings of Scripture.

But will the historical-grammatical method bring certainty regarding the
teaching of Scripture? There are, of course, numerous difficult passages which
can be understood in different ways, and although a good exegetical case can
be made for several options, no consensus presently exists. Yet even in such
cases it is still possible to be certain of the broad thrust and theological message
even though some of the details are difficult to comprehend. As Packer puts it:
'One can master the argument ... and still be unsure of the precise meaning of
occasional sentences in it.'[40] Nevertheless, the vast majority of biblical teaching
is very clear, and even those passages which at first seem confusing, can be more
easily understood when the interpreter performs a thorough analysis of the text's
genre, structure, language, and historical and cultural setting.

Indeed, the task of interpreting the Bible is apparently much simpler and
less error-prone than interpreting scientific data. Scientist Taylor Jones acknowledges that the 'Word of God is inherently more reliable than science,' and
that Scripture is much easier to interpret than nature.[41] Likewise, Robert C.
Newman admits that since general revelation is not in human language, 'it is
more liable to misinterpretation than is special revelation.'[42] David Diehi also

---

40 J.I. Packer, 'Infallible Scripture and the Role of Hermeneutics,' in Carson and Woodbridge,
    Scripture and Truth, 2nd edition, 330.

41 T. Jones, 'Science and the Bible: Guidelines for Harmonization' *TMC* 4 (Fall 1997), 2.

42 Robert C. Newman, 'Progressive Creationism,' in J.P. Moreland and John Mark Reynolds
    (editors), *Three Views on Creation and Evolution* (Grand Rapids, Michigan, Zondervan, 1999),
    131.

concedes that propositional revelation 'has a certain advantage over nonpropositional revelation.'[43] In any case, all misinterpretations and misunderstandings of Scripture result from either false presuppositions, insufficient data, or an inadequate or inconsistent hermeneutic. However, all these problems can be overcome if the interpreter is willing to thoroughly investigate the text's historical and grammatical context.

Cultural Accommodation?

Theologians of a more liberal persuasion have long believed that divine revelation necessitated the use of time-bound and erroneous statements. This position was never held by the Reformers or subscribed to by the Protestant scholastics (Lutheran or Reformed), but arose in the eighteenth century in the thought of Johann Salomo Semler and his contemporaries.[44] Nevertheless, there is now a growing trend among evangelicals to redefine inspiration and inerrancy to allow for errors when Scripture speaks on matters of history and science. Inerrancy is limited to truth concerning spiritual and moral matters. For example, Bernard Ramm, under the influence of German higher critical thinking, was convinced that 'language of accommodation' contained errors.[45] Such language 'employs the culture of the times in which it was written as the medium of revelation,'[46] and that all direct references to nature are most likely 'in terms of the prevailing cultural concepts.'[47] This is essentially another way of saying that Scripture is always wrong when it contradicts modern scientific conclusions. As Woodbridge points out, Ramm 'is actually advising [evangelicals] to consider departing from the central tradition of the Christian churches regarding the authority of Scripture.'[48] Likewise, Paul Seely believes a 'more biblical approach' to relating science and the Bible is to accept the historical-grammatical meaning of Genesis 1 but to acknowledge that 'it reflects the cosmology of the second millennium B.C., and that modern science presents a more valid picture of the universe … there is no biblical reason why the theological message in Genesis 1 cannot be

---

43 David W. Diehi, 'Evangelicalism and General Revelation: An Unfinished Agenda' *JETS* 30 (December 1987) 448. However, he attempts to nullify this concession by claiming the advantage 'is easily exaggerated.' Nevertheless, his concession is still an admission that the authority of Scripture is greater than that of general revelation.

44 Richard A. Muller, *Dictionary of Latin and Greek Theological Terms* (Grand Rapids, Michigan, Baker, 1985), 19.

45 Woodbridge, 'Some Misconceptions of the Impact of the "Enlightenment",' 264–266.

46 Ramm, *Christian View of Science and Scripture*, 48.

47 Ibid., 53. Ramm actually seems to be a bit confused on this point. He states elsewhere (Ibid., 51) that he believes the biblical writers 'do not teach *any cosmological system* or follow *any cosmogony, ancient* or *modern*. Rather their writings are prescientific and phenomenal or non-postulational' (my emphasis). Ramm's belief that Scripture is 'prescientific' is surely an attempt to insulate it from scientific criticisms, since (despite Ramm's claims to the contrary) 'prescientific' is another way of saying it is not correct.

48 Woodbridge, 'Some Misconceptions of the Impact of the "Enlightenment",' 267.

eternally valid, while the package in which it came was a temporal concession to the people of that time.'[49]

While it is true that an infinite God must in some way accommodate Himself to finite human ways of knowing in order to reveal His nature, law and gospel, this neither implies the loss of truth, nor the lessening of scriptural authority. Accommodation occurs specifically in the use of human words and concepts, and refers to the manner or mode of revelation, not to the quality and integrity of the revelation itself.[50] It is accommodation to human finitude not accommodation to error. Communication directed at mankind may involve less precision, but imprecision must not be confused with error. Inerrantists do not require scientific precision in order for a statement to be true.[51]

In any case, why stop at the possibility of errors in only those texts which relate to history and science? Why not allow for errors in spiritual, moral, and ethical matters also? If the language of accommodation does indeed allow for errors, then limiting such errors to nature and history is surely an arbitrary decision. Ramm, Seely, and others who adopt the same approach appear to accept that although much of Scripture is true, some parts are false, and the interpreter decides in which category a particular text should be placed. Thus, the standard of truth ultimately becomes whatever the interpreter decides at that time.

The Stability of Scripture and Theology

Unlike scientific data, theories and conclusions, the Scriptures have remained essentially the same for centuries, with respect to both text and canon. The Old Testament canon has been well known and generally accepted since the beginning of the Christian era, and the New Testament canon was closed in the fourth century. Although the actual texts of both testaments have undergone minor revisions as a result of textual and philological studies of newly discovered manuscripts, these changes are relatively few in number, and have not caused any significant changes in Christian belief or practice.

The central doctrines and theological motifs of Christianity have remained remarkably stable and unchanged since the time of the early church. As Michael Bauman points out, '[t]he Apostle's Creed, although it has been refined and expanded over time, has never gone through *any* extensive and fundamental changes, let alone several.'[52]

---

49 Paul H. Seely, 'The First Four Days of Genesis in Concordist Theory and Biblical Context' *PSCF* 49/2 (1997), 95.

50 Note that verses such as Isa. 55:8–9 do not imply that God's thoughts cannot be expressed in human language because they are so much higher than our own. As Carson ('Recent Developments,' 37) points out, the context shows that God's thoughts are 'higher' *in the moral realm*, and therefore 'our response must be repentance, not some kind of awareness of the ineffable.'

51 E.g. stating that the approximate value of π (*pi*) is 3 is no less truthful than saying it is 3.14159 26535897932384626. Both values are approximations but the latter is more precise.

52 Bauman, 'Between Jerusalem and the Laboratory' *JoC* 11/2 (1997), 19. My emphasis.

In relation to the doctrine of creation, W.F. Albright notes that it is 'unique in ancient literature' and that modern scientific cosmogonies 'show a disconcerting tendency to be short-lived.' Indeed, he seriously doubted whether science 'has yet caught up with the Biblical story.'[53]

What About Science?

Science has become an integral part of modern society. Many technological advances have resulted from scientific breakthroughs, and these success stories have resulted in scientists being highly regarded, and the scientific enterprise being highly valued. Thus, in the eyes of the masses, scientists command much respect and influence, and whatever they say is usually accepted without question. But is this authority warranted? How does science really work? What actually goes on?

Most people understand science as an objective and largely empirical process involving observation, analysis, hypothesizing, and testing. This is what Charles Thaxton, Walter Bradley, and Roger Olsen identified as 'operations science.'[54] Yet, when it comes to the study of origins and earth history, science works in a very different way. The process is much more subjective, involves many unprovable assumptions, and is based on a great deal of extrapolation rather than direct observation.[55] Thaxton, Bradley, and Olsen call this 'origins science.'[56] Unfortunately, most people — including most scientists — do not understand or acknowledge this difference.[57] The successful application of particular areas of scientific research does not automatically guarantee a proper understanding of origins science.

Subjectivity in Science

The subjective element of scientific study, especially in the area of origins science, is most significant when considering a biblical theology of creation, since it essentially negates the great authority usually ascribed to it. Although Forster and Marston tend toward empiricism — a belief in plain 'scientific facts' — they also acknowledge the subjective element in the scientific method:

> In observing we interpret, though we may not be aware that we are doing
> so. ... In 'seeing' the event each also 'interprets' it, not as a separate act
> but as part of the perception. An implication of this recognition that
> observation is not purely passive is that scientific discovery is creative.
> It actually involves a mixture of painstaking methodical work together

---

53 As cited by Ramm, *Christian View of Science and Scripture*, 120.

54 Charles B. Thaxton, Walter L. Bradley, and Roger L. Olsen, *The Mystery of Life's Origin* (Dallas, Lewis and Stanley, 1984), 202–206.

55 By direct observation we mean that both the cause and the effect are actually witnessed and recorded, rather than just the effect or final state.

56 Thaxton et al, *Mystery of Life's Origin*, 202–206.

57 Bernard Ramm, for example, fails to distinguish between the truth claims of modern science and the practical application of operations science (*Christian View of Science and Scripture*, 23).

with creative intuition and imagination. Seeing, then, always also involves interpreting.[58]

Unfortunately, the intuition and imagination all too often override or dominate what has actually been observed. Objective reality becomes subservient to artificial constructions or models of reality. Francis Schaeffer comments: 'One often finds that the objective reality is getting dim and that which remains is the model in the scientist's thinking.'[59] Michael Bauman agrees:

> The translation of things into numbers is, after all, a translation. Neither the words nor the numbers in scientific theories are complete and exact representations of the constitution and behaviour of the universe, much less are they the things themselves which they are intended to describe in words or embody in numbers and formulae. ... The classification of physical phenomena as suitable and useable scientific data, the arrangement of that data into groups, the translation of that data into numbers, the manipulation of those numbers via computation, and the transformation of the results of that computation into more data and new conclusions are all guided by philosophical deliberations that are prior to and apart from science's alleged empirical nature and militate against it, all of which ought to cause us to hold science's supposedly assured results with less assurance.[60]

Is Science Truly Empirical?

In reality, many conclusions of modern science are neither purely scientific nor genuinely empirical. The common perception that science deals only with verifiable facts and direct observation is utterly naïve, as is the notion that scientists are purely objective truth seekers.[61] Indeed, many of the so-called facts of nature are more 'interprefacts' than verifiable facts.[62] Even Forster and Marston admit '[t]he notion that science is "verifiable" is dead. Scientific knowledge is always partial, and even a scientific "theory of everything" never will be total knowledge.'[63]

Yet many theologians continue to treat scientific conclusions as simply 'matter of fact,' while failing to recognize the ideology behind them. Presuppositions, the need to interpret scientific data, and the selective inclusion or exclusion of data are rarely acknowledged.[64] Despite this, many continue to think that what scientists tell us is always true and reliable. Scientific analysis is assumed to be balanced and objective, and conclusions are presumed to be tested and proven.

---

58 Forster and Marston, *Reason, Science and Faith*, 367–368.

59 Francis A. Schaeffer, 'He Is There and He is Not Silent' in *Francis A. Schaeffer Trilogy* (Leicester, IVP, 1990), 313.

60 Bauman, 'Between Jerusalem and the Laboratory,' 23.

61 Schaeffer, 'He Is There and He is Not Silent' in *Francis A. Schaeffer Trilogy*, 312.

62 Arthur Holmes, *All Truth Is God's Truth* (Grand Rapids, Eerdmans, 1977), 81.

63 Forster and Marston, *Reason, Science and Faith*, 395.

64 A good example of such theologians is Bernard Ramm, *Christian View of Science and Scripture*, 24–26.

Indeed, many Christians appear to believe that what scientists say is akin to what God says! Yet in reality the situation is quite different. As Bauman points out, scientists 'sometimes appear to be narrowly informed, unteachable, and as dogmatic as any ecclesiastical or political inquisition could ever hope to be.'[65]

Another common misconception about science is the notion of falsification. It is generally believed that scientific theories are falsified and discarded if and when contrary data is discovered. However, Thomas Kuhn has categorically shown that this is not what actually happens. He points out that scientists do not 'treat anomalies as counter-instances, though in the vocabulary of philosophy of science that is what they are.'[66] He adds: 'In part this generalization is simply a statement from historic fact. ... No process yet disclosed by the historical study of scientific development at all resembles the methodological stereotype of falsification by direct comparison with nature.'[67] Ultimately, scientific theories are considered to be valid, not by rigorous testing and verification, but by their ability to explain the available data.[68] But if contrary data is discovered the theory is either modified by adjusting one or more of its parameters, or the data is ignored in the hope that a solution will be found in the future. In any case, a theory is never rejected unless there is a ready replacement.[69]

The Big Bang cosmology is a prime example of contrary data being ignored. For example, three-dimensional mapping of galaxy positions indicates that the universe is very 'clumpy,' rather than homogeneous and isotropic. James Trefil writes: 'There shouldn't be galaxies out there at all, and even if there are galaxies, they shouldn't be grouped together the way they are.' He continues: 'The problem of explaining the existence of galaxies has proved to be one of the thorniest in cosmology. By all rights, they just shouldn't be there, yet there they sit. It's hard to convey the depth of the frustration that this simple fact induces among scientists.'[70] Furthermore, William Tifft of the University of Arizona discovered that the red shifts of galaxies fall into distinct packets or quanta, like the rungs of a ladder.[71] This is like saying the speed of particles coming out of an explosion fall into distinct groups of fixed velocity, instead of being evenly distributed across a range of velocities. Tifft was ignored at first, but continued to amass data for many years. But in a major study of more than two hundred galaxies using very sensitive equipment, Bill Napier (Oxford) and Bruce Guthrie (Edinburgh) have confirmed that the phenomenon is real.[72] The

---

65 Bauman, 'Between Jerusalem and the Laboratory,' 18.

66 Thomas S. Kuhn, *The Structure of Scientific Revolutions* (Chicago, University of Chicago Press, 1996), 77.

67 Ibid., 77.

68 Ibid., 145.

69 Ibid., 77.

70 James Trefil, *The Dark Side of the Universe* (New York, Macmillan, 1988), 3, 55.

71 Red shifts are the degree to which the light from distant stars is shifted to the red end of the spectrum, which is supposed to measure the speed at which the star is moving away, and hence how far away it is.

72 See *Science* 271 (February 9, 1996), 759.

Big Bang theory has absolutely no way of explaining this phenomenon. Indeed, it totally undercuts the most basic assumption of the Big Bang cosmology — the Copernican (or Cosmological) principle.

How Does Science Progress?

Most people understand scientific progress as the accumulation of scientific knowledge where today's scientists are building on the work of the previous generation, who, likewise, built on the work of their predecessors, and so on. David Diehi, for example, states that 'general revelation continues to be progressive throughout the whole of human history. This of course is the basis for the increase in our scientific knowledge. As we investigate more deeply and fully the creation of God, he progressively unveils to us its true nature and structure.'[73] But Diehi is confusing science with general revelation. As shown in chapter 1, the two are not the same. Secondly, science as it is understood and practiced today is a relatively modern phenomenon. It is certainly not an activity that took place throughout the whole of human history. Thirdly, a review of the history of science shows that scientific advancement has been anything but a continuous and progressive unveiling of creation's true nature and structure.

Note also that scientific data is just that — data. Data does not speak for itself, so the scientist must attempt to explain its meaning and significance. Such explanation is never done in isolation, but always occurs within a framework of axioms and assumptions, and in relation to other data. Kuhn describes this framework of axioms and assumptions as a 'paradigm.'[74] All 'normal' science operates within the current reigning paradigm. Because interpretation of scientific data always takes place within a paradigm, the interpretation can only *articulate that paradigm* — it cannot correct it, although it can highlight anomalies.[75] Therefore, most scientific research is aimed at solving a current problem, rather than testing the current paradigm.[76]

New scientific theories are rarely, if ever, incremental increases in knowledge. Instead, they usually involve a major 'paradigm shift' where prior data and 'facts' are re-evaluated within the new paradigm.[77] Paradigm changes cause scientists to see the world much differently resulting in a 'scientific revolution.'[78] Not only is previous data reinterpreted, but new kinds of data are collected,[79] and much of what was once established scientific fact is thrown out.

Again, note that a paradigm is never rejected purely on the basis of anomalies. When the number of anomalies becomes intolerable, 'normal' science enters a

---

73 Diehi, 'Evangelicalism and General Revelation,' 453.

74 See Kuhn, *The Structure of Scientific Revolutions*, 43–51.

75 Ibid., 122. My emphasis.

76 Ibid., 144.

77 Ibid., 7.

78 Ibid., 111.

79 Ibid., 121.

stage of crisis.[80] This is when the current paradigm is either significantly altered or alternative paradigms are proposed. The modified reigning paradigm and the new alternatives then compete against each other, and the winner is the one which *best* explains most (but not necessarily all) of the existing scientific data. The key point to note is that a paradigm is only declared invalid and rejected if a replacement is already available. As Kuhn states: 'The decision to reject one paradigm is always simultaneously the decision to accept another, and the judgment leading to that decision involves the comparison of both paradigms with nature *and* with each other.'[81]

Henri Blocher paints a far more accurate picture of scientific progress:

> What is the progress of science, but a perpetual groping in the dark? Every day readjustments are made, periodically there are major reversals. Without going into the personal dimension of the researcher, we should denounce as utterly illusory the notion of pure objectivity, in the sense of neutrality or autonomy. No science operates without presuppositions, guide-lines and organizing models which are above ordinary verification. Ideological choices readily interfere at this basic level ...[82]

Scientific Consensus and Peer Review

It is often argued that the general consensus of scientists and the peer review process ensure the integrity of all scientific results and conclusions, and guard against faulty reasoning, over-extrapolation, poor methodology, and similar. Henri Blocher, for example, believes the agreement between many thousands of researchers is not a matter of chance or conspiracy.[83] Mark Noll also finds consensus convincing: 'If the consensus of modern scientists, who devote their lives to looking at the data of the physical world, is that humans have existed on the planet for a very long time, it is foolish for biblical interpreters to say that "the Bible teaches" the recent creation of human beings.' But again, the way scientific research is actually undertaken reveals a very different story. [84]

Firstly, consensus should never be used to determine truth since this would be committing the logical fallacy of *argumentum ad numerum*.[85] Moreover, consensus also seems to be applied rather inconsistently. For example, many Christians accept the scientific consensus that the universe is 8–15 billion years old, yet those same Christians are usually vehemently opposed to the consensus that all life came about by naturalistic evolution. Secondly, history shows that

---

80 See Ibid., 66–76.

81 Ibid., 77. Original emphasis.

82 Henri Blocher, *In the Beginning*, translated by D.G. Preston (Leicester, IVP, 1984), 22.

83 Ibid., 23.

84 For a thorough examination of the problems and limitations of peer review, see Andrew S. Kulikovsky, 'Creationism, Science and Peer Review' *JoC* 22/1 (2008), 44–49.

85 *Argumentum ad numerum* asserts that the more supporters there are for a particular proposition, the more likely that the proposition is correct.

the consensus has often been wrong — indeed, hopelessly wrong.[86] Thirdly, as Kuhn points out, scientists do not start from scratch rediscovering all the currently known scientific facts and repeating all the experiments that lead to major new discoveries. They do not personally inspect all the evidence, read through all the data, and check all the logic. Rather, as students, they learn and accept the currently held theories on the authority of their teachers and textbooks.[87] This is indoctrination, not consensus. Fourthly, much of the apparent consensus is artificial and enforced. Scientists have to choose which projects to pursue and how to allocate their time. Younger scientists need to choose which research projects will lead to tenure, gain them grants, or lead to controlling a laboratory. These goals will not be achieved by attacking well-established and widely accepted scientific tenets and theories. As a visiting fellow at Australian National University recently pointed out, many researchers feel that any new research which challenges or threatens established ideas is unlikely to be funded, and therefore, they do not even bother to put in an application.[88] Older scientists, on the other hand, have reputations to defend. Thus, Bauman concludes: 'Whether we want to admit it or not, there is a remarkably comprehensive scientific orthodoxy to which scientists must subscribe if they want to get a job, get a promotion, get a research grant, get tenured, or get published. If they resist they get forgotten.'[89] Or as science historian, Professor Evelleen Richards, puts it:

> Science…is not so much concerned with truth as it is with consensus. What counts as 'truth' is what scientists can agree to count as truth at any particular moment in time…[Scientists] are not really receptive or not really open-minded to any sorts of criticisms or any sorts of claims that actually are attacking some of the established parts of the research (traditional) paradigm — in this case neo-Darwinism — so it is very difficult for people who are pushing claims that contradict the paradigm to get a hearing. They'll find it difficult to [get] research grants; they'll find it hard to get their research published; they'll, in fact, find it very hard.[90]

In addition, scientific papers are often only taken seriously if published in particular journals, so research is often constrained by what the editors and peer reviewers of those journals will accept. Indeed, such prejudice is openly admitted and defended by Karl Giberson, editor of *Research News & Opportunities in Science and Theology*:

---

86 E.g. the phlogiston theory, formulated in 1667 by Johann Joachim Becher, stated that an additional fire-like element called 'phlogiston' was contained in all combustible bodies, and was released during combustion. The theory was an attempt to explain oxidation processes, such as combustion and the rusting of metals.

87 Kuhn, *Structure of Scientific Revolutions*, 80.

88 Leigh Baker, 'Rising Fears for Academic Freedom' *ANU Reporter* 32/7 (May 11, 2001).

89 Bauman, 'Between Jerusalem and the Laboratory,' 20.

90 Evelleen Richards, *Lateline*, Australian Broadcasting Corporation, October 9, 1998.

If an editor chooses to publish a hostile review of a book, common politeness would suggest that the author ought to have some space to respond. But editors have a 'higher calling' than common politeness, namely the editorial mission and guidelines that inform every decision as to what will be printed and what will be rejected. I have learned, since becoming the editor of Research News, common politeness is often in tension with editorial priorities.

The mission of Research News, for example, includes publishing the latest findings in science-and-religion, as reported by credible scholars in those fields. In my role as editor, I must make decisions about the 'fringe' material at or beyond the boundaries of the established science-and-religion dialogue. In my editorial judgment, the collection of ideas known as 'scientific creationism' (which is not the same as intelligent design) lacks the credibility to justify publishing any submissions that we get from its adherents.

I would go even further, in fact. The collection of creationist ideas (6,000 year old earth, no common ancestry, all the fossils laid down by Noah's flood, Genesis creation account read literally, etc.) has been so thoroughly discredited by both scientific and religious scholarship that I think it is entirely appropriate for Research News to print material designed to move our readers away from this viewpoint. For example, we might publish a negative review of a book promoting scientific creationism (or astrology, or the healing power of crystals, for that matter), while refusing to allow the author a chance to respond. Is this an unfair bias? Or is it proper stewardship of limited editorial resources?[91]

The Shifting Sands of Science

Many (including scientists) do not realize that the history of science is one of great turmoil, confusion, and revolution. Bauman points out that

> [w]hile Christian orthodoxy seems to have remained stable over two millennia, and while the constant refinement of Christian tenets in the crucible of hard reality seems not to have required any fundamental reorientation in orthodoxy, the record of science is far different. The constant testing of fundamental scientific beliefs has yielded a long series of significant reorientations, some so far reaching as to topple many, sometimes most, of the supporting pillars of any and every previous (and ardently held) scientific world view.[92]

For example, the idea that light consisted of material corpuscles was considered to be a scientific 'fact' in the eighteenth century, until Fresnel and Young in the nineteenth century suggested it was transverse wave motion. This conception of light was also considered to be scientific 'fact,' but in the early twentieth century, this was rejected in favor of the work of Planck, Einstein, and others

---

91 Karl Giberson, 'Editorial Guidelines: Prejudice or Stewardship?' *Research News & Opportunities in Science and Theology* 2/1112 (July/August 2002).

92 Bauman, 'Between Jerusalem and the Laboratory,' 19.

who characterized light as 'photons' — quantum-mechanical entities that exhibit characteristics of both particles and waves.[93]

In the field of physical chemistry, Lavoisier's discovery of oxygen and the resulting 'oxygen theory of combustion' replaced the phlogiston theory.[94] Throughout the eighteenth and into the nineteenth century, chemists universally believed that elementary atoms were held together by forces of mutual affinity, and many phenomena were explained by this belief.[95] Dalton's atomic theory also revolutionized the way chemistry was understood and practiced.[96]

However, as Kuhn notes, scientific revolutions are often 'invisible.' This is due to the fact that both scientists and students of science gain their knowledge from textbooks which (for good reasons) systematically disguise the existence and significance of scientific revolutions.[97] Indeed, when a revolution does occur the textbooks are all rewritten to include the latest scientific knowledge and to match the new scientific paradigm. These texts contain very little discussion of the historical developments that took place, and tend to contain only brief references to some of the prominent scientific pioneers. This leaves the student with the sense that science is a linear field of knowledge which is gradually and incrementally increasing as time passes. In other words, the history of science is always being rewritten. Kuhn explains: '[S]cientists are more affected by the temptation to rewrite history, partly because the results of scientific research show no obvious dependence upon the historical context of the inquiry, and partly because, except during crisis and revolution, the scientist's contemporary position seems so secure.'[98]

In light of the above, one should be very careful about accepting current scientific claims and conclusions as final. 'Science does not speak with one voice, especially over time.'[99] The fallible nature of the findings and the likelihood that current conclusions will be reversed in the future should always be kept in mind. Scientific theories, however well-grounded in 'facts,' are always based on only a partial data set. Thus, scientific theories are always vulnerable to revision or rejection in the light of new data, and '[t]oday's accepted scientific 'truth' might well turn out to be tomorrow's discarded theory.'[100]

The need to periodically overhaul and totally revise current scientific knowledge should also cause the interpreter to think long and hard before attempting to make the teaching of Scripture fit inside the current scientific consensus. Biologist Jean Pond admits that in science, new data arrives daily,

---

93 Kuhn, *Structure of Scientific Revolutions*, 12.

94 Ibid., 56.

95 Ibid., 130.

96 Ibid., 133–135.

97 Ibid., 136–143.

98 Ibid., 138.

99 Bauman, 'Between Jerusalem and the Laboratory,' 19.

100 Mark Ross, 'The Framework Hypothesis: An Interpretation of Genesis 1:1–2:3' in Joseph A. Pipa and David W. Hall (editors), *Did God Create in Six Days?* (Taylors, SC, Southern Presbyterian Press, 1999), 115.

and that scientific knowledge is provisional.[101] Indeed, this is precisely why a theology of creation based on the Bible will always be far superior than a theology based on the uncertain and provisional conclusions drawn from the limited and ever-changing data gleaned from nature.

Science and Scripture

What happens, then, when science and Scripture conflict? Unfortunately, many Christians, and especially those who are also scientists, have a generally positivistic epistemology. That is, they tend to believe only what they can objectively observe. They see the 'facts' of nature as completely objective and indisputable whereas the interpretation of Scripture is totally subjective. Thus, whenever the Bible conflicts with science, it is always the Bible that must give way.

Indeed, this tendency can be clearly seen in the writings of many professing evangelicals with a high view of Scripture. For example, Victor Hamilton writes: '...over the last few centuries science has shown that it is absurd and preposterous to think that the universe was created in one week.'[102] Davis Young confidently argues that 'evangelical scholars will have to face the implications of the mass of geological data indicating that the earth is extremely old, indicating that death has been on earth long before man, and indicating that there has not been a global flood.'[103] He notes that, in recent history, the '[a]ccumulating evidence from nature' points to the vast antiquity of the Earth and has forced theologians 'to take a much harder, more penetrating look at the biblical record than ever before.'[104] Bernard Ramm believes 'Christianity is caught between the embarrassment of simple fiat creationism which is indigestible to modern science, and evolutionism...'[105] He is also convinced that an alternative interpretation (to the traditional one) should be sought because of the 'overwhelming' evidence of geology,[106] and that outside the Garden of Eden 'were death, disease, weeds, thistles, thorns, carnivores, deadly serpents, and intemperate weather. To think otherwise is to run counter to an immense avalanche of fact.'[107] Ronald Youngblood also views the conclusions of astronomy, geology and palaeontology as overwhelming support for a universe and an earth that is billions of years old. Therefore, he suggests that a reinterpretation of the Genesis narrative is warranted.[108]

---

101 Jean Pond, 'Independence' in Richard F. Carlson (editor), *Science and Christianity: Four Views* (Leicester, IVP, 2000), 74–77.

102 Victor P. Hamilton, *The Book of Genesis 1–17*, NICOT (Grand Rapids, Michigan, Eerdmans, 1990), 53.

103 Davis A. Young, 'Scripture in the Hands of Geologists (Part Two)' *WTJ* 49 (Fall 1987), 295.

104 Davis A. Young, *Christianity and the Age of the Earth* (Grand Rapids, Michigan, Zondervan, 1982), 13.

105 Ramm, *The Christian View of Science and Scripture*, 79.

106 Ibid., 123.

107 Ibid., 335.

108 Ronald F. Youngblood, *The Book of Genesis*, 2nd edition (Grand Rapids, Michigan, Baker, 1991), 42–43.

Millard Erickson also believes scientific data is problematic: 'It is at the point of the scientific data that fiat creationism encounters difficulty. For when those data are taken seriously, they appear to indicate a considerable amount of development, including what seem to be transitional forms between species. There are even some forms that appear to be ancestors of the human species.'[109] H.W. Seaford Jr is even more confident about the superiority of scientific conclusions over the interpretation of Scripture:

> A literalistic interpretation of the creation story generates insurmountable problems for contemporary Christians who are acquainted with scientific knowledge. The human species did not begin in the ecological and cultural setting described in the opening chapters of Genesis. There were many populations of people before Adam and Eve, as literally understood. Only by allegorical interpretation can theology be noncontradictive to archaeology, biochemistry, biology, and paleoanthropology.[110]

Likewise, biologist Pattle T. Pun, although he rejects the historical nature of the Genesis account and adopts theistic evolution, admits that

> the most straightforward understanding of the Genesis record, *without regard to all the hermeneutical considerations suggested by science*, is that God created heaven and earth in six solar days, that man was created in the sixth day, that death and chaos entered the world after the Fall of Adam and Eve, that all of the fossils were the result of the catastrophic universal deluge which spared only Noah's family and the animals therewith.[111]

Roger J. Cuffey, a former consulting editor for the *Journal of the American Scientific Affiliation*,[112] goes even further and openly rejects scriptural authority regarding science and the natural world. He writes: 'I personally would temporarily accept the scientific conclusion rather than the exegetical one so long as doing so does not sacrifice the few basic spiritual concepts taught by the whole Bible.'[113]

How, then, should science affect biblical interpretation? Should science be interpreted in the light of Scripture or vice versa? The disagreement among evangelicals over the age of the earth illustrates these two different approaches. The old-earth view is built on the position that science has proved beyond reasonable doubt the great antiquity of the earth. Therefore, the true meaning of Scripture must be interpreted to show that it is not out of harmony with this

---

109 Millard J. Erickson, *Christian Theology*, 2nd edition (Grand Rapids, Michigan, Baker, 1998), 503.

110 H.W. Seaford Jr., 'Were There People Before Adam and Eve?' in R.F. Youngblood (editor), *The Genesis Debate* (Nashville: Thomas Nelson, 1986), 163.

111 Pattle P.T. Pun, 'A Theology of Progressive Creation' *PSCF* 39/1 (March 1987), 14. My emphasis.

112 The American Scientific Affiliation is a professional society for scientists who are Christians.

113 R.J. Cuffey, 'Bible-Science Symposium,' *JASA* 21/4 (1969), 108–109.

fact. On the other hand, the young-earth model is based on the position that the scientific data used to establish the 'fact' of an old earth is at best incomplete and can legitimately be interpreted to fit within a young-earth model.

But which approach is better? Milton S. Terry offers the following incisive comments:

> That certainly is a false science which is built upon inferences, assumptions, and theories, and yet presumes to dogmatize as if its hypotheses were facts. And that is a system of hermeneutics equally false and misleading which is so flexible, under the pressure of new discoveries as to yield to the putting of any number of new meanings upon an old and common word.[114]

The problem with allowing scientific 'knowledge' to influence the meaning of the text has not escaped Blocher's attention. When the Bible teaches something contrary to established scientific 'fact,' he notes the tendency to argue that God did not actually mean what the Bible appears to communicate. Blocher considers this to be subjecting the word of God to our own supposed knowledge: 'And this is what we would say: we know that the genesis of the cosmos took millions of years, *therefore* the 'seven days' must be taken allegorically; and that is conferring an unacceptable authority on scientific opinions ... You might as well say that the resurrection of Christ is a symbol because we "know" that the dead do not come back to life!'[115]

The other danger with allowing scientific conclusions to determine the interpretation of Scripture is the likelihood that these scientific conclusions will either significantly change or be abandoned altogether. As Marvin Goodman points out, 'time after time, well-intentioned Bible scholars have found how unstable and shifting the ground becomes when they embark on a course of accommodation to scientific theories.'[116] Even Davis Young admits that such concordism gives us 'a Bible that is constantly held hostage to the latest scientific theorizing. Texts are twisted, pulled, poked, stretched, and prodded to "agree" with scientific conclusions so that concordism today undermines honest, Christian exegesis.'[117]

As shown above, there are many philosophical and methodological problems associated with scientific research. Therefore, the high authority ascribed to scientists is unwarranted and the extreme level of confidence in scientific conclusions is misplaced. In contrast, the message of Scripture has always been clear, and Christian doctrine has remained amazingly stable throughout history.

Thus, it is far more prudent to start with the Bible and interpret scientific data in a biblical framework rather than a framework built upon the very limited knowledge and understanding of scientists which always seems to be changing. As Graeme Goldsworthy rightly notes,

---

114 Milton S. Terry, *Biblical Hermeneutics*, 2nd edition (Grand Rapids, Zondervan, 1974), 534.

115 Blocher, *In the Beginning*, 26. Original emphasis.

116 Goodman, 'Non-literal Interpretations of Genesis Creation' *GJ* 14/1 (Winter 1973), 34.

117 Davis A. Young, 'Scripture in the Hands of Geologists (Part One)' *WTJ* 49/1 (Spring 1987), 6.

> we also need to be reminded of the relationship of God's word to the reasoning of man the creature about what is true — one does not take a pocket flashlight and shine it on the sun to see if the sun is real! The truth of God's word cannot be subject to the puny light of man's self-centered reason. God's word created what is and must interpret what is.[118]

Thus, scientific views should never play a part in the actual interpretation of Scripture. Interpretation must be based solely on the text and its context. Indeed, if the Bible is the Scripture of God, then no other authority, including scientific reasoning, may dictate how it is to be understood.[119] In fact, it is *science* that needs to take *its* cues from biblical revelation. As Graeme Goldsworthy observes: 'Creation means that true science or knowledge needs God's revelation in his word to give it direction, and to prevent it from entering the realm of superstition and magic. Creation reminds us that modern theories which suggest that life, personhood, love and moral value are all the result of chance, have long since abandoned the realm of real science.'[120]

Yet so often this is not the case. Too many Christians feel they must conform to whatever scientists claim that science teaches about the Bible. R. Laird Harris expresses his displeasure with this situation:

> I am appalled at the freedom with which our Christian scientists are toying with the Biblical texts. I may soften that by adding that our theologians are doing so too and so the scientists naturally are taking it up. But the scientists should have a chance to hear the criticisms of various theologians rather than jumping to the first far out exegesis of Genesis that seems to meet the scientific need.[121]

Note that this does not mean or imply that an 'anti-science' position should be taken. Science can provide valuable information to illuminate and clarify a particular interpretation, as well as providing some integrity checks. Fred Howe explains:

> One should not attempt to ascertain the true meaning of biblical terms in the light of any *current scientific constructs*. Assuredly the implications of biblical terms must be studied, their full significance explored, and where necessary faulty interpretations brought into harmony with true meaning. The true meaning must be ascertained by the full use of the exegetical method alone, and then of course *illumined* or even *clarified* by any established or settled truth from the realm of science.[122]

Science and Scripture in History

Some theologians are quick to point out that interpretations based on what was thought to be the clear teaching of Scripture, have often shown to be in error by established, empirical, scientific facts. They note that certain biblical texts were used

---

118 Graeme Goldsworthy, *Gospel and Kingdom* (Carlisle, Paternoster, 1981), 49–50.

119 Blocher, *In the Beginning*, 25.

120 Graeme Goldsworthy, *According to Plan* (Leicester, IVP, 1991) 127.

121 R. Laird Harris, Letter to the Editor, *JASA* 16 (December 1964), 127.

122 Frederic R. Howe, 'The Age of the Earth Part 1: An Appraisal of Some Current Evangelical Positions' *BSac* 142 (January–March 1985), 29–30. Original emphasis.

to support the notion of a flat earth until Christopher Columbus sailed around the globe in 1492. Similarly, the Roman Catholic Church held to a geocentric cosmology which was supposedly based on the teaching of Scripture.[123]

Columbus and the Flat Earth

There is a common belief that before he made his historic voyage in 1492, Christopher Columbus, a 'simple mariner,' appeared before a crowd of dogmatic theologians and ignorant inquisitors, all of whom believed that Scripture taught the earth was flat. Columbus then set out to prove them all wrong and sailed around the globe.

While it is true that there was a meeting at Salamanca in 1491, this common understanding of what happened does not contain a shred of truth. Historian Jeffrey Burton Russell identifies Washington Irving (1783–1859), a noted American historical fiction writer, as one of the primary sources of this 'folktale.'[124] Irving created a fictitious account of a non-existent university council and let his imagination run wild.[125] Thus the whole story is 'misleading and mischievous nonsense.'[126]

Furthermore, Russell notes that the myth of the flat earth has become part of the larger myth of the 'eternal war between science (good) and religion (bad) throughout Western Society.'[127] The notion that people used to believe in a flat earth and that Scripture supported such a belief is another example of gross historical revisionism. Russell contends that 'historical scholarship is often sloppy ... [and] far too much historical scholarship consists of contorting the evidence to fit ideological models.'[128] He goes on to demonstrate that with very few exceptions, from the third century B.C. onwards, all educated people in the western world believed the earth was a globe. The notion of a spherical earth appears in the writings of Pythagoras (sixth century B.C.), Aristotle, Euclid, and Aristarchus. By the time of Eratosthenes (third century B.C.), Crates (second century B.C.), Strabo (third century B.C.), and Ptolemy (first century A.D.), the spherical shape of the earth was accepted by all educated Greeks and Romans, and the situation did not change with the advent of Christianity. Yet Irving's

---

123 As far as I have been able to determine, these two cases are the *only* examples ever cited to substantiate the claim that science has identified faulty biblical interpretation. Some may cite evolution as an example also, but the scientific data supporting this model is far from conclusive — indeed, much of it either points away from evolution or is fraudulent. See Jonathan Wells, *Icons of Evolution* (Washington D.C., Regnery, 2002).

124 The other originator being Antoine-Jean Letronne (1787–1848), an anti-religious academic, who published *On the Cosmological Ideas of the Church Fathers* (1834). See Jeffrey Burton Russell, *Inventing the Flat Earth* (London, Praeger, 1997) 49–51, 58–59.

125 Russell, *Inventing the Flat Earth*, 40–41, 52–54.

126 Jeffrey Burton Russell, 'The Myth of the Flat Earth,' Unpublished paper presented at the American Scientific Affiliation Conference, Westmont College, August 4, 1997. He notes that this was listed as the number one historical illusion some years back by the Historical Society of Britain.

127 Ibid.

128 Ibid.

fictitious version of events persists in the minds of many. This was largely due to the writings of Andrew Dickson White who, along with many later writers, have uncritically accepted and repeated Irving's account, and presented it as an example of warfare between science and Christianity.[129] While the occasional churchman did believe in a flat earth, such men were few and far between, and certainly not representative of the wider Christian church, or orthodox Christian teaching.

Copernicus, Galileo, and Heliocentrism

Around 1530, Copernicus (1473–1543), a canon of the Roman Catholic Church, constructed a heliocentric model of the universe contrary to the geocentric model proposed by Ptolemy which was the official position of the church. He was reluctant to publish it, however, for fear of being ridiculed.

Copernicus' reluctance to publish and the process against Galileo for defending the heliocentric view are commonly cited as examples of where erroneous biblical interpretation was corrected by the facts of science.

Yet Copernicus published an abstract of his theory in 1531 which seems to have been widely circulated. He received much clerical encouragement throughout his lifetime, and in 1536 Cardinal Schönberg urged Copernicus to publish the unabridged version. However, the complete work (*De Revolutionibus Orbium Coelestium*) did not appear until 1543, just before his death.

It should be noted that if Copernicus had any genuine fear of publication, it was the reaction of scientists, not the church, that worried him.[130] Again, it was a bishop and a cardinal who first urged Copernicus to publish his work, and when it finally appeared it contained a dedication to Pope Paul III.[131] Note also that at no time in history has the church ever declared Copernicus' theory to be heretical.[132] Although the book was placed on the Vatican Index, this did not occur until 1616, and it was removed again in 1620 after some minor changes.[133]

In a personal letter written in 1597 to Johannes Kepler (1571–1630), Galileo Galilei (1564–1642) stated that he was a Copernican, although he made no public admission of his belief until 1613 when he published *Letters on Sunspots*. Galileo's other major defense of Copernicanism, *Dialogue on the Two Chief World Systems*, was published in 1632.

It is commonly believed that Galileo's observations and arguments offered overwhelming support for Copernicus' theory. The stubborn, dogmatic, ignorant theologians in the Catholic Church wanted to silence Galileo in the fear that their interpretation of Scripture would be shown to be in error, and thus nullifying the church's claim as the authority in biblical interpretation.

---

129 Russell, *Inventing the Flat Earth*, 27–28, 45–47, 69–70.

130 David C. Lindberg and Ronald L. Numbers, 'Beyond War and Peace: A Reappraisal of the Encounter Between Christianity and Science' *PSCF* 39/3 (September 1987), 144.

131 Ibid.

132 W.R. Shea, 'Galileo and the Church' in D.C. Lindberg and R.L. Numbers (eds), *God and Nature* (Berkeley, University of California Press, 1986), 128.

133 Thomas Schirrmacher, 'The Galileo Affair: history or heroic hagiography?' *JoC* 14/1 (2000), 92.

Galileo was firstly warned not to teach the heliocentric theory, and then finally, silenced altogether by being brought before the Inquisition in 1633, charged with teaching heresy, and placed in house arrest.

This rendition of the Galileo controversy has been perpetuated by many historians and theologians, including David W. Diehi,[134] R. Laird Harris,[135] Mark E. Ross,[136] and most recently, by M. James Sawyer.[137] But, again, there has been much historical revisionism regarding these events. As Thomas Schirrmacher states: 'The depiction of the process against Galileo as a heroic scientist standing up against the narrow-minded dogmatism of the Christian church is based entirely on myth, not on historical research.'[138]

The famous Galileo-versus-the-church conflict began around 1611 and was prompted by

> ... a body of dissident professors at Pisa who, for further support, had allied themselves with a set of courtiers at Florence. They were all jealous of the special treatment Galileo was given [by the church and] of his large salary and of the continual favours bestowed upon him personally by the Grand Duke. In addition, the academics were furious that this braggart of an anti-Aristotelian should be in a position to promote his iconoclastic views.[139]

It is important to understand that the disagreements between scientists and theologians at this time was not a conflict between Christianity and science, but a conflict between Aristotelianism and science.[140] Galileo was a scientist who was convinced of the truth and accuracy of Scripture. His fight was against contemporary principles of biblical interpretation which were blinded by Aristotelian philosophy and which failed to do justice to the text of Scripture.[141]

---

134 Diehi, 'Evangelicalism and General Revelation,' 453.

135 R. Laird Harris, 'The Length of the Creative Days in Genesis 1' in Pipa and Hall, *Did God Create in Six Days?* 105.

136 Mark E. Ross, 'The Framework Hypothesis: An Interpretation of Genesis 1:1–2:3' in Pipa and Hall, *Did God Create in Six Days?* 116.

137 See chapter 7, 'Hardening of the Categories: Why Theologians Have opposed "New Knowledge"' in M. James Sawyer, *The Survivor's Guide to Theology* (Grand Rapids, Michigan, Zondervan, 2002).

138 Schirrmacher, 'The Galileo Affair,' 91.

139 Colin Ronan, *Galileo* (New York, Putnam's Sons, 1974). 131–132.

140 Ramm, *Christian View of Science and Scripture*, 36. Forster and Marston, (*Reason and Faith*, 293) agree that it is inaccurate to present the Galileo affair as a case of science verses religion.

141 Alister E. McGrath (*A Scientific Theology, Volume 1, Nature* [Grand Rapids, Michigan, Eerdmans, 2001], 49–50) points out that 'the development of medieval theology often shows an unsettling dependence upon certain widely-held (yet largely non-empirical) "scientific" assumptions, deriving from the Aristotelian physics of the period. The biblical exegesis and theological analysis of that period tend to reflect the unconscious incorporation of Aristotelian ideas on the basis of the implicit assumption that these were "correct". As a result, there was intense resistance to new approaches to biblical interpretation which called these settled Aristotelian presuppositions into question. Through a subtle and largely unconscious process of reasoning, a text which was originally interpreted *in the light of Aristotelian presuppositions* subsequently became regarded as *proof of these Aristotelian presuppositions.*' Original emphasis.

Note also that the Ptolemaic system 'had been denied by many high officials and Jesuit astronomers even before Galileo was born.'[142] Indeed, the Jesuits themselves '*were more Copernican than Galileo was...*'[143] In fact, hardly any experts in astronomy believed in the Ptolemaic system at that time. The choice was not between Ptolemy and Copernicus, but between Copernicus and the system proposed by Tycho Brahe.[144]

Galileo was well regarded by the church and his first defense of the Copernican system, *Letters on Sunspots* (1613), was well received and no criticism was raised. Indeed, Cardinal Barberini, who later became Pope Urban VIII and who would sentence him in 1633, was among those to congratulate Galileo on his publication.[145]

Thus, Galileo's greatest enemies were not in the church but rather among his colleagues and fellow scientists, most of whom denied the Copernican system,[146] and who were afraid of losing their position and influence.[147] Santillana writes: '[i]t has been known for a long time that a major part of the church's intellectuals were on the side of Galileo, while the clearest opposition to him came from secular ideas.'[148] Arthur Koestler adds:

> ...there existed a powerful body of men whose hostility to Galileo never abated: the Aristotelians at the Universities. ... Innovation is a twofold threat to academic mediocrities: it endangers their oracular authority, and it evokes the deeper fear that their whole laboriously constructed edifice might collapse. The academic backwoods-men have been the curse of genius ... it was this threat — not Bishop Dantiscus or Pope Paul III — which had crowned Canon Koppernigk [i.e. Copernicus] into silence. ... The first serious attack on religious grounds came also not from clerical quarters, but from a layman — none other than delle Colombe, the leader of the [Aristotelian] league ...[149]

Galileo's critics had little success at stopping him with scientific arguments, and decided that it would be much easier to silence him on the grounds of heresy, and an accusation against Galileo was filed in 1615 but was denied by the Court of Inquisition.[150]

---

142 Schirrmacher, 'The Galileo Affair,' 92.

143 Arthur C. Custance, 'The medieval synthesis and the modern fragmentation of thought' in *Science and Faith: The Doorway Papers* VIII (Grand Rapids, Michigan, Zondervan, 1984 repr.), 154.

144 Schirrmacher, 'The Galileo Affair,' 96.

145 Ibid., 92.

146 Indeed, the vast majority of scientists at that time rejected the Copernican system. See B. Barber, 'Resistance of scientists to scientific discovery' *Science* 134 (1961), 596ff; Arthur C. Custance, 157.

147 Schirrmacher, 'The Galileo Affair,' 92; Stillman Drake (editor and translator), *Discoveries and Opinions of Galileo* (New York: Doubleday, 1957).

148 Giorgie de Santillana, *The Crime of Galileo* (Chicago: University of Chicago Press, 1955), xii.

149 Arthur Koestler, *The Sleepwalkers* (London, Hutchinson, 1959), 427.

150 Ibid., 441–442.

Shortly after, Cardinal Bellarmine wrote to Paolo Antonio Foscarini, who had recently published a defense of Galileo's view from Scripture, cautioning him to treat the Copernican theory as only a hypothesis. Although Bellarmine is clearly quite skeptical, he does make the following admission:

> If there were a true demonstration that the sun is at the center of the world and the earth in the third heaven, and that the sun does not circle the earth but the earth circles the sun, then one would have to proceed with great care in explaining the Scriptures that appear contrary, and say rather that we do not understand them than what is demonstrated is false. But I will not believe that there is such a demonstration, until it is shown to me.

Thus, Bellarmine was open to the possibility that Galileo was right, but wanted physical proof.[151] However, Galileo refused to provide any proofs. The problem was that he *had no proofs*![152]

In actual fact, Galileo was not strictly an experimental scientist, and in the case of the Copernican system, he did not see the need for proof because he took it as axiomatic. Indeed, certain components of Galileo's theory could not be proven because Johannes Kepler's work had already shown them to be incorrect.[153]

When Galileo did eventually present a supposed proof for the Copernican theory — that the tides were caused by the turning of the earth — it was in fact completely erroneous.[154] Indeed, William A. Wallace has shown that Galileo knew exactly that the proof was lacking and was merely covering this fact with his rhetoric.[155] Lindberg and Numbers add:

> Galileo lacked the convincing physical proof of the mobility of the earth that his own position demanded. Every one of his telescopic observations was compatible with the modified geocentric system of Tycho Brahe. ...The trouble in which Galileo eventually found himself, and which led ultimately to his condemnation, then, resulted not from clear scientific evidence running afoul of biblical claims to the contrary (as White tells the story), but from ambiguous scientific evidence provoking an intramural dispute within Catholicism over the proper principles of scriptural interpretations ...[156]

Because of the lack of physical proof, Cardinal Bellarmine in 1616, on orders from Pope Paul V, warned Galileo not to hold or defend the Copernican theory as actual truth. There was at this stage no great hostility in the Church toward

---

151 Ibid., 447–448.

152 Schirrmacher, 'The Galileo Affair,' 95.

153 Ibid.

154 Shea, 127. Galileo also defended a number of other erroneous ideas. See Schirrmacher, 'The Galileo Affair,' 96.

155 Schirrmacher, 'The Galileo Affair' 95–96.

156 David C. Lindberg and Ronald L. Numbers, 'Beyond War and Peace: A Reappraisal of the Encounter Between Christianity and Science' *PSCF* 39/3 (September 1987), 145.

Galileo. He later had an audience with Pope Paul V, and was assured by him. Cardinal Bellarmine also wrote a letter to Galileo certifying that he had not been on trial nor condemned by the Inquisition. Again, note that Bellarmine did not actually deny the Copernican system, but simply prohibited it from being presented as fact until it could be proven.

Galileo had always been favored by Pope Urban VIII (the former Cardinal Barberini), who had even written an ode to him. This affection remained up until shortly before Galileo's trial, when Urban's friendship turned into hatred. Schirrmacher notes that this was caused by several factors, including Galileo's carelessness, arrogance, and personal attacks, as well as the political situation. In 1632, Galileo obtained the right to print his major work *Dialogo* from the Pope personally, with approval to make some minor corrections if necessary. Galileo cleverly circumvented papal censorship, and put Urban's main argument for the Copernican system into the mouth of the fool 'Simplicio,' who, in the *Dialogo* of three scientists, always asks the silly questions and defends the Ptolemaic view of the world. This greatly angered Urban.

> Not only had Galileo gone, in letter and spirit, against the agreement to treat Copernicus strictly as a hypothesis, not only had he obtained the imprimatur by methods resembling sharp practice, but Urban's favorite argument was only mentioned briefly at the very end of the book, and put into the mouth of the simpleton who on any other point was invariably proved wrong. Urban even suspected that Simplicius was intended as a caricature of his own person.[157]

Thus, Galileo was prosecuted not on religious grounds, but for disobeying papal orders, as well as for other personal and political reasons. Urban was the one who initiated the trial while the Inquisitors were apparently indifferent. The final decision lacked three signatures and two of those who signed did so under protest. Only one cardinal, the Pope's brother, zealously pushed the trial ahead.[158]

Science historian John Heilbron points out that

> Galileo's heresy, according to the standard distinction used by the Holy Office, was 'inquisitorial' rather than 'theological.' This distinction allowed it to proceed against people for disobeying orders or creating scandals, although neither articles violated an article defined and promulgated by a pope or general council. ... Since, however, the church had never declared that the Biblical passages implying a moving sun had to be interpreted in favour of a Ptolemaic universe as an article of faith, optimistic commentators ... could understand 'formally heretical' to mean 'provisionally not accepted.'[159]

Heilbron goes on to show that the general reactions of Galileo's contemporaries and later astronomers was that 'the reference to heresy in connection with

---

157 Koestler, *Sleepwalkers*, 483.

158 Schirrmacher, 'The Galileo Affair,' 96–97.

159 John L. Heilbron, *The Sun in the Church: Cathedrals as Solar Observatories* (Cambridge, Massachussets, Harvard University Press, 1999), 202–203.

Galileo or Copernicus had no general or theological significance.'[160] In any case, Galileo was not actually pronounced a heretic — the verdict was 'suspicion of heresy.'[161]

It appears, then, that the church was used by the academic community to quell what they felt was a threat to both their method of knowing and their authority. The church has been painted as an enemy of science, when, in actual fact, Galileo's scientific peers and colleagues were the greater enemies of science.

But what about the Protestant theologians? Andrew Dickson White claims that 'all branches of the Protestant Church ... vied with each other in denouncing the Copernican doctrine as contrary to Scripture.'[162] White also maintains that the theologians Martin Luther, Philip Melanchthon, and John Calvin all bitterly attacked Copernicus's theory.

In actual fact, Luther only made a single off-the-cuff remark, during a 'table talk' in 1539 (four years before the publication of Copernicus' book), in which he said, 'Whoever wants to be clever must agree with nothing that others esteem. He must do something of his own. This is what that fellow does who wishes to turn the whole of astronomy upside down. Even in these things that are thrown into disorder I believe the Holy Scriptures, for Joshua commanded the sun to stand still and not the earth [Josh. 10:12].'[163] The 'Table Talk' was based on notes taken by Luther's students, which were later compiled and published in 1566 — twenty years after Luther's death. Furthermore, the verse Luther cited (Josh. 10:12) in support of his apparent skepticism, was easily explained by Johannes Kepler using Luther's own principles of biblical interpretation,

---

160 Ibid., 203.

161 Stillman Drake, *Galileo* (Oxford: Oxford University Press, 1980), 351. The sentencing of Galileo (1633) is as follows: 'We say, pronounce, sentence, and declare that you, the above-mentioned Galileo, because of the things deduced in the trial and confessed by you as above, have rendered yourself according to this Holy Office vehemently suspected of heresy, namely of having held and believed a doctrine which is false and contrary to the divine and Holy Scripture: that the sun is the center of the world and does not move from east to west, and the earth moves and is not the center of the world, and that one may hold and defend as probable an opinion after it has been declared and defined contrary to Holy Scripture. Consequently you have incurred all the censures and penalties imposed and promulgated by the sacred canons and all particular and general laws against such delinquents. We are willing to absolve you from them provided that first, with a sincere heart and unfeigned faith, in front of us you abjure, curse, and detest the above-mentioned errors and heresies, and every other error and heresy contrary to the Catholic and Apostolic Church, in the manner and form we will prescribe to you.' From Maurice A. Finocchiaro (editor and translator), *The Galileo Affair: A Documentary History* (Berkeley, University of California Press, 1989).

162 Andrew Dickson White, *A History of the Warfare of Science with Theology in Christendom*, 2 volumes (New York, 1896) 1:126

163 This version of the remark comes from Anthony Lauterbach who dined with the Luthers. John Aurifaber's version of the same conversation uses the expression 'that fool' instead of 'that fellow' but Lauterbach's version is generally regarded as being more reliable (see Theodore G. Tappert [editor and translator], 'Table Talk,' *Luther's Works*, Vol. 54, Helmut T. Lehmann (editor) [Philadelphia, Fortress Press, 1967], xi–xxiii).

which took into account the language of appearance.[164] Since this was Luther's only recorded comment on the subject, it cannot be construed as part of a thoughtful and concerted attack on Copernicus or Copernicans. In the case of Melanchthon, although he expressed early disapproval of heliocentrism as a description of reality, he later softened his position.[165]

Calvin spoke out against the mobility of the earth in a sermon on 1 Corinthians 10–11 (dating from 1556), denouncing the propagators of such vain novelties for their contentious spirit, which undermines the quest for truth. However, it is likely that Calvin had in mind only the rotational motion of the earth as described in Cicero's *Academica*, and there is no convincing evidence that he was even acquainted with the heliocentrism of Copernicus. In any case, Calvin's dismissal of the earth's mobility is a passing remark, and it is clear that cosmological issues never entered systematically into his thought.[166]

Summary

If interpreters begin their task by assuming that the Bible is God's special, inerrant, propositional revelation to humanity in human language, then most interpretive problems will quickly disappear. Biblical interpretation is never easy, but careful and judicious exegesis is worth the effort, and gives virtual certainty or at least a very high level of confidence in one's interpretation.

Yet, so many interpreters continue to be intimidated by the truth claims of modern science, and either deny what the Scriptures apparently teach or stretch them to fit the current scientific consensus. The truth claims of science always seem to trump exegesis, regardless of how thorough it is and how well done. At this point, one would do well to heed the warning of John D. Hannah: '[In the nineteenth century] science appeared to speak with the inerrancy that we accord to Scripture alone. It behooves us to remember to be cautious not to neglect the exegesis of Scripture and the qualitative gulf between special and general revelation.'[167]

E.J. Young asks: 'Why is it so difficult to [get at the meaning the author sought to convey] with the first chapter of the Bible? The answer, we believe, is that although men pay lip service to the doctrine of creation, in reality they find it a very difficult doctrine to accept.'[168] Indeed, it appears that when considering the doctrine of creation, the difficulty is not *understanding* the teaching of Scripture, but *believing* it.

---

164 John Dillenberger, *Protestant Thought and Natural Science* (New York, Doubleday, 1960), 33.

165 Bruce T. Moran, 'The Universe of Philip Melanchthon: Criticism and Use of the Copernican Theory,' *Comitatus* 4 (1973), 14.

166 See Robert White, 'Calvin and Copernicus: The Problem Reconsidered' *CTJ* 15 (1980), 233ff, and Christopher B. Kaiser, 'Calvin, Copernicus, and Castellio' *CTJ* 21 (1985), 5–31.

167 John D. Hannah, 'Bibliotheca Sacra and Darwinism: An Analysis of the Nineteenth-Century Conflict Between Science and Theology' *GTJ* 4/1 (September 1983), 57, 58.

168 E.J. Young, *Studies in Genesis One*, 101.

CHAPTER 3

Creation and Genesis:
A Historical Survey

A nalysis of the historical development of theological motifs is, as Grant
Osborne notes, 'conspicuously absent' from most theological works and
commentaries.[1] Yet such analysis is crucial for determining a truly *biblical*
theology, in that it protects the interpreter from making the common mistake
of reading later ideas back into the biblical text.[2] Indeed, there has been a great
deal of misrepresentation of the church's historical views concerning the Genesis
cosmogony, the days of creation, and the age of the earth.[3]

The following survey outlines the major views on creation and the age of the
earth advocated by Christians and Jews throughout history, as well as analyzing
the influence of geological studies and evolutionary theory on interpretation.

While this survey is by no means exhaustive, it is nevertheless representative.[4]

---

1 Grant R. Osborne, *The Hermeneutical Spiral* (Downers Grove, Illinois, IVP, 1991), 265.

2 Ibid., 266.

3 See in particular Hugh Ross (*Creation and Time* [Colorado Springs, NavPress, 1994], 16–24;
[with Gleason Archer] 'The Day-Age Response' in D.G. Hagopian [editor], *The Genesis Debate*
[Mission Viejo, California, Crux Press, 2001], 68–70), Don Stoner (*A New Look at an Old
Earth* [Eugene, Oregon, Harvest House, 1997], 117–119), and Roger Forster and Paul Marston
(*Reason, Science and Faith* [Crowborough, East Sussex, Monarch, 1999], 188–240).

4 There has also been some outstanding historical scholarship in this area — in particular, the
work of Jack P. Lewis ('The Days of Creation: An Historical Survey of Interpretation' *JETS* 32/4
[December 1989], 433–455), David W. Hall ('The Evolution of Mythology: Classic Creation
Survives as the Fittest Among its Critics and Revisers' in Joseph. A. Pipa and David. W. Hall
[editors], *Did God Create in Six Days?* [Taylors, South Carolina, Southern Presbyterian Press,
1999], 267–305; 'What was the View of the Westminster Assembly Divines on Creation Days?'
in Ibid., 41–52.; [with J. Ligon Duncan] 'The 24-Hour View' in David G. Hagopian [editor],
The Genesis Debate [Mission Viejo, California, Crux Press], 47–52; 'The 24-Hour Reply' in Ibid.,
99–106), and Terry Mortenson ('British Scriptural Geologists in the First Half of the Nineteenth
Century: Part 1, Historical Setting' *JoC* 11/2 [1997], 221–252; 'British Scriptural Geologists
in the First Half of the Nineteenth Century: Part 2, Granville Penn (1761–1844)' *JoC* 11/3
[1997], 361–374; 'British Scriptural Geologists in the First Half of the Nineteenth Century: Part
3, George Bugg (1769–1851)' *JoC* 12/2 [1998], 237–252; 'British Scriptural Geologists in the
First Half of the Nineteenth Century: Part 4, Andrew Ure (1778–1857)' *JoC* 12/3 [1998], 362–
373; 'British Scriptural Geologists in the First Half of the Nineteenth Century: Part 5, Henry
Cole (1792?–1858)' *JoC* 13/1 [1999], 92–99; 'British Scriptural Geologists in the First Half
of the Nineteenth Century: Part 6, Thomas Gisborne (1758–1846)' *JoC* 14/1 [2000], 75–80;
'British Scriptural Geologists in the First Half of the Nineteenth Century' Unpublished Ph.D.
dissertation, University of Coventry, 1996) among others. This survey is indebted to their work
and draws heavily from it.

Early Jewish and Christian Commentators

The rabbinic writings reflect many different views concerning the creation account, and most comments tend to relate to various details in the text rather than the temporal implications of the days of creation. Nevertheless, R. Judah stated that the world 'was created in six days, for in the account of each day it is written, "and it was so".'[5]

Concerning the problem of day and night existing before the sun and moon, the Talmudic writers concluded that time was created separately, and that 'God fixed the duration of the day and night and then arranged for the appearance of the sun and moon to conform therewith.'[6]

The Jewish historian Josephus made a number of comments about the days of Creation, in book 1 of his *Antiquities of the Jews*. Although he promised a separate treatise on the days — a promise he apparently did not keep — his other comments indicate that he almost certainly understood the days literally. Regarding the first day, he wrote, 'The name he gave to one was Night, and the other he called Day: and he named the beginning of light, and the time of rest, The Evening and The Morning, and this was indeed the first day. But Moses said it was one day.'[7] He continued: 'Accordingly Moses says, that in just six days the world, and all that is therein, was made. And that the seventh day was a rest, and a release from the labor of such operations; whence it is that we Celebrate a rest from our labors on that day, and call it the Sabbath.' Furthermore, regarding the exposition of Genesis 2:4 onwards, Josephus commented, 'Moses, after the seventh day was over begins to talk philosophically,'[8] which indicates that Josephus understood the preceding passage (Genesis 1:1–2:4) not as a philosophical or theological discussion but as straightforward historical narrative.

Forster and Marston argue that the Jewish readers of Genesis 1–3 understood much of it as allegorical rather than as literal history. In support, they appeal to Philo, and the Targums.[9] Their claims, however, are without substance. Firstly, Philo was a Hellenistic Jew who could not read Hebrew.[10] Not surprisingly, his writings are almost totally free of rabbinic concerns. Instead, he resorted to 'an extensive allegorical interpretation of Scripture that made Jewish law consonant with the ideals of Stoic, Pythagorean, and especially Platonic thought.'[11] Philo was clearly more concerned with harmonizing the Old Testament with Greek philosophy, rather than with careful exegesis. Thus, to appeal to Philo

---

5 Lewis, 'The Days of Creation,' 449.

6 Abraham Cohen, *Everyman's Talmud* (New York, Schocken, 1995), 36–37.

7 Josephus, *Ant.* 1.1.

8 Ibid., 1.2.

9 Forster and Marston, *Reason, Science and Faith*, 192–8.

10 David T. Runia, 'Philo, Alexandrian and Jew,' *Exegesis and Philosophy: Studies on Philo of Alexandria* (Aldershot, Variorum, 1990), 2.

11 'Philo' in P. Achtemier (editor), *Harper's Bible Dictionary* (San Francisco, Harper and Row, 1985).

as a representative of all Jewish readers has no justification.[12] Note, however, that Philo's philosophical ideas and allegorical method had a direct impact on Christian theology through the writings of Clement of Alexandria (A.D. 150–215) and Origen (ca A.D. 185–254).

Secondly, the Targums[13] vary greatly in their literalness and in the way they expound the text.[14] Citing a relatively minor Targum edition (*Targum Neofiti*, dating from the third century A.D.) proves very little, especially since *Targum Onkelos* was actually the official version of the Babylonian Jews.

Regarding the beliefs of the Christian church, Davis Young provides a good survey of the views held by Christians over the centuries and concludes that 'the concept of a recent creation was a virtually unanimous belief of the early church. … Many of the church fathers plainly regarded the six days as ordinary days.'[15] Up until the eighteenth century, virtually the entire Christian world believed the earth was only a few thousand years old. It was not until the development of geological investigation that some churchmen began questioning this belief, and proposed alternative non-literal interpretations of the days of creation in Genesis 1.

Forster and Marston, on the other hand, claim non-literal interpretations of the creation days is *not* a modern idea, and that important mainstream church leaders had taught such views from the beginning.[16] Paul Elbert concurs and includes Irenaeus, Origen, Basil, Augustine, and Aquinas among those who viewed the days of creation as phases.[17] Yet, Forster and Marston also acknowledge that Barnabas (b. A.D. 100), Irenaeus (ca A.D. 120–202), Hippoplytus (A.D. 170–236), Methodius (A.D. 260–312), Lactantius (ca A.D. 260–330), Theophilus, and John of Damascus (ca A.D. 675–749) all understood the days as corresponding to seven ages of a seven 7,000-year world history.[18] In other words, the totality of world history could be broken down into seven ages, each of which lasts for 1,000 years. It follows, then, that all these writers believed the creation was not more than 7,000 years old.

A number of early commentators understood בְּיוֹם (*b*ᵉ*yôm*) in Genesis 2:4 as a reference to 'instantaneous' creation. Philo (ca 20–15 B.C. to A.D. 45–50) stated: 'We must think of God as doing all things simultaneously.'[19] Origen (ca A.D. 185–254), Athanasius (ca A.D. 296–373), and Augustine (A.D.

---

12 Nevertheless, Philo's philosophical ideas and allegorical method had a direct impact on Christian theology through the writings of Clement of Alexandria and Origen.

13 Aramaic paraphrases of the Old Testament.

14 'Targums' in I.H. Marshall, A.R. Millard, J.I. Packer and D.J. Wiseman (editors) *The New Bible Dictionary* (Wheaton, Illinois, Tyndale House, 1962).

15 Davis A. Young, *Christianity and the Age of the Earth* (Grand Rapids, Michigan, Zondervan, 1982), 19, 21.

16 Forster and Marston, *Reason, Science and Faith*, 38.

17 Paul Elbert, 'Biblical Creation and Science: A Review Article' *JETS* 39 (Jun 1996), 286.

18 Roger Forster and Paul Marston, *Reason and Faith* (Eastborne, Monarch, 1989), 205.

19 Philo, *De Opificio Mundi*, 13.

354–430) held a similar view and discussed how it could be harmonized with the six days.[20]

Comments on the days of Genesis are sparse in Christian writings of the second century, and, as Jack Lewis notes, there is a marked tendency to allegorize the days.[21] Theophilus (ca A.D. 115–188), in his discussion of creation, regarded the days as normal 24-hour days, but also applied various typological understandings to them. Davis Young claims that Clement of Alexandria (A.D. 150–215) interpreted the days allegorically but admits that it is unclear whether he considered the days to be literal.[22] However, the following comment from *The Stromata* indicates otherwise: 'And they purify themselves seven days, the period in which Creation was consummated. For on the seventh day the rest is celebrated; and on the eighth he brings a propitiation, as is written in Ezekiel.'[23] Even more compelling is Clement's statement in *The Stromata* 6.16:

> For the creation of the world was concluded in six days. For the motion of the sun from solstice to solstice is completed in six months — in the course of which, at one time the leaves fall, and at another plants bud and seeds come to maturity. And they say that the embryo is perfected exactly in the sixth month, that is, in one hundred and eighty days in addition to the two and a half, as Polybus the physician relates in his book *On the Eighth Month*, and Aristotle the philosopher in his book *On Nature*.[24]

Both of these comments refer to 'days' and 'months' as normal, common periods of time, implying this is what Clement had in mind when he wrote those words.

Although Origen regularly applied a non-literal hermeneutic, he 'did not usually deny the literal sense of the biblical text but used it as a vehicle to get at other "higher" meanings within a scheme of three levels of interpretation.'[25] Origen saw a triple sense in Scripture: the literal, the moral, and the spiritual. If difficulties resulted from a literal reading of Scripture, then he suggested a spiritual meaning should be sought, and he applied this hermeneutic to the days of creation.[26]

Basil (A.D. 329–379), on the other hand, rejected any allegorical interpretation of Genesis:

> For me grass is grass; … I take all in the literal sense. … It is this which those seem to me not to have understood, who, giving themselves up to

---

20 Origen, *Against Celsus* 6.49, 50, 60; *de Princ.*, 4.3.1; Athanasius, *Orat.*, 2.48–49 in *NPNF* 4, 374–375; Augustine in J.H. Taylor (editor), *St Augustine: The literal meaning of Genesis*, 2 volumes (Mahwah, New Jersey, Paulist, 1982), 1:142.

21 Lewis, 'The Days of Creation,' 435.

22 Ibid.

23 Clement, *The Stromata*, 4.25

24 Clement, *The Stromata*, 6.16.

25 Michael Stallard, 'Literal Interpretation: The Key to Understanding the Bible' *JMT* 4/1 (Spring 2000), 16.

26 Lewis, 'The Days of Creation,' 438.

the distorted meaning of allegory, have undertaken to give a majesty of their own invention to Scripture. It is to believe themselves wiser than the Holy Spirit, and to bring forth their own ideas under a pretext of exegesis. Let us hear Scripture as it has been written.[27]

Likewise, Gregory of Nyssa (A.D. 335–395) claimed in *Explicatio Apologetica in Hexaemeron* that he never resorted to allegorical interpretation, although some scholars dispute this.[28] In *Against Eunomius* he wrote: 'The creation, as we have said, comes into existence according to a sequence of order, and is commensurate with the duration of the ages, so that if one ascends along the line of things created to their beginning, one will bound the search with the foundation of those ages.'[29] While this may at first appear to indicate a belief in the day-age interpretation, the context suggests that Gregory's use of the term 'creation' refers not to creation week but to the entire time span over which the creation has existed, from the initial act 'in the beginning' up until the present day.

Of all the early commentators, Basil probably gave the clearest explanation of his interpretation of the days:

> Why does Scripture say 'one day the first day'? Before speaking to us of the second, the third, and the fourth days, would it not have been more natural to call that one the first which began the series? If it therefore says 'one day,' it is from a wish to determine the measure of day and night, and to combine the time that they contain. Now twenty-four hours fill up the space of one day — we mean of a day and of a night; and if, at the time of the solstices, they have not both an equal length, the time marked by Scripture does not the less circumscribe their duration. It is as though it said: twenty-four hours measure the space of a day, or that, in reality a day is the time that the heavens starting from one point take to return there. Thus, every time that, in the revolution of the sun, evening and morning occupy the world, their periodical succession never exceeds the space of one day.[30]

Following Basil, Ambrose (A.D. 339–397) also understood the days literally and explicitly stated that the days were of twenty-four hours in length. Regarding the first day of creation, he stated that 'one day' is used instead of 'the first day' because it is the foundation of all others things and should not to be compared to the other days.[31]

Chrysostom (A.D. 347–407) also appears to take the days literally. Commenting on Genesis 1:5, he wrote:

> Then, when he had assigned to each its own name, he linked the two together in the words, 'Evening came, and morning came, one day.' He

---

27 Basil, *Homilies on Hexaemeron,* 9.1.

28 Lewis, 'The Days of Creation,' 447.

29 *Against Eunomius,* I.24.

30 Basil, *Homilies on Hexaemeron,* 2.8

31 Ambrose, *Hexaemeron,* 3.8, 2.2.

> made a point of speaking of the end of the day and of the end of the
> night as one, so as to grasp a certain order and sequence in visible things
> and avoid any impression of confusion.[32]

Augustine was inclined to think God created all things in a moment of time,
and the days were simply introduced to aid the finite human intelligence.[33]
He wrote:

> What kind of days these were it is extremely difficult, or perhaps
> impossible for us to conceive, and how much more to say! We see,
> indeed, that our ordinary days have no evening but by the setting, and
> no morning but by the rising, of the sun; but the first three days of all
> were passed without sun, since it is reported to have been made on the
> fourth day. And first of all, indeed, light was made by the word of God,
> and God, we read, separated it from the darkness, and called the light
> Day, and the darkness Night; but what kind of light that was, and by
> what periodic movement it made evening and morning, is beyond the
> reach of our senses; neither can we understand how it was, and yet must
> unhesitatingly believe it.[34]

Therefore, Augustine interpreted the days of creation allegorically. Nevertheless,
his remarks indicate that he was not entirely happy with this view, even to the
point of reluctant acceptance, and subsequently expressed some openness to
considering other views:

> Whoever, then, does not accept the meaning that my limited powers
> have been able to discover or conjecture but seeks in the enumeration
> of the days of creation a different meaning, which might be understood
> not in a prophetical or figurative sense, but literally and more aptly, in
> interpreting the works of creation, let him search and find a solution
> with God's help. I myself may possibly discover some other meaning
> more in harmony with the words of Scripture.[35]

Note that although Augustine held to an allegorical interpretation, he did not
believe in an ancient world. In his response to the Egyptian's 'one hundred
thousand year chronology' he stated that the world was less than 6,000 years old:

> For as it is not yet six thousand years since the first man, who is called
> Adam, are not those to be ridiculed rather than refuted who try to
> persuade us of anything regarding a space of time so different from, and
> contrary to, the ascertained truth? For what historian of the past should
> we credit more than him who has also predicted things to come which
> we now see fulfilled? And the very disagreement of the historians among
> themselves furnishes a good reason why we ought rather to believe him
> who does not contradict the divine history which we hold.[36]

---

32 Chrysostom, *Homilies on Genesis*, 3.10–11.
33 Louis Lavallee, 'Augustine on the Creation Days' *JETS* 32/4 (December 1989), 460.
34 Augustine, *City of God* 11.6–7.
35 Augustine, *The Literal Meaning of Genesis*, 4.28.45.
36 Augustine, *City of God*, 18.40.

One Syriac manuscript indicates the Syrian fathers considered evening and morning (Genesis 1:5) to be true measures of time even though the sun and moon had not yet been created. They believed darkness was created first and lasted twelve hours, and then light was created and lasted twelve hours. This was called 'day' and Scripture says 'one day' rather than 'first day' so that 'it should not be thought that just as we know the days now, even so they were formed in the first instance.'[37] In other words, the term 'first' describes the relation of this day to the following days, but at that time the following days did not exist.

While all the early creeds speak of God as the maker of heaven and earth, they do not mention the six days. This should not be surprising given that the creeds were written to clarify elements of Christian doctrine, and therefore only reflect the various doctrinal controversies in the early church.[38] Nevertheless, almost all the early Gentile Christians had turned from pagan evolutionary ideas, and believed that God had created the universe either in six days or in an instant.[39]

The Middle Ages and the Reformers

Jewish commentators Rashi (Rabbi Shlomo Yitzchaki, 1040–1105), Ibn Ezra (Abraham ben Meirmâr, ca 1089–1164), Maimonides (1135–1204) and Gersonides (Levi ben Gerson, 1288–1344) rejected literal interpretations in favor of allegorical and non-chronological approaches. However, Maimonides was heavily influenced by Greek philosophy,[40] and Gersonides staunchly defended the Platonic theory of creation, and regarded human reason above Scripture as the most important criterion for determining truth.[41]

Following Barnabas, Irenaeus, Methodius, and other early church fathers, Peter Lombard (d. 1164) and Hugo of St. Victor (1097–1141), also believed God created both in an instant and in six days.[42] Arnoldus of Chartres (ca 1160), on the other hand, held to an early 'days of revelation' view where each day refers to the order in which the world was unfolded to Adam.[43]

Thomas Aquinas (1225?–1274) in his *Treatise on the Work of the Six Days*, considers many philosophical questions connected with creation. He believed in seven distinct days rather than one only, which constituted 'a succession both

---

37 A. Levene, *The Early Syrian Fathers on Genesis* (London, Taylor's Foreign, 1951), 73, 131–132.

38 Thus, the early creeds focused on the Trinity and the person of Christ, which had been the center of controversy in the early church, while the Reformation creeds focused on the differences between Protestantism and Roman Catholicism.

39 Louis Lavellee, 'Creeds and the Six Creation Days,' *Impact 235* (January 1993).

40 See William Turner, 'Teaching of Moses Maimonides' in R.C. Broderick (editor), *The Catholic Encyclopedia* (Thomas Nelson, 1990).

41 See Tamar Rudavsky, 'Gersonides' in Edward N. Zalta (editor), *Stanford Encyclopedia of Philosophy* <http://plato.stanford.edu/entries/gersonides/>.

42 Lewis, 'The Days of Creation,' 448–449.

43 Ibid., 445.

in time, and in things produced.'[44] Regarding the length of the days, Aquinas wrote: 'The words "one day" are used when the day is first established, to denote that one day is made up of twenty-four hours. Hence, by mentioning "one," the measure of a natural day is fixed.'[45]

Guillaume Salluste DuBartas (b. 1544), Francisco Suarez (1548–1617) preferred the strictly literal view of the creation days,[46] as did the Reformers Martin Luther (1483–1546)[47] and Philip Melanchthon (1497–1560). John Calvin (1509–1564),[48] and Johann Gerhard (1582–1637)[49] also rejected allegorical and figurative views, preferring a strictly literal view of the creation days. Regarding the concept of an instantaneous creation, Calvin responded:

> Here the error of those is manifestly refuted, who maintain that the world was made in a moment. For it is too violent a cavil to contend that Moses distributes the work which God perfected at once into six days, for the mere purpose of conveying instruction. Let us rather conclude that God himself took the space of six days, for the purpose of accommodating his works to the capacity of men.[50]

While it is well known that James Ussher (1581–1656), Archbishop of Armagh, interpreted the days literally, and calculated the date of creation to be 4004 B.C., John Lightfoot (1602–1675), his contemporary and the leading Hebrew scholar at that time, also interpreted the days literally and calculated a similar date of 3960 B.C. Lightfoot wrote:

> So that look at the first day of the creation, God made heaven and earth in a moment. The heaven, as soon as created, moved, and the wheel of time began to go: and thus, for twelve hours, there was universal darkness. This is called the 'evening,' meaning night. Then God said, 'Let there be light;' and light arose in the east, and, in twelve hours more, was carried over the hemisphere: and this is called, 'morning,' or 'day.' And the evening and morning made the first natural day; twelve hours, darkness, — and twelve, light.[51]

Although allegorical interpreters could still be found during the Middle Ages, they nonetheless assumed the literal meaning of the text was truthful. The allegorical hermeneutic was only applied to the text in order to discover deeper

44 Thomas Aquinas, *Summa Theologica,* I.74.2.

45 Ibid., I.74.3.

46 Lewis, 'The Days of Creation,' 453.

47 Martin Luther, 'Lectures on Genesis, Chapters 1–5' in J.P. Pelikan and H. Lehmann (editors), *Luther's Works* vol 1, US edition (St. Louis, Concordia, 1955), 5.

48 John Calvin, *Commentaries on the First Book of Moses, Called Genesis* (Grand Rapids, Eerdmans, 1948), 1.78.

49 Davis Young, *Christianity and the Age of the Earth,* 24.

50 Calvin, 1.78. See also *Institutes of the Christian Religion* (London, James Clark, 1951), 1.142.

51 John R. Pitman (editor), *The Whole Works of the Rev. John Lightfoot D.D.,* 13 volumes (London, J.F. Dove, 1822–1825), 7:373.

spiritual meanings. As Woodbridge points out, '[t]he allegorization program of most interpreters was not intended to throw disrepute on the accuracy of the biblical accounts.'[52]

It is vitally important to note that a major philosophical and theological shift was occurring in the church throughout this period. Principles and ideas external to Scripture, especially Greek philosophy, had an increasing influence on both the church and society as a whole. David Lindberg and Ronald Numbers have noted that

> [b]y the beginning of the thirteenth century, virtually all of the works of Aristotle had become available in Europe, and from this point onward we see a persistent effort to integrate Aristotelian natural philosophy, or science, with Christian theology. In the end, Christianity took its basic categories of thought, its physical principles, and much of its metaphysics and cosmology from Aristotle. By means of its power to organize and interpret human experience, Aristotelianism conquered Christendom.'[53]

Note also that it was this broad acceptance of Aristotelian thought and cosmology by the church, and the academic community that apparently led to the heliocentric controversy involving Galileo.[54]

Furthermore, due to the increasing influence and authority given to the natural sciences, many commentators started believing in the great antiquity of the earth. Episcopius (1586–1643) advocated a 'gap theory' in which a long period of time passed between Genesis 1:1 and 1:2. R. Obadiah, around 1698, argued from Psalm 90:4 that each creation day may be a thousand years.[55] This is probably why several church creeds at this time began to explicitly mention the six days of creation.[56]

The first creed mentioning the six creation days was the *Irish Articles* from the Irish Episcopal Church which were adopted in 1600. They later became the model for the Westminster Confession. Article 18 reads: 'In the beginning of time, when no creature had any being, God, by his word alone, in the space of six days, created all things ...'[57]

In the Netherlands, the Mennonites wrote their *Dordrecht Confession* in 1632, in which the first article reads: 'In this one God, who "worketh all in all," we believe. Him we confess as the Creator of all things, visible and invisible; who in six days created and prepared "heaven and earth, and the sea, and all things

52 John D. Woodbridge, 'Recent Interpretations of Biblical Authority Part 3: Does the Bible Teach Science?' *BSac* 142 (July–September 1985), 199.

53 David C. Lindberg and Ronald L. Numbers, 'Beyond War and Peace: A Reappraisal of the Encounter Between Christianity and Science' *PSCF* 39/3 (September 1987), 143.

54 This controversy was discussed in detail in chapter 2.

55 Lewis, 'The Days of Creation,' 453–454.

56 Indeed, Louis Lavellee ('Creeds and the Six Creation Days') notes: 'It was only in the 17th century that creeds first mentioned the six creation days.'

57 Ibid.

that are therein."' Later in the century, the Amish also adopted this confession, and it remains authoritative in many of these communities.[58]

The *Westminster Confession*, completed in 1646, was the core doctrinal statement of the Presbyterian Church. Article 5.1 states: 'It pleased God the Father, Son, and Holy Ghost, for the manifestation of the glory of His eternal power, wisdom, and goodness, in the beginning, to create, or make of nothing, the world, and all things therein whether visible or invisible, in the space of six days; and all very good.' The Confession also formed the basis for the *Congregational Savoy Declaration* of 1658 and the *Baptist London Confession* of 1689. Both affirmed creation in the space of six days.[59]

The Enlightenment

In the seventeenth and eighteenth centuries, most Christian naturalists based their hypotheses about earth history on an essentially literal reading of the biblical account of creation and the flood,[60] and the belief in a lengthy earth history was adhered to only by a small group of naturalists.[61] Davis Young acknowledges that 'the almost universal view of the Christian world until the eighteenth century was that the earth was only a few thousand years old. Not until the development of modern scientific investigation of the Earth itself would this view be called into question within the church.'[62]

The Enlightenment was an eighteenth-century phenomenon with philosophical roots in the seventeenth century. The human mind was freed from its philosophical and religious shackles, making it totally autonomous. McCune observes: 'It was a movement in thought, sometimes known as the Age of Reason, that was totally secular.'[63]

Sara Joan Miles has noted that the eighteenth century is generally regarded as a golden age for science while at the same time, religion began to be eroded by the rise of rationalism, materialism, deism, agnosticism, skepticism, and secularism.[64]

---

58 Ibid.

59 Ibid. Some have questioned whether the authors of the Westminster Confession really intended the statement '... in the space of six days' to be taken as a reference to 24-hour days. However, David W. Hall ('What was the View of the Westminster Assembly Divines on Creation Days?' in J.A. Pipa and D.W. Hall [editors], *Did God Create in Six Days?* [Taylors, SC, Southern Presbyterian Press, 1999] 41–52) has convincingly shown that those divines who discussed the days all held to 24-hour days.

60 Davis A. Young, 'Scripture in the Hands of Geologists (Part One),' *WTJ* 49/1 (Spring 1987), 4.

61 M.J.S. Rudwick, 'The Shape and Meaning of Earth History' in D.C. Lindberg and R.L. Numbers (editors), *God and Nature* (Berkeley, University of California Press, 1986), 309.

62 Davis Young, *Christianity and the Age of the Earth*, 25.

63 Rolland D. McCune, 'The Formation of the New Evangelicalism (Part One): Historical and Theological Antecedents' *DBSJ* 3/1 (Fall 1998), 6.

64 Sara Joan Miles, 'From Being to Becoming: Science and Theology in the Eighteenth Century' *PSCF* 43/4 (December 1991), 216.

Naturally, this kind of thinking had severe impacts on Christianity. Society became autonomous and totally free intellectually. No longer were people bound by church creeds, theological statements, revelation, or any particular worldview or presuppositions of any kind. Man was intellectually independent in an open universe of chance, relativism, and inevitable change in all areas.[65]

Secondly, the Enlightenment resulted in the destruction of the need for divine revelation. Revelation was no longer thought to be necessary since man could learn just as much about God and the world through science and reason.[66] Previously, reason was initially guided by, and subordinate to, biblical revelation, but soon the domain of biblical revelation became severely restricted — no longer was it viewed as being more authoritative than science.[67] Biblical revelation was to be understood only within the bounds of human reason, and its message and significance were essentially limited to issues of salvation and morality. Thus, Miles concludes that 'science and reason in the 18th century directly undermined the authority of Scriptural revelation by elevating the status of reason.'[68]

Thirdly, the Enlightenment also resulted in the detachment of Christianity from history.[69] Rather than Christianity being true because it is rooted in history and therefore dependent on the facts of history, theologians influenced by Enlightenment thinking became more concerned with Christianity's ability to transform lives through its morality and system of ethics. 'Theology became more concerned about spiritual "life" or the practical interests in the field of religion.'[70]

Therefore, it is not surprising to find that, during this period, various Christian scholars began to argue that Scripture may contain 'errors' regarding the natural world. This resulted in a situation where scientists no longer felt the need to align their findings with biblical teachings. Indeed, many scientists argued that their conclusions about the 'real world' should be given more authority than the 'phenomenological' statements in the Bible pertaining to the physical creation. In other words, the Scriptures should conform to what science teaches and not vice versa.[71]

It is important to emphasize, as McCune does, that Enlightenment thinkers 'refused to be bound by anything such as revelation, dogma, and tradition' and that 'the theoretical underpinnings were anti-Christian, pagan, and secular.'[72]

---

65 McCune, 'The Formation of the New Evangelicalism,' 7.

66 Ibid., 8.

67 Miles, 'From Being to Becoming,' 217–219.

68 Ibid., 224.

69 McCune, 'The Formation of the New Evangelicalism,' 8.

70 Ibid.

71 John D. Woodbridge, 'Some Misconceptions of the Impact of the "Enlightenment" on the Doctrine of Scripture' in D.A. Carson and John D. Woodbridge (editors), *Hermeneutics, Authority and Canon* (Grand Rapids, Michigan, Baker, 1995), 261.

72 McCune, 'The Formation of the New Evangelicalism,' 7.

The Modern Period

Again, up until the early nineteenth century, Jewish and Christian scholars alike agreed almost unanimously that the universe was created in six 24-hour days around 6,000 years ago.[73] However, during the nineteenth century, this consensus began to be reversed, largely because of the rise of geological study and Darwin's theory of evolution.

The Influence of Geological Study

The fundamentals of geological study (fieldwork, collection of rocks and fossils, and theory construction) were not developed until the sixteenth to eighteenth centuries,[74] and geology as a distinct discipline did not emerge until the seventeenth and eighteenth centuries, making it one of the younger sciences. Today, there are basically two broad schools of thought in geological studies. The dominant and most widely held view is uniformitarianism, where observation in the present is the key to understanding the past. The minority view is catastrophism, which postulates that the earth was shaped by major catastrophic events in the past. This is essentially the view held by 'flood geologists' and those involved in the modern creation science movement, although it is not confined to this movement.

It is often stated that young-earth creationism and flood geology originated with Seventh-Day Adventist George McReady-Price in *The New Geology* (1923), and was imported into mainstream evangelicalism by Henry M. Morris and John Whitcomb in their highly influential book, *The Genesis Flood* (1961). This understanding has become widely accepted due to Ronald Numbers's highly influential book *The Creationists*[75] and Numbers's conclusions have been regurgitated by others.[76]

Unfortunately, this is another example of the misrepresentation and revisionism that has characterized much of modern historical studies. Ross, Numbers, and Noll are wildly off the mark on this point. While McReady-Price, Morris, and Whitcomb were largely responsible for the revival of young-earth creationism and flood geology in the twentieth century (particularly in the U.S.A.), similar ideas were advocated one hundred years earlier by the 'Scriptural Geologists' in Great Britain. Even Davis Young acknowledges that flood geology (or diluvialism) 'was not the aberrant theory of a fringe group;

---

73 Ronald F. Youngblood, *The Book of Genesis*, 2nd edition (Grand Rapids, Michigan, Baker, 1991), 41.

74 Terry Mortenson, 'British Scriptural Geologists in the First Half of the Nineteenth Century: Part 1. Historical Setting' *JoC* 11/2 (1997), 228.

75 Ronald L. Numbers, *The Creationists* (Berkeley, University of California Press, 1993).

76 See, for example, Mark A. Noll, *The Scandal of the Evangelical Mind* (Grand Rapids, Michigan, Eerdmans, 1994); Hugh N. Ross, *The Genesis Question* (Colorado Springs, NavPress, 1998); and M. James Sawyer, *The Survivor's Guide to Theology* (Grand Rapids, Michigan, Zondervan, 2002).

it was mainstream natural history and was espoused by some of the ablest naturalists of the time.'[77] He explains:

> In diluvialism, Scripture provided the main outline of terrestrial history. The writings of classical historians and scattered empirical evidence from the earth provided secondary sources of information that helped fill in the detail and were believed to corroborate the biblical accounts. The biblical scheme of creation, fall, flood, and final consummation provided the main events in earth history, and the biblical materials relating to these events were typically understood in literal terms. The creation was assumed to be a recent creation in six ordinary days, and the flood was assumed to be global. Typically, the Noahic flood was the centerpiece around which the various speculative theories of the earth were constructed.[78]

Note also that a number of early church fathers, including Tertullian, Chrysostom and Augustine, believed that fossils were the remains of former living things and attributed them to the Noahic flood.[79]

In fact, numerous works on flood geology were published by the early geologists. Niels Steensen (1638–1686), a Dutch anatomist and geologist, who established the principle that sedimentary rock layers were deposited in a successive and generally horizontal fashion, stated his belief in a 6,000-year-old Earth and that organic fossils and rock strata were laid down by the flood of Noah (*Forerunner*, 1669).[80] Cambridge scholars, Thomas Burnet (1635–1715) and William Whiston (1667–1752), put forward theories on how the Noahic flood laid down the earth's surface structure.[81] Burnet's *Sacred Theory of the Earth* was originally published in 1681[82] and Whiston's *A New Theory of the Earth*, was released in 1696.

Physician and geologist John Woodward (1665–1722) invoked the flood to explain the strata and fossils in *An Essay Toward a Natural History of the Earth* (1695).[83] Alexander Catcott (1725–1779), in his *Treatise on the Deluge* (1768), invoked geological arguments to defend the Genesis account of a recent creation and a global flood which produced the geological record,[84] and Richard Kirwan (1733–1812) advocated flood geology in *Geological Essays* (1799). Yet, there were also some geologists who believed the earth was much older than mankind, and that the Noahic flood was largely a geological non-event.[85]

---

77 Davis Young, 'Scripture in the Hands of Geologists (Part One),' 23.

78 Ibid., 7.

79 Mortenson, 'British Scriptural Geologists: Historical Setting,' 228.

80 Ibid.

81 R. Porter, *The Making of Geology* (Cambridge, Cambridge University Press, 1977), 23.

82 Davis Young, 'Scripture in the Hands of Geologists (Part One),' 7.

83 Mortenson, 'British Scriptural Geologists: Historical Setting,' 228.

84 Ibid.

85 See Ibid., 228–229.

In the latter part of the eighteenth century, as a result of Enlightenment thinking, geological study became increasingly secularized. Thus in 1785 and before examining the evidence, James Hutton, a deist, proclaimed: 'the past history of our globe must be explained by what can be seen to be happening now. … No powers are to be employed that are not natural to the globe, no action to be admitted except those of which we know the principle.'[86] According to Davis Young, the '[a]ccumulating evidence from nature pointed in the direction of the vast antiquity of the Earth and forced theologians to take a much harder, more penetrating look at the biblical record than ever before.'[87] Thus, Thomas Chalmers in 1804 declared that 'the writings of Moses do not fit the antiquity of the globe.'[88]

Hutton's theory was basically uniformitarianism — the operation of slow and gradual physical processes, and he, too, believed the Noahic flood was a geological non-event.[89] In 1802, John Playfair (1748–1819), a Scottish clergyman and mathematician, published *Illustrations of the Huttonian Theory of the Earth*, which repackaged Hutton's views in a more digestible and less overtly deistic format. Playfair made no attempt to harmonize his views with Scripture nor did he attribute any geological significance to the Noahic flood.

Nevertheless, in the 1820s, old-earth catastrophist (or diluvial) geology was generally accepted by most geologists and academic theologians.[90] William Buckland (1784–1856) was the leading geologist in England in the 1820s. Although he believed the earth was very old, in his 1820 work *Vindiciae Geologicae*, he argued that geology was consistent with Genesis and offered numerous convincing proofs of the global catastrophic Noahic flood.[91] However, Buckland's convictions about the truth of Scripture soon began to waver. In his personal correspondence in the 1820s, he confessed to viewing geological data as more reliable and superior to textual evidence in determining Earth's history.[92]

Prompted by the writings of John Flemming (another Scottish minister), Charles Lyell (1797–1875) a lawyer by training, revived Hutton's ideas in his famous three-volume work, *Principles of Geology* (1830–1833). Like Hutton, Lyell was not concerned with harmonizing his views with Scripture, but saw himself as 'the spiritual savior of geology, freeing the science from the old dispensation of Moses.'[93]

---

86 As cited in A.A. Holmes, *Principles of Physical Geology*, 2nd edition (London: John Wiley, 1965), 43–44. This statement originally appeared in a paper presented to the Royal Society of Edinburgh, and was published in *Transactions of the Royal Society of Edinburgh*, 1785. It was later included in Hutton's book *Theory of the Earth* (1795).

87 Davis Young, *Christianity and the Age of the Earth*, 13.

88 Lewis, 'The Days of Creation,' 453–454.

89 Mortenson, 'British Scriptural Geologists: Historical Setting,' 229–230.

90 Ibid., 231.

91 Ibid.

92 N.A. Rupke, *The Great Chain of History: William Buckland and the English School of Geology 1814–1849* (Oxford, Clarendon Press, 1983), 41–47.

93 Mortenson, 'British Scriptural Geologists: Historical Setting,' 232.

Although Buckland had been a great defender of catastrophism, he changed his mind in light of Flemming's and Lyell's criticisms, and he too eventually concluded that the Noahic flood was tranquil and geologically insignificant.[94]

Adam Sedgwick (1785–1873), Buckland's counterpart at Cambridge University, also advocated old-earth diluvialism. In 1825, he wrote:

> The sacred record tells us — that a few thousand years ago 'the fountains of the great deep' were broken up — and that the earth's surface was submerged by the water of a general deluge; and the investigations of geology prove that the accumulations of alluvial matter … were preceded by a great catastrophe which has left traces of its operation in the diluvial detritus which is spread out over all the strata of the world.
>
> Between these conclusions, derived from sources entirely independent of each other, there is, therefore, a general coincidence which is impossible to overlook, and the importance of which it would be most unreasonable to deny. The coincidence has not been assumed hypothetically but has been proved legitimately, by an immense number of direct observations conducted with indefatigable labour, and all tending to the establishment of the same general truth.[95]

Yet, several years later, after the first volume of Lyell's *Principles* was published in 1831, Sedgwick too abandoned this view:

> Bearing upon this difficult question, there is, I think, one great negative conclusion now incontestably established — that the vast masses of diluvial gravel, scattered almost over the surface of the earth, do not belong to one violent and transitory period. It was indeed a most unwarranted conclusion. … We saw the clearest traces of diluvial action, and we had, in our sacred histories, the record of a general deluge.
>
> To seek the light of physical truth by reasoning of this kind, is, in the language of Bacon, to seek the living among the dead, and will ever end in erroneous induction. Our errors were, however, natural, and of the same kind which lead many excellent observers of a former century to refer all the secondary formations of geology to the Noachian deluge. Having been myself a believer, and, to the best of my power, a propagator of what I now regard as a philosophic heresy, and having more than once been quoted for opinions I do not now maintain, I think it right, as one of my last acts before I quit this Chair, thus publicly to read my recantation. … We ought, indeed, to have paused before we first adopted the diluvian theory.[96]

Thus, Lyell's *Principles of Geology* became highly influential and sounded the death knell for both old-earth and young-earth diluvialism.[97] By the mid to

---

94 Ibid., 231.

95 As cited in A. Hallam, *Great Geological Controversies*, 2nd edition (New York, OUP, 1989), 43.

96 Adam Sedgwick, 'Anniversary Address of the President, 1831,' *Proceedings of the Geological Society of London* 1 (1831), 312–314.

97 Mortenson, 'British Scriptural Geologists: Historical Setting,' 232.

late 1830s, virtually all geologists accepted Hutton's and Lyell's uniformitarian convictions. The only significant exceptions were the so called 'scriptural geologists' in Great Britain. These men opposed Hutton's and Lyell's uniformitarian theories as well as the catastrophic theories of Georges Cuvier and William Conybeare.[98] Despite the title ascribed to them, it is important to note that the scriptural geologists' objections to an old earth were often based on actual geological information and observation, not just on Scripture.[99] In fact, contra Davis Young and others, many of the scriptural geologists had significant geological knowledge, and a few were just as knowledgeable and capable as any of the leading geologists at that time.[100]

The most capable scriptural geologist was George Young (1777–1848), a Church of Scotland clergyman, who wrote two works on geology: (1) *A Geological Survey of the Yorkshire Coast* (1822), which was greatly revised in 1828, and (2) *Scriptural Geology* (1838), to which *Appendix to Scriptural Geology* was added in 1840. He also published six articles on geology in the respected scientific journals of his day. His writings indicate he was well read in geological and scientific journals and books. His detailed and comprehensive investigations of the geology of Yorkshire, where a great percentage of the so-called 'geological column' was exposed in the mines and on the sea coast, were praised for their accuracy by the leading old-earth geologists at the time.[101]

Young believed the rocks and fossils clearly demonstrated that most of the geological record was the result of Noah's flood and therefore did not prove that the Earth was millions of years old. Both the scientific and biblical evidence strongly convinced him that God created the world in six literal days around 6,000 years ago. Nevertheless, despite his recognized geological and biblical competence, his arguments were completely ignored by his geological opponents, even those geologists who were also ordained clergymen and knew him personally.[102]

George Fairholme (1789–1846) published two lengthy books on the subject of geology: *General View of the Geology of Scripture* (1833) and *New and Conclusive Physical Demonstrations of the Mosaic Deluge* (1837). He also published *Positions Géologiques en Vérifications Directe de la Chronologie de la Bible* (1834), a booklet critically evaluating Lyell's uniformitarianism theory, but it never appeared in English. He also wrote three other journal articles on geological issues. In 1834, he read a paper on the nature of valleys to the meeting of the main German scientific organization, and was invited to make field trips with several German scientists after that meeting, indicating the level of respect they had for his geological knowledge.[103]

---

98 Ibid., 222.

99 Ibid., 221.

100 Ibid., 222.

101 Mortenson, 'British Scriptural Geologists in the First Half of the Nineteenth Century,' Unpublished Ph.D. dissertation, University of Coventry, 1996.

102 Ibid.

103 Ibid.

Mortenson notes that Fairholme engaged in extensive geological investigations, both in Great Britain and on the European continent. He collected fossils and rock specimens and studied those in the possession of museums and leading English and European geologists. He was well read in the current works of prominent geologists and other scientists of his day, and his geological writings constantly interacted with their old-earth arguments. In many cases he quoted them liberally before respectfully presenting his reasons for rejecting their interpretations of the geological evidence. In spite of Fairholme's obvious geological competence, the three scathing published reviews of his geological writings by old-earth critics charged that Fairholme, like all the other scriptural geologists, knew nothing about geology. Yet none of his critics cited a single specific example of such ignorance. Nor did they attempt to answer his well-reasoned objections to the old-earth geological theories.[104]

William Rhind (1797–1874), a successful surgeon, wrote a number of science textbooks for teenagers. The subjects included natural history of the earth, botany, geology and physical geography, zoology, meteorology, and elementary geography. In addition, Rhind published several journal articles on geology and related issues, and three adult-level books dealing with geology. An 1833 book of excursions around Edinburgh described the geology and natural history of the area. It received two positive reviews in scientific journals, particularly for its valuable geological information. In 1842, he published *The Geology of Scotland and Its Islands*, which was the result of his own careful geological field work as well as consulting the writings of at least twenty-one other local and national geologists. These two books were purely descriptive, but in 1838 Rhind wrote *The Age of the Earth*, in which he gave his geological reasons for rejecting the old-earth theories that had recently begun to dominate the thinking of most geologists. Again, despite his geological competence, Rhind's arguments were ignored by contemporary old-earth geologists.[105]

John Murray (1786?–1851) wrote a number of journal articles and books on the subject of geology and natural history. In *The Truth of Revelation* (1831), which was greatly revised and expanded in 1840, Murray endeavored to demonstrate the truth and inspiration of the Bible by an appeal to the existing monuments, sculptures, gems, coins, and medals from ancient peoples of the Near East and elsewhere. In *Portrait of Geology* (1838), he gave geological evidence of divine design, and defended what he considered to be the clear truth of Scripture in the face of the challenges from old-earth geological theories. As well as examining geological formations in Britain and Europe firsthand, Murray also demonstrated an up-to-date knowledge of the writings of leading British and European geologists. In addition to collecting his own rock specimens and fossils, he personally examined private and museum fossil collections both in England and in France. Murray also had a more than superficial knowledge of

104 Ibid.
105 Ibid.

conchology (the study of shell creatures), a subject so important for identifying and correlating rock strata.[106]

Andrew Ure (1778–1857), a chemist, was one of the original honorary Fellows of the Geological Society of London shortly after it was founded in 1807 and was well acquainted with all the writings in books and journals of the leading geologists in his time. He also collected his own specimens and fossils, and performed chemical analyses of the composition of various kinds of rocks.[107] His book *A New System of Geology* (1829), was written for the general public. Besides giving a good general introduction to the subject, Ure proposed a theory of earth history, which sought to be faithful to the literal teaching of Genesis and to respond to old-earth geological arguments.[108] He also gave one of the earliest proposals of an ice age, which he reasoned to be a natural consequence of the flood.[109]

Granville Penn (1761–1844) was not (and never claimed to be) a geologist but was well acquainted with the geological writings of the leading geologists of the time, and read articles on geology in the leading journals.[110] He also made some of his own geological field observations on the European continent.[111] Penn's major work on geology, *A Comparative Estimate of the Mineral and Mosaical Geologies*, was published in 1822, with a supplement in 1823 that responded to the Buckland's theory on Kirkdale Cave. The second edition which was revised and expanded (two volumes) in response to various criticisms appeared in 1825.[112] Penn reaffirmed the Genesis account as literal history, understood the days of creation as 24-hour days and viewed the Noahic flood as a global, catastrophic deluge which reshaped the surface of the Earth.[113]

George Bugg (1769–1851), although he never claimed to be a geologist and had little first-hand knowledge of the subject, was also well read in the geological writings of his day. Like Penn, he had read books by the leading geologists at the time and geological articles in the journals.[114] In his large two-volume *Scriptural Geology* (1826–1827), Bugg argued for a literal six-day creation about 6,000 years ago and a global Noahic flood which produced most of the fossil bearing strata[115] and most of the physical features currently visible on the Earth's surface.[116]

---

106 Ibid.

107 Terry Mortenson, 'British Scriptural Geologists in the First Half of the Nineteenth Century: Part 4. Andrew Ure (1778–1857)' *JoC* 12/3 (1998), 363.

108 Ibid., 365–366.

109 Ibid., 367.

110 Terry Mortenson, 'British Scriptural Geologists in the First Half of the Nineteenth Century: Part 2. Granville Penn (1761–1844),' *JoC* 11/3 (1997), 362.

111 Ibid., 371.

112 Ibid., 361–362.

113 Ibid., 369.

114 Terry Mortenson, 'British Scriptural Geologists in the First Half of the Nineteenth Century: Part 3. George Bugg (1789–1851),' *JoC* 12/2 (1998), 240.

115 Ibid., 241.

116 Ibid., 245.

Thomas Gisborne (1758–1846), a respected Anglican clergyman, was also well read in the geological writings of his day. He also made his own observations in his rural parish. His book *Considerations on Modern Theories of Geology* (1837) argues for a recent, literal six-day creation and a global catastrophic Noahic flood which produced most of the strata of the Earth's crust.[117]

Again, the arguments presented by the scriptural geologists were completely ignored. Historian Charles Gillespie condescendingly suggests that '[t]heir errors cannot have seemed sufficiently damaging to science to merit professional refutation because no one bothered to refute them.'[118] Indeed, as Mortenson has documented, responses to the scriptural geologists by their contemporaries amounted to nothing more than cavalier dismissal and *ad hominem* argument.[119]

Thus, the old-earth uniformitarian views of Hutton and Lyell soon became the consensus among virtually all geologists, including those who held conservative evangelical views. However, the cost of accepting such views meant the subordination of Scripture to geological data. Rudwick observes:

> Traditionally, non-biblical sources, whether natural or historical, had received their true meaning by being fitted into the unitary narrative of the Bible. This relationship now began to be reversed: the biblical narrative, it was now claimed, received its true meaning by being fitted, on the authority of self-styled experts, into a framework of non-biblical knowledge. In this way the cognitive plausibility and religious meaning of the biblical narrative could only be maintained in a form that was constrained increasingly by non-biblical considerations.[120]

This is clearly demonstrated by the response of the New England clergy in United States. In 1849, *Bibliotheca Sacra*, the leading New England journal, published a paper by Cuvier in which he argues both for a recent creation of the earth and a universal deluge. Using Cuvier, New England clergy rejected both old-earth views and Lyell's uniformitarianism.[121] However, this situation quickly changed, and by the mid 1850s *Bibliotheca Sacra* began publishing articles clearly influenced by uniformitarian geology. Most clergy became convinced by the new 'facts' and accepted either the day-age theory or the gap theory.[122]

---

117 Terry Mortenson, 'British Scriptural Geologists in the First Half of the Nineteenth Century: Part 6. Thomas Gisborne (1758–1846)' *JoC* 14/1 (2000), 79.

118 As cited by Mortenson, 'British Scriptural Geologists: Historical Setting,' 222.

119 Ibid., 222–223.

120 Rudwick, 'The Shape and Meaning of Earth History,' 306.

121 John D. Hannah, 'Bibliotheca Sacra and Darwinism: An Analysis of the Nineteenth-Century Conflict Between Science and Theology' *GTJ* 4/1 (September 1983), 41–42. Hannah notes that the New England clergy apparently misinterpreted Cuvier as defending a young earth, since Cuvier was actually a catastrophist and believed the earth had experienced periodic catastrophes each of which left an impact in geological record. Thus, in his paper Cuvier was simply referring to the most recent catastrophe.

122 Ibid., 42.

This change in position appears to have occurred with virtually no opposition, even though a radical reinterpretation of the Genesis account was required in order to maintain the doctrine of inerrancy.[123] John D. Hannah shows that this painless transition was largely the result of the influence of Benjamin Silliman, a geologist at Yale College where the clergy of that time were trained. In 1829, Silliman affirmed that the Genesis account was strictly compatible with the facts of geology and palaeontology, but a decade later he could only assert that the correspondence between the two was approximate.[124] Wishing to maintain his deep religious commitment as well as the integrity of geology, he reinterpreted the Genesis account in terms of a day-age view, and instilled the same thinking into a generation of clergymen. Moreover, when Silliman retired, he was succeeded by James Dwight Dana, his former student and son-in-law, who continued to propagate the same old-earth views.

Others who held to old-earth views due to their convictions about the geological data included George S. Faber (1773–1854) who advocated the day-age view in his *Treatise on the Genius and Object of the Patriarchal, the Levitical, and the Christian Dispensations* (1823). Hugh Miller (1802–1856) in *Testimony of the Rocks* (1856) interpreted the six days as being six geological ages, as did F. de Rougemont, G.P. Pianciani, Delitzsch, Gultler, Secohi, and Pesnel.[125]

Thomas Chalmers (1780–1847) in his *Evidences of Christianity* (1813) advocated the 'gap theory,'[126] which was later taken up by G.W. Pember in 1876 and was greatly popularized by the notes of the *Scofield Reference Bible* and by Harry Rimmer in *Modern Science and the Genesis Record* (1937).[127] James Murphy[128] and Herbert Morris[129] also defended the gap theory in their writings.

Another view was to treat the Genesis account as merely a description of the creation of the garden of Eden. This 'local creation' theory was proposed by John Pye Smith (1774–1851) in *On the Relation Between the Holy Scriptures and Certain Parts of Geological Science* (1840), and more recently by John Sailhamer.[130]

Yet another non-literal way of dealing with the six days is the 'days of revelation' or 'pictorial-day' theory, which argues that the creation did not actually occur in six days but was merely *revealed* in six days. Advocates include P.J. Wiseman and Bernard Ramm.[131]

---

123 Ibid., 43.

124 Ibid.

125 Lewis, 'The Days of Creation,' 454.

126 The gap theory postulates a long period of time between Genesis 1:1 and 1:2.

127 Lewis, 'The Days of Creation,' 453–454.

128 James G. Murphy, *A Commentary on the Book of Genesis* (Andover: Draper, 1887).

129 Herbert W. Morris, *Science and the Bible* (Philadelphia: Ziegler and McCurdy, 1871).

130 John H. Sailhamer, *Genesis Unbound* (Sisters, Oregon, Multnomah, 1996).

131 P.J. Wiseman, *Creation Revealed in Six Days*, 3rd edition (London, Marshall Morgan & Scott, 1958); Bernard Ramm, *The Christian View of Science of Scripture* (London: Paternoster, 1955), 218–229.

Note also that the change in thinking about creation and the flood was aided by the introduction of critical biblical scholarship and liberal theology. Lindberg and Numbers point out that

> professional geologists, who embraced Charles Lyell's admonition to study geology 'as if the Scriptures were not in existence,' joined professional biblical scholars, who adapted Benjamin Jowett's advice to 'interpret the Scriptures like any other book.'... In this version of the encounter between Genesis and geology, critical biblical scholarship played as important a role in fostering scientific geology as did empirical investigation.[132]

Darwin and Evolution

Some commentators deny that evolutionary theory had anything to do with the change in views regarding the days of creation, and the age of the earth. Forster and Marston, for example, claim that the shift came as result of the empirical geological evidence alone:

> It should be noted that this was all before Darwin published the Origin of Species in 1859, and that virtually all the geologists involved rejected evolution — including Charles Lyell. There was no sense in which evolution was assumed by those who constructed the geological column, and, as we will show in a later section, some of the key geologists were evangelical Christians.[133]

However, both Hutton and Lyell were deists and therefore rejected the notion of a personal Creator God. In essence, the laws of nature became their God. In fact, in an unpublished paper written in 1794, Hutton clearly advocated a form of evolution by natural selection.[134] Lyell too, although he objected to *Lamarckian* evolution, eventually came to accept Darwinian evolution.[135]

In any case, it has long been recognized that Darwin did not invent the idea of evolution. As Livingstone notes, 'that idea was already common currency in embryological thought and in theories of social development long before Darwin's imaginative synthesis.'[136] Indeed, evolutionary ideas can be traced as far back as Thales of Miletus (640–546 B.C.) who was apparently the first to advance the idea that life originated in water, and held some views of biological evolution similar to those of modern times. Anaximander (611–547 B.C.), a student of Thales, developed these ideas further and concluded that humans evolved from fish.[137] Greek philosopher Empedocles (493–435 B.C.) believed

---

132 Lindberg and Numbers, *God and Nature*, 13.

133 Forster and Marston, *Reason, Science and Faith*, 219.

134 Paul N. Pearson, 'In retrospect: Setting the Evolutionary Record Straight On Darwin and Hutton' *Nature* 425 (16 October 2003), 665.

135 Mortenson, 'British Scriptural Geologists: Historical Setting,' 232.

136 David N. Livingstone, 'Science and Religion: Towards a New Cartography' *CSR* 26/3 (Spring 1997), 282.

137 Jerry Bergman, 'Evolutionary Naturalism: An Ancient Idea' *JoC* 15/2 (2001), 77.

that chance 'was responsible for the entire process' of human evolution. He also advocated spontaneous generation, gradual evolution by trial-and-error recombination, and natural selection as the primary mechanism of evolution.[138] Also, Aristotle (384–322 B.C.) claimed humans are the highest point of a long, continuous 'ascent with modification' of life.[139]

In France, Charles De Secondat Montesquieu (1689–1755) developed a modern theory of evolution, and Benoit de Maillet (1656–1738)[140] held that birds, mammals, and humans evolved from fish.[141] Georges-Louis Leclerc, Comte de Buffon, included discussions of evolutionary concepts in his *Historie Naturelle,* a forty-four volume encyclopedia describing everything known about the natural world. He also published *Les Epoques de la Nature* (1788) where he openly suggested that the planet was much older than the 6,000 years proclaimed by the church, and discussed 'uniformitarian' concepts very similar to those which were later formulated by Charles Lyell. John-Baptiste Lamarck (1744–1829) proposed four laws of gradual evolutionary transformation in his *Philosophie Zoologique* (1809). Étienne Geoffroy St. Hilaire (1772–1844) also discussed evolutionary concepts in *Philosophie Anatomique* (1818).

In Britain, Erasmus Darwin (1731–1802), Charles Darwin's grandfather, published a theory of evolution in *Zoonomia* (1794–1796), and the concept of natural selection was developed by William Charles Wells in 1813 and later, by Alfred Russell Wallace.[142]

Therefore, the ideas Darwin presented in *Origin of Species* were nothing new. Darwin's book was, however, highly successful in popularizing evolution by bringing it to the attention of educated people. Earlier theories of evolution were apparently not well received because at the time of their publication, the Bible and historic Christian doctrine still enjoyed a position of authority in the academy and society in general. But with the Enlightenment came autonomy, naturalism, materialism, skepticism, and liberalism, so when Charles Darwin published his ideas in 1859 the ground was much more fertile and receptive. Indeed, all 1250 copies in the first printing were sold immediately. Some copies were sent to known sympathizers, and the rest were sold to the trade, with orders for more.[143] Thus, the academy in particular was fertile ground for Darwin to push his ideas.

While theistic evolution theories are now almost unanimously rejected by evangelical theologians and philosophers,[144] this was not always the case.

---

138 Ibid.

139 Ibid.

140 His book on evolution was published posthumously in 1748.

141 Ibid., 78.

142 Ibid.

143 A. Desmond and J. Moore, *Darwin: The Life of a Tormented Evolutionist* (New York: W.W. Norton, 1994), 477.

144 See David H. Lane, 'Special Creation or Evolution: No Middle Ground' *BSac* 151 (January 1994), 11–31; _____, 'Theological Problems With Theistic Evolution' *BSac* 151 (April 1994), 155–174; Michael A. Harbin, 'Theistic Evolution: Deism Revisited?' *JETS* 40/4 (December 1997), 639–651.

Indeed, the church's response to Darwin appears to be mixed. Charles Hodge (1797–1878) of Princeton Seminary declared that Darwinism was tantamount to atheism.[145] However, Hodge primarily objected to Darwinian evolution. He and many of his Princetonian colleagues were not totally opposed to theistic evolution. A.A. Hodge, A.H. Strong, R.A. Torrey, and B.B. Warfield also accepted the possibility of theistic evolution.[146] B.B. Warfield (1851–1921) stated that evolution can supply 'a theory of the method of the divine providence.'[147]

Scottish theologian James Orr (1844–1913) felt that biological evolution was 'extremely probable, and supported by a large body of evidence.'[148] He added: '"Evolution," in short, is coming to be recognized as but a new name for "creation"…'[149]

George Frederick Wright (1838–1921), a teacher at Oberlin College who became editor of *Bibliotheca Sacra* in 1883, and Harvard botanist Asa Gray (1810–1888) were highly influential in convincing the North American Protestant community that Darwinism and Calvinism were quite compatible. Many who initially opposed Darwinism, such as James D. Dana, eventually accepted the idea even if in some modified form.[150]

Both Wright and Gray were theistic evolutionists who argued that developmentalism did not stand against Christianity, and that evolution provided proof for God's existence through design. Wright's pioneering labors, both in writing and in gaining a hearing for Gray among his fellow clergymen, were instrumental in causing Christianity and evolution to be viewed as being compatible.[151] James R. Moore writes: 'Christian Darwinism in America was as much the special creation of George Frederick Wright (1838–1921) as of Asa Gray. … No two Christian men on either side of the Atlantic were more determined to advance the cause of Darwinism.'[152]

Current Positions

In regard to creation and the age of the earth, evangelicals today generally hold to either 'young-earth creationism' or 'old-earth progressive creationism.' Those who hold to young-earth creationism interpret the Genesis creation account as

145 Charles Hodge, *What is Darwinism?* (New York: Scribners, 1874).

146 Bernard Ramm, *The Christian View of Science of Scripture* (London: Paternoster, 1955), 200–201.

147 B.B. Warfield, *Biblical and Theological Studies* (Philadelphia: Presbyterian and Reformed, 1968), 238.

148 James Orr, *The Christian View of God and the World as Centering in the Incarnation* (Grand Rapids, Michigan, Eerdmans, 1960) 99.

149 James Orr, 'Science and Christian Faith' *The Fundamentals*, vol 1, edited by R.A. Torrey et. al. (Grand Rapids, Michigan, Baker, 1972), 346.

150 Hannah, 'Bibliotheca Sacra and Darwinism,' 54–55.

151 Ibid., 48.

152 J.R. Moore, *The Post-Darwinian Controversies* (Cambridge, Cambridge University, 1979), 280, 283.

plain, descriptive, historical narrative. Those who hold to old-earth progressive creationism, on the other hand, interpret the Genesis account in a couple of different ways: The day-age view understands the creation days to be long periods of time, in the order of millions of years. This view is widely held by Christians who are also practicing scientists, as well as a several notable theologians, including J. Oliver Buswell, Jr., Harold Stigers, R. Laird Harris, Walter Kaiser, and Gleason Archer.[153]

The other major old-earth interpretation is the 'literary framework view,' which is now probably the most widely held view among theologians and commentators. This interpretation, first advocated by Arie Noordtzij from the University of Utrecht in *God's Word and the Testimony of the Ages* (1924), understands the days as merely an artistic or literary device and therefore have no correspondence with actual, physical days. Major expositions of this view have been produced by Meredith Kline, Henri Blocher, Mark E. Ross, and Lee Irons.[154]

Although the young-earth creationist position is now the minority view even among evangelicals, it still has a relatively large following including the Lutheran Church, Missouri Synod and the Wisconsin Evangelical Lutheran Synod whose doctrinal statements explicitly affirm creation in six days.[155] In addition, three Baptist bodies have confessions that affirm belief 'in the Genesis account of creation,' and one of them, the New Testament Association of Independent Baptist Churches, has added that 'the six days of creation in Genesis Chapter One were solar, that is twenty-four hour days.'[156]

Recent and current young-earth creationist theologians include Louis Berkhof (*Systematic Theology*, 1930), V. Hepp (*Calvinism and the Philosophy of Nature*, 1930), J.T. Mueller (*Christian Dogmatics*, 1934), H.C. Leupold (*Exposition of Genesis*, 1942), F. Pieper (*Church Dogmatics*, 1950), H. Hoeksema (*Reformed Dogmatics*, 1966), John Whitcomb (*The Genesis Flood*, 1961), John J. Davis (*Paradise to Prison*, 1975), and Douglas Kelly (*Creation and Change*, 1997).

---

153 J. Oliver Buswell, Jr., *A Systemic Theology of the Christian Religion* (Grand Rapids, Zondervan, 1962); Harold G. Stigers, *A Commentary on Genesis* (Grand Rapids: Zondervan, 1976); R. Laird Harris, 'The Length of the Creative Days in Genesis 1' in Pipa and Hall, 101–111; Walter C. Kaiser, *More Hard Sayings of the Old Testament* (Downers Grove, Illinois, IVP, 1992), 37; Gleason L. Archer, *Survey of Old Testament Introduction* (Chicago, Moody Press, 1996), 187–199.

154 Meredith G. Kline, 'Because It Had Not Rained' *WTJ* 20 (1958), 146–157; Meredith G. Kline, 'Space and Time in the Genesis Cosmogony' *PSCF* 48/1 (March 1996), 2–15; Mark E. Ross, 'The Framework Hypothesis: An Interpretation of Genesis 1:1–2:3' in Pipa and Hall, 113–130; Henri Blocher, *In the Beginning*, translated by D.G. Preston (Leicester, IVP, 1984); Lee Irons (with M.G. Kline), 'The Framework View' in Hagopian, 217–256.

155 Missouri Synod: 'Brief Statement of Doctrinal Position,' Article 5. Wisconsin Synod: Creed, Article II.1. and 2.

156 Lavellee, 'Creeds and the Six Creation Days.'

Summary

Although Lewis notes that interpreters have never been of one mind,[157] it is clear that the literal day view was, before the nineteenth century, the predominant view.[158]

Yet there appears to be a surprisingly strong resistance from numerous commentators to this obvious conclusion.[159] David Hall laments:

> The record of history is abundantly clear on this; yet, it is like extracting molars to convince some theologians to surrender an opinion that is in conflict with actual history. One has to question the tenacious resistance, especially when it is confronted with so much factual information. Why, I asked, would fine and godly theologians fight against history with so much energy when the case against it was so clear? The answer must provide interesting information about method.[160]

Lewis also notes that '[t]he interpretation given has never been in isolation from the general approach to Scripture of the individual interpreter.'[161] Indeed, it appears that the acceptance of an ancient earth, the minimization of the impact of the Noahic flood, the rejection of the traditional reading of the Genesis account, and its reinterpretation to fit in with the new geology, were all the result of a general trend away from Scripture as the final authority in matters of history, and towards the acceptance of scientific investigation as the most reliable record of historical information and truth in general. This can be seen, for example, in the activities of the Geological Society of London founded in 1807. The society was dominated from the beginning by those who believed in an ancient earth, and the relationship of the Genesis account to geology was never discussed in its public communications,[162] presumably because its members had little regard for its authority in matters relating to history and the natural world.

This same lack of respect for scriptural teaching appears to have also affected society in general. David Livingstone, citing the work of Frank Miller Turner, points out that there was competition for cultural power in nineteenth-century English society between the old-fashioned clergyman and the new enthusiastic scientific professional. Thus, society was also witnessing a conflict between scientists and theologians. During the Victorian era cultural power progressively

---

157 Lewis, 'The Days of Creation,' 455.

158 This is also acknowledged by Blocher (36), Davis Young ('Scripture in the Hands of Geologists (Part One)' 4) and Youngblood (41).

159 See in particular Hugh Ross (*Creation and Time* [Colorado Springs, NavPress, 1994], 16–24; [with Gleason Archer] 'The Day-Age Response' in D.G. Hagopian [editor], *The Genesis Debate* [Mission Viejo, California, Crux Press], 68–70), and Roger Forster and Paul Marston (*Reason, Science and Faith* [Crowborough, East Sussex, Monarch, 1999], 188–240).

160 David W. Hall, 'The Evolution of Mythology: Classic Creation Survives as the fittest Among Its Critics and Revisers' in Pipa and Hall, 276.

161 Lewis, 'The Days of Creation,' 455.

162 Mortenson, 'British Scriptural Geologists: Historical Setting,' 230.

passed out of the hands of the elitist clergy and into the hands of the professional scientist who became the new elite. Consequently, when people encountered agricultural or medical or social problems they progressively turned to science and scientists rather than to the church.[163]

John D. Hannah summarizes the whole situation nicely when talking about the change in attitudes of the New England clergy:

> The theory of creation changed categorically from 1856 to 1880 for [the New England] clergymen, as did the place of the Genesis account in religious orthodoxy. While it was accepted in the 1840s as describing six consecutive twenty-four hour days of creation, by the 1850s it was viewed as explicative of origins but within a Day-Age mode. By the 1870s, however, the Genesis account was perceived as truth but not a delineation of central creation truth. Hopkins says of the Genesis account: 'If this has any claim to credence, it cannot be a history of cosmogony. The creation which it designates must have been some other and some minor creation.' Reinterpretation of traditional cosmology because of claimed advances in science makes it evident to the observer in the 20th century that uniformitarian and evolutionary science not only asserted its freedom from special divine revelation but triumphed over it in the hearts of many. … [In the 19th century] science appeared to speak with the inerrancy that we accord to Scripture alone. It behooves us to remember to be cautious not to neglect the exegesis of Scripture and the qualitative gulf between special and general revelation.[164]

---

163 Livingstone, 'Science and Religion,' 272.
164 Hannah, 'Bibliotheca Sacra and Darwinism,' 57, 58.

CHAPTER 4

The Genesis Account:
Its Purpose and Function

G enesis, the book of beginnings, forms the basis of all biblical theologies, and
in particular, a biblical theology of creation. While chapters 1–2 describe
the actual creation of the universe and everything in it, chapter 3 describes
how creation became tarnished due to the curse resulting from the first couple's
rebellion against their Creator. In addition, chapters 6–9 depict the devastating
effect on all creation of God's judgment through the catastrophic global flood.

Structure of Genesis

Ten Divisions

The book of Genesis is clearly divided into ten divisions which are separated by
the construct אֵלֶּה תּוֹלְדוֹת ('ēllĕh ṭôlᵉdôt, 'these are the descendants of' or 'these
are the accounts of').[1] However, there is some disagreement over the function of
this phrase: is it a title, or a colophon (signature)?

  While most interpreters understand 'ēllĕh ṭôlᵉdôt as a title to the following
section, P.J. Wiseman claims the phrase functions in much the same way as the
colophons found on ancient Babylonian tablets. These colophons have a title,
date of writing, a serial number if part of a series, an indication if the tablet is the
last in the series, and the name of the scribe or owner. According to Wiseman,
Genesis 2:4 serves as a colophon for Genesis 1, where 'the heavens and the
earth' functions as the title, the clause 'when God created them' represents
the date, and the six days form a series with day seven identified as the end
of the series. Furthermore, the only name used is 'God' which suggests He is
the writer/author.[2] R.K. Harrison agrees: 'The colophon, which concluded the
individual tablet or the series, normally contained the name of the scribe or the
owner of the tablet, as has been remarked above, and frequently it also included
some attempt at dating. In addition, it often embodied the title given to the
narrative, and if the tablet was part of a series it furnished the serial number and
a statement as to whether the tablet did or did not conclude the series.'[3]

---

1 Gen. 2:4, 5:1, 6:9, 10:1, 11:10, 11:27, 25:12, 25:19, 36:1, 36:9, 37:2.

2 P.J. Wiseman, *Creation Revealed in Six days* (London, Marshall, Morgan and Scott, 1948), 46–47.

3 R.K. Harrison, *Introduction to the Old Testament* (Grand Rapids, Michigan, Eerdmans, 1969),
545.

This proposal, however, suffers from numerous problems. Firstly, in the case of Genesis 2:4, the preceding section is not an account of 'the heavens and the earth' which Wiseman claims is the title, but an account of the *creation* of the heavens and the earth. Secondly, the clause 'when God created them' can hardly be taken as a date.[4] Thirdly, all other instances of ʾēllĕh tôlᵉdôt in Genesis are followed by a proper noun which Wiseman claims identifies the author/owner of the tablet. However, the instance in Genesis 2:4 is followed by 'the heavens and the earth' which cannot refer to either author or owner, and to claim that the author is God in this instance, is to admit that the form which supposedly identifies these verses as colophons does not consistently hold.

Furthermore, the tôlᵉdôt clauses cannot be colophons since the last section of Genesis is not terminated by this formula. Charles Taylor attempts to explain this problem away by arguing that because Isaac and family moved to Egypt the writing method would have changed.[5] But it is difficult to imagine why a family's migration to another country would suddenly cause their writing style to change. Moreover, it is highly likely that the composer (Moses?) or final redactor of Genesis would have ensured that the final form of the text was consistent.

Taylor also suggests that the missing colophon may actually be the first few verses of Exodus:[6] 'These are the names of the sons of Israel who went to Egypt with Jacob, each with his family: Reuben, Simeon, Levi, and Judah; Issachar, Zebulun, and Benjamin; Dan and Naphtali; Gad and Asher. The descendants of Jacob numbered seventy in all; Joseph was already in Egypt.' However, the tôlᵉdôt keyword does not appear in any of these verses, making this another instance where the supposed form of the colophon does not hold.

More difficulties arise for the colophon interpretation when considering the actual content of some of the preceding sections. If tôlᵉdôt clauses are colophons then Genesis 11:27b–25:12 is the account of Ishmael. But why would Ishmael be concerned with recording the call of Abram and the covenant God made with him? Why would he wish to record the dismal prophecy in 16:11–12? Why would he record God's preference for Isaac in fulfilling His covenant with Abraham? Why would he record Abraham's willingness to send him and his mother away for the sake of Isaac? Why would he be concerned with the death of Sarah and the respect the Hittites had for Abraham? Why would he be concerned with recording the story of Isaac and Rebekah? How would he have known the details? Furthermore, the following section (25:13–18) is supposedly the account of Isaac, but this is absurd given that the entire section is devoted to *Ishmael's* descendants! Indeed, similar observations could be made regarding the accounts of Esau and Jacob.

---

4 This would also mean that the tablet was written when God created the heavens and the earth which contradicts Wiseman's theory that it was written at a much later time as a result of a revelation from God.

5 Charles A. Taylor, 'Who Wrote Genesis? Are the *Toledoth* Colophons' *JoC* 8/2 (1994), 208.

6 Ibid.

In order to evade these problems, Taylor claims the accounts of Ishmael and Esau are encapsulated within the accounts of Isaac and Jacob respectively.[7] However, this solves nothing. Firstly, why would Isaac and Jacob wish to record the family lines of their respective brothers? Secondly, Taylor is essentially admitting that the *tôlᵉdôt* clauses relating to Ishmael and Esau are not colophons.

In contrast, understanding a *tôlᵉdôt* clause to be a title to the subsequent section is far less problematic.[8] Note that *tôlᵉdôt* is the plural construct noun form of the verb יָלַד (*yālăḏ*, 'to bear'), which strongly suggests it refers to what follows rather than what precedes. As Skinner points out, the *tôlᵉdôt* clause is always followed by the genitive of the progenitor, never of the progeny.[9] In other words, the text following the *tôlᵉdôt* clause recounts what the subject of the *tôlᵉdôt* clause and his descendants went on to do in history. Thus, Wolters translates the *tôlᵉdôt* clause as '[these are the] historical developments arising out of…'[10] In the case of Genesis 2:4, the phrase 'the generations of the heavens and the earth' does not refer to the creation of the heavens and the earth but to that which was generated *from* the heavens and the earth. Furthermore, each account builds on the preceding one, and some of them cause the storyline to focus on a particular individual and their family.[11] This is shown diagrammatically in Figure 4.1.

This raises the question, however, of why the *tôlᵉdôt* clause is not found in Genesis 1:1. Hamilton's solution is to view verse 1 as both superscription and a summary statement which is functionally equivalent to 'These are the generations of…'[12] Wenham, on the other hand, argues that Genesis 1:1 – 2:3 is separate from the main historical outline of the book, and therefore should be interpreted differently.[13] Note, however, that each account carries on the story of a subject mentioned in the preceding account. Thus, Genesis 5:1 – 6:8 records the 'historical developments arising out of' the family line of Adam who had already been explicitly identified in the preceding account (Gen. 2:20). Therefore, in the case of Genesis 1, which is the first account, we would not expect to find the same *tôlᵉdôt* starting formula. By placing the creation account at the very beginning of book, the author emphasizes the point that God created *out of nothing*. In other words, the universe is a *tôlᵉdôt* of nothing. Apart from God Himself, there was no person and no thing present in the beginning from which the creation could be derived.

---

7 Ibid., 209.

8 *ʾēllēh tôlᵉdô*t is also used as a heading in Num. 3:1, Ruth 4:18, 1 Chr. 1:29.

9 John Skinner, *A Critical and Exegetical Commentary on Genesis*, ICC (Edinburgh, T & T Clark, 1910), 41.

10 A.M. Wolters, *Creation Regained* (Carlisle, Paternoster, 1996), 37.

11 Gen. 11:10 focuses the story on Shem rather than his brothers Ham and Japheth; 25:19 focuses on Isaac as opposed to Ishmael; and 37:2 singles out Jacob rather than Esau.

12 Victor P. Hamilton, *The Book of Genesis 1–17*, NICOT (Grand Rapids, Michigan: Eerdmans, 1990), 117.

13 Gordon H. Wenham, *Genesis 1–15*, WBC (Dallas, Word, 1987), 40.

Figure 4.1 — The 'accounts' of Genesis

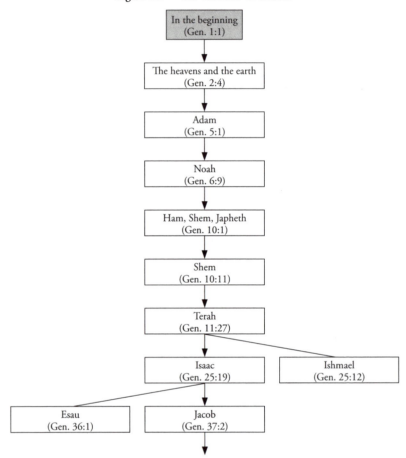

Genre of Genesis

Unlike most other world religions, Christianity (like Judaism) is distinct in that it is rooted in history, and the Bible is, above all, a book of history. As George Eldon Ladd wrote: 'The God of Israel was the God of history. ... The Bible is first of all a record of history. But history is recorded because it embodies the acts of God.'[14] Or as Graeme Goldsworthy explains, 'the whole Bible presents its message as theology within a framework of history.'[15] Thus, the biblical record describes the origin of the universe as the beginning of history, and traces the acts of God and the exploits of humanity from creation to the incarnation of Christ and the establishment of the church.

---

14   George Eldon Ladd as cited by I.E. Amaya, 'The Bible and God's Revelation in History' *JETS* 14 (Spring 1971), 68, 69.

15   Graeme Goldsworthy, *Preaching the Whole Bible as Christian Scripture* (Leicester, IVP, 2000), 24.

As a historical work, the Bible is not exhaustive — indeed much of the Old Testament focuses on a specific people group, the nation of Israel. Nevertheless, the people, places, and events that the Scriptures recount are truly historical and the biblical record is completely trustworthy. As Schaeffer argues, given that God has revealed Himself in history, what sense would it make if this revelation in history was false?[16]

Again, it is precisely because Christianity is rooted in history that much of Scripture is historical. 'God has set the revelation of the Bible in history; He did not give it (as He could have done) in the form of a theological text book.'[17] Therefore, as Decker points out, Scripture employs historical narrative deliberately, and in such a way that the 'historical basis (event) for the narrival [sic] depiction (text) is absolutely essential. The revelation value of the Bible depends on its history value ... Historical narrative explicitly appeals to history to verify what it teaches: names, places, events, dates etc. are cited. ... If these references are not trustworthy, it casts grave doubt over the theology being propounded in narrative fashion.'[18]

The historical roots of Christianity have major implications for the interpretation of Scripture and in particular, the interpretation of the book of Genesis. While most interpreters acknowledge that most of Genesis is normal Hebrew historical narrative,[19] many also view the early chapters as primarily theological rather than strictly historical.[20] Yet, there is no reason to think that history and theology are mutually exclusive. A historical account can still be packed with theological motifs and teachings. What else would one expect from a God who has revealed Himself in history? Weakening the account's historical basis appears to be based purely on the nature of the extraordinary events recorded, rather than detailed literary analysis with respect to the greater context of the book of Genesis. Yet, as V. Phillips Long warns

> Genre criticism must resist the temptation to focus exclusively on smaller units of discourse and instead must be alert to the way in which the genre of a larger discourse unit affects every smaller discourse unit within it. ... It is not wrong, of course, to study the smaller units; it is indeed useful and necessary. But final judgment on a smaller unit's import, historical or whatever, must not be passed without first considering the larger discourse of which the smaller is a part.[21]

---

16 Francis A. Schaeffer, 'The God Who Is There' in *Francis A. Schaeffer Trilogy* (Leicester, IVP, 1990), 100.

17 Ibid.

18 Rodney J. Decker, 'Realistic or Historical Narrative?' *JMT* 4/1 (Spring 2000), 59–60.

19 Richard L. Pratt (*He Gave Us Stories* [Phillipsburg, New Jersey: P & R Publishing, 1990], 282) states: 'The book of Genesis reports history from the beginning of time to the death of Joseph.'

20 Those who hold to this view do not necessarily deny that these people, places and events are historical, but merely that Genesis is not concerned with relating what actually happened with any kind of chronological order or precision.

21 V. Philips Long, *The Art of Biblical History* (Grand Rapids, Michigan: Zondervan, 1994), 46, 49.

It is no accident that Genesis 1:1, the first verse of both Genesis and the entire Bible, also sets the tone for both: 'In the beginning, God created the heavens and the earth.' This verse clearly and emphatically states that history had a beginning and this beginning originated with God. His creative acts brought about the process of human history.

While the following creation account is not a complete and exhaustive scientific discussion of how the creation came into being, it is an accurate historical summary of 'the process by which the world was prepared for the advent of man and for God's dealing with him.'[22] Humanity's relationship with, and responsibility to, their Creator is also simply and plainly stated, as is their rebellion and consequent fall.

Traditionally, the book of Genesis has been divided into two sections: primeval history (chapters 1–11) and patriarchal history (chapters 12–50).[23] However, as David Clines notes, 'it is most significant that there is no clear-cut break at the end of the Babel story. Clearly, Abrahamic material begins a new section of the Pentateuch, but the precise beginning of the Abrahamic material — and therewith the conclusion of the pre-Abrahamic material — cannot be determined. In the final form of Genesis, there is at no point a break between primeval and patriarchal history.'[24] Therefore, since the 'patriarchal' history is generally regarded as an accurate historical record, then there is no reason why the 'primeval' history should not also be accepted as an accurate historical record.

Creation and the Fall (Genesis 1–3)

As noted above, while virtually all interpreters regard Genesis 12–50 as historical narrative, many consider the early chapters — especially Genesis 1–3 — to be primarily theological rather than precise historical accounts of the creation and the fall.

Poetry or 'Exalted Prose'?

Otto Helweg claims Genesis 1 has a similar structure to Egyptian poetry. Since Moses was 'educated in all the wisdom of the Egyptians' (Acts 7:22) and the Israelites would have undoubtedly been acquainted with the basic forms of Egyptian literature then it would be logical for Moses to use such a style.[25] But this view has several problems. Firstly, while Moses was undoubtedly the editor and collator of the material in Genesis, it is quite possible that he used existing accounts recorded on clay or stone tablets by those who witnessed or partici-pated in the events. Even more likely, he drew them from oral tradition. In either case, the original author of Genesis 1 would have composed his account long

22 Merrill C. Tenney, 'The Bible and History' *JETS* 14 (Spring 1971), 78.

23 See for example William Sanford LaSor, David Allan Hubbard and Frederic W. Bush, *Old Testament Survey*, 2nd edition (Grand Rapids, Michigan, Eerdmans, 1996), 15; Alfred Edersheim, *Bible History: Old Testament* (Peabody, Massachussets, Hendrickson, 1995), 9.

24 David J.A. Clines, 'Theme in Genesis 1–11', in Richard S. Hess and David T. Tsumura (editors), *I Studied Inscriptions from Before the Flood* (Winona Lake, Indiana, Eisenbrauns, 1994), 305.

25 Otto J. Helweg, 'How Long an Evening and Morning?' *JoC* 11/3 (1997), 300.

before the establishment of Egyptian culture. Secondly, if Moses were inclined to adopt Egyptian literary techniques then would he also not be inclined to write in Egyptian hieroglyphs for the exact same reasons specified by Helweg? Yet Moses wrote in Hebrew using that language's grammar and syntax, and in the exact form of typical Hebrew historical narrative.

Nevertheless, when discussing the genre of the creation account, Bill T. Arnold claims that '[i]ts elevated style is more like poetry and the unit is unique when compared to the narrative sections you will read elsewhere in Genesis.'[26] But Arnold is quite mistaken on both points. The form of the text of the creation account is exactly the same as that found throughout the rest of the book. The only sense in which the account can be considered unique is in regard to the actual events it records. Indeed, all the accounts found in Genesis would be unique if considered against this criterion.

Neither is Genesis 1 poetry or in any sense poetic, since the distinctive elements of Hebrew poetry cannot be found anywhere in the text. Hebrew poetry regularly employs various kinds of semantic parallelism,[27] has a limited use of prose particles such as the definite article (הַ, *hă*), definite direct object marker (אֵת, *'ēt*), and relative pronoun (אֲשֶׁר, *'ăšer* and שֶׁ, *šĕ*).[28] In addition, Hebrew poetry is characteristically saturated with comparisons, personifications, anthropomorphic and symbolic language, metonymy,[29] archetypal and stereotypical language, and hyperbole, as well as generally briefer expressions.[30]

That Genesis 1 does not contain the distinctive elements of Hebrew poetry is acknowledged by Henri Blocher. Nevertheless, he argues that the few alliterations and the phrase 'beast of the field' which is elsewhere confined to poetry, suggests that the genre is 'composite' rather than normal historical narrative.[31] Therefore, for Blocher, Genesis is a 'mixed' genre — a mix of history and allegory — and he cites Matthew 21:33–41 as support, claiming that this parable summarizes centuries of history.[32]

Blocher's claims, however, do not stand up to scrutiny. Firstly, alliteration is not at all unique to poetic material[33] and the term 'beasts of the field' occurs

26 Bill T. Arnold, *Encountering the Book of Genesis* (GrandRapids, Michigan, Baker, 1998), 23.

27 For a summary, see Don Parker, *Using Biblical Hebrew in Ministry* (Lanham, Maryland, University Press of America, 1995), 149–154.

28 GRAMCORD searches reveal that the definite article *hă* is used 79 times in ch. 1 and 62 times in ch. 2, the definite direct object marker *ēt* occurs 26 times in ch. 1 and 14 times in ch. 2, and the relative pronouns *'ăšer* and *šĕ* occur 9 times in ch. 1 and 7 times in ch. 2.

29 Metonymy occurs when a figure of speech is used in place of the term normally used to express a particular idea; e.g. 'He is a real Casanova' means he is a playboy or ladies' man.

30 While Gen. 1–3 does contain some anthropomorphisms, personifications, and other figures of speech, their occurrence is not exceptional since similar elements can be found in other narrative sections in Genesis.

31 Henri Blocher, *In the Beginning*, translated by D.G. Preston (Leicester, IVP, 1984), 32.

32 Ibid., 37.

33 See Scott B. Noegel, *Puns and Pundits: Word Play in the Hebrew Bible and Ancient Near Eastern Literature* (Bethesda, Maryland, CDL Press, 2001). For examples of alliteration in Genesis, see David F. Pennant, 'Alliteration in Some Texts of Genesis' *Bib* 68/3 (1987), 390–392.

elsewhere in both narrative and prophecy.[34] Secondly, unlike Genesis 1, Matthew 21:33–41 is clearly identified as a parable (21:45–46) in which communication of history is never an important factor, and therefore, this parable adds no support at all for Blocher's view.

Similarly, Harris contends that although Genesis 1 is not formulated as poetry, it should be regarded as exalted prose since it deals with items of 'cosmic proportions.'[35] Likewise, C. John Collins claims that 'the very kind of language used here is different from what we think of as "ordinary" Hebrew narrative. ... The best term for this kind of language is "exalted prose." By this I mean that the language is "higher" than ordinary language. ...The language is stylized, very broad-stroke, and majestic in its simplicity. ...'[36]

Collins bases his conclusion on the use of the term 'lamps' instead of sun and moon, the failure to name any of the animal species, and the use of unusual terms such as רָקִיעַ (rāqîăʿ, 'expanse').[37] Both Harris and Collins, however, make their distinctions based on the nature of events covered by text, which are inherently unique. But uniqueness is hardly a valid criterion for distinguishing narrative from poetic forms. Secondly, it is highly likely that the term 'lamps' was employed to emphasize that the sun and moon were merely created instruments of light rather than gods to be worshiped — a belief held by many of Israel's neighbors. In the case of rāqîăʿ, why should it be surprising that an unusual word is used to describe a unique creative act?

It is important to recognize that while the creation account is accurate in what it relates, it is not exhaustive. Its conciseness should not be regarded as somehow indicative of poetic forms especially since 'arguments from silence are almost worthless. ... The amount of omitted information in *any* historical narrative is enormous. It is therefore rash to guess at what could *not* have been honestly omitted.'[38] Indeed, no historical narrative is a complete account including every minute detail of what actually occurred. The author simply selects and arranges the details that interest him most in order to communicate his intended message.

Wenham also believes that Genesis 1 is not normal Hebrew prose since (he claims) its syntax is distinctively different from narrative prose, given the presence of some poetic bicola and tricola.[39] However, Wenham's assertion about the account's syntax is simply not true. The syntax of Genesis 1 has all the characteristics of typical Hebrew narrative prose and is no different from

---

34 1 Sam. 17:44; Dan. 2:38.

35 R. Laird Harris, 'The Length of the Creative Days in Genesis 1' in Joseph A. Pipa and David W. Hall (editors), *Did God Create in Six Days?* (Taylors, SC, Southern Presbyterian Press, 1999), 107.

36 C. John Collins, 'Reading Genesis 1:1 – 2:3 as an Act of Communication: Discourse Analysis and Literal Interpretation' in Pipa and Hall, 140–141.

37 Ibid., 141.

38 Vern Sheridan Poythress, 'Adequacy of Language and Accommodation' in Earl D. Radmacher and Robert D. Preus (editors) *Hermeneutics, Inerrancy and the Bible* (Grand Rapids, Michigan, Zondervan, 1984), 373.

39 Wenham, *Genesis 1–15*, 10.

the syntax employed throughout the rest of Genesis.[40] While it is true that the account does contain some devices common to poetry such as bicola and tricola,[41] this merely indicates that the text was carefully composed, not that it has a poetic character.

Bruce Waltke, on the other hand, suggests the creation days are anthropomorphic.[42] But although the account does contain anthropomorphic language,[43] this does not mean or imply that the entire account is anthropomorphic. Moreover, as E.J. Young pointed out, anthropomorphisms generally take the form of a body part or body movement in order to describe God's actions. They never take the form of a temporal concept such as a day.[44]

Therefore, there appears to be no good reason to doubt that the early chapters of Genesis which discuss creation, the fall of mankind, and the global flood are any less historical or should be interpreted any differently than the rest of Genesis. As Gerhard Hasel rightly notes:

> Compared to the hymns in the Bible, the creation account is not a hymn; compared to the parables in the Bible, the creation account is not a parable; compared to the poetry in the Bible, the creation account is not a poem; compared to cultic liturgy, the creation account is not a cultic liturgy. Compared to various kinds of literary forms, the creation account is not a metaphor, a story, a parable, poetry, or the like.[45]

In fact, Steven Boyd has objectively shown, using statistical methods, that Genesis 1:1 – 2:3 is indeed historical narrative.[46] By counting each of the four finite Hebrew verb forms (preterite, imperfect, perfect and *waw*-perfect) in Genesis 1:1 – 2:3 and 96 other texts spread throughout the Old Testament (including 47 narrative and 49 poetic texts), Boyd demonstrated that preterite verb forms (also called *wayyiqtol* forms or *waw*-consecutive imperfects) clearly dominate the narrative texts, while perfect and imperfect verb forms clearly dominate the poetic texts.[47] Using logistic regression — a technique commonly used to make

---

40 This is shown below in the section entitled 'Chronological History?'

41 Umberto Cassuto (*A Commentary on the Book of Genesis*, Part One, translated by I. Adams [Jerusalem: Magnes Press, 1961], 2–14), for example, notes that the number seven, the number of perfection, is an important factor in the composition. There are seven days; v. 1 has seven words; the section following v. 1 is divided into seven paragraphs; the total number of times the words *ʾElōhîm, šāmāyim,* and *ʾ ереṣ* are repeated throughout the account are multiples of seven, etc.

42 Bruce K. Waltke, *Genesis* (Grand Rapids, Michigan, Zondervan, 2001), 75–78; Bruce K. Waltke, 'The First Seven Days' *CT* 32 (1988), 42–46.

43 e.g. God 'breathed,' in Genesis 2:7.

44 E.J. Young, *Studies in Genesis One* (Grand Rapids, Michigan, Baker, 1964), 58.

45 Gerhard F. Hasel, 'The Days of Creation in Genesis 1: Literal "Days" or Figurative "Periods/ Epochs" of Time?' *Origins* 21/1 (1994), 15–16.

46 Steven Boyd, 'A Proper Reading of Genesis 1:1–2:3' in Don DeYoung (editor), *Thousands ... Not Billions* (Green Forest, Arkansas, Master Books, 2005), 157–170.

47 There were two exceptions: (1) Exodus 33, which contains a large number of future references that are indicated by the use of the imperfect verb form. (2) Ezekiel 19, which is actually neither narrative nor poetry, but rather, an apocalyptic text. Genesis 1:1 – 2:3 has none of the features of these two texts.

predictions when two choices are involved — Boyd was able to classify each of the texts as narrative or poetry depending on its distribution of preterites. In the case of Genesis 1:1 – 2:3, it was statistically classified as narrative with a probability of 0.9999. This is an extraordinary level of confidence that amounts to virtual certainty.

In addition, James Jordan argues that the tendency to downplay the historical nature (and thus the chronology) of the creation account is to some extent a result of Gnostic thinking.[48] He posits that if the same interpretive techniques were applied to passages such as Exodus 9–10 and John 20, it would lead to the rejection of a significant portion of Israel's history, and a denial of the historical and bodily resurrection of Christ.[49]

Accommodation to Primitive Cosmology?

Some interpreters claim that the creation account accommodates the primitive cosmologies of the ancient Near East. Paul Seely, for example, believes that

> [t]he writer and first readers of Gen 1 also inherited Mesopotamian concepts about the natural world from the patriarchs and no doubt were influenced by Egyptian concepts during their stay in Egypt. Moses, in fact, was 'educated in all the wisdom of the Egyptians' (Acts 7:22; Exod 2:10). It is highly probable, therefore, that the writer and first readers of Gen 1 defined the sea in the same way that all people in the ancient Near East did, namely, as a single circular body of water in the middle of which the flat earth-disc floated and from which all wells, springs and rivers derived their water.[50]

Elsewhere, Seely writes: 'God has sometimes allowed his inspired penmen to advert to the scientific concepts of their own day. This fact in no way effaces the point and purpose of Genesis 1 to reveal the sovereign power and glory of the one true Creator.'[51] Therefore, Seely believes the Babylonian creation account, *Enuma Elish,* is an important aid to deciphering the meaning of Genesis 1.[52]

Gerhard Hasel, however, has shown that the so-called similarities between the Genesis creation account and the creation accounts of other ancient Near Eastern civilizations are greatly exaggerated and are, in reality, quite superficial.[53] Furthermore, the patriarchs became patriarchs precisely because they worshiped God, and believed Him, rather than the customs and myths of their neighbors. There is absolutely no indication in Scripture that they held any such beliefs about creation. Indeed, it is inconceivable that the Old Testament writers would seek support in their neighbors' pagan mythological works, which they would

---

48 James B. Jordan, *Creation in Six Days* (Moscow, Idaho, Canon Press, 1999), 71–87.

49 Ibid., 86–87, 92–94.

50 Paul H. Seely, 'The Geographical Meaning of "Earth" and "Seas" in Genesis 1:10' *WTJ* 59/2 (Fall 1997), 246.

51 Paul H. Seely, 'The Firmament and the Waters Above Part II: The Meaning of the "water above the firmament" in Gen 1:6–8' *WTJ* 54/1 (Spring 1992), 45.

52 Ibid., 35.

53 Gerhard F. Hasel, 'The Polemic Nature of the Genesis Cosmology' *EvQ* 46 (1974), 81–102.

surely have detested and abominated.[54] As Jewish commentator, Umberto Cassuto, writes: 'The purpose of the Torah in this section ... is thus opposed to the concepts current among the peoples of the ancient East who were Israel's neighbors; and in some respects it is also in conflict with certain ideas that had already found there way into the ranks of our people.'[55]

It is also highly unlikely that Moses and the Israelites were influenced by Egyptian concepts. Although Moses was educated as an Egyptian, he was also the recipient of divine revelation, which stands in stark contrast to any Egyptian teaching. In contrast, the Israelite people lived separately from the Egyptians — in the land of Goshen (Genesis 46:34; 47:4) — and apparently maintained their culture and customs and did not intermarry with the Egyptians. Therefore, it is highly unlikely that they would have been educated alongside the Egyptians — even more so when they became the Egyptians' slaves.

It should be kept in mind that Genesis 1 is a revelation from God, not a description of the cosmology of the Hebrews or of Moses. Indeed, as E.J. Young points out, '[i]f the [Genesis account] is of human origination, how can it have a theological message or be regarded in any sense as the Word of God?'[56]

Note also that the creation account's emphasis on fiat acts ('Let there be ... and it was so') appears to rule out any notion of a primitive anthropomorphic story which conceives of God as a human actor. When humans perform any action, they simply decide to act then proceed to do so. Humans do not make or build things by first saying 'Let there be...' and declaring 'And it was so' when a task is completed.

Walter Kaiser rightly affirms the reliability of the early chapters of Genesis when judged according to the literary conventions of their day. He adds: 'It is only when we introduce our modern conventions and criteria that we begin to allege that the writer was more primitive than ourselves and that he erred in several areas, such as historical, scientific and cultural areas.'[57]

A Literary Framework?

An increasing number of commentators are now suggesting the days of creation do not represent a chronological sequence but a literary framework. Specific interpretations following this principle are dealt with in later chapters, but some preliminary observations regarding the literary framework are given here.

Proponents of this view do not deny the historicity of the people, places, and events described, only the chronological ordering. For example, C. John Collins argues that the narrative can still be historical without being chronological.[58] Likewise, David F. Payne considers the sequence in both Genesis 1 and 2 to

---

54 Cassuto, *Commentary on the Book of Genesis*, I:8.

55 Ibid., 7.

56 E.J. Young, *Studies in Genesis One*, 50.

57 Walter C. Kaiser, *The Old Testament Documents* (Downers Grove, Illinois, Intervarsity, 2001), 83.

58 C. John Collins, 'Reading Genesis 1:1 – 2:3,' 140.

be 'dramatic' rather than chronological.[59] He believes Genesis 1–11 'presents a kaleidoscope of events rather than a connected history.'[60]

Based on the absence of the article before each 'day' and before the numerals of days one to five, both David Sterchi and Ronald Youngblood argue that the syntax does not necessarily imply or require a chronological sequence, although they admit that chronology is not excluded.[61] They also argue that this allows for the possibility of a random or literary order.[62]

In response, Benjamin Shaw notes that when יוֹם (yôm, 'day') is accompanied by a number, the Hebrew is syntactically odd. In fact, when yôm is modified by a number, the number has the definite article while yôm itself is anarthrous (has no article), yet the reference is still understood to be definite.[63] James Stambaugh concurs:

> It appears that numbers in the Hebrew language have a definitive quality in themselves. Kautzsch refers to them as substantives,[64] yet the meaning is the same. A substantive is a noun that one can touch, such as a chair. He cites many examples where the number and noun occur without the article, yet the meaning is definite. There are 13 other occurrences similar to Genesis 1, where the noun does not have the article but is with a number. In each of these other occurrences, the English translation uses the definite article.[65]

Furthermore, both Sterchi and Youngblood fail to consider the significance of the *waw*-consecutive וַיֹּאמֶר (wāyyōʾmĕr, 'and … said') introducing each new day, which clearly indicates both chronological sequence, and an implicit progression of the account as a whole.[66] That is, the fundamentals of time, space, and matter are created *ex nihilo*, the initial 'deep' is divided by an expanse, and the waters below are gathered together to form seas so that dry land can appear. Vegetation is then created and animals are formed, and then finally, mankind is

---

59 David F. Payne, *Genesis One Reconsidered* (London: Tyndale, 1964), 17.

60 Ibid., 19.

61 David A. Sterchi, 'Does Genesis 1 Provide a Chronological Sequence?' *JETS* 39/4 (December 1996), 533; Ronald F. Youngblood, *The Book of Genesis*, 2nd edition (Grand Rapids, Michigan, Baker, 1991), 26. Sterchi suggests the article before 'sixth' and 'seventh' is emphatic.

62 E.J. Young (*Studies in Genesis One*, 65) states that even if Genesis 1 is schematic, it does not necessarily follow that it is figurative or not a record of what actually happened. It does not prove that the days are non-chronological.

63 This is probably due to the fact that yôm plus the article is idiomatic for 'today.' See Benjamin Shaw, 'The Literal Day Interpretation' in Pipa and Hall, 219. The exception is when a preposition is also attached — then both yôm and the number have the article, e.g. Num 7:18.

64 GKC § 134a

65 James Stambaugh, 'The Meaning of "Day" in Genesis' *Impact* 184 (October 1988). See Num. 11:19; I Sam. 1:1; 1 Chron. 12:39; 2 Chron. 20:25; Ezra 8:15, 32; Neh. 2:11; Dan. 1:12, 14,15; 12:12, 13, and Jonah 3:4.

66 GKC § 49a–b.

formed from the ground. It would make no sense for God to create in any other order. As Hess explains:

> Each day accomplishes something new, bringing about a greater completion of the work of creation. Each day begets the next. As has been observed, the events of the first three days are a necessary background for and correspond to what occurs in the fourth through to the sixth day … Indeed, it points to a perspective in which each day of creation, as each generation of humanity, progresses in the unfolding of a divine plan.[67]

Similarly, Leupold understands Genesis 1 as a record of successive creative acts which remove four deficiencies or instances of incompleteness. The account clearly progresses from providing an environment suitable for life to a climax which is the creation of humanity.[68] It is progressive revelation which gets fuller and clearer.[69]

It must also be asked why the author would choose a clearly chronological framework (a week) to communicate something that is supposedly non-chronological? Thus, E.J. Young concludes that '[i]t is questionable whether serious exegesis of Genesis one would in itself lead anyone to adopt a non-chronological view of the days for the simple reason that everything in the text militates against it.'[70]

In regard to Genesis 2–3, Blocher sees a chiasm[71] in Genesis 2:4 – 3:24:[72]

A   Garden planted and man commissioned to cultivate it (2:4b–17)

   B   No mate found among beasts, so woman formed (2:18–25)

      C   Snake tempts woman (3:1–5)

         D   Man and woman eat forbidden fruit and hide from God (3:6–8)

      C'   Woman blames snake (3:9–13)

   B'   Beasts are cursed, and the woman will be dominated by her mate (3:14–19

A'   Expulsion from the garden to cultivate the ground (3:20–24)

Yet a closer analysis of the text reveals that such schemas are artificial and arbitrary. The following table sets out the significant elements of each paragraph with possible correspondences underlined:

---

67 Richard S. Hess, 'Genesis 1–2 in its Literary Context' *TynB* 41 (1990), 152.

68 H.C. Leupold, *Exposition of Genesis*, 2 volumes (Grand Rapids, Michigan, Baker, 1949), 1:38.

69 Ibid., 25. Derek Kidner (*Genesis*, TOTC [London: Tyndale, 1967], 55.) also concludes that Genesis 1 is a narrative story with sequence.

70 E.J. Young, *Studies in Genesis One*, 100.

71 Chiasm (or chiasmus) is a Jewish literary device which employs an inverted parallelism of words and/or thoughts in a phrase, sentence, verse or larger literary structure. The term 'chiasm' is derived from the Greek letter X. See Nils W. Lund, *Chiasmus in the New Testament* (Peabody, Massachusetts, Hendrickson, 1992).

72 Blocher, *In the Beginning*, 28–29.

A	No shrub/plant of the field existed, and there was no man to cultivate the ground.	A′	Woman is named Eve.
			Animal skin used to clothe Adam and Eve.
	Man formed from the ground.		
	God breathes life into man.		Acknowledgment of problem of mankind 'knowing good and evil.'
	Garden planted.		God decides to not allow man and woman to live forever.
	Tree of life and tree of knowledge of good and evil established.		
	Rivers of Eden described.		Man and woman driven from garden to cultivate the ground.
	Man placed in garden to cultivate it.		Access to tree of life inhibited by cherub and flaming sword.
	Man warned not to eat from tree of knowledge of good and evil.		
B	Companion for man sought among animals.	B′	Snake cursed above all other animals.
	Formation of woman from man.		Promise of enmity between woman and snake and their respective seeds.
	Man accepts woman as suitable mate.		
			Woman suffers increased pain in childbirth.
			Woman will desire to control man but he will dominate her.
			Cursing of ground leading to frustration when cultivating it.
			Man destined to return to dust.
C	Snake described as the most shrewd animal.	C′	God calls Adam because he is hiding.
	Snake tempts woman.		God queries Adam regarding the source of his knowledge of his nakedness.
			Adam blames the woman.
			Woman blames snake.
D	Man and woman eat the forbidden fruit.		
	They become aware of the their nakedness and try to cover themselves.		
	Because of their guilt feelings, they hide from God.		

Clearly, many correspondences are missing and those that do exist are arbitrary and/ or relatively insignificant. Thus, there are really no legitimate grounds for taking this passage as a chiasm. Indeed, none of the Talmudic writers saw any such parallelism, nor does this view have any significant support in the history of interpretation.

John J. Collins warns that '[m]any conservative biblicists have invoked literary criticism as a way of avoiding unwelcome historical conclusions. ... It should be clear that such evasions will not work. ... "Story" is not "history." It is essentially fiction, material which in some measure has been invented.'[73]

There is no denying the creation narrative has a literary character and form. However, there is a tendency for many interpreters to de-emphasize the historical correspondence, and over-emphasize the literary attributes.

Chronological History?

There is an overwhelming amount of internal evidence suggesting that Genesis 1–2 records real historical events. Indeed, Walter Kaiser points out that

> The writer used the rubric 'These are the generations (i.e., histories) of ...' (KJV) ten times throughout the book, six times in the first eleven chapters and four times in the remainder of the book. Since the historical nature of the patriarchal narratives of Genesis 12–50 is usually conceded to be 'substantially accurate' even by many non-evangelical scholars, we believe it is fair to argue that the writer wanted to indicate that the prepatriarchal material is of similar nature.[74]

Regarding the straightforward nature of the language employed in the creation account, Calvin stated: 'It must be remembered, that Moses does not speak with philosophical acuteness on occult mysteries, but states these things which are everywhere observed, even by the uncultivated, and which are in common use.'[75] Gerhard von Rad writes: 'Genesis I presents the results of concentrated theological and cosmological reflexion in a language which is concise and always utterly direct in expression. Its statements are not allusive and charged with a hidden meaning ... but are everywhere clearly contoured and mean exactly what they say.'[76] Likewise, Herman Bavinck affirms that the creation account presents no 'saga or myth or poetical fantasy' but 'presents history, which deserves faith and trust. And for that reason, Christian theology, with but few exceptions, has held fast to the literal, historical view of the account of creation.'[77] Derek Kidner, also, notes the inescapable impression that the characters of Genesis 'are people of flesh and blood' and 'the events actual and the book itself a unity.'[78]

---

73 As cited in Grant R. Osborne, *The Hermeneutical Spiral* (Downers Grove, Illinois, IVP, 1991), 420.

74 Walter C. Kaiser Jr., 'Legitimate Hermeneutics' in Norman L. Geisler (editor), *Inerrancy* (Grand Rapids, Zondervan, 1979), 145. See also Kaiser, *The Old Testament Documents*, 82–83.

75 John Calvin, *Genesis* (London, Banner of Truth, 1965). 84.

76 Gerhard von Rad, *Old Testament Theology*, vol. 1 (Edinburgh, Oliver and Boyd, 1962), 141.

77 As cited by E.J. Young, *Studies in Genesis One*, 43.

78 Kidner, *Genesis*, 22. Unfortunately, many interpreters do a poor job of interpreting narrative, and especially the creation account. Common errors include allegorizing (interpreting text in a manner which completely ignores its original meaning or in a manner which is completely arbitrary), and decontextualizing (ignoring historical or literary context).

Note also that the creation account contains all the usual grammatical markers one would expect to find in historical narrative. Gesenius' Hebrew grammar states: 'One of the most striking peculiarities in the Hebrew *consecution* of tenses is the phenomenon that, in representing a series of past events, only the first verb stands in the perfect, and the narration is continued in the imperfect.'[79] Indeed, this is exactly what we find in Genesis 1: The first verb, בָּרָא (*bārā'*, 'created'), is a Qal perfect, which is then followed by a series of Qal imperfects, including וַיֹּאמֶר (*wayyō'mer*, 'and ... said'), וַיַּרְא (*wayyar'*, 'and ... saw') and וַיְהִי (*wayᵉhî*, 'and ... was').

At the higher literary level, typical elements of Hebrew narrative include (1) point of view, (2) characterization, (3) dialogue, (4) narration framework or glue, (5) plot, and (6) repetition.[80] Indeed, all of these elements are clearly exhibited in the early chapters of Genesis. The point of view is clearly that of an observer on earth. The Serpent is characterized as shrewd and cunning. Dialogue occurs between God and Adam, Adam and Eve, and the Serpent and Eve. The grammatical constructions outlined above form the narration framework, and the plot involves the creation of mankind in the image of God in a pristine universe, mankind's rebellion against his Creator, and the cursing of creation as a consequence. The account also contains a great deal of repetition.[81]

In addition, many other Scriptures make allusions to the historicity of the Genesis account.[82] This led Leupold to conclude that '[t]he account as it stands expects the impartial reader to accept it as entirely literal and historical. The use made of it in the rest of Sacred Scriptures treats every part referred to as sober fact, not as a fancy-picture.'[83] Similarly, Allan MacRae considers the passage to be 'as factual and literal as any section anywhere in the Bible.'[84] Indeed, 'Hebrew history taught and accepted the historicity of Adam.'[85]

Blocher, on the other hand, argues that Genesis 1–2 cannot be a literal historical account because Revelation 2:7 presupposes that the Tree of Life still survives, but if the flood was universal it would surely have been destroyed. Furthermore, the geographical region of 'Eden' is never referred to in later

---

79 GKC § 49.a.1. Original emphasis.

80 *Point of view* is the perspective from which the narrator is describing the events. *Characterization* refers to people who are represented in the story. *Dialogue* is the reported direct speech of the characters. *Narration* is the explanatory text which either provides additional background information regarding the events or facilitates the unfolding of the plot. *Plot* is the interaction between characters in their circumstances directed toward a goal. See Don Parker, *Using Biblical Hebrew in Ministry* (Lanham, Maryland, University Press of America, 1995), 120–131.

81 e.g. 'And God said ... and it was so.' 'And God saw that is was good.' 'There was evening and there was morning — the [Xth] day.' Richard L. Pratt adds: '[p]erhaps the most common technique Old Testament [narrative] writers employed was *repetition*' (245). Original emphasis.

82 e.g. Exod. 20:9–11, 31:17; Ps. 8, 104; Matt. 19:4–6; Mark 13:9; Luke 3:38; John 1:3,10; Rom. 8:19–22; Col. 1:16; 2 Pet. 3:5 and Heb. 4:4, 11:3.

83 Leupold, *Exposition of Genesis*, 1:104.

84 Allan A. MacRae, 'The Principles of Interpreting Genesis 1 and 2' *BETS* 2/4 (1959), 2.

85 W.R. Eichhorst, 'The Issue of Biblical Inerrancy in Definition and Defense' *GJ* 10 (Winter 1969), 14.

biblical texts, and neither is there any mention of the garden being destroyed or removed.[86] But Blocher's argument is, again, an argument from silence. As stated above, one cannot legitimately make such conclusions given the amount of material that is normally left out of historical narrative. Furthermore, regarding the Tree of Life, Blocher actually has it the wrong way around: it is the reference in Revelation which is apparently not literal.[87]

Therefore, both the grammatical structure and the narrative style of Genesis 1–2, as well as the allusions to the creation events found in other Scriptures, all suggest that the account is a positive record of things as they actually happened.

The Author's Intent

The belief that the creation account is primarily theological rather than historical, is becoming increasingly popular.[88] Waltke, citing Charles Hummel, posits that the Genesis 1–2 is not a purely descriptive account answering the 'what?' 'how?' and 'what is?' Instead, it is prescriptive in that it answers the 'who?' 'why?' and 'what ought to be?'[89] Therefore, many commentators argue that the Genesis account of creation and the fall talk in general theological terms rather than describing actual historical events.

For example, John Jefferson Davis claims that the biblical writers were more concerned with the results of God's creative work rather than with material processes.[90] Similarly, Bernard Ramm states that Scripture 'tells us emphatically *that* God created, but is silent as to *how* God created. … It informs us that the stars, and the flowers, and the animals, and the trees, and man are creatures of God, but how God produced them is nowhere a matter of clear affirmation in Scripture.'[91] Therefore, he believes the main purpose of the creation account 'is theological and religious' — it communicates that the universe has its origin in God, and serves as a prohibition against idolatry.[92]

Such a reductionistic view, however, simply does not align with what the Scriptures actually state. As Walter Kaiser responds, '[this is] an obvious slighting of the phrase repeated ten times, "and God said"…'[93] Indeed, God's creative activity is precisely described using the verbs 'created,' 'made,' 'said,' 'called,' 'set,' 'formed,' 'caused,' 'took,' 'planted,' and 'blessed.' Furthermore, these activities are described from start to finish, and spread out over a period of six days. In other words, the Genesis account describes exactly how God

---

86 Blocher, *In the Beginning*, 116–117.

87 Cf. Rev 22:1–2. John is describing what he saw in his vision.

88 One would expect history to precede theology, since theology only exists because of real things and real events.

89 Waltke, 'The First Seven Days,' 45.

90 John Jefferson Davis, 'Response to Nelson and Reynolds' in Moreland and Reynolds, 82.

91 Bernard Ramm, *The Christian View of Science of Scripture* (London, Paternoster, 1955), 70. Original emphasis.

92 Ibid., 149–150.

93 Kaiser, 'Legitimate Hermeneutics,' 147.

created, the order in which He created, and the timing of His creative acts. If, on the other hand, all the author intended to communicate was that 'God is the creator of everything,' then the first verse would be enough.[94]

There is no doubt that Genesis makes a significant theological contribution, but to say that Genesis is primarily theological rather than historical is to set up a false dichotomy; history and theology are *not* mutually exclusive. 'The fact is that the whole Bible presents its message as theology within a framework of history.'[95]

Payne also claims that Genesis shows no interest in the mechanics of creation. However, he explains the divine fiats as mere references to the agent.[96] Yet, this explanation stands against Psalm 33:6 and 2 Peter 3:5 which explicitly affirm that God created by His Scripture.

Similarly, Arnold claims '[t]he important lesson from Genesis 1 is that [God] did in fact create it, and that he made it orderly and good in every respect.' He adds: 'If it were important to know how long it took God to create the world, the Bible would have made it clear.'[97] Yet the creation account seems quite explicit in this matter: it took six days during which God created before evening, paused until the morning of the following day, and then resumed His acts of creation. What else could the author have said to make himself clearer?

John Jefferson Davis also claims that Genesis communicates theological truths about God against a backdrop of polytheistic ancient Near Eastern cultures.[98] Likewise, Vern Poythress claims that God is primarily interested in attacking polytheism and pagan myths,[99] and Wenham declares that the account 'is a polemic against the mythico-religious concepts of the ancient Orient.'[100]

Hasel has shown that the creation account is to some extent polemical, but only in regard to the creation of the luminaries, the purpose of the creation of mankind, and the method of creation 'by word.'[101] In every other respect, however, the tone is not polemical — indeed, quite the opposite. Umberto Cassuto writes: 'The language is tranquil, undisturbed by polemic or dispute; the controversial note is heard indirectly, as it were, through the deliberate, quiet utterances of Scripture.'[102] Blocher adds: 'The style of the prologue is amazing for its deliberate simplicity, its ascetic style. It shows not the slightest trace of rhetoric.'[103] Of course, the fact that Genesis records the truth, implies that it may also serve as a polemic, although this is not the primary purpose.

---

94 John J. Davis, *Paradise to Prison* (Salem, Wisconsin, Sheffield Publishing, 1998 repr.), 75.

95 Graeme Goldsworthy, *Preaching the Whole Bible as Christian Scripture* (Leicester, IVP, 2000), 24.

96 Payne, *Genesis One Reconsidered*, 7.

97 Arnold, *Encountering the Book of Genesis*, 23.

98 John Jefferson Davis, 'Response to Nelson and Reynolds,' 82.

99 Vern Sheridan Poythress, 'Response to Nelson and Reynolds' in Moreland and Reynolds, 91.

100 Wenham, *Genesis 1–15*, 37.

101 Hasel, 'The Polemic Nature of the Genesis Cosmology,' 81–102.

102 Cassuto, *Commentary on the Book of Genesis*, I:7.

103 Blocher, *In the Beginning*, 31.

Blocher claims the Genesis account is a literary arrangement used to communicate a *theology of the Sabbath*.[104] Although the days should be understood as ordinary 24-hour days, they form part of a larger figurative whole.[105] The advantage of such an approach is that it escapes the exegetical and scientific problems of interpreting the days as ages, and avoids chronological difficulties in the text such as the occurrence of an 'evening' and a 'morning' before the creation of the sun, moon and stars on day four. Blocher believes the form of Genesis 1–2 is exactly what would be expected if the author wanted to communicate such a view.[106] However, it is presumptuous to assume that a particular author living in a vastly different culture and at a time far removed from the present, would write according to twenty-first century expectations.[107] In addition, if this is all Genesis 1 intends to communicate, it leaves an abundance of 'spare' data. Why is there so much excess detail? Blocher is also inconsistent in viewing the creation account as merely a vehicle for communicating a theology of the Sabbath. This is because he later argues that the absence of any reference to the days of creation in the Sabbath commandment, in Deuteronomy 5:12–15, suggests the days referred to in the Sabbath commandments of Exodus 20:11 and 31:17 should not be taken as too close a link to creation.[108] But if the creation week is fundamental to a theology of the Sabbath, then surely the creation week would also be mentioned in Deuteronomy 5:12–15?

One has to question the motives of those who take a reductionistic view of the creation account. It appears that the reason for such views is a perceived threat from the conclusions of the natural sciences. For example, advocates of the literary framework view consider the *gap theory* and the *day-age theory* to be inadequate, yet they are still convinced that the claims of modern biology, geology and astronomy are true. Therefore, a *non-concordist* view is taken; Genesis 1 is not meant to be harmonized with science. This means that 'as far as the time frame is concerned, with respect to both the duration and sequence of events, the scientist is left free of biblical constraints in hypothesizing about cosmic origins.'[109]

As David Roth incisively point out, however, Genesis does not simply present God as *a* creator, or as merely *creative*, but as *the* Creator. This concept is so tightly coupled with actual history, that separating God the Creator from its historical basis makes the whole concept meaningless:

> The assertion that God is the Creator is much more historically specific — much more tied-in with the intricacies of real world history — than many modern commentators allow for. ... God is the Creator. That

---

104 Ibid., 50. Blocher does, however, affirm that the events of creation (i.e. the creation of seas, land, plants, animals, and man) were historical.

105 Ibid.

106 Ibid., 51.

107 Blocher does not even consider what one would expect to read if the creation week was, in fact, a literal chronological record.

108 Ibid., 48.

109 Meredith G. Kline, 'Space and Time in the Genesis Cosmogony' *PSCF* 48 (March 1996), 2.

is specific. Too specific, in fact, to dismiss the possibility of conflict between the Bible and our culture's sciences. Attempts to bring these two together nearly always means subordinating the articulations of the Holy Spirit to those of the sciences. Where this two-world approach is used … you can never exegetically establish that God is *the* Creator. Oh, you might genuinely believe that he is the Creator. But you could not derive it exegetically. Not from Genesis 1, anyway. … In the end, the very attempt to save Genesis from 'too much' specificity, empties it of any real specific religious meaning too! … the problem with the modern approach boils down to the fact that what God created *is* the real world. This world that God is said to have created, here in Genesis 1, is the same world that the rest of Scripture takes place in.[110]

In the final analysis, those who claim the creation account is primarily theological, do so for reasons apart from what the text says, and usually to avoid the perceived conflict with modern science.

Yet, the author's intent and purpose for writing is surely expressed in the text itself. How else can a reader know the author's intention apart from what the author actually states in the text? The meaning of the text must be discovered first, before there can be any hope of determining the author's intent. As Norman Geisler states: 'Purpose does not determine meaning. Rather, meaning determines purpose.'[111] An interpreter discovers the meaning and hence the purpose of the text by studying the individual verses and their context. Suggestions of intent and purpose which are not directly derived from the text itself, can only come from the interpreter's imagination. Therefore, ascribing an intent and purpose which is not directly derived from the text, is to subordinate Scripture to the imagination of the interpreter.

Such denials of intended meaning and purpose through literary criticism appear to be endemic in all modern historical studies. As historian G.R. Elton observed: 'In battling against people who would subject historical studies to the dictates of literary critics we historians are, in a way, fighting for our lives. Certainly, we are fighting for the lives of innocent young people beset by devilish tempters who claim to offer higher forms of thought and deeper truths and insights — the intellectual equivalent of crack.'[112]

The Message of Creation and the Fall

What, then, do the early chapters of Genesis intend to communicate? As shown above, these chapters are a historical account of the origin of the universe and everything in it, the creation of mankind in the image of God, mankind's rebellion against their Creator, and the resulting judgment against them and the distortion of the rest of creation.

---

110 David L. Roth, 'Genesis and the Real World' *Kerux* 9/2 (September 1994), 34, 35.

111 Norman L. Geisler, 'The Relation of Purpose and Meaning in Interpreting Scripture' *GTJ* 5/2 (Fall 1984), 229.

112 G.R. Elton, *Return to Essentials: Some Reflections on the Present State of Historical Study* (Cambridge: Cambridge University Press, 2002), 49.

These chapters are also theologically packed since they reveal that God is personal, not a deistic force, that He is uncreated and self-existent, that He is sovereign and all-powerful, and that He is holy and righteous and detests sin.

Furthermore, the account describes the initial and intended relationship between God and mankind, the relationship between man and woman, and the relationship between mankind and the rest of creation. Yet, man's sin has broken or warped these relationships. Mankind is therefore in need of reconciliation — a need which is fulfilled by Christ's propitiating death on the cross. Thus, the account of creation and the fall form the basis for 'salvation history.'

In addition, Arnold notes that the controversial questions of creation and evolution, and the age of the Earth are not the main concern of the creation account.[113] Indeed, it is highly unlikely that the original readers would have asked these questions since the text itself clearly provides answers to both.

It is important to note that this account is a divine revelation from God. No other observers were present when God created the universe (Job 38:4), therefore God revealed this knowledge to humanity via the special revelation of Scripture. As Waltke points out: 'Because of man's limitation as a creature, he must receive this knowledge by revelation from the creator. Moreover, because of the noetic effects of sin, he needs to be reborn before he can comprehend that revelation.'[114] Waltke goes on to argue that since the prophets received theological revelation from God, it follows that historical details may also be revealed by divine revelation.[115] Furthermore, as Davis observes, the author makes no attempt to glorify himself for his own insight. This is not his own cosmogony, nor did he discover God through natural revelation, but through special revelation from God Himself.[116]

---

113 Arnold, *Encountering the Book of Genesis*, 23.

114 Bruce K. Waltke, 'The Creation Account in Genesis 1:1–3 Part I' *BSac* 132 (January 1975), 28.

115 Bruce K. Waltke, 'The Creation Account in Genesis 1:1–3 Part IV' *BSac* 132 (October 1975), 331.

116 John J. Davis, *Paradise to Prison*, 27.

CHAPTER 5

Formation, Re-creation or Creation *Ex Nihilo*?

Although the Bible emphatically states that God created the heavens and the earth, much disagreement remains over the mechanism, the mode, and the material used (if any). These disagreements revolve around the meaning and significance of the first two verses of Genesis, their relationship to each other, and to the rest of the chapter. Was the scope of creation a limited geographical area or the entire universe? Was pre-existing material used to create the universe? Did creation involve mainly natural processes?

In the Beginning

The various interpretations of what actually happened 'in the beginning' revolve around the following points of contention surrounding Genesis 1:1–2.

1. In the beginning God created the heavens and the earth.

2. Now the earth was formless and empty, darkness was over the surface of the deep, and the Spirit of God was hovering over the waters.

(1) In verse 1, what do the terms אֵת הַשָּׁמַיִם וְאֵת הָאָרֶץ (*ēt hăšāmāyim weēt hā'āreṣ,*) refer to? (2) Is בְּרֵאשִׁית (*berēšît*) in the absolute state ('In the beginning') or the construct state ('In the beginning of' = 'When ... began')? (3) What is the semantic nuance of *berēšît*? Does it describe a point in time or a period of time? (4) What is the relationship between verse 1 and verse 2? Is verse 1 a title or summary of the account? Is verse 2 subordinate to verse 1, or vice versa? (5) Is there a time gap between verse 1 and verse 2?

Regarding (1), many interpreters take *ēt hăšāmāyim weēt hā'āreṣ* as a merism[1] denoting 'the universe' since Hebrew had no word to express such a concept.[2] However, this seems unlikely for two reasons: firstly, as Cassuto has pointed out, the Israelites regarded the heavens and the earth as two separate

---

1 A merism (or merismus) is a rhetorical device used to describe the whole by enumerating its parts (usually those parts which define the boundaries of the whole). For example, 'day and night,' 'seedtime and harvest' and other instances in Gen. 8:22.

2 Ronald F. Youngblood, *The Book of Genesis*, 2nd edition (Grand Rapids, Michigan, Baker, 1991) 23; John H. Sailhamer, *Genesis Unbound* (Sisters, Oregon, Multnomah, 1996) 56–57; See also Douglas J. Moo, *2 Peter, Jude*, NIVAC (Grand Rapids, Michigan, Zondervan, 1997), 169.

entities and did not have a concept of a unified world until much later when an appropriate term was immediately coined.[3] Secondly, אֶרֶץ (*'ereṣ*, 'the earth') is specifically referred to as a separate entity in a circumstantial clause in the very next sentence. This singling out of the 'earth' distinguishes it from the supposed merism that is meant to refer to the universe as a whole. E.W. Bullinger identifies this as an instance of 'anadiplosis' and the very first figure of speech used in the Bible: '[I]t is used to call our attention to, and emphasize, the fact that, while the first statement refers to two things, "the heavens and the earth"; the following statement proceeds to speak of only one of them, leaving the other entirely out of consideration.'[4] In other words, if 'the heavens and the earth' means 'the universe,' then it seems odd, given that this is an account of creation, that the author would describe the nature of *'ĕrĕṣ* without first defining specifically what *'ĕrĕṣ* is and where it came from. Nevertheless, while it is unlikely that *ēt hāšāmāyim wᵉēt hā'ārĕṣ* means 'universe' as conceived by modern writers, it does appear to carry the idea that God has created every physical and invisible thing, and the following circumstantial clauses in verse 2 describe the initial state of all these physical and invisible things on the earth and in the heavens above, both seen and unseen.[5] Therefore, the use of the terms 'heavens' and 'earth' is quite deliberate and meaningful since they indicate an explicit affirmation that God created *ex nihilo* every visible and invisible thing.

Again, as indicated by the rest of the chapter, this first act of creation was only the beginning of the creative process. The dry land and the sun, moon and stars and so on were not yet created or formed. The language is also geocentric in that the description is given from the point of view of an observer on earth. This is why the terms 'heavens' and 'earth,' were used, even though planet earth itself is insignificant with respect to the entire universe. This should not be surprising since Scripture was written to humans who live on this planet. As A.M. Wolters puts it, 'the Scriptures here [Genesis 1] use both 'heaven' and 'earth' in broad and narrow senses. It is the broad sense that is meant in the opening statement that God created heaven and earth. The focus of the narrative then immediately turns to the earth ... and heaven in that original sense (presumably heaven as the place of God's throne and the home of the angels) is no longer spoken of.'[6]

Genesis 1:1, then, describes God's initial creative act. Genesis 1:2 focuses on and describes the state of the earth and the yet to be developed environment in which God's creatures are to live. Genesis 1:3, on the other hand, begins the account of how God transformed this undeveloped environment into a place which was perfectly suited for life.

---

3 Umberto Cassuto, *A Commentary on the Book of Genesis, Part One*, translated by I. Adams (Jerusalem, Magnes Press, 1961), 20.

4 E.W. Bullinger, *Figures of Speech Used in the Bible* (Grand Rapids, Michigan, Baker, 1968), 251.

5 This concept appears to be affirmed by Paul is his letter to the Colossians (1:16): 'For by him all things were created: things in heaven and on earth, visible and invisible, whether thrones or powers or rulers or authorities; all things were created by him and for him.'

6 A.M. Wolters, *Creation Regained* (Carlisle, Paternoster, 1996), 19.

The Gap Theory

The gap theory was proposed to provide a way of harmonizing Scripture with the claims of modern geology, which views the world as billions of years old. This is done by insisting there is a time gap of indeterminable length between verse 1 and verse 2.

Verse 1 declares that God created the universe in the beginning, while verse 2 picks up the story at a much later time. Therefore, gap-theorists believe that God created a perfect world which He later cursed due to Satan's rebellion described in Isaiah 14:12–17 and Ezekiel 28, making it *become* תֹהוּ וָבֹהוּ (*tōhû wābōhû*, 'without form and void'). A flood (known as 'Lucifer's Flood') has been suggested as the method for this destruction and some believe 2 Peter 3:5–7 is a reference to such a flood. Thus, Genesis 1:3 – 2:3 describes God recreating the earth in six normal days as indicated by the use of the word 'replenish' in Genesis 1:28 (KJV).

Gap-theorists argue that since *ṭōhû wābōhû* in Jeremiah 4:23 and Isaiah 34:11 describes a state effected by God's judgment then so must Genesis 1:2.[7] Allen P. Ross argues that the *waw*-disjunctive of Genesis 1:2 goes against the idea of a 'formless and void' intermediate creation and cites Isaiah 45:18 as stating that God did not make this world formless and void. He also views darkness as representing evil and death and therefore not conducive to life.[8] Ross claims that חֹשֶׁךְ (*ḥōšĕk*, 'darkness') is not used in Scripture for something good, but frequently in conjunction with divine judgment.[9] Ross also claims that הָיְתָה (*hāyᵉtāh*) has the sense of 'became' rather than 'was' and therefore describes a transition to a chaotic state, although he offers no philological support for this rendering.[10]

However, Waltke shows that appealing to Jeremiah 4:23–26 and Isaiah 34:11 to support the notion of God destroying the original creation in judgment is a *non sequitur*[11] and that appealing to Isaiah 14 and Ezekiel 28 for additional support is dubious given that neither of these passages, nor any other passages in Scripture, contain an explicit statement describing such an event.[12] In regard to the connection between verses 1 and 2, both Davis and Waltke point out the *waw* introducing verse 2 is more precisely a *waw*-disjunctive, which never introduces an independent sequential clause.[13] The beginning of verse 2, then, is best translated, 'Now the earth …' This is also supported by the LXX's use of δέ (*de*) which is very frequently used as a transitional particle.[14]

---

7 Bruce K. Waltke, 'The Creation Account in Genesis 1:1–3 Part II' *BSac* 132 (April 1975), 139.

8 Allen P. Ross, *Creation and Blessing* (Grand Rapids, Michigan, Baker, 1996), 106.

9 Ibid., 722.

10 Ibid., 719.

11 Waltke, 'The Creation Account in Genesis 1:1–3 Part II,' 142.

12 Ibid., 143.

13 John J. Davis, *Paradise to Prison* (Grand Rapids, Michigan, Baker 1975), 44. See also Waltke, 'The Creation Account in Genesis 1:1–3 Part II,' 140. Waltke actually refers to it as a *waw*-conjunctive.

14 BAGD 'δέ' 2.

Note also that Psalm 104:19 and Isaiah 45:7 indicate that physical darkness is not inherently evil, and 'replenish' in Genesis 1:28 is not a possible rendering for מָלֵא (*mālē'*).[15] Moreover, the destruction in 2 Peter 3:5–7 clearly refers to the Noahic flood not a hypothetical 'Lucifer's Flood.'[16]

Pre-creation Chaos Theory

Rather than understanding Genesis 1:1 as a description of God's first basic act of creation, some interpreters either (1) understand the entire verse as a summary or title for the rest of the chapter, or (2) take בְּרֵאשִׁית (*bᵉrē'šît*) as a construct ('In the beginning of …' or 'When … began').[17] It is important to note that neither of these options imply an absolute beginning or creation *ex nihilo*.

In the case of (1), verse 2 is understood as circumstantial to verse 3 rather than to verse 1. Indeed, Bruce Waltke believes this is the only view that fully satisfies the Hebrew grammar.[18] He compares Genesis 1:1–3 with Genesis 2:4–7 and concludes that they follow the same pattern: an introductory summary statement, then a circumstantial clause that is followed by the main clause, which he claims reflects normal Semitic thought and is consistent with Hebrew grammar and Semitic literature.[19]

Leupold, on the other hand, points out that Genesis 1:1 cannot be a title because the connective conjunction וְ (*wᵉ*) in verse 2 suggests a grammatical dependency.[20] In addition, Rooker notes that although the correspondence between Genesis 1:1–3 and Genesis 2:4b–7 is similar, it is not the same, and the long circumstantial clauses in Genesis 2:4b–6 'indicate that the styles of the two narratives are distinct.'[21]

Because Waltke understands verse 1 as a title to the account, he concludes that *ēt hăšāmayim wᵉēt hā'āreṣ* refers specifically to the *ordered cosmos*.[22] Based

---

15 *TWOT* 1:505.

16 E. Blum, *2 Peter*, EBC (Grand Rapids, Michigan, Zondervan, 1981).

17 See for example: 'In the beginning of creation, when God made heaven and earth, the earth was without form and void, with darkness over the face of the abyss …' (NEB); 'In the beginning, when God created the heavens and the earth, the earth was a formless wasteland and darkness covered the abyss …' (NAB); 'When God began to create the heaven and the earth — the earth being unformed and void, with darkness over the surface of the deep …' (NJV); 'In the beginning when God created the heavens and the earth, the earth was a formless void and darkness covered the face of the deep…' (NRSV).

18 Bruce K. Waltke, 'The Creation Account in Genesis 1:1–3 Part III' *BSac* 132 (July 1975), 226. However, earlier on in the article (217) he admits that taking Genesis 1:2 as a circumstantial clause connected to v. 1 is not only syntactically possible but is the majority view held by commentators throughout history.

19 Ibid., 226–7. Waltke simply asserts this without offering any specific examples or any other justification. Note also that James Barr (*The Semantics of Biblical Language* [Oxford, OUP, 1961]) has warned against drawing interpretive conclusions based on linguistic elements.

20 H.C. Leupold, *Exposition of Genesis*, 2 volumes (Grand Rapids, Michigan, Baker, 1975), 1:42.

21 Mark F. Rooker, 'Genesis 1:1–3: Creation or Re-creation? Part II' *BSac* 149 (October 1992), 414.

22 Waltke, 'The Creation Account in Genesis 1:1–3 Part III', 218. Waltke appeals to Childs and Skinner for support, but fails to give any real linguistic justification for his view.

on this understanding of 'the heavens and the earth' he goes on to argue that verse 2 cannot be a circumstantial clause because it would contradict verse 1: 'God created the organized heavens and earth; the earth was unorganized.'[23] But taking verse 1 as a title also sets up a contradiction between the first two verses: How can it be said that God created the earth when in fact it already existed in some form? Moreover, a survey of the usage of *ēt hăšāmāyĭm wᵉēt hāʾāreṣ* shows that in some cases it clearly does not refer to the complete and ordered cosmos.[24] The chief thrust appears to be that of 'totality' rather than that of organization.[25]

Waltke's view also implies that בָּרָא (*bārāʾ*, 'created') in verse 1 is not a reference to creation *ex nihilo* since Genesis 1:3–31 is understood as a *re-creation* of the earth from *pre-existing material*.[26] But although *bārāʾ* does not necessarily imply creation *ex nihilo*, it is well suited to communicate this idea, especially since it only ever occurs with 'God' as its subject.[27] If Moses intended to state that the earth was formed out of pre-existing material, then he would surely have used one of several better-suited words available to him.[28] Furthermore, as Leupold points out, '[w]hen no existing material is mentioned ... no such material is implied.'[29] This appears to be the case in Genesis 1:1, especially since *bārāʾ* is used with בְּרֵאשִׁית (*bᵉrēʾšît*, 'In the beginning'), and creation *ex nihilo* is indicated by a number of other Scriptures.[30]

Based on their usage in Jeremiah 4:23 and Isaiah 34:11, Waltke believes *tōhû wābōhû* ('formless and void') denotes the very antithesis of creation — material that is completely chaotic, without shape or order.[31] Yet a closer look reveals that both instances relate to God's judgment. Jeremiah 4:23 contains a verbal allusion to Genesis 1:2 in order to portray judgment as a reversal of creation, such that the earth will be transformed back into its raw unformed state. However, the allusion only works one way — Jeremiah's use of this phrase says nothing about its meaning and significance in Genesis 1:2. Similarly, Isaiah 34:11 is part of a pronouncement of judgment against Edom, and the terms 'chaos' and 'desolation' (NIV) depict the resulting state of Edom's kingdom, not the state of creation after God's initial creative act.

David Tsumura's detailed analysis of *tōhû wābōhû* and its use in Scripture, shows that it refers to a desolate and uninhabited place, rather than some chaotic

---

23 Ibid., 219.

24 Exod. 20:11; Hag. 2:6.

25 A GRAMCORD search reveals 12 occurrences outside of Gen. 1:1. Deut. 4:26; 30:19; 31:28 all refer to heaven and earth (i.e. all creation) as witnesses. 2 Kgs 19:15 and Isa. 37:16 relate to the totality of God's dominion. Jer. 23:24 refers to God's omnipresence. See also Wenham, *Genesis 1–15*, 15.

26 Waltke, 'The Creation Account in Genesis 1:1–3 Part IV' *BSac* 132 (October 1975), 335–6.

27 *TWOT* 1:127.

28 e.g. יָצַר (*yāṣar*, 'form', 'fashion'), עָשָׂה (*ʿāśāh*, 'make', 'produce', 'prepare').

29 Leupold, *Exposition of Genesis*, 1:40–1.

30 Ps. 33:6, 9; 148:5, Prov. 8:22–7, Rom. 4:17, Heb. 11:3.

31 Waltke, 'The Creation Account in Genesis 1:1–3 Part III' 220.

state.[32] Sailhamer also considers the idea of a chaotic, amorphous mass unlikely and suggests, along with Leupold, that it is best understood as an uninhabitable stretch of wasteland or wilderness, unsuitable for life.[33] Robert Ouro adds:

> The main reason why the author describes the earth as *tohu wabohu* is to inform the audience that the earth 'is not yet' the earth such as they know it … it is necessary to use literary language and figures common to the audience to communicate to human beings the theme of creation. Therefore, the author uses in this verse language originating in his life experience (desert, empty, uninhabited, unproductive places) to explain the initial situation or condition of the earth.[34]

According to Waltke, this initial chaotic state of the heavens and the earth, along with the darkness which covered 'the deep,' is thoroughly evil and completely contrary to God's nature. Therefore, it is inconceivable to Waltke that God would initially create the earth in such a state. He does not see it as good in any way and maintains that its existence is a mystery since the Bible never says God created the world in this state.[35] But if God did not create the darkness and the deep, then who did? Rooker observes that when God named the darkness 'night' in Genesis 1:5, He never gave any indication that it was evil or undesirable.[36] In any case, Isaiah 45:7, using the same words found in Genesis 1, states that God *did* create the darkness. Rooker also points out that all three clauses in verse 2 begin with *waw* plus the subject noun, which means they are all co-ordinates (i.e. parallel). To be consistent, Waltke would also have to view the Spirit hovering over the deep as evil or undesirable.[37]

Waltke also argues that because God only ever creates by His word in the rest of the account, and because God did not speak until verse 4, He could not have created the darkness and the deep.[38] But this is too weighty a conclusion to be based on an argument from silence. The omission may be due to the fact that creation by divine fiat appears to carry the implication that the fiat is directed toward some other existing entity. However, the point of Genesis 1:1 is to clearly and categorically state that God alone was there when the world was created, and that He alone was the source of creation. In any case, other Scriptures such as 2 Peter 3:5 and Psalm 33:6 (which Waltke himself cites to support his view!) do affirm that God created the heavens and the earth by His word.

Other interpreters, however, hold to a pre-creation chaos scenario by reading *bᵉrēʾšît* in verse 1 as a construct noun. This is the view of the translators of the

---

32 David T. Tsumura, *The Earth and the Waters in Genesis 1–2* (Sheffield, Sheffield Academic Press, 1989), 326–328.

33 John H. Sailhamer, *The Pentateuch as Narrative* (Grand Rapids, Michigan, Zondervan, 1992), 84; Leupold, *Exposition of Genesis*, 1:46.

34 Robert Ouro, 'The Earth of Genesis 1:2: Abiotic or Chaotic? Part 1' *AUSS* 35/2 (1998), 276.

35 Waltke, 'The Creation Account in Genesis 1:1–3 Part IV,' 338, 339.

36 Rooker, 'Genesis 1:1–3: Creation or Re-creation? Part II,' 421.

37 Ibid., 422.

38 Waltke, 'The Creation Account in Genesis 1:1–3 Part III,' 220–221. Waltke cites Ps. 33:6, 9 and Heb. 11:3 as support.

NRSV, NAB, NEB, and NJV. Proponents of this interpretation have offered two arguments: (1) a lexical statistical analysis of its usage, and (2) the absence of the article.[39]

But when *rēʾšît* occurs in the construct state, it has either a pronominal suffix (e.g., Numbers 18:12; Job 8:7), a vowel contraction (e.g., Deuteronomy 11:12), or is part of a chain of constructs terminated by a definite absolute noun (e.g., Jeremiah 26:1; 27:1), yet none of these indicators are present in Genesis 1:1.

Although *bᵉrēʾšît* in Genesis 1:1 does not have the article, it would be a fallacy to claim that it is in the construct state because construct nouns never occur with the article. Indeed, only one of the fifty occurrences of *rēʾšît* in the absolute state (excluding Genesis 1:1) has the article (Nehemiah 12:44).[40]

Furthermore, the author of the account used the infinitive construct in Genesis 2:4 which unambiguously communicates a pre-existing state which is to be developed. Therefore, if the author really intended the reader to take *bᵉrēʾšît* as a construct, why did he not use this less ambiguous construction?[41]

Other evidence suggesting *bᵉrēʾšît* is in the absolute state includes the accentuation in the Masoretic Text which has the accent normally used to indicate an absolute noun,[42] and the allusion John 1:1 makes to Genesis 1:1, followed by the declaration in John 1:3 that '[t]hrough him all things were made; without him nothing was made that has been made.' Therefore, Genesis 1:1–3 is best understood as depicting a transformation of an uninhabitable earth into a place fit for man, rather than a reversal of a chaotic state.[43]

Limited Geography Theory

In his book, *Genesis Unbound*, John Sailhamer adopts a rather unique view of the creation account in order to harmonize it with the truth claims of modern science. Sailhamer acknowledges that the creation account is historical narrative,[44] and admits that Genesis 1 appears to indicate that God made the whole world and everything in it, as well as the sun, moon, and stars in six days.[45] However, Sailhamer believes Genesis 1:1 refers to the creation of the entire functioning universe, including the sun, moon, and stars in the heavens, and the plants and animals on earth.[46] He goes on to argue that Genesis 1:2 onwards describes God preparing the land for man and woman to inhabit — the same land promised to Abraham and his descendants and the same land given to the Israelites after their wandering in the desert.

---

39 See Waltke, 'The Creation Account in Genesis 1:1–3 Part III,' 222.

40 Search performed with GRAMCORD on Groves-Wheeler Westminster Morphological Text v. 3.1.

41 Waltke, 'The Creation Account in Genesis 1:1–3 Part III,' 223.

42 Victor P. Hamilton, *The Book of Genesis 1–17*, NICOT (Grand Rapids, Michigan, Eerdmans, 1990), 107.

43 Mark F. Rooker, 'Genesis 1:1–3: Creation or Re-creation? Part I' *BSac* 149 (July 1992), 333.

44 John H. Sailhamer, *Genesis Unbound* (Sisters, Oregon, Multnomah Books, 1996), 28.

45 Ibid., 89.

46 Ibid., 14.

Sailhamer's view is really a variation of the gap theory: He argues that 'beginning' (רֵאשִׁית, *rēʾšît*) can refer to an indefinite and most probably long period of time, and cites Genesis 10:10, and Jeremiah 28:1 for support. According to Sailhamer, *bᵉrēʾšît* tells us that God created the universe over a period of time, rather than a single instant. Yet Qal perfect verbs which refer to actions (such as *bārāʾ*, 'created') rather than states of being, indicate an *event* not a process.[47] Furthermore, Sailhamer argues that the Hebrew words רֵאשָׁה (*rišāh*, 'beginning time') or תְּחִלָּה (*tᵉchilāh*, 'beginning' or 'first') would be more appropriate for communicating a single event, resulting in a translation like 'The first thing God did was to create the universe.'[48] However, both these words do not necessarily refer to an event but can also refer to a period of time.[49] Moreover, the resulting statement would not rule out the existence and activities of anyone or anything else, and the notion of a unique self-existent God bringing everything into being *ex nihilo* (John 1:3) would be lost.

Regarding the Scriptures Sailhamer cites as support, the instance in Genesis 10:10 carries no temporal reference at all and thus provides no support for his claim. While it is certainly true that *bᵉrēʾšît* is occasionally used in the way Sailhamer describes (e.g. Jeremiah 28:1), it is important to note that *all* instances outside Genesis 1 are in the construct state.[50] As shown above, the instance in Genesis 1:1 is in the absolute state and is therefore grammatically independent of the verbal clause ('God created …').

In fact, even if *bᵉrēʾšît* was understood as Sailhamer suggests, there is no basis for claiming that the unspecified period of time refers to a *long* period. Zedekiah reigned for eleven years so 'in the beginning of the reign of Zedekiah' most likely refers to the first few years of his reign. So the 'beginning' refers to a relatively small amount of time in relation to the total time in which the king reigned. Therefore, with respect to the six days of creation, even with Sailhamer's own reasoning, 'the beginning' could at most refer only to the first couple of days, not to a long period of time.

Again. it appears that the motivation behind Sailhamer's interpretation is the desire for harmonization with modern scientific conclusions: 'Given what appears to be true about the age of the earth, it is likely that millions or billions of years transpired during this time of "the beginning".'[51] Like many others, Sailhamer has given too much priority to the truth claims of modern science rather than allowing the text to speak for itself.

---

47 *IBHS* 30.1b.

48 Sailhamer, *Genesis Unbound*, 40–41.

49 E.g. For *rišāh* see Ezek. 36:11. For *tᵉchilāh* see Ruth 1:22; 2 Sam. 21:9, 10; Ezra 4:6; Eccles. 10:13; Isa. 1:26; Dan. 9:23.

50 In Jer. 28:1, for example, *bᵉrēʾšît* is the first element of a construct chain and is followed by מַמְלֶכֶת (*mămᵉlēḵet*) and terminated by the proper name צִדְקִיָּה (*ṣiḏᵉqiyyāh*).

51 Sailhamer, *Genesis Unbound*, 105. See also his comments regarding the formation of the fossil record in the supposed period of time indicated by 'the beginning' (33).

Regarding the meaning of ʾ*ĕrĕṣ* ('earth', 'land'), Sailhamer argues that the instance in verse 2 is a reference to the Promised Land.[52] Indeed, he claims that a reader familiar with the theme and purpose of the Pentateuch would naturally understand the land of Genesis 1 as referring to the Promised Land.[53] Yet this appears to be a very spurious claim, considering that none of the Talmudic commentators understood Genesis 1 in this way — and they could hardly be accused of ignorance regarding the theme and purpose of the Pentateuch!

Regarding the meaning of *tōhû wāḇōhû*, Sailhamer objects to rendering it as 'formless and empty,' stating that, when properly understood, it refers to a desolate and uninhabitable wasteland — the initial state of the garden. However, understanding *tōhû wāḇōhû* in this way does not preclude the idea of a formless and empty place, since a formless and empty place would also be a desolate and uninhabitable wasteland. In any case, Genesis 1:2 and 1:9 make it clear that there was no dry ground at all until day three, so it is difficult to imagine how even a desolate and uninhabitable garden could be in view at this point.

Since Sailhamer believes the entire functioning universe, including the sun, was created 'in the beginning,' he claims that God's pronouncement 'Let there be light' (Genesis 1:3) does not refer to the creation of light but to sunrise, and cites Exodus 10:23, Nehemiah 8:3, and Genesis 44:3 as support.[54] Nehemiah 8:3 indicates that אוֹר (ʾ*ôr*, 'light') can refer to sunrise, but unlike Genesis 1:3, ʾ*ôr* has the article prefixed. Exodus 10:23 makes no reference at all to the sunrise, and Genesis 44:3 uses a verbal form, unlike Genesis 1:3. Nevertheless, if this divine fiat merely resulted in sunrise, then was this the very first sunrise? If so, then this would lead to all kinds of scientific problems, which Sailhamer is apparently trying to avoid. If not, then why is the sunrise not mentioned in this way on every day given that the evening and morning which terminate each day are repeatedly mentioned? If the sun had been rising as normal on every other day for millions or billions of years prior to the first day of the creation week, then what is so significant about this particular sunrise that it deserves a mention at all?

This interpretation also forces Sailhamer to adopt a very questionable rendering of Genesis 1:14: 'Let the lights in the expanse be for separating the day and night …' He appears to suggest that the syntax of verse 14 is much different from that of verse 6 and goes on to argue that this supposed difference indicates that the lights already existed (i.e. they were created 'in the beginning') and that God merely appointed them 'to separate' on day four.[55] Yet, the Hebrew syntax of verse 14 and verse 6 (and v. 3) are identical. The fiat in each verse begins with יְהִי (y*ᵉhî*, 'Let there be …'), the jussive form of הָיָה (*hāyāh*), which can only refer to the occurrence of an event or the bringing of something into existence.[56] Given the context, the latter meaning was clearly intended.

---

52 Ibid., 48–49.

53 Ibid., 52.

54 Ibid., 112–113.

55 Ibid., 131–132.

56 See entry for הָיָה in BDB, Holladay.

In all these verses the jussive is followed by the subject and identifies what the speaker is willing into existence. In the case of Genesis 1:14, the subject is מְאֹרֹת (*mᵉʾōrōṯ*, 'luminaries'). If verse 14 simply states that God appointed the luminaries to the task of separating day and night, then one would surely expect the fiat to begin with the jussive form of בָּדַל (*bāḏal*, 'separate'). Therefore, the rendering 'Let there be lights … for the purpose of separating…' makes much better sense syntactically. This retains the expression of purpose but does not assume the pre-existence of the lights. Indeed, this is the traditional rendering and is supported by all the major translations[57] as well as the LXX.[58]

In addition, if verse 14 expresses what Sailhamer claims, then verses 15–16 make little sense. If the sun and moon were created millions of years beforehand during the 'beginning' but were only appointed to shine light on the earth on day four, then what were they doing all this time? Verse 16 is even more problematic, since it explicitly states that God 'made' (Heb. עָשָׂה, *ʿāśāh*) the sun, moon and the stars on day four. Thus, in view of Genesis 1:3 and 1:14, it appears that although the phenomenon of light pre-existed, the sun, moon, and stars, as light sources, did not.

Sailhamer's limited-geography interpretation involves a number of other fanciful ideas, such as a belief that the sky was still empty of life on day two.[59] But this is absurd if birds and other flying creatures had supposedly been flying around for millions of years.

In regard to the creation of the seas on day three, Sailhamer makes a point of noting that the text clearly says 'one place' not 'many places,' and interprets this to mean that the seas were formed in and alongside of the Promised Land. In other words, the waters which were gathered into one place on day three are actually the lakes and seas which border the Promised Land today, namely, the Sea of Galilee, the Dead Sea, and the Mediterranean Sea.[60] But this is surely a tortuous reading of the text. These three bodies of water are not in one place at all. Indeed, the Promised Land adjoins only a very small part of the Mediterranean Sea, which extends far beyond the Middle East. Furthermore, Sailhamer considers the creation of sea creatures on day five to be a populating of these 'local' seas, rather than the initial global creation of sea creatures.[61] Again, such a belief is surely absurd: how could the Atlantic be filled with life for millions of years, while the Mediterranean Sea remained devoid of life?

Sailhamer also seems to assume the geography of the 'land' in Genesis 1 is more or less what we observe in the Middle East today. He does not consider

57 NIV, NASB, RSV, NRSV, NET, KJV, ASV.

58 The LXX reads: γενηθήτωσαν φωστῆρες ἐν τῷ στερεώματι τοῦ οὐρανοῦ εἰς φαῦσιν τῆς γῆς … 'Let there be lights in the firmament of the heavens, for the purpose of illuminating the earth …' Note also that γενηθήτωσαν is the third person plural aorist passive imperative form of γίνομαι, which is specifically used to refer to the bringing of something into existence, either directly or indirectly. See entry for γίνομαι in BAGD.

59 Sailhamer, *Genesis Unbound*, 122.

60 Ibid., 126.

61 Ibid., 139.

the role catastrophic events such as the global flood in the time of Noah, would have played in dramatically reshaping the earth's geography.

The most significant biblical problem Sailhamer must overcome is the statement in Exodus 20:11: 'For in six days the LORD made the heavens and the earth, the sea, and all that is in them, but he rested on the seventh day.' Sailhamer claims that this verse does not use the merism 'the heavens and the earth' to describe the work of the sixth day because that phrase is followed by a list.[62] He also argues that Exodus 20:11 refers to Genesis 1:2 – 2:4 rather than Genesis 1:1.[63] Yet Exodus 20:11 contains *exactly the same* phrase in the Hebrew as Genesis 1:1, which suggests a definite link between the two verses. Exodus 31:17 also contains this exact same phrase. In this instance, no additional terms follow making it a clear reference to the entire creation, so Sailhamer's distinction does not hold.

Sailhamer also claims that the use of עָשָׂה ('*āsāh*, 'do', 'make', 'form') in Exodus 20:11 instead of *bārā'*, indicates that this verse does not refer to the creation of the universe.[64] However, there are several verses (e.g. Exodus 31:17; 2 Kings 19:15; 2 Chronicles 2:12; Isaiah 37:16) which use '*āsāh*, yet clearly refer to the creation of the universe. Therefore, *bārā'* and '*āsāh* can be used interchangeably.[65]

Creation Ex Nihilo

Traditionally Genesis 1:1 is said to refer to the original state of the earth just after God created it. This is also the view held by Luther and Calvin and supported by the Gesenius-Kautzsch-Cowley (GKC) Hebrew grammar.[66]

Waltke, who holds to the pre-creation chaos theory, dismisses this view, based on the supposed similarity between Genesis 1:1–3 and 2:4–7 as discussed previously,[67] and Isaiah 45:18, which declares that God 'did not create it to be empty [Heb. יָצַר, *yāṣar*], but formed it to be inhabited.'[68]

But note that the intent of Isaiah 45:18 is to communicate *purpose*: God did not create the earth *to be* empty, but *to be* inhabited. Indeed, the Qal infinitive לָשֶׁבֶת (*lāšebet*, 'to dwell') indicates that purpose is in view.[69] Therefore, this verse describes God's intended purpose for the earth. It does not exclude the possibility that God created the earth initially uninhabitable before transforming it into an environment which can support life.

---

62 Ibid., 106.

63 Ibid., 107.

64 Ibid.

65 Note that in Gen. 1:27 and 2:3 *bārā'* is employed when '*āsāh* would usually have been used instead.

66 Rooker, 'Genesis 1:1–3: Creation or Re-creation? Part I,' 318. GKC construes verse 2 as a circumstantial clause of verse 1 (see 142.c).

67 Waltke, 'The Creation Account in Genesis 1:1–3 Part III,' 226–227.

68 Ibid., 220.

69 *IBHS*, 605ff.

In regard to the supposed grammatical parallel with Genesis 2:4–7, Rooker cites Judges 8:11 and Jonah 3:3 as better grammatical parallels to Genesis 1:1–2, since both contain a *waw*-disjunctive clause containing הָיְתָה (*hāyᵉtāh*, 'was'). This kind of clause qualifies a term in the preceding independent clause. In other words, the independent clause makes a statement and the *waw*-disjunctive clause parenthetically describes an element in the independent clause.[70] In the case of Genesis 1:1–2, verse 1 is the independent clause and verse 2 makes parenthetical statements concerning the earth in its initial state just after God brought it into existence.

The terms 'formless and empty,' therefore, do not refer to some chaotic and evil situation, but to the result of God's initial and basic creative act.[71] As Wolters observes, '*formless* means "unformed," not "deformed".'[72] Indeed, Hamilton's survey on the use of *tōhû* in the Old Testament concludes that it generally describes something which has no substance or reality.[73]

This fits in well with Genesis 1:1–2 and 2 Peter 3:5, which suggest that God's initial act was to create a gigantic ball of water referred to as 'the deep' (Heb. תְהוֹם, *tᵉhôm*).[74] The 'earth' in Genesis 1:2 is formless (i.e. it has no substance or reality) since it is, at this stage, indistinguishable from the rest of 'the deep.' Not until day two, when the expanse is created, does the 'earth' become distinct and begin to take shape, and on day three dry land finally appears.[75]

In light of the above, understanding Genesis 1:1–2 as a description of God's initial and basic creative act, appears to be the only interpretation that does justice to the text, the context, and the historic Christian doctrine of creation *ex nihilo*.

The Mode and Mechanism of Creation

Theistic Evolution

Theistic evolution is the view that God used the process of macro-evolution[76] to create every living organism. God is always in the background and is not actively involved in maintaining His creation, nor does He dynamically create new life. In essence, theistic evolution borders on deism since the god of the theistic evolutionist is distant and impersonal.

Theistic evolution comprises the following basic beliefs: (1) the first human couple shared a common ancestor with the apes; (2) the first human couple were highly evolved hominids, who were imparted with God's image; (3) death,

---

70 Rooker, 'Genesis 1:1–3: Creation or Re-creation? Part II,' 416.

71 Wolters, *Creation Regained*, 19.

72 Ibid., 20. Original emphasis.

73 Hamilton, *Book of Genesis 1–17*, 109.

74 Seely ('The Firmament and the Waters Above Part II: The Meaning of the "water above the firmament" in Gen 1:6–8' *WTJ* 54/1 [Spring 1992], 39) claims *tᵉhôm* means a 'deep sea,' but this is clearly not the case given that it refers to the 'depths of the earth' in Psalm 71:20.

75 Wolters, *Creation Regained*, 20.

76 The transition of biological organisms from one kind to another through genetic mutation and natural selection.

decay, and suffering are an integral part of the world God created, and therefore, the teaching that physical death is a direct consequence and penalty of Adam's sin is denied; (4) the penalty for sin is 'spiritual death.'

Theistic evolution attempts to reconcile the competing viewpoints of creation and evolution, and its proponents argue that the creation–evolution controversy is a false dichotomy. David H. Lane notes that Asa Gray, a distinguished biologist, professing Christian, and a contemporary of Charles Darwin, 'sought to reconcile the natural teleology (design) of evolution with natural theology. Gray's attempt to promote an "evolutionary teleology" was motivated by his desire to demonstrate the purpose or design behind evolution.' But as Lane points outs, Gray's theory conflicted with Darwin's perception of evolution, which destroyed any idea of teleology which implied a Designer.[77] Darwin wrote, 'There seems to be no more design in the variability of organic beings and in the action of natural selection, than in the course which the wind blows: Everything in nature is the result of fixed laws.'[78]

Theistic evolution is supposed to be a strictly scientific account of origins. However, as Lane rightly notes, it is clearly a theological explanation designed to accommodate Darwinism. In fact, Boyd admits that the 'wholly natural process' is really 'the Act of God' from start to finish. But how can this process be 'wholly natural' yet still involve some divine intervention, which makes it no longer strictly naturalistic?

Douglas Spanner even considers his 'theology of evolution' as superior to traditional Christian teaching on creation.[79] Similarly, John Stott suggests the traditional doctrine of the special creation of mankind could be replaced:

> It seems perfectly possible to reconcile the historicity of Adam with at least some (theistic) evolutionary theory. Many biblical Christians in fact do so, believing them to be not entirely incompatible. To assert the historicity of an original pair who sinned through disobedience is one thing; it is quite another to deny all evolution and to assert the separate and special creation of everything, including both subhuman creatures and Adam's body. The suggestion (for it is no more than that) does not seem to me to be against Scripture … [W]hen God made man in His image, what He did was to stamp His likeness on one of the many 'hominids' which appears to have been living at the time.[80]

In a similar vein, Blackmore and Page posit that '[t]here may have been an original couple, somehow different from the other evolved hominids, on whom God bestowed His Spirit and who subsequently rebelled.'[81]

---

77 David H. Lane, 'Special Creation or Evolution: No Middle Ground' *BSac* 151 (January, 1994), 19.

78 Nora Barlow (editor), *The Autobiography of Charles Darwin 1809–1882* (London, Collins, 1958). 87.

79 Lane, 'Special Creation or Evolution: No Middle Ground.' 28.

80 John R. Stott in *Church of England Newspaper*, June 17, 1968, cited in N.M. de S. Cameron, *Evolution and the Authority of the Bible* (Exeter, Paternoster, 1983), 63.

81 Vernon Blackmore and Andrew Page, *Evolution: The Great Debate* (Oxford, Lion, 1989), 170.

All such views, however, run into trouble with Genesis 2:7 which states that the man was formed from the dust of the ground and became a living being (נֶפֶשׁ חַיָּה, *nĕpĕš ḥăyyāh*), like the other creatures (cf. Genesis 1:24), when God breathed the 'breath of life' into the man's nostrils. This would seem to rule out any interpretation which sees man as genetically derived from some previously existing living forms.

Theistic evolution also seems to cast doubt upon God's omniscience, omnipotence, and efficiency. Why would an omniscient God, who surely knows exactly what He wants, create a scenario where nature aimlessly gropes around trying to find the path of least resistance in an upward direction? Why would an omnipotent God employ such a wasteful and cruel method to 'create' life? Indeed, Blackmore and Page are also troubled by the cruelty built into their proposed 'instrument of creation,' natural selection: 'Why has God designed a process which requires the strong to usurp the weak?' They reply: 'if there is cruelty and waste, it is a necessary sacrifice for the greater glory of the higher human forms.' This sounds far more like the teaching of Karl Marx, than the God of the Bible.

Jacques Monod, a Nobel Prize recipient in molecular biology, and an atheist, has been highly critical of Christians who advocate theistic evolution:

> Selection is the blindest, and most cruel way of evolving new species, and more and more complex and refined organisms ... the more cruel because it is a process of elimination, of destruction. The struggle for life and the elimination of the weakest is a horrible process, against which our whole modern ethic revolts. An ideal society is a non-selective society, it is one where the weak are protected; which is exactly the reverse of the so-called natural law. I am surprised that a Christian would defend the idea that this is the process which God more or less set up in order to have evolution.[82]

Rather than being an evil and a curse arising as a result of the fall as Scripture teaches (Genesis 2:17), death is credited as being an integral part of God's plan to 'evolve' His creation. Yet Blackmore and Page argue that '[t]he doctrine of the Fall does not require us to believe that a single pair existed as the only human beings and we can regard Adam as the "federal" head of humanity.'[83] Again, such views contradict the teaching of Scripture. Acts 17:26 states that God 'made from one man every nation of men, that they should inhabit the whole earth.' Indeed, this truth was foundational to Paul's message of salvation to the Gentiles.

The Bible states that God considered the creation to be 'very good' (Genesis 1:31). It was exactly what He wanted and was implicitly perfect given that on the seventh day He ceased His creative activities, blessed that day and made

---

82 Jacques Monod, Interview broadcast by the Australian Broadcasting Commission on June 10, 1976, as a tribute to Monod and entitled 'The Secret of Life,' cited in Ken Ham, 'The Relevance of Creation,' *Ex Nihilo* (Casebook II), 8.

83 Blackmore and Page, *Evolution: The Great Debate*, 170.

it holy. But the perfection of creation was spoiled by mankind, who, as free agents, rebelled against God and brought death and suffering into the world as a consequence. Therefore, the logical implication of theistic evolution is that God made the world in a fallen state, which means that the theory cannot properly account for the fall of mankind. If there is no fall, there is no basis for the propitiatory death of Christ, or the gospel itself for that matter.

Furthermore, theistic evolution naturally suffers from the numerous scientific problems of all evolutionary scenarios — especially the absence of a mechanism which can create new genetic information.[84] This is especially problematic for the brand of theistic evolution which sees God as merely 'lighting the fuse,' but remaining totally uninvolved in the way evolution progresses. However, God could be invoked to create supernaturally such new genetic information when necessary to ensure that evolution progresses the way He wants it go. This would, however, mean that the theory is no longer 'strictly scientific' — a distinctive characteristic of theistic evolution and held up as one of its main attractions.

Progressive Creation

Ramm summarizes progressive creationism as God directly creating higher and higher forms of life over millions of years of geological history.[85] While theistic evolution teaches 'creation from within,' with divine activity 'immanental in Nature,' progressive creation teaches 'the transcendental activity of God.'[86] With theistic evolution, original cells in the prehistoric waters continuously evolve in an unbroken line to mankind. With progressive creation, '[t]here is no continuum of life from amoeba to man, but the great phyla and families come into being only by the creative act of God.'[87] Thus, Ramm warns that equating progressive creationism with theistic evolution is 'careless' and 'a failure to understand a position.'[88] Yet, despite Ramm's claims to the contrary, progressive creationism has more in common with theistic evolution than its proponents would like to admit.

Regarding the mechanics of progressive creationism, Ramm writes:

> If dry land is to appear, the Spirit sets those laws of geology to work which will produce dry land. If the seas are to swarm with fish the Spirit initiates whatever is necessary for that to be realized. In the process of time, the Spirit works through-and-through Nature, the command of God is fulfilled. The laws of Nature, under the direction of the Holy Spirit, actualize over a period of time and through process, the plan of God.[89]

---

84 See for example Michael J. Behe, *Darwin's Black Box* (New York, Simon & Schuster, 1998); Walter J. Remine, *The Biotic Message* (St. Paul, 1993); Lee R. Spetner, *Not By Chance* (Judaica Press, 1998).

85 Bernard Ramm, *The Christian View of Science of Scripture* (London, Paternoster, 1955), 181.

86 Ibid., 147.

87 Ibid., 147.

88 Ibid., 76.

89 Ibid., 78.

Like theistic evolution, God's *modus operandi* in progressive creation is 'the laws of nature, under the direction of the Holy Spirit.' Again, God is construed as an impersonal actor working through nature, which is suggestive of deism.

Comparing progressive creation to the two flavors of theistic evolution shows how minor the differences are. The form of theistic evolution that has God merely lighting the fuse to a bomb, which is somehow destined to bring about order and life with an ability to progress upwards, differs from progressive creationism only in timing. Instead of a one-time creation of a pregnant mass which has the potential to produce and sustain life, God creates over a period of time. The only difference is the timing and frequency of God's creative actions.

Similarly, the version of theistic evolution which has God regularly creating new genetic information to drive the evolutionary process, differs from progressive creationism only in regard to the level at which God creates. Rather than creating new genetic information and material, God creates new species or genera.

Progressive creationism also suffers from the same theological problems as theistic evolution. It is driven via the laws of nature, including natural selection as a result of disease, suffering and death, implying a fallen state before the fall. In other words, it cannot properly account for the biblical account of the fall.[90]

Fiat Creation

Put simply, fiat creation means that God created by His word, and when He spoke, His commands were immediately executed (Psalm 33:9; 2 Peter 3:5). Divine fiat implies an immediate consequence. When God said, 'Let there be light,' light came into being. When God said, 'Let there be an expanse,' the expanse was created. When God said, 'Let dry ground appear,' dry ground appeared. When God said, 'Let the land produce vegetation,' vegetation appeared. When God said, 'Let there be lights in the expanse,' the lights were created and began to shine upon the earth. When God said, 'Let the water teem with living creatures, and let birds fly above the earth,' living creatures appeared in the water, and birds flew above the earth. When God said, 'Let the land produce living creatures,' living creatures appeared immediately. When God said 'Let us make man in our image, in our likeness,' He went ahead and made man in His image and likeness.[91]

The divine fiats of Genesis 1 are issued using the jussives יְהִי (*yᵉhî*, 'Let there be'), יִקָּווּ (*yĭqāvû*, 'Let … be gathered'), תֵּרָאֶה (*tērā'ĕh*, 'Let … appear'), תַּדְשֵׁא (*tăd°šē'*, 'Let … produce'), יִשְׁרְצוּ (*yĭšr°ṣû*, 'Let … teem'),

---

90 The problem of death before the fall will be covered in greater detail in a later chapter.

91 Note that the divine fiats are unique to the biblical account of creation when compared with other ancient Near Eastern cosmogonies. See David T. Tsumura, 'Genesis and Ancient Near Eastern Stories of Creation and Flood: An Introduction' in Richard S. Hess and David T. Tsumura (editors), *I Studied Inscriptions from Before the Flood* (Winona Lake, Indiana, Eisenbrauns, 1994),31.

תוֹצֵא (*tôṣē'*, 'Let ... bring forth'), which are all 'jussives of command.' — that is, they indicate a command.[92]

Furthermore, each divine fiat is immediately followed by וַיְהִי־כֵן (*wāyᵉhî-kēn*, 'And it was so').[93] There are two instances outside of Genesis 1 where this clause occurs (Judges 6:38; 2 Kings 15:12), and in both cases the clause indicates fulfillment and completion. Therefore, the presence of this clause immediately after a divine fiat is uttered strongly indicates that the command issued was immediately completed.[94]

Note also that the New Testament (John 1:3) presents Christ as both the agent in creation ('through him') and the necessary element ('without him nothing came into being').[95] Indeed, creation was for Christ, and He is its sustainer (Colossians 1:16). Given that the commands of Christ which resulted in a miracle were almost always instantaneous,[96] there is no reason not to think that each of the divine fiats in Genesis 1 had an immediate fulfillment. Indeed, as David Fouts points out, 'the only impediment to universal obedience seems to be sourced in the sinfulness of humanity'[97] yet humanity was not present at this point — nor had they sinned. Fiat creation, then, with instantaneous results is the most likely scenario described by the Genesis account.

This is reinforced by the fact that God's acts of creation are clearly supernatural and miraculous, transcending the normal laws governing the universe, and miraculous and supernatural acts are more or less instantaneous. Indeed, this is what makes them unexplainable in normal terms.

Summary

The Genesis account of creation describes God supernaturally bringing into being all that exists *ex nihilo* (out of nothing). That these creative acts were by definition supernatural implies that they were essentially instantaneous, and that there is no completely naturalistic explanation which can describe what actually occurred.

---

92 *IBHS* 34.3a, b. Note that there is no fiat for the initial creation of the heavens and the earth (Gen. 1:1). This may be due to the fact that uttering a fiat appears to carry the implication that the fiat is directed toward some other existing entity. However, the point of Gen. 1:1 is to clearly and categorically state that God alone was there when the world was created, and He alone was the source of creation.

93 In some cases, semantically equivalent phrases are used instead of 'And it was so' — e.g., 'and there was light' (v. 3), 'So God created the great creatures of the sea ...' (v. 21).

94 David M. Fouts, 'Selected Lexical and Grammatical Studies in Genesis One.' Paper presented at annual meeting of the Evangelical Theological Society, Colorado Springs, 2001.

95 Hamilton, *Book of Genesis 1–17*, 144.

96 See for example Matt. 8:3; 20:34; 21:19; Mark 1:42; 5:42; 10:52; Luke 1:64; 5:13; 8:44; 13:13; 18:43; John 2:7–10; 4:50–53; 5:8; 6:5–12; 9:6–7; 11:43–44, etc.

97 Fouts, 'Selected Lexical and Grammatical Studies in Genesis One.'

CHAPTER 6

The Days of Creation:
God's Creative Activities

God's creative activity is divided into six 'days.' The following is an analysis of God's creative acts on each day.

The First Day

The first question that must be answered is when does the first day begin? The two options are: (1) with the creation of light (Genesis 1:3), or (2) 'In the beginning' (Genesis 1:1).

As shown in chapter 5, verse 1 is a main clause grammatically connected to verse 2, which contains three circumstantial clauses describing the apparent result of God's initial act of creation. Verse 3, then, resumes the narrative by describing the creation of light. This indicates that the first day began not with the creation of light but 'in the beginning' with God's very first creative act in verse 1.[1] Therefore, our analysis of the first day begins with verse 1.

Creation of the Raw Materials

God's first creative act appears to be the creation *ex nihilo* of 'the heavens and the earth,' the initial matter of creation. This initial matter includes everything visible and invisible both here on earth and in the heavens. At this point, however, the earth itself has no definite form and is indistinguishable from the rest of 'the deep,' and therefore cannot support any form of life. This is hinted at in Psalm 102:25 which states that 'in the beginning' God merely 'laid the foundations of the earth.' According to Genesis 1, these 'foundations' were used to construct an environment suitable for vegetation as well as both animal and human life.

---

1 This view is also favored by E.J. Young (*Studies in Genesis One* [Grand Rapids, Michigan, Baker, 1964], 89). In addition, the rabbinic interpreters believed that ten things were created on day one: heaven and earth, *tohu* and *bohu*, light and darkness, wind and water, the duration of the day and the duration of the night (*Chag.* 12a) which implies that they also understood day one as beginning with verse 1.

Although the text makes no explicit statement, it is reasonable to conclude that God not only created matter, but also time. Indeed, the time of God's first creative act was 'in the beginning' — there was no time before this time.[2]

From a scientific perspective, physicist Russell Humphreys suggests that on the first day God created a three-dimensional space containing a ball of liquid water large enough to contain all the mass of the universe.[3] This is not inconsistent with it being called 'the deep' and having a surface (Genesis 1:2).[4] Indeed, 2 Peter 3:5 states that the earth was originally formed 'out of water and by water,' and one of the rabbinic tractates affirmed a similar belief.[5] In addition, David Tsumura points out that the watery beginning described in Genesis 1:2 'could well be a reflection of the universal understanding of water as a basic element of the cosmos.'[6]

Alternatively, 'the deep' may refer to a massively deep layer of water covering or surrounding the surface of the barren and desolate earth which was, at this point, simply an unformed chunk of silicon and other basic elements. The waters would continue to cover the desolate earth until day three, when dry land would finally appear.

Creation and Separation of Light

God's second creative act on the first day was the creation of light. It is important to note that light is an independent phenomenon apart from any light source. Furthermore, it is reasonable to conclude that God not only created visible light, but also the entire spectrum, including both visible and invisible electromagnetic radiation.

Thus, what God created on the first day was not just visible light, but the entire electromagnetic spectrum itself, apart from any light sources. Indeed, it would make little sense for God to create a light source if the electromagnetic spectrum did not yet exist. This would be analogous to creating a musical instrument if there was no such thing as sound. If this is the case, the creation of light was also *ex nihilo* and instantaneous as indicated by the phrase 'and there was light' which serves the same function as 'and it was so' which follows the divine fiats in subsequent verses.

God Himself divided the light from the darkness and called the period of light 'day' and the period of darkness 'night.' The fact that only light is declared to be 'good' has led some to conclude that darkness (חֹשֶׁךְ, *ḥōšĕk*) is *not* good or is in some way inherently evil. While darkness is often used as a metaphoric

---

2　The idea of God being outside of time is denied by some Christian philosophers, especially those who argue for the *A-theory* (or *tensed view*) of time (e.g. William Lane Craig, 'God and Real Time' *RelS* 26 [1990], 336). Nevertheless, all admit that God does not experience time as we do.

3　Approximately 2 light years in diameter.

4　D. Russell Humphreys, *Starlight and Time* (Green Forest, Arkansas, Master Books, 1994), 70.

5　*Chag.* 77a. See also Psalm 24:1–2: 'The earth is the LORD's, and everything in it, the world, and all who live in it; for he founded it upon the seas and established it upon the waters.'

6　David T. Tsumura, *The Earth and the Waters in Genesis 1–2* (Sheffield: Sheffield Academic Press, 1989) 165.

description of evil (Isaiah 5:20) or a withholding of divine blessing (Job 10:20–22; 18:18), it is also an instrument of divine judgment (Exodus 10:21–23; 1 Samuel 2:9; Isaiah 45:7), and a way in which God manifests Himself (Deuteronomy 5:22–23). Moreover, Psalm 139:12 affirms that light and darkness are the same in God's eyes. Physical darkness, then, is not inherently evil even though the term 'darkness' can be used to indicate the presence of evil. It may be that only light is declared to be 'good' because it was a necessary precondition to sustain both the animal and vegetable life created on subsequent days.

Evening and Morning

If the first day involves only the creation of light itself and not light sources such as the sun and moon, how can there be an 'evening' and a 'morning'? Allan MacRae asks: 'Is it possible that the words evening and morning here are used not in a literal, but in a figurative sense? … Do these words indicate a literal evening and a literal morning, or do they merely describe the beginning and the end of each period?'[7] He goes on to conclude that these terms must be metaphorical:

> Moreover, we should note that the chapter is written from the viewpoint of God. There is no human observer present until near the end of the sixth day. When would it be evening to God and when would it be morning to God? When it is evening in Texas, it is morning in China, and vice versa. God, of course, is not at any particular point of the earth. He is always aware that it is evening in some parts of the earth and morning in others, so that it is quite meaningless to speak of each of these days as having a literal evening and then a literal morning. It is quite clear that the phrases must be used figuratively here and simply indicate the beginning and end of a period of time, whatever its length may be.[8]

Mark Ross also believes the terms are metaphors, as do Roger Forster and Paul Marston, in keeping with their metaphorical hermeneutic.[9]

Perry G. Phillips argues from Psalm 90:6 — a psalm written by Moses — that 'morning' and 'evening' could have a figurative meaning in Genesis 1.[10] However, Psalm 90:6 is an example of hyperbole or overstatement commonly used in Hebrew poetry for emphasis. In the case of Psalm 90:6, the lifetimes of humans are pictured as grass springing up in the morning and then withering in the evening in order to emphasize the relative brevity of human life compared

---

7 Allan A. MacRae, 'The Scientific Approach to the Old Testament Part 2' *BSac* 110 (April–June 1953), 135–136.

8 Ibid., 136.

9 Mark E. Ross, 'The Framework Hypothesis: An Interpretation of Genesis 1:1 – 2:3' in Joseph A. Pipa and David W. Hall (editors), *Did God Create in Six Days?* (Taylors, SC, Southern Presbyterian Press, 1999), 120; Roger Forster and Paul Marston, *Reason and Faith* (Eastbourne, Monarch, 1989), 222.

10 Perry G. Phillips, 'Are the Days of Genesis Longer Than 24 Hours? The Bible Says, "Yes!" ' *IBRIRep* 40 (1990).

with the eternity of God. 'Morning' and 'evening' have their usual literal meaning — this is what gives the verse its emphatic sense. Although grass does not really spring up in the morning only to die in the evening, it may as well do so when compared with the eternity of God.[11]

Alternatively, Sailhamer uses Joel 3:15–16 to argue that the sun and moon are synonymous with, or are included in, the 'heavens.'[12] This passage, however, mentions the sun and moon in conjunction with the stars, and as usual 'heavens' occurs together with 'earth.' The Hebrew wording is also different: Joel 3:16 has שָׁמַיִם וָאָרֶץ (šāmāyim wāʾāreṣ, 'heavens and earth') whereas Genesis 1:1 has אֵת הַשָּׁמַיִם וְאֵת הָאָרֶץ (ʾēṭ haššāmāyim wᵉʾēṭ hāʾāreṣ), 'the heavens and the earth.'

Clyde McCone proposes yet another interpretation by claiming there is 'a considerable number of biblical references to indicate that the light of the first day was spiritual and that its source was God.' However, he only cites 2 Corinthians 4:6, and adds: 'The subsequent separation of light from darkness is not the distinction between evening and morning. Rather, it is an absolute and permanent separation between spiritual light and spiritual darkness.'[13] But 2 Corinthians 4:6 simply uses the creation of light as an analogy for spiritual enlightenment, and the two events are never equated.[14] Such an eccentric interpretation cannot be sustained, since it moves the account away from history and into allegory when there is no justification for doing so.

With respect to 'evening' and 'morning,' taking these terms as literal references — even without the sun — does not necessarily lead to a contradiction. Indeed, there are two possible solutions: (1) a temporary directional light source illuminated the earth for the first three days; or (2) the terms 'evening' and 'morning' are general references to particular periods or events during the day rather than specific references to the rising and setting of the sun.[15]

According to Lewis, the rabbinic interpreters held that God created a primeval light not dependent on the sun, which came into existence at God's command but was later withdrawn and stored up for the righteous in the messianic future.[16] One rabbi wrote: 'The Holy One, blessed be He, enwrapped Himself in light like a garment, and the brilliance of His splendor shone forth from one end of the Universe to the other.'[17]

The Syrian fathers, as reflected in a Syriac manuscript in the Mingana collection, also considered 'evening' and 'morning' as literal references even though the sun and moon had not been created. They concluded that darkness

---

11 Hyperbole is also used in Ps. 30:5.

12 John H. Sailhamer, *Genesis*, EBC (Grand Rapids, Zondervan, 1976), 23.

13 R. Clyde McCone, 'Were the Days of Creation Twenty-Fours Hours Long?' in R.F. Youngblood (editor), *The Genesis Debate* (Grand Rapids, Michigan, Baker, 1990), 25.

14 2 Cor. 4:6 reads: 'For God, who said, "Let light shine out of darkness," made his light shine in our hearts to give us the light of the knowledge of the glory of God in the face of Christ.'

15 The following is mostly drawn from Andrew S. Kulikovsky 'Evenings and Mornings' *JoC* 16/2 (2002), 83.

16 Jack P. Lewis, 'The Days of Creation: An Historical Survey' *JETS* 32/4 (December 1989), 449.

17 *Gen. R.* III.1.

was created first and lasted twelve hours, before light was created which also lasted twelve hours and was called day.[18]

R.L. Dabney also believed in a temporary light source: 'What it is, whether a substance, or an affection of other substance, is still unknown. Hence it cannot be held unreasonable, that it should have existed before the sun; nor that God should have regulated it in alterations of day and night.'[19] More recent advocates include Umberto Cassuto, E.J. Young, John J. Davis and Victor P. Hamilton.[20] Hamilton writes: 'The creation of light anticipates the creation of sunlight. Eventually the task of separating the light from the darkness will be assigned to the heavenly luminaries (v. 18). It is unnecessary to explain such a claim as reflecting scientific ignorance. What the author states is that God caused the light to shine from a source other than the sun for the first three "days".' He adds: 'The Bible begins and ends by describing an untarnished world that is filled with light, but no sun (cf. Rev. 22:5). Should not the one who is himself called "light" (1 John 1:5) have at his disposal many sources by which he dispatches light into his creation?'

Furthermore, Revelation 21:23 and 22:5 may also indicate that there will be no physical sun and moon illuminating the New Jerusalem,[21] even though Archer claims there is no reference to light anywhere else in Scripture which is not connected with the sun, moon, and stars or as a result of combustion.[22]

Meredith Kline, however, objects to this view: 'Why would God create such a vast cosmic order only to discard it three days (or ages) later? Why create a replacement cosmos to perform the very same functions already being performed perfectly well by the original system?'[23] Not only does this appear to be an arbitrary dismissal, it is also a straw-man argument. God would not have created and discarded 'a vast cosmic order,' only a temporary directional light source, and that source may have been some manifestation of Himself, given that Genesis 1:4 states that God Himself 'separated the light from the darkness.' Therefore, the idea of a temporary supernatural light source for the first three days is not an unreasonable explanation and appears to match what the text says. As Young affirms: 'That the heavenly bodies are made on the fourth day

---

18 A. Levene, *The Early Syrian Fathers on Genesis* (London, Taylor's Foreign, 1951), 73, 131–132.

19 R.L. Dabney, *Lectures in Systematic Theology* (Grand Rapid, Michigan, Zondervan, 1972), 252.

20 Umberto Cassuto, *A Commentary on the Book of Genesis*, 2 volumes, translated by Israel Adams (Jerusalem, Magnes Press, 1961), 1:44; E.J. Young, *Studies in Genesis One*, 95; John J. Davis, *Paradise to Prison* (Grand Rapids, Michigan, Baker, 1975), 49; Victor P. Hamilton, *The Book of Genesis 1–17*, NICOT (Grand Rapids, Michigan, Eerdmans, 1990), 121, fn. 7.

21 See also Psalm 104:2 and 1 John 1:5.

22 Gleason L. Archer, 'A Response to The Trustworthiness of Scripture in Areas Relating to Natural Science' in Earl D. Radmacher and Robert D. Preus (editors) *Hermeneutics, Inerrancy and the Bible* (Grand Rapids, Michigan, Zondervan, 1984), 322–323. Archer also states 'there is no scientific evidence for photosynthesis resulting from cosmic light' but this is a moot point, since it is a question of the light *source* not the *kind* of light. The temporary light source would have radiated the same kind of light as the sun does today.

23 Meredith G. Kline, 'Space and Time in the Genesis Cosmogony' *PSCF* 48/1 (1996), 9.

and that the earth had received light from a source other than the sun is not a naïve conception, but is a plain and sober statement of the truth.'[24]

Alternatively, rather than actually describing particular events, the terms 'morning' and 'evening' may simply refer to particular (short) periods of time during the day. As with most words, these terms can have different shades of meaning depending on the context. The word 'evening' usually describes the short period of time when the sun is sinking below the horizon. However, it is also often used to generally describe the period of time at the end of the work day, that is, between finishing work and going to bed. Indeed, it is during this period of time that most people have their 'evening' meal, yet this does not necessarily mean that they actually eat it while the sun is setting! Similarly, 'morning' can refer to any time before midday, not just the short period of time when the sun is emerging from the horizon.

Note also that sunset and sunrise can occur at vastly different times of the day depending on the country and the season. For example, for about a month during summer, the town of Gällivare which is situated in Lapland (northern Sweden) inside the Arctic Circle, experiences sunlight twenty-four hours a day. Conversely, for about a month during winter, Gällivare experiences perpetual darkness.[25] Sunset and sunrise never occur during these respective periods, so 'evening' and 'morning' in this sense never occur! But the absence of sunlight or the absence of darkness does not mean that there is no concept of evening or morning (or daytime and nighttime) during this period. Rather than referring to sunset and sunrise, 'evening' and 'morning' serve as simple references to the beginning and ending of the work day.

This idea fits very well with the context of Genesis 1. Each day of creation describes the activities of God on that day and is terminated by the phrase 'And there was evening, and there was morning — the [Xth] day.' Thus, God worked for a period of time before finishing (marked by the term 'evening'), and began a period of inactivity which continued until 'morning' when he began working again. In other words, the term 'evening' refers to the beginning of the period when God was inactive, and the term 'morning' refers to the termination of God's inactivity and the beginning of the next day's work.

The relationship between light and the light sources (sun and moon) is further discussed under day four.

The End of the Day

The description of the first day, like the descriptions of subsequent days, ends with וַיְהִי־עֶרֶב וַיְהִי־בֹקֶר (*wăyᵉhî ᵉrĕḇ wăyᵉhî ḇōqĕr*, 'And there was evening and there was morning') followed by a designation of the day. The *waw*-consecutives indicate that this phrase does not refer to the composition of a day but to the sequence of events following God's creative acts. Again, God's creative acts occurred during the daytime and were followed by 'evening' which marked

---

24 E.J. Young, *Studies in Genesis One*, 95.

25 The north and south poles experience six months of daylight and six months of darkness.

the beginning of a period of inactivity lasting until 'morning,' the beginning of the next day and the time at which God resumed His creative activity. As Chrysostom wrote long ago, 'when he had assigned to each its own name, he linked the two together in the words, "Evening came, and morning came, one day." He made a point of speaking of the end of the day and of the end of the night as one, so as to grasp a certain order and sequence in visible things and avoid any impression of confusion.'[26]

The Translation of the Cardinal

It is interesting to note that, unlike the following days, the designation of the first day employs a cardinal (יוֹם אֶחָד, yôm 'ĕḥāḏ, 'one day') rather than an ordinal (yôm ri'šôn, 'first day'). Waltke and O'Connor point out that the indefinite noun yôm with the indefinite cardinal numeral for 'one' in Genesis 1:5 has 'an emphatic, counting force' and a 'definite sense' having the force of an ordinal number which allows it to be rendered as 'the first day.'[27] But while 'ĕḥāḏ can be rendered as 'first' it is usually done so only if it has the article (as in Genesis 2:11) or if it modifies a noun which has the article (as in Genesis 8:5).[28] Therefore, 'one day' is the more likely meaning.

On the first day of creation there were no other days to which this day could be compared. Thus, the cardinal was probably used in the designation of the first day in order to define precisely what constituted a 'day' and to reinforce that this first day was exactly the kind of day we all experience at this time.[29]

Thus, the above analysis suggests that the first day included the creation *ex nihilo* of 'the heavens and the earth' in their initial unformed state, and the creation *ex nihilo* of light including the entire electromagnetic spectrum.

The Second Day

On the second day, God creates an 'expanse' in the midst of the 'waters.' Two questions can be raised at this point: (1) What exactly is the expanse? (2) What in particular are the 'waters' which were divided resulting in waters above the expanse and waters below it?

The Waters Above

Leupold claims the 'waters above' are the clouds,[30] as does Davis Young who also claims Proverbs 8:28 indicates that 'above' (מֵעַל, mā'al) 'may be used simply

---

26 Chrysostom, *Hom. on Gen.,* 6.14.

27 *IBHS*, 15.2.1a.

28 Exceptions to this rule include Ezra 1:1, Dan. 9:1, Jonah 3:4 (with yôm), and 1 Chr. 25:28 uses a cardinal for 'twenty-first.'

29 The early Syrian fathers (see A. Levene, *The Early Syrian Fathers on Genesis* [London, Taylor's Foreign, 1951], 73, 131–132) held a similar view, as does David M. Fouts ('Selected Lexical and Grammatical Studies in Genesis One,' Paper presented at ETS annual meeting, Colorado Springs, 2001). See also Andrew Steinman's recent paper ('אחד as an Ordinal Number and the Meaning of Genesis 1:5' *JETS* 45/4 [December 2002], 577–584) which reaches virtually the same conclusion.

30 H.C. Leupold, *Exposition of Genesis* vol. 1 (Grand Rapids, Michigan, Baker, 1942), 63.

to indicate that clouds are very high up in the sky.'[31] But such a claim has no justification. Like Genesis 1, the language of Proverbs 8:28 is surely 'earth-centric' — a description relative to a person standing on the earth who would have very little idea about how high the clouds actually are. Indeed, clouds may form at a wide range of altitudes including very close to the ground. In this instance the clouds are simply 'above.' Yet, as E.J. Young pointed out, the waters are not just 'above' but *above the expanse*.[32] The waters 'above the expanse' are referred to again only once in Scripture (Ps. 148:4). With so little information it is impossible to determine precisely what these waters were, what they were for, or what happened to them.

The Expanse

Numerous commentators, including Calvin, A. Clarke, George Bush, R.S. Candlish, Keil and Delitzsch, Fausset and Brown, and Ellison and Payne have suggested רָקִיעַ (*rāqîă'*, 'expanse') is the earth's atmosphere.[33] However, the expanse cannot be equated with the atmosphere, since verse 14 states that the sun, moon and stars are set *in the expanse* (בִּרְקִיעַ, *bîr'qîă'*), and verse 20 states that birds and other flying creatures are to fly 'over the *surface* of the *expanse of the heavens*' (עַל־פְּנֵי רְקִיעַ הַשָּׁמָיִם, *'al-p'nêh r'qîă' hăššāmāyǐm*) rather than '*in* the expanse.'

Other commentators, such as Paul H. Seely, have argued that the writer of Genesis understood the expanse to be a solid dome over-arching the earth.[34] But the notion that the *rāqîă'* represented a solid dome came from the Latin Vulgate's use of *firmamentum* and the use of στερέωμα (*stereōma*, 'solid body') in the LXX. These translations merely reflected the Greek view of the cosmos at the time the translation was done.[35]

Seely, however, objects: 'The basic historical fact that defines the meaning of *rāqîă'* in Genesis 1 is simply this: all peoples in the ancient world thought of the sky as solid. This concept did not begin with the Greeks.'[36] After a survey of ancient Near Eastern cosmologies, Seely concludes:

31 Davis A. Young, *Creation and the Flood* (Grand Rapids, Michigan, Baker, 1977), 123.

32 E.J. Young, *Studies in Genesis One*, 90 fn.94.

33 John Calvin, *Genesis* (Grand Rapids, Eerdmans, 1948) 78–79; A. Clarke, *The Old Testament* (New York, Hunt and Eaton, n.d.) 1.31; George Bush, *Notes on the Book of Genesis* (New York, Ivison, Phinney, 1860), 33; R.S. Candlish, *Commentary on Genesis* (Grand Rapids, Zondervan, repr.), 25; Carl F. Keil and Franz Delitzsch, *Biblical Commentary on the Old Testament, The Pentateuch* (Grand Rapids, Eerdmans, 1949), 1.52; A.R. Fausset and D. Brown, *A Commentary on the Old and New Testaments* (Grand Rapids, Eerdmans, 1948), 5; H.L. Ellison and D.F. Payne, 'Genesis,' in F.F. Bruce (editor) *The International Bible Commentary* (Grand Rapids, Zondervan, 1979), 115.

34 Paul H. Seely, 'The Firmament and the Water Above Part I: The Meaning of *rāqîă'* in Gen. 1:6–8' *WTJ* 53/2 (Fall 1991), 227–240.

35 R. Laird Harris, 'Bible and Cosmology,' *BETS* 5 (1962), 11–17; Frederic R. Howe, 'Part 1: The Age of the Earth: An Appraisal of Some Current Evangelical Positions' *BSac* 142 (January 1985), 29.

36 Seely, 'The Firmament and the Water Above Part I,' 228.

Considering that the Hebrews were a scientifically naive people who would accordingly believe the *rāqîă‛* was solid, that both their Babylonian and their Egyptian background would influence them to believe the *rāqîă‛* was solid, and that they naturally accepted the concepts of the peoples around them so long as they were not theologically offensive, I believe we have every reason to think that both the writer and original readers of Genesis 1 believed the *rāqîă‛* was solid. The historical meaning of *rāqîă‛* in Gen 1:6–8 is, accordingly, 'a solid sky.'

Seely's analysis, however, does not justify this conclusion. Firstly, in light of Job 26:7–10, it appears that the Israelites did indeed have some sophisticated knowledge of the world. In contrast to virtually all ancient cosmologies, verse 7 states that the earth is suspended over nothing. Verse 8 states: 'He wraps up the waters in his clouds, yet the clouds do not burst under their weight.' This clearly indicates that the Israelites knew the clouds consisted of large amounts of water vapor. Verse 9 states: 'He covers the face of the full moon, spreading his clouds over it.' Not only does this statement suggest the Israelites knew the moon lay much deeper in the sky than the clouds, but also the use of the term פְּנֵי (*p‛nê*, 'face,' 'surface') suggests they believed the moon itself was more than just a flat disk mounted on a 'solid dome' over-arching the world, but had some depth to it.[37]

Secondly, it is highly unlikely that the Israelites would have had any knowledge of, or any interest in, other ancient Near Eastern cosmologies. The Israelites came from a single family whose descendants had lived in an isolated community in Egypt (the land of Goshen) for centuries. Even if they had come in contact with such knowledge, why would they take any interest in it, especially if these other cosmologies denied what their own cosmology clearly taught? It is also unlikely that they would have learnt such beliefs from the Egyptians due to their separatism and subsequent bondage. While Moses, having been 'educated in all the wisdom of the Egyptians,' was the exception (Acts 7:22) it is clear that he still maintained his identity as an Israelite, and there is no reason to think that he accepted the entire Egyptian worldview including their cosmology in preference to the traditions handed down from his own ancestors.

Note also that the semantic ranges of *stereōma* and *firmamentum* do not match *rāqîă‛*. The Hebrew word *rāqîă‛* refers to something flexible or malleable which has been stretched out. As Livingston puts it: 'The emphasis in the Hebrew word *raqia* is not on the material itself but on the act of spreading out or the condition of being expanded.'[38] *Stereōma* and *firmamentum*, on the other hand, refer to something hard, solid and inflexible.[39] Indeed, Seely admits that his historical etymology of *rāqîă‛* and *rāqă* 'does not absolutely prove that *rāqîă‛* in Genesis 1 is solid …'[40]

---

37 *p‛nê* is used frequently throughout the Old Testament and always refers to a part of the exterior or surface structure of an object, including a human body.

38 George Herbert Livingston, *Genesis*, BBC (Kansas City, Missouri, Beacon Hill Press, 1969), 32.

39 See BAGD, Louw-Nida.

40 Paul H. Seely, 'The Three Storied Universe' *JASA* 21/1 (1969), 19.

In light of the above, it appears that the 'expanse' was created 'in the midst of' (בְּתוֹךְ, *bᵉtôk*)[41] the waters of verse 2 which is the 'deep' (תְהוֹם, *tᵉhôm*).[42] Note also that if Humphreys is correct in identifying the 'deep' as a massive ball of water created on the first day, then it would appear that God created the 'expanse' by dividing these waters which resulted in 'waters above' and 'waters below.' As indicated by the term 'expanse' (*rāqîă'*), the size of the division would have increased rapidly as God caused the waters above to expand outwardly, as indicated by numerous Scriptures.[43] But what becomes of the 'waters above'? The Bible does not say exactly. Psalm 148:4 does contain a reference to them, so they presumably still exist. The waters below the expanse, on the other hand, appear to have become the foundations of the earth — its core and mantle.[44] In fact, some Scriptures mention both the stretching out of the heavens and the laying of the earth's foundations together as though they were complementary events.[45]

What, then, is the 'expanse'? In Genesis 1:14 the writer of Genesis states that the sun, moon, and stars are placed by God '*in* the expanse of the heavens.' The preposition *bᵉ* implies that the expanse is where the sun, moon, and stars are located — that is, *interstellar space*.

The Third Day

On the third day God caused the appearance of dry land and vegetation.

Creation of Dry Land

Dry land is brought about by God gathering the waters under the heavens (that is, the waters below the expanse) into one place, which somehow results in the appearance of dry land. Rather than a reference to a single large body of water, Wenham suggests 'one place' stands in contrast to the state when the waters were everywhere and there was no dry land.[46] Indeed, verse 10 indicates there were multiple seas.

If we assume that the primeval earth after the creation of the expanse was a barren, desolate, and unformed chunk of rock covered by water, then it would appear that God caused the waters to 'be gathered to one place' by changing the earth's topography by forming mountains and valleys.

However, Hamilton argues that the two jussives in Genesis 1:9 ('Let the water … be gathered …' and 'let dry ground appear') suggest that the gathering of the waters and the emergence of dry land should be understood as independent events, because if the author intended to convey a simultaneous, sequential or

---

41 Note that *bᵉtôk* means 'in the midst,' 'between.'

42 *tᵉhôm* usually refers to the very deepest part of an ocean or river.

43 Job 9:8, 37:18; Ps. 104:2; Isa. 40:22, 42:5, 44:24, 45:12, 48:13, 51:13; Jer. 10:12, 51:15; Zech. 12:1. See also Humphreys, *Starlight and Time*, 66–68.

44 Humphreys, *Starlight and Time*, 77.

45 Zech. 12:1; Isa. 51:13.

46 Gordon J. Wenham, *Genesis 1–15*, WBC (Dallas, Word, 1987), 20.

causal relationship then a different (less ambiguous) construction would surely have been used.[47]

Indeed, if we assume that 'the deep' was a massive ball of water then two separate events seem to be implied. The deep was divided by the expanse on the second day and the waters below the expanse become the raw material from which the dry land emerges on the third day. Now, if the raw material from which the dry land emerges was purely the waters below the expanse, then there would be no need to gather the waters into one place — they were all that existed at this point in time. Therefore, it may be that God (1) caused earth's watery foundations to be transformed into other basic elements and compounds such as silicon and carbon, and (2) separated these elements from the rest of the waters which resulted in the appearance of dry land. In other words, the primeval earth comprised of the waters below the expanse — a large ball of water with similar dimensions as the earth today. Some of these waters were transformed into other compounds and were separated from the rest of the waters, which resulted in the formation of dry land. Indeed, 2 Peter 3:5 contains a striking allusion to this kind of scenario: 'But they deliberately forget that long ago by God's word the heavens existed and *the earth was formed out of water and by water.*'[48]

Creation of Vegetation

God's second creative act on the third day involves the creation of vegetation on the newly formed dry land. The land is to produce seed-bearing plants, and trees with seed-bearing fruit. Not only does God create a diversity of vegetation but also the capability for the vegetation to reproduce itself.[49]

The Fourth Day

According to Genesis 1:14–16, God created the sun, the moon, and the stars on the fourth day.

Evening and Morning Without the Sun?

As noted previously, the creation of the sun and moon on the fourth day presents a problem: how could there have been an evening and a morning for the first three days when the light sources which mark the evening and morning did not yet exist? This has led interpreters, such as Millard Erickson and numerous others, to conclude that the sun, moon, and stars were created on the first day but did not appear until the fourth day.[50] Likewise, Hugh Ross

---

47 Hamilton, *Book of Genesis 1–17*, 125. The author could have said: 'Let the waters be gathered to one place so that dry land can appear.'

48 Emphasis mine. A.M. Wolters (*Creation Regained* [Carlisle, Paternoster, 1996] 20) also takes this verse as a reference to the third day of creation.

49 Alan Hayward (*Creation and Evolution* [London, Triangle, 1985] 194) argues that 'according to their kinds' refers to fruit etc., not reproduction. However, this is a selective reading of the text. Gen. 1:11 mentions *seed-bearing* plants and fruit containing *seed*, and seed is clearly indicative of reproduction.

50 Millard J. Erickson, *Christian Theology* 2nd edition (Grand Rapids, Michigan, Baker, 1998), 408.

posits that the sun, moon and stars were actually created 'in the beginning' and that verse 16 is a parenthetical note referring back to day one.[51] Yet, in light of the context, the *waw*-consecutive Qal imperfect וַיַּעַשׂאֱלֹהִים (*wăyyăʿăś ʾĕlōhîm*, 'and God made') in verse 16 clearly indicates that the following description is an elaboration of the event mentioned in verse 14: 'And God said, "Let there be lights in the expanse of the sky ..."' Therefore, this clause refers to the same event as verse 14 rather than a subsequent and, therefore, different event. This rules out the idea that God had made the sun, moon, and stars at an unspecified time in the past before the atmosphere cleared on day four, allowing the lights to be seen.

Ross also claims that all the planets, including earth, started with opaque atmospheres of hydrogen, helium, methane, and ammonia which would not have allowed any sunlight, moonlight or starlight to reach the surface. Thus, on day (period) four, God merely caused this atmosphere to dissipate so that the sun, moon and stars would appear in the sky.[52] Gleason Archer maintains a similar position. He suggests the sunlight was filtered through cloud cover dense enough to inhibit determination of the exact time of sunrise, sunset and length of the solar year, yet still allowed photosynthesis to occur.[53]

Jonathan Sarfati, a physical chemist, points out however that hydrogen could not be held by Earth's gravity, that methane and ammonia would be photolyzed quickly, and that all these gases are transparent anyway![54] In the case of cloud cover, even the thickest clouds still allow enough light through in order for an observer to distinguish between day and night even if they could not tell the exact time of sunrise and sunset, so Archer's suggestion is dubious at best.

Furthermore, if God intended to say that the sun, moon and stars merely 'appeared' on the fourth day then why did the author not use the Niphal form of רָאָה (*rāʾāh*, 'see') in the same way He described the appearance of dry land? Moreover, verses 17–18 state that, after God made these lights He 'set' or 'put' (נָתַן, *nāṯăn*) them in the expanse. This also rules out any notion of the lights merely 'appearing.'

Sailhamer, on the other hand, admits that creation of the sun, moon and stars is the obvious sense of the text, although he rejects this view because, in keeping with his local creation interpretation, he too believes 'the heavens and the earth' in verse 1 includes the sun, moon and stars.[55]

---

51 Hugh N. Ross, *The Genesis Question* (Colorado Springs, Navpress, 1998), 44.

52 Ibid., 26–27.

53 Archer, 'A Response to The Trustworthiness of Scripture in Areas Relating to Natural Science,' 322–323. Archer fails to deal with any of the meteorological or botanic implications of his view. For example, if the earth was surrounded by a blanket of cloud for the first three days (three long periods of time according to Archer) then the resulting weather conditions would be horrific. Also, many plant species require direct sunlight to survive.

54 Jonathan Sarfati, 'A Review of The Genesis Question' *JoC* 13/2 (1999), 24.

55 Sailhamer, *Genesis*, 33; Sailhamer, *The Pentateuch As Narrative* (Grand Rapids, Michigan, Zondervan, 1992). 92. See also ch. 5 for a critique of Sailhamer's local creation interpretation.

Sailhamer claims that יְהִי...לְהַבְדִּיל (yᵉhî...lᵉhăbᵉdîl, 'let there be … to separate') indicates the lights already existed (that is, were created on day one) and that God merely appointed them 'to separate' on day four.[56] But note that the Hebrew syntax of verse 14 is identical to that of verse 6 (and v. 3). The fiat in each verse begins with יְהִי (yᵉhî, 'Let there be …'), the jussive form of הָיָה (hāyāh), which can only refer to the occurrence of an event or the bringing of something into existence.[57] Given the context, the latter meaning was clearly intended. In all these verses the jussive is followed by the subject and identifies what the speaker is willing into existence. In the case of Genesis 1:14, the subject is מְאֹרֹת (mᵉʾōrōṯ, 'luminaries'). If verse 14 simply states that God appointed the luminaries to the task of separating day and night, then one would surely expect the fiat to begin with the jussive form of בָדַל (bāḏăl, 'separate'). Therefore, the rendering 'Let there be lights … for the purpose of separating …' makes much better sense syntactically. This retains the expression of purpose but does not assume the pre-existence of the lights. Indeed, this is the traditional rendering and is supported by all the major translations[58] as well as the LXX.[59]

Davis Young also claims the sun, moon, and stars already existed on the fourth day but he argues that they merely came into a particular relationship with the earth.[60] But in what way have the sun, moon, and stars come into a different relationship with the earth? Verse 14 states that they divided the day and night, and served as signs for days, years, and seasons. If this function was only allocated on the fourth day or period, then what were they doing before this time? Furthermore, verse 17 indicates that God placed these light sources *in the expanse* on this day. Where were they prior to this?

Note that any interpretation which advocates the existence of the sun, moon, and stars prior to the fourth day implies that the fourth day is unique among the creation days in that nothing was actually created or formed on this day. As Kline states,

> … this proposal is guilty of foisting an unwarranted meaning on the language affirming God's making and positioning of the luminaries. In the accounts of the other days, everybody rightly recognises that the same language of divine fiat and creative fulfilment signifies the bringing into existence of something new, not just a visual detecting of something that was there all the while. There is no more excuse for *reducing divine acts of production into human acts of perception* in day four than there would be elsewhere.[61]

---

56 Sailhamer, *Genesis*, 34.

57 See BDB, Holladay.

58 NIV, NASB, RSV, NRSV, NET, KJV, ASV.

59 The LXX reads: γενηθήτωσαν φωστῆρες ἐν τῷ στερεώματι τοῦ οὐρανοῦ εἰς φαῦσιν τῆς γῆς …: 'Let there be lights in the firmament of the heavens, for the purpose of illuminating the earth …'

60 Young, *Creation and the Flood*, 128–129.

61 Kline, 'Space and Time in the Genesis Cosmogony,' 8.

He continues:

> ... the primary declaration that the luminaries were made cannot be
> eliminated as a day four event in that way no more so than the statement
> in the day two account that God made the firmament may be reduced
> to the idea that a previously existing firmament began to perform its
> stated purpose of dividing between the waters above and below (Gen.
> 1:6, 7). Moreover, this minimalist view of day four would share the fatal
> flaw of all views that eliminate the forming of the luminaries from the
> happenings of day four: it would leave day four with no new contri-
> bution, for all the functions mentioned there are already said to be
> operative in day one.[62]

The Sun and Moon as the New Dividers

What, then, did God actually do on the fourth day? As indicated in the
discussion of the first day, when light was created, *God Himself* divided it from
the darkness (v. 4), possibly using a temporary directional light source. But on
the fourth day, God created the sun and moon for this purpose. As Cassuto puts
it, 'throughout those first three days God caused light to shine upon the earth
from some other source without recourse to the sun; but when He created the
luminaries He handed over to them the task of separation ...'[63]

It must be asked, however, why the sun was not created until the fourth day?
If a temporary light source was used, then why? Why create a temporary light
source then replace it with the sun?[64] It may be that this section of the account
is somewhat polemical. Indeed, referring to the sun as the 'greater light' and the
moon as the 'lesser light' strongly indicate polemical concerns, since the terms
'sun' and 'moon' are similar in other Semitic languages and represent pagan
gods. It appears, then, that in His creative work, God wished to emphasize
that He is the source of everything including the sun and the moon, and the
light which they radiate. Nevertheless, Genesis 1 is intended to be a historical
narrative account of what God actually did during the creation week, so any
polemical points are only incidental.

The Fifth Day

On the fifth day, God created aquatic life to fill the seas and winged creatures to
fly 'above the earth across the expanse' (Genesis 1:20).

Creation of Aquatic Life

The aquatic life is described as שֶׁרֶץ נֶפֶשׁ חַיָּה (*šěrěṣ něpěš ḥǎyyāh*, 'a swarm
of living, breathing creatures') which includes not only fish, but other sea
creatures such as whales, sharks, and other large species, both extinct and
alive today.

---

62   Ibid.

63   Cassuto, 1:44.

64   Ross, 'The Framework Hypothesis,' 121.

Creation of Winged Creatures

The term עוֹף ('ôp) is usually rendered as 'birds' but can actually describe any winged creature including insects and the like.[65]

As shown above, the term 'expanse' refers to interstellar space. But in light of verse 20, this would imply that birds were flying through space.[66] However, most English translations do a poor job of rendering עַל־פְּנֵי רְקִיעַ הַשָּׁמָיִם ('ăl-p'nêh r'qîă' hăššāmāyĭm). 'Across' appears to be a dubious rendering of the preposition 'ăl ('on,' 'over')[67] and p'nêh ('face,' 'surface') is often not translated. In verse 2, the exact same phrase is translated 'over the surface,' so in verse 20 it would be better rendered as 'over the surface of the expanse of the heavens.' This language appears to be phenomenological. An observer on earth looking up at the sky and watching a bird fly past can easily determine the approximate distance to the bird since it is an objective and well-defined entity. Yet the same observer could not determine the distance to the beginning of interstellar space (the expanse) because its boundaries are not so well-defined — at least from the perspective of an observer on earth. Nevertheless, the observer can perceive that the boundary of interstellar space is much further away than the bird. Therefore, to the observer looking up at the sky, the bird flies 'over the surface of the expanse of the heavens' (that is, inside the Earth's atmosphere), rather than in the expanse itself.

The Sixth Day

The sixth day sees the advent of animate creatures, both animals and humans.

Creation of Land-Dwelling Living Creatures

God declared that the land should 'produce living creatures.' The verb יָצָא (yāṣār, 'come out') is in the *Hiphil* form which indicates 'the subject as causing an object to participate indirectly as a second subject in the notion expressed by the verbal route.'[68] Thus, the sense here is: 'Let the land cause living creatures to come out …'

These 'living creatures' (נֶפֶשׁ חַיָּה, *nĕpĕš ḥăyyāh*) are those which have the 'breath of life.' This includes livestock and other domesticated animals (בְּהֵמָה, *b'hēmāh*), creatures that move along the ground (רֶמֶשׂ, *rĕmĕś*) and all other wild or undomesticated animals (חַיָּה, *ḥăyyāh*). These broad and somewhat

---

65 See entry for עוֹף in BDB, Holladay, *HALOT*.

66 Modern translations have rendered 'ăl-p'nêh r'qîă' hăššāmāyĭm in various ways: 'above the earth across the expanse of the heavens' (NIV); 'above the earth in the open expanse of the heavens' (NASB); 'above the earth across the dome of the sky' (NRSV); 'above the earth across the face of the firmament of the heavens' (NKJV).

67 *HALOT* lists 'across' as a possible rendering but the only instance it cites is Gen. 1:20 — the very instance that is in dispute! A GRAMCORD search reveals that עַל־פְּנֵי occurs 205 times in the OT and 31 times in Genesis. It is invariably rendered as 'on/over the surface/face of,' 'throughout,' 'near,' 'facedown.'

68 *IBHS* 27.1e.

overlapping terms appear to cover all of the land dwelling, air breathing creatures, that is, land-dwelling creatures with a respiratory system.[69]

The general terms used when describing the land-dwelling animals, and the reference to 'their kinds' suggest that it is highly unlikely that God initially created the many different species we presently observe. Rather, He most likely created various kinds of creatures such as a 'dog kind,' a 'cat kind,' a 'horse kind' corresponding to what modern taxonomists define as a *genus*. Through speciation processes, these *genera* later split into the species and varieties now observed today.[70] For example, 'big cat' species such as the lion, tiger, and jaguar may have all descended from one of the offspring of the original 'proto-cat' while the smaller, sleeker cat species such as the leopard, puma and cheetah may have descended from a different offspring.[71]

Creation of Humans to be God's Image-Bearers

God's second creative act on the sixth day sees His creative work reach a climax: God makes man in His own image. As God's image-bearers, humans are personal, moral, and spiritual beings. We have volition, freedom of choice, self-consciousness, self-transcendence, self-determination, and rationality.[72]

Note that the human body is also part of the image of God. In the indictment against murder in Genesis 9:6, God declared that humans who murder another human will also die by the hands of men, 'for in the image of God has God made man.' Therefore, in this instance, as William Dyrness points out, the image of God is grounded in the human body.[73]

In addition, verse 27 indicates that the image of God is not restricted to just the male or to just the female. The true expression of God's image is reflected in *both* the male and the female, *together*.

Furthermore, as God's image-bearers, humans were created to have communion with God and with each other. Dyrness points out that 'the image, if not essentially relationship, is made for community and finds its highest expression therein. Man is created in and for covenant and fellowship. ... It is this capacity for relationship that characterizes the image of God.'[74] Thus, the

---

69 C. John Collins ('Reading Genesis 1:1–2:3 as an Act of Communication: Discourse Analysis and Literal Interpretation' in J.A. Pipa and D.W. Hall [editors], *Did God Create in Six Days?* [Taylors, SC, Southern Presbyterian Press, 1999], 136) argues that the listing of the land animals in vs. 24–5 is not exhaustive, e.g., it does not include dinosaurs. But this claim is unjustified in light of the generic semantics of *nĕpĕš ḥāyyāh*. Since flying creatures and aquatic life were created on the fifth day, the only organisms which are not covered in the creation account are non-flying insects, beetles, arachnids, centipedes, worms, and micro-organisms.

70 Speciation processes include gene loss, genetic drift, and genetic recombination. These are well-defined, well-documented natural processes which have been observed and are not related to molecules-to-man evolution.

71 See Donald A. Batten, 'Ligers and wolphins? What next?' *Creation* 22/3 (June–August 2000), 28–33.

72 Charles Lee Feinberg, 'The Image of God' *BSac* 129 (July 1972), 246.

73 William A. Dyrness, 'The *Imago Dei* And Christian Aesthetics' *JETS* 15/3 (Summer 1972), 162.

74 Ibid., 171.

image of God includes all aspects of the human being; spiritual, psychological, moral, emotional, physical and relational.

It is on this basis and the fact that all humanity came from Adam and Eve, the first man and the first woman, that racism should be seen as truly scandalous. All human beings are related to one another and all are image bearers of God regardless of their skin color or physical characteristics.[75] In fact, Scripture never talks about 'races,' but about 'nations,' 'tribes,' 'clans,' and 'families.'[76] The variation in human characteristics and skin color presently observed is merely a result of 'genetic drift' and/or loss of genetic information brought about by environmental pressure and/or inter-breeding as a result of isolation.[77]

Mankind's Dominion

God blesses the first couple and commands them to multiply, fill the earth and 'subdue' it, and to 'rule' over the entire animal kingdom (v. 28). The verb 'subdue' (כָּבַשׁ, *kābaš*) refers to the cultivation and manipulation of the land to suit mankind's purposes. Similarly, the verb 'rule' (רָדָה, *rādāh*) indicates humanity's pre-eminence over all other living creatures, and their ability to control and harness them. Note, however, that neither *kābaš* nor *rādāh* carries any notion of destruction or devastation. This command should not be taken as a license to plunder, spoil, or destroy that which God has given us to rule.

Neither is there any need for mankind or other living creatures to hunt and kill each other. God, in His wisdom and providence, provided food and sustenance for His animate creatures. Mankind was given 'every seed-bearing plant on the face of the whole earth and every tree that has fruit with seed in it' for food, while other living creatures were simply given 'every green plant for food' (vs. 29–30).

The 'Very Good' Creation

In Genesis 1:31, God looks upon everything He made and declared it to be 'very good.' But what exactly did He mean by this? In what way is the creation 'very good'? Like many adjectives, 'good' is a relative term. How does one decide whether something is 'good'? What standard of comparison is to be used? Jesus told the religious leaders it was lawful to do 'good' on the Sabbath (Matthew 12:12) but the psalmist and Paul both state that no-one does 'good' (Psalm 14:1; 53:1 and Romans 3:12). Clearly, 'good' refers to mankind's standard of goodness in the first instance, and God's standard in the second. Given the context, it would seem that when God declared His particular creative works

---

75 Note that there is very little difference at all between the various people groups living on Earth. The color of one's skin simply depends on the amount of melanin produced by the body which is encoded in that person's genes.

76 See Josh. 7:14

77 Genetic drift is the concentration of a particular gene or set of genes in a particular population. Loss of genetic information involves the degeneration of a particular gene or set of genes such that functional information is lost from the entire population.

to be 'good,' and the completed creation to be 'very good,' He was using His own absolute standard of goodness. Indeed, everything God creates is 'good' (1 Timothy 4:4).

In verse 31, the adjective טוֹב (*ṭôḇ*, 'good') is followed by מְאֹד (*mᵉʾōd*), an adverb which often strengthens and intensifies the verb and is usually rendered as 'very', 'greatly', or 'exceedingly.'[78] However, when *mᵉʾōd* follows an adjective it may cause it to function as an absolute superlative.[79] Given the context of Genesis 1:31 and the absence of a verb, this is the most likely meaning.[80] Thus, the creation was not merely 'good' but *exceedingly* good — so good that it could not be improved or made any better. In other words, when God had completed His creative activity and looked at what He had made it was exactly as He intended. It was *perfect*. As von Rad writes:

> Verse 31 contains the concluding formula of approval for the entire work of creation. This formula 'Behold, it was very good' is of great importance within the terse and plain language of the author. It could also be translated 'completely perfect,' and rightly refers more to the wonderful purposefulness and harmony than to the beauty of the entire cosmos. This statement, expressed and written in a world full of innumerable troubles, preserves an inalienable concern of faith: no evil was laid upon the world by God's hand; neither was His omnipotence limited by any kind of opposing power whatever. When faith speaks of creation, and in so doing directs its eye toward God, then it can only say that God created the world perfect.[81]

The Seventh Day: The Sabbath

'Resting' or 'Ceasing' from Work?

On the seventh day God finished His creative work and 'rested' (Genesis 2:2). This should not be understood as indicating that God was somehow tired and fatigued as a result of His creative activities. The Qal form of שָׁבַת (*šāḇaṯ*) does not inherently mean 'rest' but rather 'stop,' 'cease' or 'desist.'[82] Moreover, *šāḇaṯ* is further qualified by מִכָּל־מְלַאכְתּוֹ אֲשֶׁר עָשָׂה (*mikāl-mᵉlāʾkᵉtô ʾᵃšer ʾāśāh*, 'from all His work He had done'). Indeed, humans do not work for six days before becoming tired, causing them to sleep/rest for one whole day before resuming work. Rather, we recover from our fatigue and tiredness every night throughout the week.

---

78 In this case it would strengthen the elided copulative verb 'was.'

79 An absolute superlative is used to describe an object which excels in some quality, state or condition. See *IBHS* 14.5a-b. For examples, see Exod. 9:18, 9:24; Num. 12:3; Deut. 28:54.

80 Indeed, Waltke and O'Connor list Gen. 1:31 as an example of this function in their grammar. See *IBHS* 14.5b.

81 Gerhard von Rad, *Genesis: A Commentary*, OTL, rev. ed. (Philadelphia, Westminster Press, 1973), 61.

82 See entry for שָׁבַת in BDB, Hollady, *HALOT*. See also Gen. 8:22; Josh. 5:12; Neh. 6:3; Job 32:1; Prov. 22:10; Isa. 14:4.

In Exodus 20:11, however, the verb נוּחַ (*nûăḥ*) is used to refer to God's resting. Rather than a reference to the ceasing of work, the Qal form describes the notion of 'settling,' 'remaining' or 'stopping.'[83] That *nûăḥ* cannot mean 'resting from work' is shown in Genesis 2:15: 'The LORD God took the man and put [*nûăḥ*] him in the Garden of Eden to work it and take care of it.' Clearly *nûăḥ* cannot mean 'resting from work' because the man was put into the garden to 'work it.' Therefore, 'rested' is an inadequate rendering, and in the context of Exodus 20:11 a better rendering would be 'stopped.'

Exodus 31:17, although very similar to Exodus 20:11, includes an additional clause: 'and was refreshed.'[84] Unlike *šāḇăṭ*, נָפַשׁ (*nāpăš*, 'refresh oneself') does imply a recovery from tiredness and fatigue. But note that fatigue and tiredness are distinctive consequences of bodily existence. Since God has no body, and in the light of the verses discussed above, *nāpăš* cannot refer to God being literally refreshed after being tired from His creative activities. Rather, this appears to be an anthropomorphism. God was refreshed in that, after a short stoppage, His desire, excitement, and enthusiasm for interacting with His creation was reignited. Leon Morris writes: 'So we should think of the rest as something like the satisfaction that comes from accomplishment, from the completion of a task, from the exercise of creativity.'[85]

Purpose of the Sabbath

What, then, is the purpose of the Sabbath? Firstly, it must be emphasized that the Sabbath is a special day, a day different from all others, a day which God blessed and made holy, a day when no work was done.

Secondly, the Sabbath is always dedicated to, or directed toward, God.[86] The Israelites were forbidden to work on the Sabbath because that would cause their time to be filled with self-centered worldly pursuits (Exodus 35:2) instead of giving God the worship and attention He deserves.

Thirdly, the Sabbath served as a reminder that God provided for His people in the desert (Exodus 16:26–9). Each day God sent them manna and quail. Each morning the people were to go out and collect enough food for that day. They were not to keep any for the next day and if they did it would go off, become infested with maggots and stink. However, no manna or quail was sent on the Sabbath so God allowed the people to collect extra on the sixth day to keep for the Sabbath and it did not go bad or become infested.

Fourthly, the Sabbath was to serve as an everlasting covenant between God and Israel to remind them that He is the Creator and Sustainer of the universe (Exodus 31:16–17).

Fifthly, the Sabbath was given as a sign to remind the people that God made them holy. Human beings are different from all other creatures — we are made

---

83 See entry for נוּחַ in BDB.

84 NASB, NLT, ESV, NKJV, KJV. Cf. NIV: '… he abstained from work and rested.'

85 Leon Morris and D.W. Burdick, *Hebrews and James*, EBC (Grand Rapids, Michigan, Zondervan, 1996), 41.

86 e.g. Exod. 16:23–25, 20:10; Lev. 23:3; Deut. 5:12.

in the image of God. Thus, human beings are the only animate creatures which stop working to enjoy their environment and the fruits of their labor, and to engage in recreational activities. We are the only creatures that can relate to and reflect upon our Creator.

Lastly, the Sabbath was to be kept by *everyone* and *every creature* in the land, not just the Israelites (Deuteronomy 5:14).

Note that although Sabbath observance requires that the people do no work, this did not mean that they were to do nothing. On the contrary, the people were to celebrate (Exodus 31:16), to read and hear the Scripture of God (Acts 15:21), to teach and to be taught (Acts 13:42–4), and to do good (Matthew 12:12), as Jesus did on several occasions.[87]

The purpose of the Sabbath, then, was to worship God, to reflect upon what He has done, to read and discuss His Scripture, and to celebrate life. It was a time when the people were to focus on their relationship with their Creator. This is clearly illustrated in Mark 2:27:

> A   The *Sabbath* was made
>   B   for *man*,
>   B′   not *man*
> A′   for the *Sabbath*.
>   So the Son of Man is Lord even of the Sabbath.

Note that the chiastic structure emphasizes man over the Sabbath itself, and the 'Son of Man' (Jesus Christ) is Lord of the Sabbath. Thus, the Sabbath is merely a platform from which man can focus his attention on God and maintain his relationship with his Creator.

The Sabbath as a 'Type' of the Kingdom of God

The Sabbath rest is also mentioned in Hebrews 4. In this context, the notion of 'rest' is first mentioned in Hebrews 3:11, which is part of a quotation from Psalm 95:7–11, regarding the unbelief of the Israelites after they fled Egypt (3:18). God punished them by not allowing any adult, over twenty years old,[88] to enter His 'rest' (Numbers 14:28–35), which was the Land of Canaan, the promised land.

In Hebrews 4:1, the author states that the promise of entering God's rest still stands. However, verses 2–3a make it clear that he is now talking about *entering the kingdom of God*, rather than possessing the land. Because of this, the 'Promised Land' is set up as a *type* of the kingdom, and both may be referred to as 'God's rest.'

In Hebrews 4:4, the author quotes Genesis 2:2 in order to point out that the invitation to enter God's 'rest' has not just been there since the time of the exodus, but has actually been there ever since the creation of the world.

The Greek word translated 'rested' is κατέπαυσεν (*katepausen*), an aorist active indicative verb, and the same word used in the LXX to render the Hebrew

---

87   e.g. Matt. 12:1–12; Mark 3:2–5; Luke 13:10–14; John 5:5–9.

88   The only exceptions were Caleb and Joshua.

וַיִּשְׁבֹּת (*wăyyĭšbōt*) — a *waw*-consecutive imperfect (or *wayyiqtol* form) — in Genesis 2:2. In biblical Greek, the aorist indicative can have an *ingressive* sense, that is, the focus is on the *beginning* of the action or an *entrance into a state*.[89] Therefore, both the author of Hebrews and the translators of the LXX understood that on the seventh day '… God *began* to rest.' Similarly, the Hebrew *waw*-consecutive imperfect not only usually expresses a perfective action when it follows a perfect verb (as is the case in Genesis 2:2), but can also express a similar ingressive meaning.[90]

Therefore, God's 'rest' should be viewed as a long period of time *beginning* with the seventh day of creation, not as *equivalent* to the seventh day.[91] Note also that this reference to creation confirms that the author has gone beyond the events of the exodus, and that the kingdom of God is now in view. Thus, the 'rest' referred to in Hebrews 4 is actually a picture of the kingdom of God.

The Days of Creation and Time

No Relation

Interpreters who view the days of creation as merely a literary framework or some form of anthropomorphism believe there is no real connection between the days and actual time. While most affirm the Genesis account refers to real historical events, they do not consider it to be a detailed historical and chronological record of the actual events as they occurred.[92]

A Prophetic Overview of World History

Many of the early church fathers including Barnabas, Irenaeus, Hippoplytus, Methodius, Lactantius, Theophilus, and John of Damascus all understood the days as corresponding to seven ages of a 7,000-year world history.[93] In other words, the totality of world history could be broken down into seven ages, each of which lasts for 1,000 years.

It should be added that no notable theologian or commentator currently holds this view.

Instantaneous Creation

Hilary of Poitiers believed that creation was a single instantaneous act: 'For, although according to Moses there is an appearance of regular order in the fixing of the firmament, the laying bare of the dry land, the gathering together of the waters, the formation of the heavenly bodies, and the arising of living

---

89 Wallace, *Greek Grammar*, 558.

90 *IBHS* 33.3.1a. Another example of the ingressive use is Gen. 4:5: 'but for Cain and for his offering He had no regard. So Cain became very angry and his countenance fell' (NRSV).

91 See for example Paul Ellingworth, *The Epistle to the Hebrews*, NIGTC (Grand Rapids, Michigan, Eerdmans, 1993), 249.

92 For example, John H. Walton (*Genesis*, NIVAC [Grand Rapids, Michigan, Zondervan, 2001], 108) simply affirms that Genesis 1 teaches the creation of time and nothing more.

93 Forster and Marston, *Reason and Faith*, 205.

things from land and water, yet the creation of the heavens, earth, and other elements is seen to be the work of a single moment.'[94]

Likewise, Augustine was inclined to think God created all things in a moment of time, and the days were simply introduced to aid the finite human intelligence.[95] He wrote:

> What kind of days these were it is extremely difficult, or perhaps impossible for us to conceive, and how much more to say! We see, indeed, that our ordinary days have no evening but by the setting, and no morning but by the rising, of the sun; but the first three days of all were passed without sun, since it is reported to have been made on the fourth day. And first of all, indeed, light was made by the word of God, and God, we read, separated it from the darkness, and called the light Day, and the darkness Night; but what kind of light that was, and by what periodic movement it made evening and morning, is beyond the reach of our senses; neither can we understand how it was, and yet must unhesitatingly believe it.[96]

Like the previous view, this one also is not currently accepted by any notable theologian or commentator.

A Historical Revelation

P.J. Wiseman and Bernard Ramm understood the days of Genesis 1 not as days of creation but as days of *revelation concerning the creation*. Thus, God did not actually create the heavens and the earth and all that is in them in six days but, rather, He took six days to reveal the basic outline of how He created.

Again, this view has largely been abandoned by modern interpreters and commentators.

A Historical Process

The traditional view is to understand the Genesis account as a historical process by which God creates over a period of time. However, advocates disagree over the length of the period. The predominant view, until about 200 years ago, was that God created everything in six normal days (Exodus 20:11). But due to the naturalistic ideas coming out of the 'Enlightenment,' the total length of time is now claimed to be billions of years.[97]

There is also some disagreement over the extent to which God is actively involved in the creation. Theistic evolutionists see God as merely starting the ball rolling then stepping back. Progressive creationists understand God as periodically creating new organisms over a long period of time. Young-earth creationists, on the other hand, understand God to be actively involved throughout the entire creation week, which is a normal seven-day week. In any case, Scripture is consistent in affirming that things were created by God's word not through any mediated natural process.

---

94   As cited by Lewis, 'The Days of Creation: An Historical Survey,' 448.

95   Louis Lavallee, 'Augustine on the Creation Days' *JETS* 32/4 (December 1989), 460.

96   Augustine, *City of God*, 11.6–7.

97   See the discussion in chapter 3.

CHAPTER 7

The Days of Creation: Meaning and Significance

What, then, is the meaning and significance of the creation days? What kind of days are they? What is their relationship to history? The history of interpretation reveals that the days have been understood in numerous ways and the following sections survey and evaluate the major views.

Days of Revelation

The 'Days of Revelation' interpretation, also known as the 'pictorial day' view, treats the days of Genesis 1 not as days of creation but as days of revelation. Each day is a normal day in which God revealed a particular scene of creation. They represent days in the life of the prophet who received the vision or the message, not actual time delineations during the original creative period. In other words, rather than actually creating the universe in six days, God simply *revealed* His works of creation in six days.[1] Although the days of creation are understood as literal days, they are used as a time frame for God revealing to the author His works of creation. Advocates of this view argue that since God revealed the unknown future in visions, it is logical to conclude that God would also reveal the unknown past in similar visions.

Although this view was adopted by J.H. Kurtz in the nineteenth century, and by Augustus H. Strong and Bernard Ramm in the early twentieth century,[2] P.J. Wiseman (1888–1948) was probably the most well-known proponent and popularizer. Wiseman, who considered creation in six days to be a serious misrepresentation,[3] argued that 'God said' indicates that it is a 'record of what God *said to man*…'[4] and therefore 'the first page of the Bible must refer to six days during which God did something in relation to creation after *man was on the earth*.'[5]

---

1 P.J. Wiseman, *Creation Revealed in Six Days* (London. Marshall, Morgan and Scott, 1948), 33ff.

2 J.H. Kurtz, *Bible and Astronomy*, 3rd German edition (1857); Augustus H. Strong, *Systematic Theology* (Philadelphia, Judson Press, 1956), II:393–397; Bernard Ramm, *The Christian View of Science of Scripture* (London, Paternoster, 1955), 151, 218–229.

3 Wiseman, *Creation Revealed in Six days*, 18.

4 Ibid., 39. Original emphasis.

5 Ibid. Original emphasis.

Objections

Davis points out that Scripture only rarely employs visions to reveal past events — Daniel 7:1–14 being the only possible example.[6] Historical events are almost always revealed in historical narrative like that found in the rest of Genesis. Accounts of visions are also clearly identified by the text, yet no such indication can be found in Genesis 1–2. Nor is there any philological evidence to suggest that *bārā'* and *'āśāh* (עָשָׂה) (Genesis 2:3) can mean anything close to 'reveal.' Exodus 20:11 also affirms that God 'made' (*'āśāh*) the heavens and the earth and everything in them in six days, suggesting real action rather than mere revelation. For these reasons, very few, if any, scholars now hold this view.

Anthropomorphic Days

C. John Collins understands the days to be 'analogical' or 'anthropomorphic' in the sense that they express God's activity in terms common to human experience. However, his view is, to some extent, eclectic.

Although Collins affirms that the account is historical in the sense that it refers to real space-time events, he stops short of accepting it as a strictly chronological description of God's actions in time.[7] To him, the account is only broadly consecutive[8] and has an unspecified relation to time as we experience it.[9]

Collins argues that the first day of creation begins at Genesis 1:3. Verses 1–2 describe the initial creation event as background material, and this initial event occurred at 'some unspecified time before the beginning of the first day' because 'each day begins with "and God said ..."' and because 'verse 3 is the first place the normal Hebrew narrative tense appears.'[10] This view is somewhat similar to the 'gap theory.'[11]

> [T]he fact that 1:1–2 is not part of the first day tells us that we don't have to take the creation week as the first 'week' of the universe ... the purpose of the creation story [is] to describe how God prepared the earth as the ideal place for humans to live, love, and serve ... This means that, however we interpret the days, we have no obligation to read Moses as claiming that God began his creative work of the first day at the very beginning of the universe — or even at the very beginning of the earth.'[12]

---

6 John J. Davis, *Paradise to Prison* (Grand Rapids, Michigan, Baker, 1975), 54.

7 C. John Collins, 'Reading Genesis 1:1 – 2:3 as an Act of Communication: Discourse Analysis and Literal Interpretation' in Joseph A. Pipa and David W. Hall (editors), *Did God Create in Six Days?* (Taylors, SC, Southern Presbyterian Press, 1999), 140–141.

8 i.e. they probably overlap to some extent.

9 Collins, 'Reading Genesis 1:1 – 2:3 as an Act of Communication.' 146.

10 C. John Collins, *Science and Faith: Friends of Foes?* (Wheaton, Illinois, Crossway, 2003), 82.

11 The gap theory was discussed in chapter 5.

12 Collins, *Science and Faith*, 83.

Like the literary framework view, he holds to parallels between the first three and second three days: days 1–3 describe the creation of locations, and days 4–6 describe the creation of inhabitants of these locations:

Day 1	Light and dark	Sun and moon	Day 4
Day 2	Sea and sky	Marine and winged animals	Day 5
Day 3	Fertile earth	Land animals and humans	Day 6

Collins argues that the Sabbath commandments in Exodus 20:11 and 31:17 do not support the ordinary day view because God's creative work is totally different to ours, and therefore our work week is only *like* God's — not identical: 'The point of similarity, the analogy, is the fact that during the creation week God was "working on" the earth to make it just right for man to live on … In his Sabbath he is no longer doing this, but now keeps it all in being … It follows from this that length of time has no bearing on the analogy.'[13] According to Collins, the occurrence of שָׁבַת (*šābāṯ*, 'cease'), נוּחַ (*nûăḥ*, 'rest') and נָפַשׁ (*nāpăš*, 'refresh oneself') in Exodus 23:12 demonstrates that physical rest and refreshment is in view. Because all three of these verses refer to the working week and the Sabbath rest, Collins reasons that humans are to rest and refresh themselves on the Sabbath because that is what God did. Thus, Collins concludes that these references to the days of creation are not literal but merely analogical in the sense that 'they have a point of similarity, with a basis in our experience, by which we can understand something about God and his historical activity.'[14] Thus, Collins concludes that, because day 7 is analogical, the other six days must also be analogical.

Objections

Asserting that the first day does not begin until verse 3 stands against the grammar of the Hebrew text. As Gesenius' Hebrew grammar states: 'One of the most striking peculiarities in the Hebrew *consecution* of tenses is the phenomenon that, in representing a series of past events, only the first verb stands in the perfect, and the narration is continued in the imperfect.'[15] This is exactly what we see in Genesis 1:1–3. Verse 1 employs the perfect (or *qatal*) form of the verb (as do the three parallel circumstantial clauses in v. 2), whereas verse 3 employs the imperfect (or *wayyiqtol*) form. This is a clear and objective marker of historical narrative in Hebrew and indicates that the narrative begins in verse 1 rather than verse 3.

There are also problems with Collins' locations–inhabitants scheme for the days of creation. Light (and darkness) are not locations; the expanse was created on day two, not the sea and sky; and the birds and other flying creatures live on the earth rather than in the sky (they merely *fly* in the sky).

---

13 Collins, *Science and Faith*, 86.
14 Collins, 'Reading Genesis 1:1–2:3,' 139 fn. 19.
15 GKC § 49.a.1. Original emphasis.

In addition, if the purpose of the analogy has nothing to do with time, then what *is* its purpose? If it is just to 'set a pattern for the human rhythm of work and rest'[16] and the length of time has no bearing, then why mention the days at all? And are we to work for six hours, six days, six weeks, six months, or six years before stopping to observe the Sabbath 'day'? Collins' argument for analogical days based on the Sabbath rest is nothing more than special pleading. It is abundantly clear that the primary purpose of the reference to the days of creation was to set the length of time. An analogy, by definition, uses something in the real world to explain some abstract concept. The author is using the real historical creation week to set a pattern and duration for mankind's working week. If the days are not real historical days then there is no analogy, and the reference is meaningless.

Day-Age View
The day-age view attempts to harmonize Scripture with the consensus of modern science. Although held by some notable commentators and theologians, it is typically held by Christians who are trained in the sciences, and who hold to either progressive creation or theistic evolution.

Proponents of the day-age view argue that the creation days are not actual 24-hour periods but figures of speech used to describe long undefined periods of time. Kidner asserts that the days are 'instruments of truth,' because they turn long ages into 'days,' enabling us to see a totality that is normally too big for us.[17] Archer believes the creation week simply signifies the successive phases of creation, and does not constrain it to seven literal days.[18]

Regarding the presence of 'evening' and 'morning' in the description of the days, Allan MacRae asks:

> Is it possible that the words evening and morning here are used not in a literal, but in a figurative sense?... Do these words indicate a literal evening and a literal morning, or do they merely describe the beginning and the end of each period?...Moreover, we should note that the chapter is written from the viewpoint of God. There is no human observer present until near the end of the sixth day. When would it be evening to God and when would it be morning to God? When it is evening in Texas, it is morning in China, and vice versa. God, of course, is not at any particular point of the earth. He is always aware that it is evening in some parts of the earth and morning in others, so that it is quite meaningless to speak of each of these days as having a literal evening and then a literal morning. It is quite clear that the phrases must be used figuratively here and simply indicate the beginning and end of a period of time, whatever its length may be.[19]

---

16 Collins, *Science and Faith*, 89.

17 Derek Kidner, *Genesis*, TOTC (Downers Grove, Illinois, IVP, 1975) 57–58.

18 Gleason L. Archer, 'A Response to The Trustworthiness of Scripture in Areas Relating to Natural Science' in Earl D. Radmacher and Robert D. Preus (editors), *Hermeneutics, Inerrancy and the Bible* (Grand Rapids, Michigan, Zondervan, 1984), 329.

19 Allan A. MacRae, 'The Scientific Approach to the Old Testament Part 2' *BSac* 110 (April 1953), 135, 136.

MacRae later concludes that as far as the actual length of the creation days is concerned, 'Scripture is silent on this particular matter,'[20] and Paul Elbert adds: 'The six days of creation refer to six specific phases in the development of the universe. Phases, not twenty-four-hour days, is the perspective here ...'[21]

Can םוי Refer to an Age or Period?

Since םוי (yôm) has a large semantic range and can refer to periods of time greater than twenty-four hours, is there any justification for taking the instances in Genesis 1 to mean 'age' or 'period' rather than a normal 24-hour day? Given that the most common and basic meaning is in reference to a 24-hour day or the period of daylight during a 24-hour day, the burden of proof surely lies with those who claim the Genesis days are something other than normal days. And as Mark Ross rightly notes, 'if we are to conclude that the seven-day work of creation is not a literal description of the elapsed time for the creation period, and was not intended as such by the Biblical author, this must be for exegetical, not scientific reasons.'[22]

R. Laird Harris, Walter Kaiser, Gleason Archer, and Millard Erickson all affirm that the instances of yôm in Genesis 1 most likely refer to long periods of time.[23] Hugh Ross even suggests the days are most naturally understood as long ages,[24] and that no other Hebrew word apart from yôm can mean long period.[25] What then is the exegetical evidence supporting the day-age interpretation?

Hugh Ross appeals to 2 Peter 3:8 (an allusion to Psalm 90:4) to suggest that because 'a day is like a thousand years and a thousand years are like a day,' God's days are not our days.[26] But rather than defining the meaning of 'day,' these verses are similes[27] which indicate that God is eternal, is not constrained by time, and does not experience the passage of time as humans do.[28]

Similarly, Paul Elbert argues that yôm may refer to an unspecified period of time:

> [T]he interpretation of the day as a linguistic metaphor for an unprescribed period of time or phase is surely in contextual coincidence

---

20 Ibid., 138.

21 Paul Elbert, 'Biblical Creation and Science: A Review Article' *JETS* 39 (Jun 1996), 285.

22 Mark Ross, 'The Framework Hypothesis: An Interpretation of Genesis 1:1–2:3' in Pipa and Hall, 117.

23 R. Laird Harris, 'The Length of the Creative Days in Genesis 1' in Pipa and Hall, 101–111; Walter C. Kaiser, *More Hard Sayings of the Old Testament* (Downers Grove, Illinois, IVP, 1992), 37; Gleason L. Archer, *Survey of Old Testament Introduction* (Chicago, Moody Press), 187–199. Millard J. Erickson, *Christian Theology*, 2nd edition (Grand Rapids, Michigan, Baker, 1998), 408. Hugh N. Ross, *The Genesis Question* (Colorado Springs, NavPress, 1998), 65.

24 Hugh N. Ross, *Creation and Time* (Colorado Springs, NavPress, 1994), 143. However, it seems that other 'progressive creationists' disagree with Ross. Gleason Archer (*A Survey of Old Testament Introduction*, 181) writes: 'From a superficial reading of Genesis 1, the impression received is that the entire creative process took place in six 24-hour days.'

25 Hugh Ross, *The Genesis Question*, 65.

26 Hugh Ross, *Creation and Time*, 45.

27 As indicated by the presence of the comparative 'like.'

28 See Willem A. VanGemeren, *Psalms*, EBC (Grand Rapids, Michigan, Zondervan, 1991).

with the entire narrative and in keeping with what the text would have meant in the mind of the author of Genesis (as far as we are able to discover it) as he attempts to describe monumental events in simple straightforward language that he and his thoughtful readers in the ancient world would best understand and appreciate.[29]

Not only does Elbert's argument beg the question, but Davis notes that even when *yôm* is used to refer to something other than a literal day, it still refers to a time period of specified duration.[30]

These kind of arguments are quite common among day-age advocates but they are exegetically unjustified. John Walton explains:

> It is not unusual for an interpreter to claim something like, 'The word day can mean an extended, indefinite period of time,' and then follow up with a series of supportive references. The problem is that invariably most if not all of these references will be examples of [*yom* with a prefixed preposition and/or demonstrative pronoun]. Unfortunately, one cannot pull the word *yom* out of that setting and still retain the meaning it has in that setting.[31]

In the case of Genesis 1, Skinner adds: 'The interpretation of *yôm* as aeon ... is opposed to the plain sense of the passage, and has no warrant in Hebrew usage (not even in Ps. 90:4) ... If the writer had had aeons in his mind, he would hardly have missed the opportunity of stating how many millenniums each embraced.'[32]

Contra Hugh Ross, there were other lexical choices available to the author which are far better suited to expressing the idea of an age or long period of time. For example, דּוֹר (*dōr*) is used in various combinations to express the idea of an age or period of time.[33] The word עוֹלָם (*ʿōlām*) could also have been used.[34]

Moreover, the concept of an age does not necessarily have to be expressed in a single word. The same concept could be described by expressions such as: 'After many, many years...' or 'After many, many generations...'

Evening and Morning

Hugh Ross also argues that the presence of 'evening' (עֶרֶב, *ĕrĕḇ*) and 'morning' (בֹקֶר, *ḇōqĕr*) which terminate the descriptions of each day are merely

---

29 Elbert, 'Biblical Creation and Science' 286.

30 John J. Davis, *Paradise to Prison*, 53. For example, the 'day' God created the heavens and the earth (Gen. 2:4) is still limited to six days and the days of man are limited to 120 years (Gen. 6:3).

31 John H. Walton, *Genesis*, NIVAC (Grand Rapids, Michigan, Zondervan, 2001), 81.

32 John Skinner, *A Critical and Exegetical Commentary on Genesis*, 2nd edition, ICC (Edinburgh, T & T Clark, 1930), 21.

33 e.g. Isa. 51:9; Deut. 32:7. See also *TWOT*, 1:186–187

34 Allan A. MacRae (*TWOT*, 2:673) states: 'The LXX generally translates *ʿōlām* by *aiōn* which has essentially the same range of meaning ... Both words came to be used to refer to a long age or period ...' *HALOT* likewise gives the rendering 'long time, duration (usually eternal, eternity, but not in a philosophical sense).'

metaphorical and do not imply a literal 24-hour day.[35] What then do they actually represent? In the case of Psalm 90:5–6, VanGemeren suggests a metaphorical usage indicating the beginning and ending of an unspecified period of time.[36] The situation described in this text is clearly hyperbolic (grass does not ordinarily spring up in the morning only to disappear in the evening), and the immediate context suggests the theme is the *brevity of life*. Note that 'morning' still means morning, and 'evening' still means evening — indeed, if the literal meanings are not accepted this word picture would fail to communicate what the author intended.[37]

Moreover, the syntax of the clauses that contain *ĕrĕb* and *bōqĕr* rule out any possibility of them merely referring to the beginning and ending of an unspecified time period. Both *ĕrĕb* and *bōqĕr* are immediately followed by the Qal *waw*-consecutive imperfect verb *wăyᵉhî* and act as subjects for these verbs: 'And then evening came, and then morning came' (or 'And then there was evening and then there was morning').[38] Therefore, evening occurred *after* God's creative activities on that day and *before* the following morning. But if 'morning' and 'evening' merely referred to the beginning and ending of a (long) period of time, the situation becomes incoherent. If a long period of time were being described, the earth would remain illuminated for millions of years while God created, and then become engulfed in darkness for millions of years before being illuminated again in preparation for the next phase of creative activity. If each 'day' were a long time period, then it would have been light for half of this long period and dark for the other half. Under these conditions, the existence of any form of life would be virtually impossible, not to mention the implication of such a view on astronomy and the structure of the solar system.

The Sabbath of Day Seven

Both Hugh Ross and Archer argue the Sabbath of day seven is still continuing. They go on to argue that since the seventh day is obviously a long period, and given the parallelism of the account, it is reasonable to conclude the first six days were also long periods.[39] But this same logic could just as easily be applied in reverse: day seven is a literal day because the first six are literal days. In any case, Hoeksema demonstrates that this reasoning is ultimately self-defeating. If the Sabbath simply means that God ceased His creative activity on the seventh day, then the seventh day lasts forever, because God never creates again. This

---

35 Hugh N. Ross, *Genesis One: A Scientific Perspective* (Sierra Madre, California, Wisemen Productions, 1983), 16; Hugh N. Ross , *Creation and Time*, 46. Note, however, that Mark Van Bebber and Paul Taylor (*Creation and Time: A Report on the Progressive Creationist Book by Hugh Ross* [Gilbert, Arizona, Eden Communications, 1996], 68) demonstrate that Ross misrepresents his sources.

36 VanGemeren, *Psalms*, 90:5–6.

37 i.e. 'though in the *beginning* [the grass] springs up new, by the *end* it is dry and withered.'

38 My translation.

39 Hugh N. Ross and Gleason L. Archer, 'The Day-Age View' in D.G. Hagopian (editor), *The Genesis Debate* (Mission Viejo, California, Crux Press), 145–146.

would mean the other days of the creation week were also eternal, which is, of course, absurd.[40]

Creation of the Sun on Day Four

The creation of the sun on the fourth day is also a problem for the day-age view, since vegetation created on day three could not have survived for a long period of time without sunlight.[41] Harris's solution to this problem is to take וַיַּעַשׂ (*wayyăś*, 'and … made') in Genesis 1:16 as a pluperfect, resulting in the translation 'God had made …'[42] However, the context makes it clear that the *waw*-consecutive imperfect form marks the beginning of an elaboration of the event *just mentioned* ('And God said, "Let there be lights in the expanse of the sky …"' v. 14) rather than a different event altogether. It would also mean that the lights were created on day three even though the description of day three makes no reference to them. This is a major oversight given the importance and significance of the sun and moon. It would also imply that day four was unique in that nothing was actually created. Thus, Harris's suggestion of a pluperfect rendering is unsustainable.

Archer, on the other hand, believes the sun was created on day one but the sunlight was filtered through cloud cover dense enough to inhibit determination of the exact time of sunrise, sunset and the length of the solar year, yet still allow photosynthesis to occur.[43] However, this interpretation does not do justice to the text. There is simply no lexical justification for translating עָשָׂה (*'ăśăh*) as 'reveal.'

Science and the Day-Age View

Although the intent is to harmonize Scripture and science, the day-age view is *just as much at odds with modern science as any other creationist view*. The geological ages do not harmonize with the days of creation[44] and there are many discrepancies between the two:

> There are far more differences between the Genesis account and the geological record than there are similarities. And these differences are quite significant … Genesis says there were grasses and fruit trees before there were any animals at all; geology reports a wide variety of animals already in the Cambrian period, while the flowering plants did not appear until the Cretaceous period, 400 million years later … fish and birds were created on the same day, the fifth day; geology reports fish

---

40 Herman Hoeksema, *Reformed Dogmatics* (Grand Rapids, Michigan, Reformed Free Publishing, 1966), 180.

41 John J. Davis, *Paradise to Prison*, 55.

42 Harris, 'The Length of the Creative Days in Genesis 1,' 108.

43 Archer, 'A Response to The Trustworthiness of Scripture,' 322–323. Archer fails to deal with any of the meteorological or botanical implications of this view. For example, if the earth was surrounded by a blanket of cloud for the first three days (three long periods of time according to Archer) then the resulting weather conditions would be horrific. Also, many plant species require direct sunlight to survive.

44 John J. Davis, *Paradise to Prison*, 55.

already in the Ordovician period and finds birds first in the Jurassic
period, some 300 million years later … Genesis reports the creation of
the birds on the fifth day and of the creeping things on the sixth day;
geology reports reptiles already in the Pennsylvanian period, while birds
appeared only in the Jurassic period, about 100 million years later.[45]

In addition, Richard Niessen points out that the existence of symbiotic relationships[46] in nature also rules out the day-age view. He cites examples such as the
yucca plant and yucca moth, flowers requiring bees for pollination/reproduction,
and the Calvaria tree and dodo bird. According to Genesis 1, plants were created
on day three (vv. 9–13), birds on day five (vv. 20–23) and insects on day six
(vv. 24–5). While it is possible for symbionts to survive short periods of time
without their dependents, they could not survive the great time periods implied
by the day-age theory.[47]

In order to avoid these discrepancies, Hugh Ross and Davis Young suggest
that the days of creation also overlap, making the events ascribed to each
particular day not necessarily unique to that day.[48] As Davis Young explains,
'It is a great mistake to insist that not a single animal could possibly have been
created before all the plants were created simply because the third day reports
on plants and the fifth and sixth report on animals. To insist on this kind of
conclusion is to overlook the fact that Moses is speaking very generally.'[49] But
this is surely begging the question, and Young is simply reading his own view
into the text. Young adds: 'the creation of plants generally preceded the creation
of animals.'[50] However, Young's claim lacks coherence: either plants were created
first or they were not — there is no other possibility. Again, the descriptions of
God's activities on each day all begin with a *waw*-consecutive, 'And God said…'
and close with two *waw*-consecutives, 'And then there was evening and then
there was morning…'[51] clearly indicating that each day is a consecutive and
completed event which rules out any possibility of overlap.

In the final analysis, interpreting the days as long ages cannot be sustained.
It allows the ever-changing conclusions of science to override the well-attested
usage of the common Hebrew word *yôm* in its context, and, as Hamilton also
points out, it takes extreme liberty with the phrase 'there was evening and there
was morning — the [*X*th] day.'[52]

45 J.W. Klotz, *Modern Science in the Christian Life* (St. Louis, Concordia, 1961), 111–112.
    Likewise, Henry Morris ('A Response to The Trustworthiness of Scripture in Areas Relating to
    Natural Science,' in Radmacher and Preus, 341) claims there are twenty-three discrepancies.

46 Symbiosis is a biological term used to describe the existence of mutually beneficial relationships
    between two animals or an animal and a plant.

47 Richard Niessen, 'Theistic Evolution and the Day-Age Theory' *Impact* 81 (March 1980).

48 Hugh N. Ross, *Genesis One*, 12.

49 Davis A. Young, *Creation and the Flood* (Grand Rapids, Michigan, Baker, 1977), 116.

50 Ibid., 117.

51 My translation.

52 Victor P. Hamilton, *The Book of Genesis: Chapters 1–17*, NICOT (Grand Rapids, Michigan,
    Eerdmans, 1990), 54.

Intermittent Day View

The intermittent day view, a variation of the day-age view, was proposed by Robert Newman and Herman Eckelmann in order to avoid some of the above noted problems. They suggest that 'each day opens a new creative period, and therefore each day is mentioned in Genesis 1 after the activities of the previous creative period have been described, but before those of the next period are given.'[53] Thus, the days were 'sequential but not consecutive' and 'the creative activity largely occurs between days rather than on them.'[54] In other words, each creation day was a 24-hour day that introduced a particular creative activity of God. The creative activity was not confined to that day, since each day was followed by a long period of time in which the activity continued. Therefore, although the beginning of the creation of vegetation preceded the beginning of the creation of land animals, the appearance of vegetation may have continued after the animals began to appear: 'It is not necessary to suppose that the fruit trees … were created before any kind of animal life, which would contradict the fossil record understood as a chronological sequence. Instead, we assume that the creative period involving land vegetation began before the creative periods involving sea, air and land animals of sorts big enough to be noticed by an average human observer.'[55]

An early exegetical defense of a view very similar to this can be found in F. Hugh Capron, *The Conflict of Truth*,[56] and a similar concept has also been proposed by Alan Hayward in *Creation and Evolution*.[57]

Objections

This view is just as problematic as the day-age theory. Although most of the creative activities are said to take place during the long period of time between days, the text clearly indicates that God created on the actual days. In fact, the account gives not the slightest indication that creative activity occurred at any time apart from the days mentioned.

Secondly, although proponents of this view claim the creative activity mentioned on a particular day was not confined to that day, the supernatural and miraculous tone of the account, along with the presence of expressions such as 'And there was light,' 'And it was so' suggest the creative acts were immediate not long and slow processes.

Thirdly, regarding the proposition that long periods of time elapsed between creative days, the syntactical relationships within the account indicate otherwise. The *waw*-consecutive imperfect verb forms that hold the account together

---

53   Robert C. Newman and Herman J. Eckelmann Jr., *Genesis One and the Origin of the Earth* (Downers Grove, Illinois, IVP, 1977), 64–65.

54   Ibid., 74.

55   Ibid., 79.

56   F. Hugh Capron, *The Conflict of Truth* (Cincinnati, Jennings and Pye, 1903), 162–99.

57   Alan Hayward, *Creation and Evolution* (London, Triangle, 1985).

point toward a tight sequence of events. The daylight hours of each day ended at evening, and night time ended with the advent of the morning of the new day. As soon as a particular day had finished, the subsequent day began, so there is simply no room for any time gaps between days.

Literary Framework View [58]

This view has become increasingly popular among many scholars in recent years. Advocates of the literary framework view consider the gap theory and the day-age theory inadequate, yet are still convinced the claims of modern geology and cosmology are true. Therefore, a *non-concordist* view is taken; Genesis was never intended to be harmonized with science. The appeal of this interpretation is that it not only avoids the problems relating to the creation of the sun, moon, and stars on day four, but also the exegetical and scientific problems of interpreting the days as ages.

Henri Blocher, for example, views the creation week as an artistic arrangement and anthropomorphism that should not be taken literally. He claims the author's intention was to provide a theology of the Sabbath not a chronology.[59] Although the days should be understood as ordinary 24-hour days, they form part of a larger figurative whole.[60] As McCone, another framework advocate, explains, 'To make the "days' of creation "days' of time is to bring the Creator down into the framework of his creation so that we can understand and explain creation rather than know the Creator.'[61]

Furthermore, Blocher believes the form of Genesis 1–2 is exactly what would be expected if the author wanted to communicate such a view.[62] However, this kind of argument surely begs the question, and most interpreters would disagree since the history of interpretation indicates that the overwhelming majority of interpreters understood the text as communicating a chronological sequence.[63] It is also quite presumptuous to assume that a particular author living in a vastly different culture and at a time far removed from the present, would write according to *our* expectations. Furthermore, it must be asked what one would expect to read if the creation week was, in fact, a literal, chronological record?

---

58 Much of the following material has been drawn from Andrew S. Kulikovsky, 'A Critique of the Literary Framework View of the Days of Creation' *CRSQ* 37/4 (March 2001), 237–244.

59 If this is all the Genesis 1 is supposed to communicate it leaves an abundance of 'spare' data. Why so much excess detail? In any case, Blocher basically contradicts himself when he later states that the absence of the reference to the days in Deut. 5:12–15 suggests that Exod. 20:11 and 31:17, should not be taken as too close a link to creation. See Henri Blocher, *In the Beginning*, translated by D.G. Preston (Leicester, IVP, 1984), 48.

60 Blocher, *In the Beginning*, 50.

61 R.C. McCone, 'Were the Days of Creation Twenty-Four Hours Long? No' in Ronald F. Youngblood (editor), *The Genesis Debate* (Grand Rapids, Michigan, Baker, 1990), 16.

62 Blocher, *In the Beginning*, 51.

63 See chapter 3, 'Creation and Genesis: An historical survey.'

Parallels Between the Days

Most commentators on Genesis have pointed out the apparent parallels between the first three days and the second three days. For example, Youngblood proposes the outline presented in Table 7.1.[64]

Day 1	Let there be light (1:3).	Let there be lights (1:14).	Day 4
Day 2	Let there be an expanse . . . to separate water from water (1:6).	Let the water teem with creatures and let birds fly above the earth (1:20).	Day 5
Day 3	Let dry land appear (1:9). Let the land produce vegetation (1:11).	Let the land produce living creatures (1:24). Let us make man (1:26). I give you every seed bearing plant . . . and every tree that has fruit with seed in it . . . for food (1:29).	Day 6

Table 7.1: Suggested correspondences between days

Several suggestions have been made regarding the relationship of the second triad to the first. Some proponents believe that each day in the first triad describes a realm while the corresponding day in the second triad describes the population of that realm. Kline, on the other hand, understands the second triad as proclaiming kings to rule over the kingdoms described in the first triad. Either way, the relationship is not consistent across all days. If we take the second triad as describing the population of the realms in the first triad, then in what way do the lights 'populate' the electromagnetic spectrum of which visible light is a part? On day five, sea creatures live in the 'waters below' but birds do not live in the 'waters above' or the 'expanse.' On day six, land is populated by creatures and mankind, but also by vegetation which was created on day three. If we take Kline's view that the second triad describes kings that rule over kingdoms, then who is the king on day six: the living creatures or mankind? On day five, in what way do birds rule over the 'waters above' or the 'expanse'?

Two-Register Cosmology

Kline, however, goes even further with his 'Two Register Cosmology'[65] (see Table 7.2) which envisions a heavenly level (upper register) and an earthly level (lower register),

---

64 Ronald F. Youngblood, *The Book of Genesis*, 2nd edition (Grand Rapids, Michigan, Baker, 1991), 25. Blocher (*In the Beginning*, 51–52) presents a similar view.

65 See Meredith G. Kline, 'Space and Time in the Genesis Cosmogony' *PSCF* 48 (March 1996), 2–15.

where the lower register relates to the upper register as replica to archetype.[66] Kline is not entirely clear what these two registers or levels actually represent, but it appears they refer to the visible and invisible realms respectively.[67]

	v. 1	v. 2	Days 1–6	Day 7
upper register	heaven	Spirit	fiats	God's Sabbath
lower register	earth	deep	fulfillments	Sabbath ordinance

Table 7.2: Correspondences between upper and lower registers

Kline claims that the use of 'the heavens and the earth' is the first indication of the two-register cosmology: heaven is the invisible realm and earth is the visible realm. Yet he earlier claims that the term is not just a merism[68] but two *concrete* components that form the physical world. But if 'the heavens' are upper register how can they also be concrete?

These two registers are said to be re-emphasized by (1) the Spirit hovering over the deep, (2) the fiats and fulfillments of the six days, and (3) God's rest on the seventh day. Table 7.3 shows how Kline also divides the days into two triads:[69]

First Triad	**Level**	**Second Triad**
day one	Upper	day four
day two	upper { } lower	day five
day three	Lower	day six

Table 7.3: Triads of creation days

The creative acts of the first three days supposedly mirror characteristics of the invisible heaven. For example, the day light created on day one was a replica of the 'Glory-light.'[70] The expanse of day two was so much like its archetype that they both shared the name 'heaven.' Kline claims the trees and fruit of day three are used in Scripture as a figure for the cosmos. Their high spreading branches are a realm for the birds of heaven, and are comparable to the expanse in which the birds fly (Genesis 1:20) — a towering image pointing to the overarching Spirit-heaven above. Daniel 4:10–12 is cited as support, but this is actually part

---

66 See Table 1 in Kline 'Space and Time.' He also sees the same kind of two-register cosmology in Job and Revelation. However, these books are completely different in both form and function to the Genesis prologue. Revelation is apocalyptic and Job is wisdom literature. They are completely different genres and not at all comparable.

67 Ibid., 5.

68 Ibid., 4. A merism (or merismus) is a pair of antonyms, which together signify a totality.

69 See Table 2 in Kline 'Space and Time.'

70 Kline never actually defines what he means by 'Glory-light.'

of a prophetic vision concerning King Nebuchadnezzar, which does not speak at all about the cosmos.

The first members of each triad are meant to relate to the heaven (upper level): light on day one, and light sources on day four. However, Kline is again inconsistent. The upper level is supposed to represent the invisible realm, but both light and light sources are physical and very visible! The third members are meant to relate to the earth (lower level): land and vegetation on day three, and the land animals and man on day six. The second members are meant to serve as links between the first and third members. These middle units combine both upper and lower levels: the sky and sea on day two, and birds of the air and fish of the sea on day five. Here again, Kline is inconsistent, since both sky and birds are physical and visible.[71]

An even closer analysis of the text shows the so-called parallels and literary devices are far from what is claimed, if they exist at all.

Day One and Day Four
Kline holds that in terms of chronology, day four is contemporaneous with day one, and describes the astral apparatus that accounts for the day and night. He claims the luminaries (kings) of day four rule over the light and dark (kingdoms) of day one, thus regulating the cycle of light and darkness. He thus concludes the narrative sequence is not chronological.[72]

However, Kline is very selective in his treatment of the text. On day one, God Himself separates light from darkness, and calls the light 'day' and the darkness 'night.' On day four, God creates light sources[73] to separate 'day' from 'night' (as opposed to 'light' and 'darkness') and to give 'light' to the earth. This implies that 'light' pre-existed. The light sources were to govern the 'day' and 'night,' which implies that 'day' and 'night' also pre-existed. Therefore, day one must have preceded day four.

Day Two and Day Five
Following the principle of 'kings' ruling over 'kingdoms,' the birds and fish of day five are said to rule over the sky and sea of day two, respectively.[74] But Kline erroneously identifies the 'expanse' and 'waters below the expanse' of day three, with the habitats of birds and sea creatures, respectively. This critical error causes his whole framework to collapse. On day two, God creates the expanse and calls it 'sky' (שָׁמַיִם, šāmāyim). Again, the expanse cannot be equated with the atmosphere, since verse 14 states that the sun, moon and stars are set *in the expanse* (בִּרְקִיעַ, birᵉqiăʿ), which implies that the expanse is where the sun, moon and stars are located — that is, *interstellar space*.[75] As

---

71 Although the boundaries of the sky are indeterminate, it is certainly visible in a phenomenological sense.

72 Kline, 'Space and Time,' 7–8.

73 i.e. in the expanse, which did not exist yet!

74 Kline, 'Space and Time,' 6.

75 D. Russell Humphreys, *Starlight and Time* (Green Forest, Arkansas, Master Books, 1994), 58–59.

noted in the previous chapter, 'above the earth across the expanse of the sky' (Genesis 1:20) is an inaccurate translation of the underlying Hebrew. It is better translated 'over the surface of the expanse of the heavens.' To an observer looking up at the sky, birds fly *over the face* of the expanse (that is, in earth's atmosphere), not *in* the expanse.

In addition, the 'waters' (מַיִם, *māyĭm*) of day two are the same as those of day one. However, on day five the sea creatures were to fill the 'water in the seas' (הַמַּיִם בַּיַּמִּים, *hămmăyĭm băyyămmîm*), which were created on day three (v. 10). But according to Kline's schema, day three is contemporaneous with day six, not day five! Furthermore, the sea creatures were commanded to 'be fruitful' (פְּרוּ, *pᵉrû*), 'increase in number' (רְבוּ, *rᵉbû*) and 'fill' (מִלְאוּ, *mĭlᵉʾû*) the seas, and the birds (or winged creatures in general) were commanded to 'increase on the land' (יִרֶב בָּאָרֶץ, *yĭrᵉb bāʿărĕş*). Despite Kline's claim to the contrary, there is no philological or contextual evidence to indicate that God intended birds to rule or govern anything. In fact, in nature, birds reproduce 'on the earth' (v. 22). Birds merely fly in sky — they do not live, rule, or populate it.

It should also be noted that the focus of day two is the creation of the *expanse* between the waters, *not the waters themselves*, which were already in existence at the beginning of day two. It should also be asked why the waters *below* the expanse are singled out? Kline makes no mention of the waters *above* the expanse, presumably because they do not fit into his pattern. Indeed, the lack of correspondence between day two and day five completely undermines the entire schema.

Day Three and Day Six

Continuing the 'kings' and 'kingdoms' theme, Kline notes that humanity has been commissioned by God to rule over the creation.[76] But Kline is again highly selective in his presentation of the relationship between the two days. Humanity was not commissioned to rule over the land, the seas, and the vegetation created on day three, but over the land animals created that same day, and over the fish and birds created the previous day! Humanity was not told to 'rule' the earth, but to 'fill' and 'subdue' it.

Humans along with those animals which have 'the breath of life,' were also given specific vegetation for food. But again, this provision does not imply any notion of 'ruling.'

Again, Kline fails to integrate the many details of both days. On day three, why does God specifically call dry ground 'land' and gathered waters 'seas'? On day six, what is the significance of the commission to increase, fill the earth, and subdue it? Why is there no parallel on day three? Why the repetition concerning man created in the image of God and our task of ruling over the animal kingdom?

Even if Kline's so-called parallelism is accepted, E.J. Young points out that there is still an implicit chronology in the account: day one/day four → day

---

76 Kline, 'Space and Time,' 6.

two/day five → day three/day six.[77] Note that the sun and moon are placed *in the expanse* on day four, which (according to Kline's framework) occurs *at the same time as day one*. This would imply the expanse existed *before* day one/day four, but this clearly contradicts verses 6–8 which state that the expanse was created on day two!

In regard to the 'there was evening and there was morning — the [Xth] day' pattern, Kline argues that 'when we find that God's upper level activity of issuing creative fiats from his heavenly throne is pictured as transpiring in a week of earthly days, we readily recognize that, in keeping with the pervasive contextual pattern, this is a literary figure, an earthly, lower register time metaphor for an upper register, heavenly reality.'[78] But this is inconsistent with the rest of his interpretation, where lower register elements such as the 'earth' (Genesis 1:1), the 'deep' (Genesis 1:2), and the fulfillments of the six days, are all concrete, not figurative. If Kline views the creation days as figurative, why does he not view the creation of land (day three) and the creation of animals and man (day six) as figurative, since these are all part of the lower register? Kline's belief that the pattern of days is simply a detail in the creation-week picture[79] is far too simplistic and all too convenient.

The Sabbath of Day Seven

Regarding day seven, Kline believes it exclusively relates to God and the upper register:

> It is precisely the (temporary) exclusion of man from this heavenly Sabbath of God that gives rise to the two-register cosmology. At the Consummation, God's people will enter his royal rest, the seventh day of creation (Heb. 4:4, 9, 10), but until then, the seventh creation day does not belong to the lower register world of human solar day experience. It is heaven time, not earth time.[80]

The unending nature of day seven differentiates it from solar days, which Kline claims is confirmed by the treatment of God's rest in Hebrews 4:

> If the seventh day were not an unending Sabbath-rest for God but a literal day, would the next day be another work day, introducing another week of work and rest for him, to be followed by an indefinite repetition of this pattern? Are we to replace the Sabbath-Consummation doctrine of biblical eschatology with a mythological concept of cyclic time? In the Genesis prologue the unending nature of God's Sabbath is signalized by the absence of the evening-morning formula from the account of the seventh day.[81]

But arguing for a long Sabbath based on the missing 'and there was evening and there was morning — the [Xth] day' is an argument from silence, which

---

77 E.J. Young, *Studies in Genesis One* (Grand Rapids, Michigan, Baker, 1964), 69.

78 Kline, 'Space and Time,' 7.

79 Ibid., 10.

80 Ibid.

81 Ibid.

Poythress describes as 'worthless' given that 'the amount of omitted information in *any* historical narrative is enormous' and therefore, it would be 'rash' to claim that certain information 'could *not* have been honestly omitted.'[82]

Kline's appeal to Hebrews 4:3–4 is also misguided. As noted in chapter 6, God's 'rest' refers to the kingdom of God. The author merely quotes Genesis 2:2 in order to explain that the invitation to enter God's 'rest' has not just been open since the time of the exodus, but has been open ever since the creation of the world because that is when God ceased His creative work and began resting. Thus Paul Ellingworth suggests God's rest in Genesis 2:2 is a long period of time *beginning* with the seventh day of creation, not that the Sabbath *is* the seventh day.[83] Nowhere in the text is it equated with the seventh day of creation, nor is there any grammatical or contextual data suggesting any such equation.

Blocher, on the other hand, argues for a non-literal Sabbath based on Jesus' statement in John 5:19. Concerning the Son doing 'what He sees the Father doing,' Blocher argues that Jesus' reasoning is only sound if the Father acts during the Sabbath — only then, would the Son also have the right to act on the Sabbath.[84] Therefore, he concludes the Sabbath must be something other than a literal day. But as Frederic Howe points out, John 5:17 indicates that this "work" is closely identified with the mission of the Messiah. No contextual evidence allows this to reflect back to the work of God in creation.'[85] And, in any case, Blocher's argument fails because the sense of שָׁבַת (*šābaṭ*, 'cease', 'rest') on day seven is the ceasing of *creative* work, not the ceasing of all work, so there is no reason why day seven should be understood as anything other than a literal day.

Other Objections

The literary framework view appears to be based more on imagination than on the biblical text. Indeed, Mark Ross openly admits that this interpretation is not the first impression one gets from the text.[86] The parallels and relationships either are artificial, stretched, or non-existent, and the syntactical relationship between the days are not taken into account. The whole approach appears to be arbitrary and inconsistent, and shows little regard for the genre of the text.[87]

Furthermore, if the days are indeed a literary device then it should be possible to find similar schemas in other biblical or ancient Near Eastern writings. Yet no

---

82 Vern Sheridan Poythress, 'Adequacy of Language and Accommodation' in Radmacher and Preus, 373.

83 Paul Ellingworth, *The Epistle to the Hebrews*, NIGTC (Grand Rapids, Michigan, Eerdmans, 1993), 249.

84 Blocher, *In the Beginning*, 57.

85 Frederic R. Howe, 'The Age of the Earth Part 2: An Appraisal of Some Current Evangelical Positions' *BSac* 142 (April 1985), 124.

86 Mark Ross, 'The Framework Hypothesis,' 113.

87 The genre of the creation account is clearly historical narrative. See chapter 4, 'Creation and the Fall: Genre and message of the Genesis account.'

such parallel can be found. In fact, E.J. Young pointed out that the framework interpretation of Genesis 1 originated with Arie Noordtzij as late as 1924,[88] so the question must be asked how this rather eccentric interpretation managed to escape the attention of thousands of commentators (including the Talmudic commentators) over the centuries?

Note also that the driving force behind the framework interpretation is the desire to divorce the theology of Genesis from its historical basis. This separation of history and theology allows scientists to be 'free of biblical constraints in hypothesizing about cosmic origins' with regard to the time frame, and the order and sequence of events.[89]

By viewing the text of Genesis 1 as something other than historical narrative, advocates of the framework hypothesis unwittingly cast doubt on the historicity of the people and events described. In other words, although proponents of the framework hypothesis still believe that the people and events in Genesis 1 are truly historical, they have no exegetical basis for doing so, because ultimately this interpretation implies that the events described in the creation account never actually happened — or at least never happened in the way they are described.

Literal Day View

This interpretation has been the orthodox position of the church throughout history up until the early nineteenth century,[90] and virtually everyone agrees that this is the most natural reading of the text. Nevertheless, most interpreters — including evangelicals — now reject this view. This change did not occur overnight but over a period of about 300 years. Nor did the change occur as a result of conclusive contradictory exegetical evidence, but as a result of accepting the truth claims of scientists over the propositional revelation of Scripture. Many interpreters have uncritically accepted scientists' claims of superior knowledge, precision, and objectivity, and naïvely placed their faith in the verification and peer review process.[91] Therefore, they are convinced that modern science has shown that a recent creation is not only scientifically impossible but goes against an enormous amount of empirical data. For example, evidence from geology and astronomy is said to indicate an age of the universe in the order of billions, not thousands of years. Thus, many commentators have felt compelled to reinterpret the creation account in the ways outlined above.

As shown in chapters 1 and 2, the propositional truth of Scripture must always take precedence over the speculations and ideological interpretations of raw empirical data. The Bible must be allowed to speak for itself, instead of being squeezed to fit the latest scientific consensus.

---

88 E.J. Young, *Studies in Genesis One*, 44.

89 Kline, 'Space and Time' 2.

90 See chapter 3, 'Creation and Genesis: An historical survey.'

91 For a detailed explanation of the limitations of the peer review process see Andrew S. Kulikovsky, 'Creationism, Science and Peer Review' *JoC* 22/1 (2008), 44–49.

The meaning of יוֹם

There is no doubt that יוֹם (*yôm*, 'day') can refer to something other than a 24-hour day.[92] But does it refer to a non 24-hour day in Genesis 1? Elsewhere, whenever a number modifies *yôm* it always refers to a literal 24-hour day, and the presence of וַיְהִי־עֶרֶב וַיְהִי־בֹקֶר (*wăyᵉhî-ĕrĕb wăyᵉhî-bōqĕr*, 'and then there was evening, and then there was morning'), strongly suggests a 24-hour day was meant. Wenham admits: 'There can be little doubt that here "day" has its basic sense of a 24-hour period. The mention of morning and evening, the enumeration of the days, and the divine rest on the seventh show that a week of divine activity is being described here.'[93] Blocher also acknowledges that the numbered days and the mention of 'evening' and 'morning' diminishes the possibility of a metaphorical day, and considers a 24-hour day the most obvious understanding.[94]

The use of *yôm* in Deuteronomy 4:32 offers another clue to its meaning in Genesis 1. In this text, *yôm* is part of a temporal phrase: אֱלֹהִים אָדָם עַל־הָאָרֶץ מִן־הַיּוֹם אֲשֶׁר בָּרָא (*min-hăyyôm ᵃšĕr bārā ᵉlōhîm ādām āl-hā ārĕṣ*, 'from the day that God created man on the earth'). This same phrase occurs twenty-three times in the Old Testament and clearly refers to a normal 24-hour day,[95] implying that 'the day God created man on the earth' (day six) was also a normal 24-hour day.

The actual description of the first day also suggests a 24-hour day. In Genesis 1:5, 'day' is defined as the period of light, and 'night' as the period of darkness. The description is then terminated by 'and there was evening and there was morning — one day.' Therefore, a day ('one day') is defined as period of light and a period of darkness separated by an evening and a morning — a literal 24-hour day.[96] Indeed, Thomas Aquinas stated: 'The words "one day" are used when the day is first established, to denote that one day is made up of 24 hours. Hence, by mentioning "one," the measure of a natural day is fixed.'[97] Ambrose also noted that the term 'one day' was used because 'on it the foundation of things was laid.'[98]

Likewise, John Stek admits:

> Surely there is no sign or hint within the narrative [of Genesis 1] itself
> that the author thought his 'days' to be irregular designations — first

---

92 The use of *yôm* in Genesis 2:4 is often cited as such an example. But in this case, *yôm* has a prefixed preposition (*bᵉyôm*), and stands in a construct relationship with the infinitive form of *ᶜāśāh*, i.e. literally 'in the day of making.' This causes it to function as a temporal clause which the NIV renders as 'when.' See BDB, Holladay and GKC §114e.

93 Gordon H. Wenham, *Genesis 1–15*, WBC (Dallas, Word, 1987), 19.

94 Blocher, *In the Beginning*, 44–45.

95 GRAMCORD search using Groves-Wheeler Westminster Morphological Text v. 3.1.

96 The use of 'day', 'days' and 'night' in Genesis 1:14–18 can *only* possibly refer to literal 24-hour days.

97 Aquinas, as cited by Jack P. Lewis, 'The Days of Creation: An Historical Survey' *JETS* 32/4 (December 1989), 451–452.

98 Lewis, 'The Days of Creation: An Historical Survey,' 447.

a series of undefined periods, then a series of solar days — or that the 'days' he bounded with 'evening and morning' could possibly be understood as long aeons of time. His language is plain and simple, and he speaks in plain and simple terms of one of the most common elements in humanity's experience of the world.[99]

Hamilton concurs: 'And whoever wrote Gen. 1 believed he was talking about literal days.'[100]

As noted earlier, *yôm* can only refer to something other than a normal day when situated in certain contexts. Hasel explains: '[E]xtended, non-literal meanings of this Hebrew term have special linguistic and contextual connections which indicate clearly that a non-literal meaning is intended. If such special linguistic connections are absent, the term *yôm* does not have an extended, non-literal meaning; it has its normal meaning of a literal day of 24-hours.'[101] It is important to note that none of these 'special linguistic connections' can be found in Genesis 1. Indeed, in their entries under *yôm*, the standard Hebrew lexicons explicitly cite Genesis 1:5 as an example of where this word refers to a 24-hour day.[102] Therefore, when it comes to deciding on the meaning of *yôm* in Genesis 1 '[t]he burden of proof … is on those who do not attribute to *yôm* … its normal and most common interpretation…'[103]

Those who reject the literal day view have put forward various counter arguments. Newman and Eckelman, for example, write:

> that yom means a twenty-four-hour day when used with ordinal numbers (1st, 2nd, 3rd, etc.), has the advantage that no clear counter-example can be cited with yom meaning a long period of time. The force of this observation is greatly reduced, however, when one considers that the Bible has no occasion to mention several long periods of time which might be numbered, except the days of creation. In any case, it is not clear why an adjective such as an ordinal number should change the range of meaning of the noun yom.[104]

However, such arguments surely beg the question. In order to claim that Genesis 1 is unique, Newman and Eckelmann must *assume* that the days refer to long periods of time, which is actually what they need to prove. Again, if the author of Genesis 1 intended to communicate a long period of time, several better linguistic options were available.[105]

---

99 John H. Stek, 'What Says the Scripture?' in H.J. Van Till, *Portraits of Creation* (Grand Rapids, Michigan, Eerdmans, 1990), 237–8.

100 Hamilton, *Book of Genesis: Chapters 1–17*, 53.

101 Gerhard F. Hasel, 'The Days of Creation in Genesis 1: Literal "Days" or Figurative "Periods/ Epochs" of Time?' *Origins* 21/1 (1994), 18.

102 See entries for יוֹם in Holladay, BDB, *HALOT*. See also *TDOT* 4:7–32 and *THAT* 1:707–26.

103 Hamilton, *Book of Genesis: Chapters 1–17*, 53.

104 Newman and Eckelmann, 61–62. This argument is echoed by Walter L. Bradley and Roger Olsen ('The Trustworthiness of Scripture in Areas Relating to Natural Science' in Radmacher and Preus, 299), and Hugh N. Ross, *Creation and Time*, 46–7.

105 e.g. דוֹר (*dôr*, 'period', 'age') or עוֹלָם (*'olam*, 'long duration').

Newman and Eckelmann also fail to understand why an ordinal number adjective should modify the semantic range of yôm. This is a surprising comment, and shows a great deal of linguistic naïvety. An adjective's primary purpose is to modify the noun!

Collins, on the other hand, questions the grammatical basis of claiming that yôm modified by a number equates to a literal day. Although every instance of yôm modified by a number refers to a 24-hour day, Collins correctly points out that this alone is not enough to form a valid inductive argument. As Collins explains, an explanation of *why* this construction must refer to a literal 24-hour day is required:

> For a lexical argument such as this one, this explanation would be in terms of the combinational rules of the Hebrew word ym 'day' and the kinds of words with which it is being combined. For this argument to be good, then, we must propose a combinational rule for the Hebrew word ym when it is modified by a number. We would then have to show that the rule applies in every case; and to do that we would have to show that it was the *rule*, and not the *context* of the other usages, which secured the interpretation of ym.[106]

In other words, one must explain why the numeral, apart from any other contextual factors, constrains the meaning of yôm to a 24-hour day. Such an explanation has yet to be given.

Note, however, that this offers little comfort to those who believe the days of Genesis 1 refer to long periods of time. Although the occurrence of yôm with a modifying numeral fails as a strictly grammatical argument for literal days, this construction does form a solid *contextual* argument. In other words, in a context where yôm is modified by a numeral it always, without exception, refers to a literal 24-hour day, and never refers to anything like a long period of time.[107] In fact, Numbers 29:12–35 also describes a numbered sequence of days, all of which clearly refer to normal 24-hour days.

Others claim that Hosea 6:2, Isaiah 9:14, and Zechariah 14:7 are clear exceptions to the belief that yôm modified by a number always refers to a literal day.[108]

In the case of Hosea 6:2, the text reads: 'After two days he will revive us; on the third day he will restore us, that we may live in his presence.' However, this verse is set in poetic parallelism — and parallelism of a very specific kind. This

---

106 C. John Collins, 'Reading Genesis 1:1–2:3 as an Act of Communication,' 148–149. Original emphasis. Similarly, Hugh Ross (*Creation and Time*, 46–7) also contends there is no rule of Hebrew grammar relating to ordinals attached to yôm denoting a 24-hour day.

107 An important example of a grammatical rule based on a contextual argument is the Granville Sharpe rule in Hellenistic Greek grammar. This rule states that when the definite article is followed by two singular, non-proper, substantives separated by και ('and'), then the two substantives always refer to the same thing or person.

108 See Perry G. Phillips, 'Are the Days of Genesis Longer than 24 Hours? The Bible Says, "Yes!"' *IBRIRep* 40 (1991); Hayward, *Creation and Evolution*, 164; Don Stoner, *A New Look at an Old Earth* (Eugene, Oregon, Harvest House, 1997), 46–48.

particular parallelism is a common Semitic device, which takes the form X //
X + 1.[109] Given that these instances are part of a well-defined Semitic device,
they must be interpreted in accordance with that device. In this case, the use of
'two days' and 'three days' communicates that the restoration mentioned in the
previous verse will happen quickly and surely.[110] Therefore, these instances must
refer to normal days as opposed to long periods, otherwise the literary device
would lose its meaning. In other words, the restoration would *not* be quick and
certain if the days were long periods of time.

There may also be a subtle prophetic allusion to the restoration of humanity
after the death and resurrection of Christ — especially since much of Hosea
serves to prophetically illustrate future events. Again, this demands that the days
be taken as 24-hour days.

In the case of Isaiah 9:14 (9:13 in the Hebrew), Phillips simply asserts that
'one day' ('single day,' NIV, NASB) is 'clearly figurative' but offers no exegetical
justification. On the contrary, there is no reason to think that this 'day' is
anything other than a normal day.

Don Stoner cites Zechariah 14:7 as another exception: 'It will be a unique
day, without daytime or nighttime — a day known to the LORD. When evening
comes, there will be light.' Stoner believes this 'unique day' refers to the New
Jerusalem, the eternal state. But if this is a reference to the eternal state — an
infinite period of time — it can hardly be described as 'unique!'

The 'day' in question is surely the same as that mentioned in verses 1, 4, and
6, and it is clear from verse 5 that on 'that day' the Lord will come. In other
words, it describes a specific time at which a space-time *event* occurs in the
future. How can the coming of the Lord take a long period of time? It is an
event: at one moment on that day, He will be absent — in the next moment He
will have returned. Therefore, the 'unique day' in Zechariah 14:7 does indeed
refer to a literal 24-hour day.

Evening and Morning

Walter Bradley and Roger Olsen consider עֶרֶב (*ĕrĕḇ*, 'evening') and בֹּקֶר
(*bōqĕr*, 'morning') to be figurative.[111] Similarly, Hugh Ross claims these
words may be used metaphorically and cites the Brown-Driver-Briggs (BDB)
Hebrew lexicon and the *Theological Wordbook of the Old Testament* (*TWOT*) as
support.[112] However, the 'metaphorical' renderings for *ĕrĕḇ* and *bōqĕr* listed
in BDB and *TWOT* only apply if clearly inferred from the context or literary
genre, or if they are modified by various prepositions. None of these situations
apply to Genesis 1.

---

109 See W.M.W. Roth, 'The Numerical Sequence x/x+1 in the Old Testament,' *VT* 12 (1962),
    300–1. For more examples, see Job 5:19; Proverbs 6:16; 30:15, 18; Amos 1:3, 6, 9.

110 See H. Ronald Vandermey, *Hosea*, Everyman's Bible Commentary (Chicago, Moody, 1981).

111 Bradley and Olsen, 'The Trustworthiness of Scripture in Areas Relating to Natural Science,'
    300.

112 Hugh N. Ross, *Creation and Time*, 46.

In any case, note that in Genesis 1 both 'evening' and 'morning' are immediately preceded by the *waw*-consecutive Qal imperfect וַיְהִי (*wăyĕhî*, 'and there was', 'then came'). Considering this clause always comes *after* the description of God's creative activity, and evening *precedes* morning, it is unlikely that it refers to the beginning and ending of a given day. Rather, it most likely marks the period of time between sunset and sunrise when no creative activity was taking place.[113]

Nevertheless, Otto Helweg insists that 'and there was evening and there was morning,' which terminates the description of each day, does not necessarily refer to a 24-hour day, but may also refer to a long or indefinite period.[114] He argues that the vision of Daniel 8 covers a long period of time, and in Daniel 8:26, the Hebrew for 'evenings and mornings' is actually singular. Therefore, he concludes that this is an instance of 'evening and morning' referring to an indefinite epoch. However, David Fouts points out that using the singular is normal practice for these Hebrew words. The singular forms are commonly used as collectives and translated as plurals, which appears to be the case in Daniel 8:26. The same clause is used in Daniel 8:14, which is the antecedent of Daniel 8:26. This instance also has a singular form yet should be translated as a plural since it is modified by the number '2,300', so Helweg's objection is invalid.[115]

In addition, the reference to evening and morning before the creation of the sun has caused many to reject the literal day interpretation,[116] but this conclusion is unwarranted. Although the sun was not created until day four, light *was* created on day one. As discussed earlier, light could have come from a temporary light source since all that is required for sunset and sunrise to occur is a directional light source, and a rotating earth — none of which are precluded by the text.[117] Alternatively, the terms 'evening' and 'morning' may simply refer to a particular time during a normal day rather than actual lighting conditions.[118]

The Events of Day Six

Another objection raised against the literal day view is that the events of day six could not have been completed in less than twenty-four hours.[119]

---

113 Hamilton, *Book of Genesis: Chapters 1–17*, 121.

114 Otto J. Helweg, 'How Long and Evening and Morning?', *JoC* 11/3 (1997), 300.

115 David M. Fouts, 'How Short an Evening and Morning?', *JoC* 11/3 (1997), 304.

116 e.g. Wenham, *Genesis 1–15*, 40. Roger Forster and Paul Marston (*Reason, Science and Faith* [Crowborough, East Sussex: Monarch, 1999], 252) claim that E.J. Young admitted the first three days were 'non-solar' and therefore not 24-hour days. However, Young's statement regarding the non-solar nature of days 1–3 does not mean that he rejected the 24-hour view and understood them to be long time periods. Rather, Young simply stated that the first three days were not governed by the sun. See E.J. Young, *Studies in Genesis One* (Grand Rapids, Michigan, Baker, 1964), 103–104.

117 See sections on day one and day four.

118 See discussion of days one and four in chapter 6.

119 Hugh N. Ross, *Creation and Time*, 51. Also Youngblood, *The Book of Genesis*, 44–45; Archer, 'A Response to The Trustworthiness of Scripture' 325; and Hayward, *Creation and Evolution*, 164–165.

A close reading of Genesis 1–2 reveals the following events occurred on day six:

- God creates land animals (1:24–25).
- God creates Adam (2:7).
- God planted a garden (2:8–9).
- God places Adam into the garden (2:15).
- God gives Adam instructions regarding the Tree of the Knowledge of Good and Evil (2:16–17).
- God brought the animals to Adam to be named (2:19–20).
- God sedated Adam (2:21).
- God removes bone and tissue from Adam's side (2:21).
- God closes the wound (2:21).
- God creates Eve (2:22).
- God brings Eve to Adam (2:22).
- Adam calls Eve 'woman' (2:23).
- God instructs Adam and Eve in regard to their work and dominion (1:28–29).

Note that most of these events are direct supernatural actions of God, implying that they were completed more or less instantaneously.

The naming of all the land animals and birds in such a short period of time, on the other hand, does pose a problem. How could Adam have named millions of different species in less than twelve hours?[120]

There are several factors that need to be considered which may not be immediately obvious to the casual reader. Firstly, Adam did not have to go out and round up or track any of these animals. Genesis 2:19 clearly states that *God brought the animals to Adam*. Secondly, although many objectors have claimed that the species Adam had to observe and name would have numbered in the millions, the actual number would almost certainly have been only a small fraction of this.

Note that Scripture explicitly states that Adam named all the 'livestock' (בְּהֵמָה, *bᵉhēmāh*), the 'birds of the air' (עוֹף הַשָּׁמַיִם, *ʿôp haśśāmāyim*) and all the 'beasts of the field' (חַיַּת הַשָּׂדֶה, *ḥayyāṭ haśśādeh*). There is no indication that Adam named the fish in the sea, or any other marine organisms, nor any of the insects, beetles, and arachnids. In fact, of the two million known species, 98 percent are invertebrates, which include a variety of animals from sponges, worms, and jellyfish, to mollusks and insects. The remaining 2 percent are vertebrates and number

---

120 Regarding the actual number of species on earth, R.M. May ('How many species are there on Earth?' *Science* 241 [1988], 1441) writes: 'At the purely factual level, we do not know to within an order of magnitude how many species of *plants and animals* we share the globe with: *fewer than 2 million are currently classified*, and estimates of the total number range from *under 5 million to more than 50 million*.' My emphasis.

approximately 40,000 species.[121] This number is further reduced when the 25,000 marine vertebrates[122] and 4,000 amphibians[123] are discounted since they clearly do not fit into any of the categories of animals listed in Genesis 2:20.

In addition, assuming that speciation has been an ongoing occurrence since creation, the 11,000 vertebrate species in question would have most likely descended from a much smaller number of proto-species, equivalent to what taxonomists call a *genus*[124] and what the Genesis account calls a 'kind.'[125] Since many *genera* contain dozens — even hundreds — of species, it is far more likely that Adam had to name only a couple of thousand of these proto-species — a task which could easily have been achieved in a few hours.[126]

It is important to note that the purpose of parading all the animals before Adam was not merely so that he would give them names but to reinforce the fact that he was entirely different from the rest of creation, and that none of these animals could ever serve as a physical, emotional, intellectual, or spiritual companion.

Other objections against the sixth day being a normal day include Adam's capability for linguistic communication and his sense of 'loneliness.' Critics argue that a period of time much longer than twenty-four hours is required to learn a language and to feel a sense of loneliness.

In the case of linguistic communication, it appears that Adam's linguistic abilities were inherent, not acquired. Because Adam was immediately able to communicate with his Creator, one can only assume that God pre-programmed this ability into Adam's brain at the moment of his creation.

The second objection is due to a misreading of the biblical text. Genesis 2:18 states that it was not good for Adam to be 'alone' (Heb. לְבַדּוֹ, *lᵉḇadô*). Being 'alone' is not the same as being 'lonely.' The latter requires some time; the former does not.

Day Seven: The Sabbath

Many interpreters have argued that the lack of the terminating formula 'And there was evening and there was morning — the [Xth] day' directly implies that the seventh day has not yet ended and still continues.[127] For example, R. Laird Harris, argues:

---

121 David Burnie, 'Animal' Microsoft® Encarta® Online Encyclopedia 2002, <http://encarta.msn.com>.

122 James W. Orr 'Fish' Microsoft® Encarta® Online Encyclopedia 2002, <http://encarta.msn.com>.

123 David Burnie 'Vertebrate' Microsoft® Encarta® Online Encyclopedia 2002, <http://encarta.msn.com>.

124 Or possibly the higher taxonomic order known as a *family*.

125 See Pete J. Williams, 'What does *min* mean?' *JoC* 11/3 (1997), 344–352.

126 Assuming Adam had to name 2,500 proto-species (*genera*), and he named a single proto-species every five seconds, it would take him approximately three hours and forty-five minutes to complete the task even if we include a five-minute break every hour.

127 e.g. Hugh N. Ross, *The Genesis Question*, 63–65; Davis A. Young, *Creation and the Flood*, 85–86; Youngblood, *The Book of Genesis*, 45; C. John Collins, 'Reading Genesis 1:1–2:3 as an Act of Communication,' 137; Gleason L. Archer, *Encyclopedia of Bible Difficulties* (Grand Rapids, Michigan, Zondervan, 1982), 62.

> Now if God's seventh day is an eternal day, as argued in the Psalms and Hebrews and yet it is paralleled to man's seventh day Sabbath, it follows that our weekdays cannot be duplicates of God's days of creation and rest, but are symbolic thereof. It seems to be an inescapable conclusion that our seventh day 24-hour Sabbath is symbolic of God's eternal Sabbath of rest from creation. If so, then there is no reason at all to deny that our particular six 24 hour days of labor are symbolic of, not equivalent to, God's six long days of creative labor.[128]

However, Herman Hoeksema has highlighted the futility of such an argument:

> It has sometimes been alleged that the seventh day, the day of God's rest, certainly must have been a longer period, seeing that the Lord God is still resting of His work of creation, and that therefore it is exegetically very well conceivable that also the six days of creation were long periods. But against this it may be remarked, in the first place, that this argument annihilates itself. For if this were the significance of the seventh day, then the seventh day lasts forever. God never creates again. In that case also the other days of the creation week were everlasting. And this last supposition is, of course, nonsense. But, in the second place, this certainly is not the significance of God's rest on the seventh day. This rest was a hallowing, through which the Lord God, together with His creature that was created in His image, rejoiced in all the works of His hands. And this certainly was not an everlasting day, although the rest of God was [an] image of the eternal rest in His tabernacle. But the day itself was twenty-four hours. Also the first sabbath was a common day.[129]

Poythress also asserts that day seven is unending,[130] but elsewhere he contradicts himself by arguing that the Hebrew tenses used in Genesis 2:2–3 indicate that the seventh day is in the past.[131] But if the seventh day is in the past, how can it also be unending?

Furthermore, arguing for a long Sabbath based on the missing terminating formula is an argument from silence — its absence does not necessarily imply that it did not happen. Indeed, Poythress himself has pointed out that such arguments are 'worthless.'[132]

In contrast, Jack Lewis points out that '[t]he hallowing of the seventh day (Gen. 2:1–2) presupposes the literal character of the six days. Primarily interested

---

128 Harris, 'The Length of the Creative Days in Genesis 1,' 110. Other commentators, including Hugh Ross, Davis Young, and Meredith Kline, cite the reference to the creation sabbath in Hebrews 4 as added support for this argument. See A.S. Kulikovsky ('God's Rest in Hebrews 4:1–11' *JoC* 13/2 [1999], 61–62) for a refutation.

129 Hoeksema, *Reformed Dogmatics*, 180.

130 Vern Sheridan Poythress, 'Response to Nelson and Reynolds' in J.P. Moreland and John Mark Reynolds (editors), *Three Views on Creation and Evolution* (Grand Rapids, Michigan, Zondervan, 1999), 92.

131 Poythress, 'Response to Newman' in Moreland and Reynolds, 149. In actual fact, Poythress is incorrect on this point as well. For a full discussion of this verse and its quotation in Hebrews 4, see Kulikovsky 'God's Rest in Hebrews 4:1–11'.

132 Poythress, 'Adequacy of Language and Accommodation,' 373.

in declaring the power of God, the writer of Genesis would have known nothing of the millennia now assumed by geologists and palaeontologists.'[133]

Exodus 20:11 and 31:17

Both Exodus 20:11 and 31:17 clearly state that God created the universe 'in six days.'[134] Of course, those who interpret the days non-literally disagree and have presented numerous arguments to the contrary.

Poythress, for example, claims that on the basis of Exodus 20:11, the creation week is analogous to, not identical with, man's work week.[135] Similarly, Gordon Wenham asserts that this verse draws attention to the correspondence between God's work and man's, and God's rest as a model for the Sabbath, but adds that this does not imply that the six days were the same as human days.[136]

Neither Exodus 20:11 nor 31:17, however, contain anything that could possibly indicate an analogical comparison or correspondence. On the contrary, the use of כִּי (ki, 'for,' 'because') to link the creation week to the working week indicates that the creation week forms the *basis* of, and establishes the pattern for, both the working week and the observance of the Sabbath.[137] In fact, if the reference to the six days were merely an analogy, and 'day' can refer to an indefinite period of time, then this commandment would become incoherent. The reader would be unable to determine whether humans are meant to work for six days, six weeks, six months, or six years, before taking leave.

W.G.T. Shedd presents a slightly more sophisticated objection:

> the seven days of the human week are copies of the seven days of the Divine week. The 'sun divided days' are images of the 'God-divided days.' This agrees with the Biblical representation generally. The human is a copy of the Divine; not the Divine of the human. Human fatherhood and sonship are finite copies of the trinitarian fatherhood and sonship. Human justice, benevolence, holiness, mercy, etc. are imitations of corresponding Divine qualities. The reason given for man's rest upon the seventh solar day is, that God rested upon the seventh creative day. Ex. 20:11. But this does not prove that the Divine rest was only twenty-four hours in duration; any more than the fact that human sonship is a copy of the Divine, proves that the latter is sexual.[138]

---

133 Lewis, 'The Days of Creation: An Historical Survey,' 433.

134 The structure of six days, followed by a seventh day, is also found in *Enuma Elish* (Tablet V, lines 16–17) and twice in *The Gilgamesh Epic* (Tablets XI, lines 127–30 and 142–6) with each occurrence clearly referring to literal 24-hour days. See James B. Pritchard, *The Ancient Near East vol. 1: An Anthology of Texts and Pictures* (Princeton, PUP, 1958), 36, 69.

135 Poythress, 'Response to Nelson and Reynolds,' 93.

136 Wenham, *Genesis 1–15*, 40. See also Bradley and Olsen, 'The Trustworthiness of Scripture in Areas Relating to Natural Science' 300, and Kline, 'Space and Time'; Blocher, *In the Beginning*, 57; C. John Collins, 'Reading Genesis 1:1–2:3 as an Act of Communication,' 142.

137 This interpretation was also given in one of the midrash. See Lewis, 'The Days of Creation: An Historical Survey,' 450.

138 W.G.T. Shedd, *Dogmatic Theology* (Grand Rapids, Michigan, Zondervan, 1971), 477.

Nevertheless, Shedd's argument suffers from two fatal problems: Firstly, his distinction between a 'human week' and a 'divine week' is artificial. If God stands outside of time (or, at least, does not experience time as humans do), then what exactly is a 'divine week'? Indeed, the very concepts of daytime and nighttime, evening and morning, are meaningless to an eternal, omnipresent God. These concepts are unique to the human experience.[139] Secondly, the idea of sonship does not inherently communicate a genetic relationship. An adopted son is just as much a son. And God the Son does not stand in a genetic relationship to God the Father.

Similarly, Archer argues that Exodus 20:11 does not demonstrate that the creation days were twenty-four hours, any more than the eight-day celebration of the Feast of Tabernacles (Leviticus 23:33–43) proves the wilderness wanderings, under Moses, lasted for eight days.[140] But these two situations are clearly not comparable. The Feast of Tabernacles served to remind the Israelites that their ancestors lived in tents when God brought them out of Egypt. The people were to live in tents for seven days 'so [their] descendants will know that [God] had the Israelites live in [tents] when [He] brought them out of Egypt' (v. 43). In contrast, the people were to work for six days and rest on the seventh '[f]or in six days the LORD made the heavens and the earth, the sea, and all that is in them, but he rested on the seventh day' (Exodus 20:11). In the case of the Feast of Tabernacles, the point of correspondence is explicitly stated as the act of living in booths, but for the working week the point of correspondence is explicitly stated as the duration of six days, so Archer's objection is invalid. Therefore, there is no reason not to see a direct correspondence between the creation days and the working week.

Blocher, however, attempts to minimize the significance of the two Exodus references by arguing that the absence of a reference to creation in Deuteronomy 5:12–15 suggests the Exodus verses should not be taken as too close a link with creation.[141] Note, however, that Deuteronomy is merely Moses' sermon on the Law (which is recorded in Exodus) — not the Law itself — and Blocher actually contradicts himself since one of the central theses of his own interpretation of the creation account, and the references to it in Exodus, is that it teaches a 'theology of the sabbath.'[142]

Blocher also argues that Exodus 31:17 is figurative since it uses figurative language in stating that 'God was refreshed.'[143] But this conclusion does not follow: the presence of a simple anthropomorphism does not imply the entire verse is anthropomorphic or figurative in any way.[144]

---

139   Of course, this human experience ultimately became part of the divine experience through the incarnation, but this just reinforces the point. Even God must take the form of a human in order to experience time.

140   Archer, 'A Response to The Trustworthiness of Scripture,' 329.

141   Blocher, *In the Beginning*, 48.

142   Blocher, *In the Beginning*, 50.

143   See also Hayward, *Creation and Evolution*, 163–164.

144   Blocher, *In the Beginning*, 48.

Yet another attempt to minimize the significance of Exodus 20:11 comes from C. John Collins, who claims that rendering עָשָׂה ('āśāh) as 'made' (which implies ontological origination) is misleading since it refers back to the same verb in verse 9, where the sense is working *on* something rather than *creating* it. Thus, Collins argues that verse 11 has nothing to do with ontological origination, and cannot be used to set up an identity between our work week and the length of the creation days.[145] This, however, is a very selective treatment of the text. The six days are explicitly linked to Genesis 1 and so it is clear that ontological origination is in view. Moreover, ontological origination does not necessarily imply *ex nihilo* acts of creation and, in any case, 'āśāh is used twelve times throughout Genesis 1–2.[146]

Not only is the literal day view the traditional interpretation of the church; the above analysis demonstrates that it is also the most exegetically sound, and the objections raised against it have little or no substance.

The Days of Creation and the Age of the Earth

Although the Scriptures give relatively few absolute temporal references and indicators, by applying elementary arithmetic to those temporal markers that are given — in particular, the genealogies of Genesis, Matthew, and Luke — it is possible to arrive at an approximate age of the earth. Indeed, this is precisely what Bishop James Ussher and John Lightfoot did in the sixteenth century when they arrived at creation dates of 4004 B.C. and 3960 B.C. respectively, and an age of the earth of approximately 6,000 years.

Because both Ussher and Lightfoot had made some dubious assumptions in their calculations, even the most conservative interpreters tend to reject these dates. Nevertheless, the approach they used is sound and may at least provide a 'ballpark' figure. Therefore, those who accept the literal-day view generally believe that the earth is about 6,000 to 10,000 years old.

On the other hand, there are many interpreters who believe the earth is much, much older. Regarding the date of the creation of mankind, most of these interpreters would more or less agree with those who adopt a young-earth position. Where they disagree with young-earth proponents, is the timing and sequence (and in some cases, the historical reality) of the creation events.

Those who hold to an old-earth interpretation generally do so because they are convinced that science has proved that the earth is billions of years old. Again, the level of authority the interpreter gives to scientific conclusions plays a big part in determining their final position.

Some young-earth proponents have attempted to minimize the scientific arguments by arguing that God created the universe with the 'appearance of age.' This line of argument may be appropriate in some cases. For example, Adam and Eve were created as adults and the trees in the garden of Eden were

---

145 C. John Collins, 'Reading Genesis 1:1–2:3 as an Act of Communication,' 142.

146 GRAMCORD search using Groves-Wheeler Westminster Morphological Text v. 3.1.

apparently producing fruit as soon as God had planted them and caused them to grow (Genesis 2:8–17). However, arguing that God created starlight en route so that it would not take billions of years to reach earth, or that He created fossils in the ground to fool unbelievers, or to test the faith of Christians, has rightly received much scorn, since it implies that God is deceptive because He has presented us with a history of creation (as inferred from the creation itself) that is false. This has been pointed out most forcefully by those who reject the literal 24-hour day view. However, these same people ironically make the very same mistake when they attempt to reinterpret the days of creation as anything other than literal, historical 24-hour days. Why did God use language which so strongly suggests a supernatural creation in six consecutive days, if he really intended to communicate a creation resulting in a combination of natural and supernatural events, and over a very long time period? Does this not also make God deceptive?

While some interpreters have appealed to various Scriptures in support of an old earth, Poythress (who himself believes in an old earth) admits that 'the alleged "biblical hints" of an old earth are quite weak and should be dropped from the argument.'[147]

A more sophisticated argument is given by Kline, who contends that, according to Genesis 2:5, God did not produce the plants of the field before he had established an environment with a watering system — the natural, normal precondition for plant life. Therefore the assumption underlying Genesis 2:5 is clearly that a *natural* mode of divine providence was in operation during the creation days. Because the literal solar-day interpretation entails each new creative act transpiring within a few hours or a day, the absence of vegetation or anything else at any given point would not last long enough to occasion special consideration of the reasons for it. Within that time-frame such a question would be practically irrelevant. So Kline concludes that Genesis 2:5 reflects an environmental situation that has lasted for a significant period.[148] In other words, Genesis 2:5 suggests that Genesis 1 is not a literal chronological account, and so there is no reason to deny the vast ages of the earth and universe proclaimed by modern science.

While Kline's interpretation of Genesis 2:5 is discussed in detail in the next chapter, Joseph Pipa highlights the completely arbitrary methodology involved:

> Moses' style in chapters two and three is as figurative if not more so than chapter 1 (description of the creation of man; a talking serpent; God's making clothing): why are not these acts made symbolic? Why are not chapters two and three made non-literal? ... Or why do we allow for supernatural intervention later in the Pentateuch (the plagues, crossing the Red Sea, the clothing of the children of Israel not wearing out) but

---

147 Poythress, 'Response to Newman,' 151.

148 Meredith G. Kline, 'Because it had not yet rained' *WTJ* 20 (1958), 149–150.

demand that only ordinary providence has been at work in the midst of the omnipotent creating work of God? It seems to me the method has no exegetical brakes. Each decision is made on the basis of the presuppositions of the interpreter.[149]

In contrast, there are several verses which suggest the earth is relatively young. The genealogy of Jesus in Luke 3:23–38 traces His ancestry right back to Adam. As Ussher and Lightfoot calculated (using the genealogy as a chronology), this would place the creation of Adam at around 6,000 to 7,000 years ago. Matthew 19:4 and Mark 10:6 state that 'at the beginning, the Creator [Gk. ὁ κτίσας ἀπ ἀρχῆς] "made them male and female,"' which is an obvious allusion to the creation account.[150] It is important to note that these verses tie the actual creation of Adam and Eve to the 'beginning' of creation rather than at some long indeterminate period afterwards. This alone rules out any notion of creation over a long period of time including theistic evolution and progressive creation, regardless of whether that view takes the form of a pictorial day interpretation, a day-age interpretation, or a literary framework interpretation.

Another example can be found in Isaiah 45:18: 'For this is what the LORD says — he who created the heavens, he is God; he who fashioned and made the earth, he founded it; he did not create it to be empty, but formed it to be inhabited ...' Note that this verse explicitly states that God's purpose was never to have an empty earth, but always to have it inhabited. Yet, if there were billions of years between the formation of the land on day three and the creation of mankind and the animals on day six, then this would surely be contrary to the Creator's intentions. If God's plans can never be thwarted, then why did He wait so long to populate the earth?

Summary

The position most in line with the exegetical data, the theology of God and man, and the context is that the days of creation are a sequence of normal 24-hour days which occurred in history around 6,000 to 10,000 years ago. In other words, the days of creation are a record of the very first week of the history of the universe.

Walton acknowledges that 'it is extremely difficult to conclude that anything other than a twenty-four-hour day was intended. It is not the text that causes people to think otherwise, only the demands of trying to harmonize with

---

149 Joseph A. Pipa, 'From Chaos to Cosmos: A Critique of the Non-literal Views of Genesis 1:1–2:3' in Pipa and Hall, 196–197.

150 Most English translations render ἀπὸ more literally as 'from'. This places the focus more on the duration of time since the beginning of creation rather than on the beginning itself. Nevertheless, both renderings place the creation of Adam and Eve at the beginning of creation.

modern science.'[151] This is clearly evident in the thinking of Bernard Ramm, who argued that because 'such a great array of geologists and theologians accept a metaphorical interpretation of the word day, the case for the literal day cannot be conclusive nor the objections to the metaphorical interpretation too serious.'[152] In light of the above (and the discussion of scientific methodology in an earlier chapter), it would be very difficult to honestly maintain Ramm's position.

---

151 Walton, *Genesis*, 81.

152 Ramm, *Christian View of Science of Scripture*, 145.

CHAPTER 8

Creation of Humanity and the Garden of Eden

Genesis 2:4–25 contains a detailed description of the creation of the first couple and their home — the Garden of Eden. God forms Adam from the dust of the earth and places him in a garden of paradise that supplied all his needs except one — the need for a suitable companion. So God creates a companion from Adam's own flesh.

The relationship between Genesis 1 and Genesis 2, however, has caused considerable controversy in the history of interpretation. Although they contain some common elements, the two chapters are quite different from each other. Chapter 2 has a very different structure to both chapter 1 and other ancient Near Eastern accounts.[1] While most liberal interpreters take these chapters as two different and somewhat contradictory accounts, those with a high view of Scripture see them as complementary but disagree over how they are to be harmonized. How then do these two chapters relate to one another? Where do the events described in chapter 2 fit into chapter 1?

Relationship Between Genesis 1 and Genesis 2

A Complementary Unit

Sailhamer and Blocher consider chapters 1 and 2 a unity.[2] Likewise, Hess and Cassuto argue that literary and comparative approaches show that the two accounts complement each other. Genesis 1 is a broad outline whereas Genesis 2 is an elaboration which focuses on mankind.[3]

Sailhamer understands the beginning of chapter 2 as a description of the condition of the land before the creation of mankind. It resembles the description of the land in Genesis 1:2 and focuses on the parts of the land that

---

1 Michael J. Kruger ('An Understanding of Genesis 2:5' *JoC* 11/1 [1997], 107) points out that 'All ancient near-Eastern creation accounts make substantial reference to the formation of the Sun, Moon, stars, oceans and seas, whereas these factors are entirely absent in Genesis 2.'

2 John H. Sailhamer, *The Pentateuch as Narrative* (Grand Rapids, Michigan, Zondervan, 1992), 81. _____, *Genesis*, EBC (Grand Rapids, Michigan, Zondervan, 1990), 19, 31; Blocher, 30–31.

3 Richard S. Hess, 'Genesis 1–2 in its Literary Context' *TynB* 41 (1990), 144, 152; Umberto Cassuto, *A Commentary on the Book of Genesis*, 2 volumes, translated by I. Adams (Jerusalem, Magnes Press, 1961), 1:89–92.

were to be directly affected by the fall (Genesis 3:8–24). Although Sailhamer erroneously identifies the 'land' of Genesis 1 with the Promised Land, he is correct in that the narrative points to the fact that before mankind was created (v. 7), the results of human rebellion and the effects of the fall had 'not yet' been felt on the land.[4]

The creation of man and woman is the concern of the whole of chapter 2. What the author had stated as a simple fact in chapter 1 (man, male and female, created in God's image) is explained and developed throughout the narrative of chapter 2.[5]

Chronological Issues

There is an apparent contradiction between the chronological order of the events in chapter 2 compared with chapter 1. Genesis 2 suggests that mankind was created before vegetation, whereas Genesis 1 clearly indicates that vegetation was created before mankind.

Rather than attempting to sort out the relative chronologies of the two chapters, Sailhamer believes it is better to understand 2:4b–14 as a summary of the events of chapter 1, which means it should not be read in chronological harmony with it. These verses simply state that before there were any wild plants, before there was any rain, before mankind had to work the ground, God made man from the ground, planted a garden for him, and placed him there to maintain it.[6]

Kline uses the two chapters to argue for a non-chronological thematic interpretation, supporting his literary framework view.[7] According to Kline, Genesis 2:5–6 clearly implies that 'a natural mode of divine providence was in operation during the creation "days."'[8] He goes on to argue that if all the creative acts of day one occurred sequentially in a short period of time, then 'the absence of vegetation or anything else at any given point would not last long enough to occasion special consideration of the reasons for it. Within that time-frame such a question would be practically irrelevant.'[9] Therefore, Kline concludes that holding to a strictly chronological interpretation leads not only to Scripture standing against science, but Scripture standing against Scripture.[10]

Because the effect of this watering was beneficial, Kline suggests it must relate to a new development, not something concurrent with the situation described in verse 5, otherwise verse 6 would be affirming the presence of a water supply necessary for the growth of vegetation while verse 5b says the absence of vegetation was due to the lack of such a water supply. Therefore, he

---

4 Sailhamer, *Genesis*, 40.

5 Ibid., 41.

6 Ibid., 43–44.

7 Meredith G. Kline, 'Space and Time in the Genesis Cosmogony' *PSCF* 48 (1996), 2–15.

8 Ibid., 13.

9 Ibid.

10 Ibid., 14.

translates the Qal imperfect יַעֲלֶה (yă‘ᵃlĕh, 'ascend,' 'rise') in verse 6 with an inceptive or ingressive nuance: 'but a mist *began* to rise.'[11] He takes אֵד (’ēḏ), which is normally translated 'mist' or 'vapour,' as 'rain cloud,' since it answers to the previous lack of rain in verse 5b.[12]

Kline argues that if ’ēḏ is not rain, the absence of which was the problem, then the citing of the absence of rain in verse 5b would be irrelevant.[13] Therefore, the springing forth of plants (at least the wild plants that need only rain, not cultivation) is taken for granted in Genesis 2:6 as a consequence of the provision of the prerequisite water, a consequence occurring before the creation of man (v. 7). Kline also believes the planting of the garden (v. 8) should be located before the creation of man, since וַיִּטַּע (wăyyiṭṭă‘, 'and he planted') is a *waw*-consecutive Qal imperfect which can be rendered as a pluperfect ('and he had planted'). In the absence of rainfall, man can dig irrigation ditches to bring water to cultivated land, so the absence of man was added to the absence of rain, to complete the explanation of the absence of vegetation in Genesis 2:5b. This interpretation, however, has serious problems which make it untenable. Kline understands the plants mentioned in Genesis 2:5 as those created on day 3.[14] According to Kline, these plants had not yet appeared because there was no watering system and no man to cultivate them.[15] Yet, this view implies that no plant life appeared on earth until after humans appeared which does not square with in any version of earth history, theistic or atheistic.[16]

Grudem's solution is to view the statement in Genesis 2:5 as an explanation of the general time frame in which God created mankind:

> Genesis 2:5 does not really say that plants were not on the earth because the earth was too dry to support them ... If we adopt that reasoning we would also have to say there were no plants because 'there was no man to till the ground' (Gen 2:5), for that is the second half of the comment about no rain coming on the earth. Moreover, the remainder of the sentence says that the earth was the opposite of being too dry to support plants: 'streams came up from the earth and watered the whole surface of the ground' (Gen 2:6 NIV).

Therefore, Grudem concludes that 'Genesis 2:4–6 sets the stage ... The statements about lack of rain and no man to till the ground do not give the *physical reason* why there were no plants, but only explain that God's work of

---

11 Ibid.

12 E.J. Young (*Studies in Genesis One* [Grand Rapids, Michigan, Baker, 1964], 62), on the other hand, argues that ’ēḏ could not refer to 'mist' or 'rain' because of the verb וְהִשְׁקָה (wᵉhishqāh, 'drink'). Mist or rain could moisten the ground, but not cause it to drink. He goes on to cite Albright's suggestion (William F. Albright, 'The Predeuteronomic Primeval' *JBL* 58 [1939], 102) that ’ēḏ refers to subterranean ground-water.

13 Kline also cites Job 36 and 38:25–30 for support. However, R.L. Alden (*TWOT* 1:17) notes that 'mist' is not demanded here and that 'stream' would also fit.

14 Meredith G. Kline, 'Because It Had Not Rained' *WTJ* 20 (1958) 146–157.

15 Kline, 'Space and Time in the Genesis Cosmogony' *PSCF* 48/1 (1996) 12.

16 Kruger, 'An Understanding of Genesis 2:5' 109.

creation was not complete.'[17] But Grudem's approach surely neglects the syntax and content of the verse 5. The causal conjunction כִּי (*kî*, 'for,' 'because') clearly indicates the reason why these plants had not appeared — there was no rain and no man to cultivate the ground.

Kruger, on the other hand, argues that Genesis 2 does not contradict Genesis 1 by teaching that man came before plants, because Genesis 2:5 deals only with specific types of plants ('shrub of the field' and 'plant of the field') and only in regard to a specific location (the Garden in Eden). These plants — the shrub of the field and the plant of the field — are those which require cultivation by mankind in order to grow.[18]

Kruger's explanation also has problems. Firstly, there is nothing in the immediate context of Genesis 2:5 suggesting that the author had in mind a specific geographical location. Indeed, the preceding temporal clause suggests the setting to be the entire earth, and the Garden of Eden is not mentioned until verse 8. Secondly, Kruger does not deal with the fact that the absence of these plants was not only a result of the absence of mankind but also the lack of rain.

Genesis 2:4b–6 as a Backdrop to the Creation of the First Human Couple

Genesis 2:4b–9 may be translated and diagramed as follows:

(a) When the LORD God made the earth and the heavens,
(b)   every shrub of the field had not yet appeared on the earth and
(c)   every plant of the field had not yet sprung up,
(d)   for the LORD God had not sent rain on the earth
(e)   and there was no man to work the ground,
(f)   but springs came up from the earth
(g)   and watered the whole surface of the ground.
(h) The LORD God formed the man from the dust of the ground and breathed into his nostrils the breath of life, and the man became a living being.
(i) Then the LORD God planted a garden in Eden towards the east; and there he put the man he had formed.
(j) And then the LORD God made all kinds of trees grow out of the ground — trees that were pleasing to the eye and good for food. In the middle of the garden were the Tree of Life and the Tree of the Knowledge of Good and Evil.

Note that (a)–(g) (vv. 4b–6) are subordinate to the main narrative which does not begin until (h) (v. 7).[19] This initial section briefly describes the environment and the state of the earth on day six just before God created Adam and Eve.

---

17 Wayne A. Grudem, *Systematic Theology* (Grand Rapids, Michigan: Zondervan, 1994), 303.

18 Kruger, 'An Understanding of Genesis 2:5,' 107.

19 More precisely, (a) is a temporal clause, (b)–(c) are subordinate to (a), and (d)–(g) are subordinate to (b)–(c).

The expressions 'shrub of the field' (שִׂיחַ הַשָּׂדֶה, *sîaḥ haśśādeh*) and 'plant of the field' (עֵשֶׂב הַשָּׂדֶה, *ēśeb haśśādeh*) are not all-inclusive botanical descriptions. Indeed, the combination of כֹל...טֶרֶם (*kōl ... ṭerem*, 'every ... not yet') demonstrates that although God had previously created dry land and vegetation, *not every* 'shrub of the field' and *not every* 'plant of the field' had appeared *at this point in time*.[20] In other words, some shrubs and plants were still yet to appear.

Note that *sîaḥ* is a general term used to refer to a shrub, bush, or plant.[21] *ēśeb*, on the other hand, refers to non-woody vegetation such as weeds, grass, vegetables, and cereals which grow during the rainy season (but not perennials).[22] These terms stand in contrast to the all-encompassing use of דֶּשֶׁא (*dēše*, 'vegetation')[23] and עֵץ (*ēṣ*, 'trees') in Genesis 1:11. A 'shrub of the field,' then, probably refers to any non-edible, uncultivated plant growing in the wild, including thorns, thistles and cacti,[24] whereas a 'plant of the field' refers to any non-woody, edible plant which requires human cultivation, including cereal crops, rice, vegetables and herbs. Indeed, in Genesis 3:17–18, God told Adam he would have to work the ground 'in painful toil' in order to produce 'plants of the field' for food.

Again, the two reasons why these certain shrubs of the field and certain plants of the field had not yet appeared were: (1) God had not yet caused it to rain, and (2) there were no humans around to cultivate the ground. Such conditions may have been adequate for certain wild plants, but at least some of the plants of the field required either natural rainfall and/or man's attention in order for them to grow. In contrast, unproductive and inedible shrubs of the field such as thorns and thistles appeared only when Adam began to work the ground after his rebellion against God and the subsequent cursing of the ground (Genesis 3:17–19). In this sense, the shrub of the field in Genesis 2:5 anticipates the more detailed explanation in Genesis 3:18. These shrubs do not appear in the fields until after humanity's creation and fall.[25] Not until Adam was expelled from the garden did he begin working the ground (Genesis 3:23). As Cassuto remarks: 'Man, who was no longer able to enjoy the fruits of the Garden of Eden, was compelled *to till the ground* ...'[26] Adam was now forced to labor for his food by working the ground for the rest of his life even though much of his labor would be in vain due to the inadvertent production of thorns and thistles and the like. In other words, because *sîaḥ* in the Old Testament refers to non-

---

20 Surprisingly, virtually all English translations of v. 5 appear to leave כֹל (*kōl*, 'every') untranslated.

21 See entry for שִׂיחַ in BDB.

22 See entry for עֵשֶׂב in Holladay.

23 While *dēše* most commonly refers to 'grass' it can also function as a general reference to vegetation as in Gen. 1:11 and Isa. 15:6. See entry for דֶּשֶׁא in Holladay and *TWOT* 1:199.

24 Apart from Gen. 2:5, Scripture contains three other occurrences of *sîaḥ* (Gen. 21:15; Job 30:4, 7) all of which refer to wild unproductive and uncultivated bushes or shrubs.

25 Victor P. Hamilton, *The Book of Genesis 1–17*, NICOT (Grand Rapids, Michigan, Eerdmans, 1990),154; U. Cassuto, *Commentary on the Book of Genesis*, 1:102; Sailhamer, *Genesis*, 40.

26 Cassuto, *Commentary on the Book of Genesis*, 1:102.

productive, inedible plants such as thorns and thistles, and because these came about as a result of the fall of humanity, then the absence of humans to work the ground meant that thorns and thistles and the like were yet to appear. Likewise, because *ēśĕḇ* refers to non-woody vegetation such as weeds, grasses which grow during the rainy season, and vegetables and cereals which require cultivation, then the absence of rain and the absence of humans to irrigate and cultivate the ground would mean that these kinds of plants would not yet have appeared.

This raises the question of *why* the absence of rain resulted in the absence of certain shrubs and plants of the field — especially since verse 6 states that 'streams' (אֵד, *ʾēḏ*) came up from the earth and watered the whole surface of the land. Why was this water supply not adequate?

There has been some contention over the meaning of *ʾēḏ*. Does it refer to mist,[27] rain-clouds,[28] flooding,[29] springs,[30] or something else? Albright's suggestion that *ʾēḏ* refers to subterranean ground-water is the most convincing among the options,[31] and Holladay also describes *ʾēḏ* as a 'subterranean freshwater stream.'[32] This would imply that *ʾēḏ* water was part of the subterranean water table and explains how it could water 'the whole surface of the ground' (v. 6): a rising water table would moisten the top soil and feed the root systems of most trees, shrubs and plants. In fact, Genesis 2:10 states that a single 'river' watered the garden, rather than rain. This could also indicate that water was drawn up from a subterranean source. When the water level river rose, so would the water table, which would provide sufficient water for most types of vegetation, but not all. Those unproductive and inedible shrubs of the field which had not yet appeared would only do so as a result of God cursing the ground. Those shrubs which require rain would not spring up until rain eventually came.[33] Similarly, some plants of the field would only appear as a result of Adam working the ground after his banishment from the garden.

Creation of Adam

As noted earlier, verses 4b–6 form the backdrop to the main thread of chapter 2 — the creation of the first human couple and their idyllic environment. The main thread does not begin until verse 7, which opens with אֱלֹהִים אֶת־הָאָדָם

27　See entry for אֵד in BDB.

28　M. Dahood, 'Eblaite i-du and Hebrew ʾed, 'Rain Cloud' *CBQ* 43 (1981) 534–538.

29　R. Laird Harris, 'The Mist, the Canopy and the Rivers of Eden' *BETS* 11 (1968), 178.

30　Gordon H. Wenham, Genesis 1–15, WBC (Waco, Texas, Word, 1987) 58.

31　William F. Albright, 'The Predeuteronomic Primeval' *JBL* 58 (1939), 102.

32　See entry for אֵד in Holladay.

33　Apart from Gen. 2:5, the first mention of rain in the Old Testament is Gen. 7:4. Note the contrast between these two occurrences: In 2:5, God 'had not sent rain on the earth.' In 7:4, God 'will send rain on the earth.' This strongly suggests that the advent of the flood was the very first time it had ever rained. This would also explain the sudden appearance of the rainbow and its subsequent appointment as a sign that God would never again destroy the earth by flood. Admittedly this is an argument from silence — but the silence is rather deafening!

וַיִּיצֶר יְהוָה (wăyyîṣĕr Yᵉhwāh ʾᵉlōhîm ĕt-hāʾāḏām, 'The LORD God formed the man'). The waw-consecutive Qal imperfect wăyyîṣĕr marks the beginning of the new thread and moves the overall storyline forward.

Unlike the rest of creation, the first couple were formed directly by the hand of God. It was God Himself who crafted Adam from the dust of the earth and Eve from Adam's side. He created our inmost being and knit us together in our mother's womb (Psalm 139:13), and it was He who breathed life into our inanimate bodies (Genesis 2:7).[34]

The creation of mankind truly is the climax of God's creative activities and humans alone are made in the Creator's own image (Genesis 1:26).[35] We are indeed 'fearfully and wonderfully made' (Psalm 139:14).

Nevertheless, many interpreters — including some who hold to a high view of Scripture — have attempted to harmonize the biblical account of humanity's creation with the conclusions of secular anthropology and archaeology by arguing that the first couple were not directly created by God but were actually descended from pre-Adamic ape creatures.

Pre-Adamites?

The first serious suggestions of pre-Adamites originated from Isaac La Peyrère, a Jewish convert to Catholicism, who published *Systema Theologicum ex Pre-Adamitarum Hypothesi* in 1655. However, his doctrine was regarded as heretical and he was forced to publicly recant, although he still held to his beliefs.[36]

Nevertheless, many professing evangelicals hold to similar views. John Jefferson Davis claims that 'extinct hominid forms displayed characteristics intermediate between modern man and earlier primates,'[37] but in doing so demonstrates his complete ignorance of the facts. The fossil record includes both primates and humans, but nothing that could be called 'intermediate.'[38]

Regarding the supposed appearance of modern man from more primitive types, Aviezer posits that this resulted in a 'dramatic surge of cultural advances … followed by a long period of gradual technological and artistic development …'[39] He adds: 'This relatively recent revolution can be associated with the biblical statement that God blessed man, telling him to "fill the land and subdue it" (1:28).'

---

34 Note that in Isa. 42:5 'breath' and 'life' are arranged in a synonymous parallelism: 'This is what God the LORD says — he who created the heavens and stretched them out, who spread out the earth and all that comes out of it, who gives breath to its people, and life to those who walk on it.'

35 See also the discussion of day six in chapter 6.

36 Marvin L. Lubenow, 'Pre-Adamites, Sin, Death and the Human Fossils' *JoC* 12/2 (1998), 222.

37 John Jefferson Davis, 'Response to Nelson and Reynolds' in J.P. Moreland and John Mark Reynolds (editors), *Three Views on Creation and Evolution* (Grand Rapids, Michigan, Zondervan, 1999), 81.

38 See especially Marvin L. Lubenow, *Bones of Contention* (Grand Rapids, Michigan, Baker, 1992).

39 N. Aviezer, *In the Beginning: Biblical Creation and Science* (Hoboken: KTAV, 1990), 101.

Although biblical dates indicate that Adam was culturally a neolithic man, Paul Seely believes that anthropologists have clearly proven that man existed before 10,000 B.C. Therefore, Seely's solution is to simply regard Genesis 2–3 as figurative and purely symbolic: 'The underlying history really happened; but the form in which that history is portrayed is purely imaginary.'[40]

Ronald Youngblood also seems to accept the idea of pre-Adamites which had no covenant relationship with God and only animal intelligence.[41] Adam and Eve, the first humans in the biblical sense, emerged only several thousand years ago, but scientists are free to date pre-Adamites as living long before this time.[42] Similarly, Gleason Archer also believes they had no covenant relationship and thinks that God destroyed them before He created Adam.[43] John Stott agrees, and adds that Adam was merely the first human specifically created in the image of God.[44]

Forster and Marston are also open to some form of theistic evolution of 'pre-Adamites' which brought about the appearance of the first human couple.[45] They deny that Adam is a literal single individual and suggest that אָדָם (ā\d{d}ām) should be taken as a generic reference to humanity as opposed to a personal proper name.[46] In support of this they point out that 'ā\d{d}ām always occurs with the definite article (ה, hă) up until Genesis 5:1, which they claim is the first time it is used as a proper name.[47] However, it is quite common in Hebrew to use the definite article with a common noun to refer to a specific and unique person, place or object. Waltke and O'Connor write: 'Sometimes, through usage, the article not only points out a particular person or thing, but it also elevates it to such a position of uniqueness that the *noun + article* combination becomes the equivalent of a *proper name*.'[48] Note that both 'ā\d{d}ām and hă'ā\d{d}ām are used in Genesis 1:26–7. Verse 26 uses the anarthrous (articleless) ā\d{d}ām, and appears to refer to both man and woman, given the third person plural form of the jussive 'let *them* rule …' (יִרְדּוּ, yi\r{r}ĕdû). However, verse 27 employs hă'ā\d{d}ām, but the presence of the direct object particle with a third person singular masculine suffix (אֹתוֹ, 'ōtō, 'him') indicates that this refers, again, to only Adam, even though the next sentence (which does not use either 'ā\d{d}ām or hă'ā\d{d}ām) clearly refers to both Adam and Eve. Therefore, it appears that the actual uses of 'ā\d{d}ām and hă'ā\d{d}ām indicate the very opposite of what Forster

---

40 Paul H. Seely 'Adam and Anthropology: A Proposed Solution' *JASA* 22/3 (September 1970), 89.

41 R.F. Youngblood, *The Book of Genesis*, 2nd edition (Grand Rapids, Michigan, Baker, 1991), 47.

42 Ibid., 48.

43 Gleason L. Archer, *A Survey of Old Testament Introduction* (Chicago, Moody, 1964), 187–189.

44 John R.W. Stott, *Understanding the Bible* (Glendale, California, Regal, 1972), 63.

45 Roger Forster and Paul Marston, *Reason, Science and Faith* (Crowborough, East Sussex, Monarch, 1999), 440–443.

46 Ibid., 283–284.

47 Ibid., 293. In actual fact, Gen. 4:25 is the first clear use of 'ā\d{d}ām as a proper noun.

48 *IBHS* 13.6. See also the examples listed there.

and Marston claim: the anarthrous 'ādām appears to be used as a collective noun referring to mankind in general (or at least Eve as well as Adam), while hā'ādām refers to a specific man, Adam.

That hā'ādām refers to a single historical individual is demonstrated in Genesis 3:9–10. God called out to 'the man' (hā'ādām) and he answered (וַיֹּאמֶר, wăyy'ōmĕr), 'I heard you (שָׁמַעְתִּי, šāmă'tî) ... I was afraid (וָאִירָא, wā'îrā') ... I hid (וָאֵחָבֵא, wā'ēhābē').' All these verb forms are singular and communicate the utterings of a single individual. Therefore, in Genesis 1–3, hā'ādām ('the man') refers not just to a specific man but to the one and only man at this time: Adam.

To his credit, Bernard Ramm writes:

> There are problems with [the pre-Adamite] theory before it can be a good option. It seems too much like having our cake and eating it. We can admit all that the anthropologists say; and then announce that it has nothing to do with the biblical account of man. We can have the antiquity of man, and the recency of Adam! But who is to tell where one leaves off and the other begins? Certainly, if pre-Adamism leads to the breakdown of the unity of the race, we have theological problems with the imputation of sin through the fall of one man.[49]

Marvin Lubenow points out that '[t]he pre-Adamite concept was born in Biblical scepticism and heresy. It then moved into mainstream science and became a justification for racism and slavery ... with the continued discovery of human fossils of alleged great age, pre-Adamism has moved into the church and become one of the major apologetic methods used in the harmonization of science and the Scriptures.'[50] Lubenow is not the first to point this out. Science historian David Livingstone also noted that pre-Adamism is 'born in infidelity and is nurtured in skepticism.'[51]

Lubenow observes that most interpreters who hold to the existence of pre-Adamites also believe that human death began with the biblical Adam who lived around 10,000 years ago. Thus, all human fossils which date before this time (using conventional methods) are actually pre-Adamites, and therefore less than human.[52] However, Lubenow's thorough survey of the human fossil record prior to ten thousand years ago shows that there is a great deal of evidence of moral evil: 'Evidence of virtually every type of premature death, trauma, disease, and sin which we could reasonably expect the human fossils to show is found in the fossil record before 10 ka [10,000 years ago]. We find in them the conditions we would expect to find after the Fall of Adam, not before.'[53]

---

49 Bernard Ramm, *The Christian View of Science and Scripture* (Grand Rapids, Michigan, Eerdmans, 1954), 316–317.

50 Lubenow, 'Pre-Adamites, Sin, Death and the Human Fossils,' 223.

51 As cited in ibid., 222.

52 Ibid., 225.

53 Ibid., 230.

In any case, Scripture clearly states that the first man — Adam — was created out of the dust of the ground (Genesis 2:7; 1 Corinthians 15:45–49) not from a highly evolved ape. 'This could not refer to or include a former animal ancestry, since it is to dust that man returns — and this is not a return to an animal state (Gen 3:19).'[54]

Creation and Propagation

Mankind was created on the sixth day of creation, and on the seventh day God ceased all His creative activity. How, then, are we to explain the propagation of the human race?

This question is best answered by the *Traducian theory* which views the entire human race as created immediately in Adam and Eve. In the beginning, the first couple *were* the human race, and both body and spirit are propagated from them through natural generation.[55] In other words, when Adam and Eve were created they constituted the entire human race. The image of God is manifested by both male (Adam) and female (Eve), and no other humans existed at this time. When Eve conceived and gave birth to a child, that child, like his parents before him, had both body and spirit and was an image bearer of God. The same characteristics would also apply to the child's offspring.

Garden of Eden

The section describing the Garden of Eden (vv. 8–14) begins with the Qal *waw*-consecutive וַיִּטַּע (*wăyyiṭṭăʿ*, 'and … planted'). Some see this section as presenting a chronological discrepancy since it implies that Adam was created before vegetation, and so have opted for non-chronological thematic interpretations.[56] But note that the Garden of Eden is in focus here — not the general creation of all plants on day three — so the chronology of Genesis 1 would not be violated.[57]

The Garden Itself

The garden itself was located in the eastern part of the area known as 'Eden.'[58] It was in the garden that God placed Adam whom he had just created. The garden was not only the first couple's home but also their place of work. It was their responsibility to tend to it and maintain it (Genesis 2:15). Yet, there is no indication that Adam and Eve were confined to the garden. Indeed, the only way they could carry out their mandate — 'Be fruitful and increase in number;

---

54 Charles C. Ryrie, 'The Bible and Evolution' *BSac* 124 (January 1967), 66.

55 See Henry C. Thiessen, *Lectures in Systematic Theology*, revised by Vernon D. Doerksen (Grand Rapids, Michigan, Eerdmans, 1979), 165–167.

56 e.g. Kline, Blocher, and Futato.

57 Cassuto (*Commentary on the Book of Genesis*, 1:107) agrees that after God created mankind, He planted the garden. Alternatively, *wăyyiṭṭăʿ* could be taken as *pluperfect* rather than consecutive, which would make it a circumstantial clause subordinate to the second half of v. 8. Again, this avoids any chronological clashes with chapter 1.

58 Heb. בְּעֵדֶן מִן קֶדֶם (*bᵉʿēḏen min qēḏem*). Literally, 'in Eden, on the side of the east.'

fill the earth and subdue it. Rule over the fish of the sea and the birds of the air and over every living creature that moves on the ground' (Genesis 1:28) — was for them to venture outside the garden, and for their descendants to leave the garden and migrate to the extents of the earth.

Contra Ramm, the idyllic conditions were not limited to the garden.[59] Isaiah 51:3 includes a synonymous parallelism which indicates that Eden itself was just as perfect and tranquil as the garden: 'The LORD will surely comfort Zion and will look with compassion on all her ruins; he will make her deserts like Eden, her wastelands like the garden of the LORD.' Indeed, God pronounced the entire creation 'very good,' not just the garden.

Regarding the growth of the trees in the garden, Genesis 2:9 states explicitly that God Himself 'made all kinds of trees grow out of the ground.' This stands in contrast to the passive creation of the rest of the world's plants on day three ('Let the land produce vegetation' [Genesis 1:11]) and, contra MacRae,[60] suggests some kind of supernatural accelerated growth rather than natural germination and growth. Indeed, accelerated growth was necessary since the trees in the garden were meant to supply the first couple with their food. This was no unique event either, since God would later cause a vine to supernaturally grow in order to provide Jonah with shade (Jonah 4:6). Therefore, the growth of trees in the garden is not a creation of new types, but a description of God's personal involvement in supernaturally creating a paradise for His greatest creature — mankind.

Rivers of Eden

A river which originated in Eden flowed through the garden and watered it. After exiting the garden the river divided into four branches (Heb. רֹאשׁ, $rō'š$, 'headwater'), but were these branches part of an estuary (that is, one river flowing into four) or part of a tributary (that is, four rivers flowing into one)? The word $rō'š$ most commonly means 'head' but can also refer to a 'beginning.'[61] Either way, the use of $rō'š$ in this context strongly suggests that the four branches are the *beginning* or the *source* of four different rivers: the Pishon, the Gihon, the Tigris, and the Euphrates.[62] In other words, the four branches formed an estuary of the river which flowed through Eden.

The problematic geographical description of the rivers has caused many scholars to view the garden as mythical imagery rather than a reference to

---

59 Contra Ramm (233), who states: 'Ideal conditions existed only in the Garden. There was disease and death and bloodshed in Nature long before man sinned.'

60 Allan A. MacRae, 'The Scientific Approach to the Old Testament, Part 3' *BSac* 110 (July 1953), 237.

61 BDB, Holladay.

62 E.A. Speiser (*Genesis*, ICC [New York: Doubleday, 1964], 19–20) argues that יֹצֵא מֵעֵדֶן ($yōṣē'$ $mē'ēden$) in Genesis 2:10 means 'rise in' rather than 'flow from' implying that the river was formed by four converging branches just outside the garden. However, similar constructions in Exod. 25:32 and 37:18 indicate the opposite.

a real historic place.[63] Nevertheless, many others have tried to find a way of harmonizing the account with known geography. James Montgomery Boice, for example, posits that 'there is no doubt that Moses was using names and places at least partially known to his contemporaries. The Tigris and Euphrates were known then and are known to this day. Moses speaks of Havilah as a land of gold, resin, and onyx. He speaks of Cush, generally regarded as a section of Arabia and Ethiopia. Asshur is the land of Assyria.'[64]

Scripture describes the Pishon as winding through the entire land of Havilah, which abounds with fine gold, as well as aromatic resin and onyx. Munday argues that the reference to Havilah points to the Arabian peninsula:

> As a place name, Havilah is used in Gen 25:18 and 1 Sam 15:7. In the first, Ishmael's descendants settled the area 'from Havilah to Shur, near the border of Egypt.' In the second, 'Saul attacked the Amalekites all the way from Havilah to Shur, to the east of Egypt.' The Desert of Shur, in size at least three days' journey, lay just east of the Red Sea during the Exodus (Exod 15:22). Havilah must have lain at the other end, to the east, of the Amalekite range of habitation … 1 Sam 15:7 quoted earlier indicates that Havilah was the eastern extremity of the Amalekite range; thus, Havilah is to be located in Arabia east of Edom. This is consistent with the accepted derivation of the word Havilah from a West Semitic root meaning 'sand' and hence 'land of sand.'[65]

He concludes that the Pishon, because of its association with Havilah, 'is consistent with a location somewhere in Arabia, most likely its northern half somewhere eastward of Edom and Moab. The probability is that the Pishon coursed through the eastern half of northern Arabia, adjacent to the Mesopotamian valley, a region traditionally proposed as the garden site. The Pishon may have been the Wadi Batin.'[66] However, not only is the Wadi Batin river not part of a four-branched estuary, it is particularly straight and does not wind about at any point as it makes its way to the sea. Nor are there any other rivers in the region which would fit the biblical description. Thus, it is not surprising that James admits: 'The "land of Havilah"' is equally an enigma in spite of repeated attempts to locate it in various parts of Arabia and the Nubian desert.'[67]

---

63 See for example Cassuto, *Commentary on the Book of Genesis*, 1:118. John Skinner, *A Critical and Exegetical Commentary on Genesis*, ICC (New York, Scribner, 1910), 62. H.E. Ryle, *The Book of Genesis* (Cambridge, Cambridge University Press, 1921), 32. Y.T. Radday, 'The Four Rivers of Paradise,' *HS* 23 (1982), 23–31. J.L. McKenzie, 'The Literary Characteristics of Genesis 2–3' *TS* 15 (1954), 555. D.E. Burns, 'Dream Form in Genesis 2.4b–3.24: Asleep in the Garden,' *JSOT* 37 (1987), 3–14.

64 James Montgomery Boice, *Genesis: An Expositional Commentary 1:1–11:32* (Grand Rapids, Michigan, Zondervan, 1982), 102.

65 John C. Munday Jr., 'Eden's Geography Erodes Flood Geology' *WTJ* 58/1 (Spring 1996), 138–139.

66 Ibid., 141.

67 E.O. James, *The Tree of Life: An Archaeological Study* (Leiden, E.J. Brill, 1966), 74.

The second river is the Gihon. It passed through the whole land of Cush (usually associated with the land Ethiopia). But the land of Cush lies a long way to the southwest of Mesopotamia and on the other side of the Red Sea! Munday, however, understands the land of Cush as a reference to the land of the *descendants* of Cush, a son of Ham. Therefore, he claims the Gihon 'probably was a river flowing from Kassite country in the Zagros mountains into the Tigris-Euphrates system near the Gulf.'[68] This speculative understanding is inferred from Genesis 10:6–10. But, like the Pishon, neither of Munday's suggestions (that is, the Karun River or Kerkha River) are part of a four-branch estuary.

The third river, the Tigris, flowed along the east side of Asshur. Munday observes that in Scripture and elsewhere Asshur usually designates the Assyrian nation, the region of Assyria or its capital city.[69] He concludes: 'Without any doubt, the word here refers to the capital city of Assyria ... Geographically, Asshur is located on the west bank of the Tigris River, in perfect correspondence with Genesis 2:14.'[70] Likewise, Hamilton notes that Asshur could refer to the Assyrian empire or the capital of the empire, but since the Assyrian empire extended on both sides of the Tigris, it is more likely a reference to the capital city.[71] Yet neither the Assyrian empire nor the city of Asshur would have existed when the source for this account was written. One could argue that Moses inserted the reference for clarification, but it is doubtful a reference to Assyria would have had much meaning or significance to Moses' audience, the Israelites — especially since they had just spent the last 400 years in captivity, and would have known very little about the world outside of Egypt. Furthermore, stating that a river flows on the east side of any given city is a particularly odd way of describing its path: stating that the Rhine river passes to the east of the city of Bonn says virtually nothing about its course. Thus, the description would make much more sense if Asshur was actually a much larger area.

The fourth and last river mentioned is the Euphrates. Nothing more is said about it, and along with the Tigris, most conservatives assume it is the same river which flows from southeastern Turkey to the Persian Gulf bearing the same name.

It should be clear from the above discussion that the description of the geography of Eden and the garden corresponds to no place on earth at this time or in recent history. What, then, does the account mean? In light of the genre analysis in chapter 4, the account is certainly not myth or allegory. But if it purports to be history, does it not present false propositions and thus negate the claims of inerrantists? The only way inerrancy could be saved is if the earth's geography had dramatically changed after the account of Eden had been constructed. The most obvious explanation of how such a change could

---

68 Munday suggests the Gihon was perhaps the Karun River, or possibly the Kerkha River.

69 Munday, 'Eden's Geography Erodes Flood Geology,' 142.

70 Ibid., 143.

71 Victor P. Hamilton, *The Book of Genesis 1–17*, NICOT (Grand Rapids, Michigan, Eerdmans, 1990), 170.

have occurred is by means of the global catastrophic flood described in Genesis 6–9.[72] But if the geographical description was no longer applicable then why did Moses include it when he wrote/edited/constructed the book of Genesis? The geographical description was most probably included simply to reinforce that the original author believed the garden was a real and physical place on this earth,[73] and to highlight the perfect and sufficient state of the pristine earth.

Once the garden was complete, Adam was instructed to work and till the ground. God did not intend Adam to be idle but instead gave him work and a purpose. As Leupold puts it, 'work and duty belong to the perfect state.'[74]

Note also that the mention of Adam reinforces the historical veracity of the account. Adam is clearly viewed by the New Testament writers as a truly historical figure, so if Adam is a real physical person but Eden and the garden are allegorical, how can a literal something be placed into and tend to an allegorical/mythical anything?

Two Trees

In the middle of the garden there were two special trees: the *Tree of Life* and the *Tree of the Knowledge of Good and Evil*. Very little is said about either of these trees. Given that Adam is permitted to eat from *any* trees in the garden *except for the Tree of the Knowledge of Good and Evil*, it seems fair to assume that Adam could and most probably did eat the fruit of the Tree of Life. However, in Genesis 3:22–23, God banishes Adam and Eve from the garden for eating from the Tree of the Knowledge of Good and Evil in order to stop them from also taking and eating the fruit of the Tree of Life. What, then, was the purpose of these trees and what effect did their fruit have?

The Tree of Life

The 'Tree of life,' Cassuto points out, 'serves as a common simile for things from which the power of life flows.'[75] Therefore, it appears that the Tree of Life provided the first couple with a supernatural, life-sustaining fruit.[76] However, Blocher objects: 'The entire Bible ... excludes the idea of any supernatural effect attached to any kind of food. It does not permit us to understand in literal terms what we read about the tree of life.'[77] But apart from this argument from

---

72 The flood and its effects are discussed in detail in chapter 10.

73 The region of Asshur and the post-flood Tigris and Euphrates rivers were most probably named by Noah or his sons after the pre-flood 'originals' much like the rivers Thames and Trent in Ontario, Canada were named by the English settlers after those rivers in England which bear the same name.

74 H.C. Leupold, *Exposition of Genesis*, 2 volumes (Grand Rapids, Michigan, Baker, 1942), 1:126.

75 Cassuto, *Commentary on the Book of Genesis*, 1:109.

76 Prov. 3:18, 11:30, 13:12, 15:4 use the term 'tree of life' as a metaphor for things which have life-giving power. Cassuto (*Commentary on the Book of Genesis*, 1:109) also notes that in the Hebrew 'Tree of life' has the article, so this tree was apparently well known to readers.

77 Blocher, *In the Beginning*, 123–124.

silence, Blocher offers no support for his assertion. What Scriptures prohibit the concept of a life-sustaining fruit?

Robert Starke also objects to the idea of a supernatural, life-sustaining fruit: 'the entire Genesis record, and likewise all of Scripture, excludes the idea of an element of any kind possessing, in and of itself, magical power.'[78] Derek Kidner concurs: 'the Old Testament has no room for blind forces, only for the acts of God.'[79] This is surely a straw man argument. The fruit is no more magical than the bronze serpent which Moses made in the desert (Numbers 21:9), nor are there any blind forces at work. Rather, the fruit was merely the means by which God performed a supernatural act. In the same way, the bronze serpent was the means by which God healed those who had been bitten by the venomous snakes.

Blocher, on the other hand, believes the whole account is non-literal and metaphorical. He points to Proverbs 3:18, 11:30, and 13:12 as obvious allusions to the Tree of Life in Genesis, and believes that this strongly suggests a non-literal interpretation.[80] Yet, in each of the verses the Tree of Life is used as the predicate of a metaphor: that is, 'X is a Tree of Life.' In other words, character-istics of the Tree of Life are used to describe the subject of the metaphor, but these metaphors say absolutely nothing about the Tree of Life itself.

Blocher also notes that Revelation 2:7 (and 22:2,14,19) presuppose the Tree of Life still survives. But given that the universal flood would surely have destroyed it, and that the geographical region of 'Eden' is never referred to in later biblical texts, nor is there any mention of the garden being destroyed or removed, Blocher concludes the account cannot be literal.[81] However, this line of argument fails on multiple counts. Firstly, Revelation records an apocalyptic vision, not a historical or futuristic account, so one cannot legitimately read its statements as a straightforward description of the future. Therefore, Blocher's assertion that Revelation presupposes the Tree still exists is false. Secondly, if the universal flood had surely destroyed the Tree of Life, then why would it not also have destroyed the entire garden? Thirdly, the Garden of Eden is indeed mentioned in later texts.[82]

The Tree of the Knowledge of Good and Evil

Blocher adds that in Revelation 2 and 22 'the tree of life is obviously a symbol'[83] and then concludes that if the Tree of life is a symbol, so is its counterpart, the Tree of the Knowledge of Good and Evil.[84] But since Blocher's premise is false, his conclusion does not follow.

---

78 R. Starke, 'The Tree of Life: Protological to Eschatological' *Kerux* 11/2 (September 1996), 24.

79 Derek Kidner, *Genesis* (Downers Grove, IL: InterVarsity Press, 1967), 62.

80 Blocher, *In the Beginning*, 124.

81 Blocher, *In the Beginning*, 116–117.

82 Apart from the reference in Gen. 4:16, Eden is also explicitly referred to in Isa. 51:3; Ezek. 36:35 and Joel 2:3, and alluded to in Ezek. 28:13; 31:9, 16, 18.

83 Blocher, *In the Beginning*, 125.

84 Ibid.

The phrase 'Knowledge of Good and Evil' refers to moral autonomy. This conclusion is based on the use of these terms as a legal idiom referring to judicial judgments.[85] Man is forbidden to decide for himself what is and is not in his best interests — that is God's prerogative alone (compare Ezekiel 28:2). The consequence of eating the forbidden fruit was certain death: 'for in the day that you eat of it you shall die' (Genesis 2:17, NRSV). Yet, as reported in Genesis 3, the first couple did not immediately die when they took the fruit. On the contrary, it appears they lived on for many hundreds of years. How, then, are we to understand this pronouncement?

Many conservative commentators have suggested that this is a reference to 'spiritual death' rather than the physical death of the body.[86] As a result of taking the fruit, Adam and Eve died spiritually. Ephesians 2:1–9 is often cited in support of this view. Such an interpretation is, however, highly problematic. What exactly is meant by the term 'spiritual death'? If we take the term literally, it can only reasonably mean that the spirit of a non-Christian is dead. Thus, the very thing that differentiates humans from animals is no longer living, making an unbeliever no different to an animal. This goes against Genesis 1:26, which teaches that all humanity is uniquely created in the image of God. Positing two kinds of death — physical and spiritual — creates a false or artificial distinction. As Hebrews 9:27 teaches, each person is destined to die once, and then face judgment.

Ephesians 2:1, 5 teaches that non-Christians are dead in their sins. This is clearly not a reference to physical death, so in what way are these people 'dead'? In this case, being 'dead in your transgressions and sins' appears to refer to our natural state of separation from God before accepting the gospel. All human beings are destined to experience eternal separation from God (i.e., hell) if they continue in their life of sin, apart from God's will.

In any case, the apparent timing problems of Genesis 2:17 can still be resolved. Firstly, as noted in the discussion of Genesis 2:4, בְּיוֹם ($b^e y\hat{o}m$) is an idiom for 'when,' so a fixed point in time is not in view. Secondly, the finite verb is a Qal imperfect (or *yiqtol*) form implying an action which is (1) dependent upon the event of Adam and Eve eating the fruit, and (2) in the future with respect to the time that they ate. Thirdly, the Hebrew (תָּמוּתכִּי בְּיוֹם אֲכָלְךָ מִמֶּנּוּ מוֹת, *kî b^e yôm 'ăkāl^e k mimmĕnû môt tāmût*) literally reads: 'for in the day of your eating of it, dying you shall die.' When the infinitive absolute precedes a finite verb of the same stem (as is the case here), it strengthens or intensifies the verbal idea by emphasizing 'either the certainty (especially in the case of threats) or the forcibleness and completeness of an occurrence.'[87] In other words, the emphasis

---

85 W.M. Clark, 'A Legal Background to the Yahwist's Use of "Good and Evil" in Genesis 2–3' *JBL* 88 (1969), 266–278.

86 See for example Walter L. Bradley, 'Response to Paul Nelson and John Mark Reynolds' in J.P. Moreland and John Mark Reynolds (editors), *Three Views on Creation and Evolution* (Grand Rapids, Michigan, Zondervan, 1999), 77.

87 GKC § 113n. Note also that Gen. 2:17 is cited as a specific example. See also *IBHS* 35.3.1 b–f.

is on the *certainty* of their death rather than its precise timing or chronology.[88] This is demonstrated in 1 Kings 2:37–46: Shimei could not possibly have been executed 'on the day' he exited his house since he was not killed until after he had traveled from Jerusalem to Gath, located his missing slaves, and traveled back to Jerusalem.

Note also that this verse does not teach that Adam would become mortal as a result of eating the fruit. This would imply that the first couple possessed inherent immortality before the fall, but this is contradicted in 1 Timothy 6:16 — only God is inherently immortal. Rather, it was the life-sustaining fruit of the Tree of Life that prevented the first couple from dying — a privilege they were denied as a consequence of disobeying God and eating from the Tree of the Knowledge of Good and Evil.

Adam and Eve

God never intended for Adam to be alone. No animal was a suitable helper and mate. As a social creature made in the image of God, Adam needed a spiritual, intellectual, emotional, and biological companion, so God created Eve from Adam's own flesh.

Note that when God formed Eve, He did not take Adam's head or his foot, but rather one of his ribs, indicating that the woman is not superior or inferior to the man, but his equal.[89]

Chronological Issues

Some interpreters believe that Genesis 2:18–19 contradicts 1:24–27. Based on their shallow understanding of Hebrew and Greek grammar, Forster and Marston object to 'interpreting "and" (*wa*) as "also" and "formed" (*yatsar*) as the pluperfect "had formed"' in Genesis 2:19. They add: 'The NIV is the only version we can find which renders it thus, and, as the Hebrew is a simple past tense, its motivation is plainly theological not linguistic. It is hardly a "straight-forward" reading, and the Septuagint rendering ("God further formed") shows that the Jews never took it thus.'[90] In actual fact, Hebrew has no such thing as a simple past tense. The Hebrew verb is a *waw*-consecutive Qal imperfect which may be legitimately rendered as a pluperfect — especially in light of the context of Genesis 1. Furthermore, the Septuagint (LXX) uses an aorist active indicative functioning as a constative aorist, which simply refers to the fact of the action (as a whole) in past time without saying anything about the kind of action involved or its precise timing.[91]

---

88 Hamilton, *The Book of Genesis 1–17*, NICOT (Grand Rapids, Michigan, Eerdmans, 1990), 172. Alternatively, the imperfect/*yiqtol* form could be taken *ingressively*: 'when you eat of it you will begin to die.'

89 Note also that the rib bone has an amazing capacity to self-regenerate. See Carl W. Wieland, 'Regenerating Ribs' *Creation* 21/4 (September 1999), 46–47.

90 Forster and Marston, *Reason Science and Faith*, 269. Note that both the NET and ESV have 'had formed' as an alternative rendering in the footnotes.

91 See Wallace, *Greek Grammar*, 557–558.

Mark Futato, on the other hand, acknowledges that the *waw*-consecutive Qal imperfect וַיִּצֶר (*wăyyiṣĕr*) in verse 19 may be taken as a pluperfect ('had formed'), but claims this is not the obvious syntactic choice.[92] Nevertheless, 2:18–19 should be read in the light of 1:24–27. Indeed, Futato himself admits that a pluperfect rendering can be used 'when there is lexical repetition or when knowledge of the real world leads to the conclusion that an explanation of a previous event or situation is being provided.'[93] In this case, Genesis 1 provides this knowledge — animals were made before Adam.

God displayed the animals to Adam for two reasons. Firstly, '[t]he naming of something or someone is a token of lordship.'[94] In naming the animals, Adam was merely exercising his lordship over them, since humans are created in the image of God to exercise dominion over all living creatures and the earth itself. Secondly, seeing all these animals caused Adam to recognize that none of them would make a suitable partner and companion.

History or Allegory

In keeping with their allegorical hermeneutic, Forster and Marston deny the historicity of the account. Rather than relating a series of actual historical events they claim that it merely teaches that 'Mankind alone was created with an in-built urge to create conceptual language in "naming" animals' and that '[n]o animal can have a truly personal relationship with a human person in the way epitomised by marriage.'[95] They continue: 'In some instances [the apostle Paul's] arguments actually make sense only if some of the Genesis account is *intended* as a kind of allegory. If it is purely literal reporting of historical events, then why should it imply anything about how we should live now?'[96]

Regarding the formation of Eve, they ask:

> Why should God put Adam into a deep sleep to do it? Since it was (presumably) miraculous anyway, he could surely have done it painlessly with Adam awake — on a local rather than a general anaesthetic principle? Secondly, if Adam had been asleep, how did he know that Eve was 'bone of his bone,' as soon as he saw her? God might, of course, have told him – though one then wonders why the text does not mention it.[97]

Apart from the fact that Forster and Marston do not seem to understand what allegory is, their criticisms are easily answered. The reason God caused Adam to sleep in order to remove a rib appears to be to emphasize that Adam was an actual real person and that Eve was indeed built from Adam's own flesh

---

92 Mark D. Futato, 'Because It Had Rained: A Study Of Gen 2:5–7 With Implications For Gen 2:4–25 And Gen 1:1–2:3' *WTJ* 60/1 (Spring 1998), 10–11.

93 Ibid., n. 34.

94 Cassuto, *Commentary on the Book of Genesis*, 1:130.

95 Forster and Marston, *Reason Science and Faith* (Crowborough, East Sussex, Monarch, 1999), 283.

96 Ibid., 285.

97 Ibid., 284.

— a fact that would have been immediately obvious to him when he first saw her — especially just after viewing all the animals. Indeed, Adam explicitly acknowledges her origin in Genesis 2:23.

Forster and Marston also cite 1 Corinthians 11:8 as support for a non-literal reading of the creation of Eve, stating that Paul's argument 'carries weight only if Genesis is about a meaning deeper than anatomy.'[98] To claim that a straight-forward reading reduces the meaning, significance, and details of the creation of Eve to the level of 'anatomy' is surely a straw man. The meaning of these events is clearly communicated: Adam and Eve are both God's creatures and Eve is the only suitable partner for Adam since she was formed from his own flesh. Paul's argument in 1 Corinthians 11 fits nicely with this straightforward meaning.

In addition, 1 Timothy 2:11–15 mentions Adam and Eve specifically in an obvious reference to Genesis 1–3.[99] However, the most devastating refutation of Forster and Marston's non-literal view of Adam comes from the apostle Paul in Romans 5:12–14:

> Therefore, just as sin entered the world through one man, and death through sin, and in this way death came to all men, because all sinned — for before the law was given, sin was in the world. But sin is not taken into account when there is no law. Nevertheless, death reigned from the time of Adam to the time of Moses, even over those who did not sin by breaking a command, as did Adam, who was a pattern of the one to come.

How could sin and death enter into the physical world through the actions of a figurative and non-physical man?

Marriage and Nakedness

Although men and women are quite different, there is still a psychological and physiological relationship between the two. They are spiritually, mentally, emotionally, and sexually compatible. Therefore, a man will leave his parents and cleave to his wife and the two 'shall become one flesh.' In addition, when a man and a woman marry, a new family — the most basic social structure — is formed.

The unity of mankind is manifested not only in the fact that they are made of the same flesh, but also in the marriage relationship and its consummation in the act of sexual intercourse where male and female 'become one flesh.' Indeed, it is through this act that the human race procreates.

Genesis 2 concludes by stating that the man and woman were not ashamed even though they were both naked. Hamilton points out that nakedness in the Old Testament is always connected with some form of humiliation, and

---

98 Ibid., 286.

99 Forster and Marston, of course, have a different (unorthodox) understanding of this passage. They argue that it 'actually has *more* force not less if we see the Genesis account as a divinely inspired allegory intended to teach us truth about humanity.' However, this will be dealt with in more detail in chapter 12.

in particular, of guilt.[100] At this point in time, before sin had entered into the world, the first couple was innocent and experienced perfect communion with God. There was no humiliation and no guilt (either guilt feelings or true moral guilt). It was not until they ate the forbidden fruit that they began to experience such feelings and cover their nakedness (Genesis 3:7).

Summary

Genesis 2 is a simple historical account which focuses on the sixth day of creation when God created both the animals and the first human couple. God first formed the man from the dust of the ground and breathed life into him.

God never intended Adam to be alone so He showed him all the beasts of the field and all the birds of the air — not just so that Adam could name them and therefore exercise his dominion over them, but also to cause him to recognize that none of them was a suitable companion. Therefore, God made the woman from Adam's own flesh and the two lived in perfect harmony with each other and with their Creator.

Adam and Eve were perfect human beings in a perfect world. They had a unique relationship with their Creator and enjoyed perfect communion with Him. This blissful state sets up a vivid contrast to Genesis 3. Although they had everything they needed they still coveted what they could not have. They took the forbidden fruit and ate it — and the resulting state is the exact opposite of what they had in the beginning.

---

100 Hamilton, *Genesis 1–17*, 181. See Gen 2:25; Isa 20:4; 47:3; Mic 1:11; Nah 3:5.

CHAPTER 9

The Fall and Its Effects

Despite their unique, intimate relationship with their Creator and the perfect, tranquil environment, Adam and Eve desired more. Although they had everything they could possibly want or need they coveted the forbidden fruit. Their covetousness caused them to disobey their Creator and, as a result, they lost everything. As John Milton put it, it was 'Paradise Lost.'

The Fall

Like the preceding chapters, Genesis 3 is a historical account which describes real people in a real place in real history. This is not mythology or allegory. Indeed, there are numerous Scriptures which explicitly refer to the historical nature of the events and characters of Genesis 3 and the unity of the account itself.[1]

While Blocher rightly acknowledges that 'in the debate on the "historicity of the content" of Genesis 3 nothing less than the gospel is at stake',[2] he believes 'the real problem is not to know if we have a historical account of the fall, but the account of a historical fall.'[3] Blocher tries to divorce the historical characters and events from the vehicle in which they are communicated (that is, historical narrative). Thus, he affirms that the characters and events are fully historical, but that the account itself is not. He believes that, because there were no eyewitnesses and because of the problem of transmission, the account of the fall is 'an imaginative projection into the past, starting from the conditions of the writer's present experience.'[4] Blocher goes on to quote Paul Ricoeur: 'Every effort to save the letter of the story as a true history is vain and hopeless. What we know, as men of science, about the beginnings of mankind leaves no place for such a primordial event.'[5]

Not only does Blocher illegitimately allow science to overrule Scripture, he fails to consider the role of divine revelation. Although no human eyewitnesses were

---

1 e.g. 1 Chr. 1:1; Isa. 51:3; Ezek. 28:13, 31:9, 36:35; Hos. 6:7; Joel 2:3; Luke 3:38; Rom. 5:14; 1 Cor. 15:22, 45; 2 Cor. 11:3; 1 Tim. 2:13, 14; Jude 1:14; Rev. 12:9; 20:2.

2 Henri Blocher, *In the Beginning*, translated by D.G. Preston (Leicester, IVP, 1984), 170.

3 Ibid., 157.

4 Ibid.

5 As cited by Blocher, *In the Beginning*, 157.

present, God has revealed knowledge of these events to the original author. In fact, given that human senses are not always reliable, knowledge gained through divine revelation would be superior to any other. Furthermore, if the account of the fall (or any other part of Scripture) is a human reconstruction, how can it be regarded in any sense as the word of God? How can a historical event be known except through historical accounts? Blocher's approach to the historicity of Genesis 1–3 is semantic subterfuge at best, and incoherent at worst.

On the other hand, it should be noted that while the account of the fall is true, it is not necessarily exhaustive in its description: '[Moses] emphasizes just those points which need to be stressed, in order that the reader may be properly prepared to understand the account of the fall.'[6]

The Serpent

In keeping with their non-literal allegorical hermeneutic, Forster and Marston consider the account of the temptation by the serpent as non-literal: 'We have little doubt, then, that the "tree of life," the "serpent" and the other imagery in these passages is intended as pure symbolism (and not literally as well) both in Revelation 20–22 and in Genesis 2–3. It deals with real events and issues, but describes them in figurative terms.'[7] But Forster and Marston's position surely begs the question. If these characters and events are symbolic, how could they possibly know that they correspond to real historical characters, objects and events?

The comparison of the serpent with the rest of the 'beasts of the field' (Genesis 3:1) and the physical nature of the curse he received (Genesis 3:14) strongly indicate a literal, historical creature. Indeed, a traditional Jewish interpretation also appears to view the serpent as a literal creature.[8]

As for the identity of the serpent, some early Jewish expositions infer that it is Satan,[9] although in general, it was seen as representing an evil influence without being explicitly identified as the ultimate source or cause of evil. Indeed, 'the author of Genesis seems to intentionally underplay the role or identification of the serpent.'[10] Nevertheless, the serpent is explicitly identified as Satan in the New Testament.[11] As Blocher rightly notes, 'Scripture itself leaves us in no doubt; the snake is the devil.'[12]

---

6 E.J. Young, *Studies in Genesis One* (Grand Rapids, Michigan, Baker, 1964), 75.

7 Roger Forster and Paul Marston, *Reason, Science and Faith* (Crowborough, East Sussex, Monarch, 1999), 282.

8 *Jubilees* 3:17–28.

9 *Wisdom of Solomon* 2:23–24.

10 John H. Walton, *Genesis*, NIVAC (Grand Rapids, Michigan, Zondervan, 2001), 209.

11 Rev. 12:9; 20:2.

12 Blocher, *In the Beginning*, 151. Note, however, that Blocher believes the snake is symbolic of Satan and everything said about the snake applies to the devil (152). But the snake is cursed 'above all the animals' and made to crawl on its belly, so how do the specific curses placed on the snake apply to Satan?

Boice, on the other hand, posits that the creature that tempted Eve was not a serpent but merely became a serpent as a result of God's judgment. He sees the tempter as an 'upright creature, not totally dissimilar to Adam and Eve themselves.'[13] But this position cannot be sustained. Genesis 3 explicitly and repeatedly refers to the tempter as 'the serpent.' Furthermore, God cursed 'the serpent' (v. 14) and the effect of that curse was that the serpent would now crawl on his belly. There is no indication in the text that the tempter would *become* a serpent.

The serpent is described as 'more crafty [Heb. עָרוּם, 'ārûm] than any of the wild animals the LORD God had made' (3:1). Note that 'ārûm is not necessarily a negative description but is often employed to denote shrewdness and prudence.[14] Thus, the cleverness of the serpent indirectly indicates the subtlety and deceptiveness in the words and overall approach of Satan. Leupold notes that '[s]uch cleverness may well make this creature the most subtle vehicle of Satan's evil devices.'[15]

Temptation and Rebellion

The serpent approaches Eve and questions God's instructions regarding the Tree of the Knowledge of Good and Evil: 'Did God really say, "You must not eat from any tree in the garden"?' With this remark, Satan sows the seeds of doubt in Eve's mind. The serpent goes on to directly contradict the words of God: 'You will *not* surely die.' By questioning and contradicting God's words, and by telling half truths, the serpent is able to convince Eve that taking the forbidden fruit will allow her to be like God Himself.

Note that the tree was not inherently evil. The reason it was 'off-limits' was purely due to God's prohibition. The first couple were forbidden to decide for themselves what is and is not in their best interests — that was God's prerogative alone (cf. Ezekiel 28:2). Thus, Adam and Eve's sin was a transgression of the law of God — the law prohibiting them from eating the fruit of the Tree of the Knowledge of Good and Evil (cf. Hosea 6:7).

Again, Forster and Marston regard this whole story as a divinely inspired allegory.[16] But such an interpretation reveals that Forster and Marston clearly have little understanding of what an allegory entails. Allegories use completely different symbols for the elements they intend to represent, like the one found in Daniel 8. The ram with two horns is symbolic of the kings of Media and Persia (v. 20)[17] and it certainly does not represent any real historical ram running around beating up all the other animals! Thus, if the Genesis account

---

13 James Montgomery Boice, *Genesis: An Expositional Commentary 1:1 – 11:32* (Grand Rapids, Michigan, Zondervan, 1982), 129.

14 See entry for עָרוּם in BDB.

15 H.C. Leupold, *Exposition of Genesis*, 2 volumes (Grand Rapids, Michigan, Baker, 1942), 1:142.

16 Forster and Marston, *Reason, Science and Faith*, 279–285.

17 Note also that when allegory is used in Scripture the meaning of the allegory is always clearly expounded by other Scriptures.

is an allegory and Adam and Eve are symbolic elements, then they cannot be historical figures as well. Yet the Scriptures clearly teach that they are indeed historical![18] Moreover, if Adam and Eve are allegorical symbols, then how is it that they give birth to Cain and Abel, an event which the New Testament also treats as historical?[19]

Furthermore, if the tree is part of an allegory then what does it mean when its fruit is described as 'good for food'? Blocher claims the fruit is representative of the forbidden 'knowledge' and therefore demonstrates that humans always exercise their autonomy in their use of the created order.[20] However, Blocher appears to be playing fast and loose with the definition of 'allegory' at this point. If the account is allegorical and the fruit is representative of an abstract concept like forbidden knowledge, then it cannot also be representative of the created order. Blocher cannot have it both ways.

Effects of the Fall

Genesis 3:7–19 describes the catastrophic and shocking results of the first couple's rebellion against their Creator. Note that God's judgments on each of the transgressors involve both a function and a relationship.[21] Adam and Eve's task of tending the garden and their mandate to partake of the Tree of Life were withdrawn and the couple were banished from the garden. Moreover, God's curse resulted in the distortion of the physical creation — a distortion which was instigated by divine fiat (Genesis 3:14–19). As Schaeffer explains:

> The abnormality of the external world was brought about by divine fiat. Putting it into twentieth-century terminology, we can say this: the universe does not display a unity of cause and effect in a closed system; God speaks and something changes. We are reminded here of the long arguments that date back to the time of Lyell and Darwin concerning whether there could be such a thing as catastrophe — something that cuts across the uniformity of cause and effect. Scripture answers this plainly: yes, God spoke and that which He had created was changed.[22]

Schaeffer goes on to note that non-Christian philosophers 'almost universally agree in seeing everything as normal, assuming things are as they have always been.' Yet, a Christian 'sees things now as not the way they have always been. And, of course, this is very important to the explanation of evil in the world.'[23]

---

18 e.g. Luke 3:38 (where Adam is part of a genealogy!); Rom. 5:14; 1 Cor. 15:22, 45; 1 Tim. 2:13–14; Jude 1:14.

19 e.g. Matt. 23:35; Heb. 11:4; 1 John 3:12; Jude 1:11.

20 Blocher, *In the Beginning*, 140.

21 Victor P. Hamilton, *The Book of Genesis 1 – 17*, NICOT (Grand Rapids, Michigan, Eerdmans, 1990), 196.

22 Francis A. Schaeffer, 'Genesis in Space and Time' in *Complete Works of Francis A. Schaeffer*, 2nd edition, 5 volumes (Wheaton, Illinois, Crossway, 1985), 2:67.

23 Ibid., 2:68.

The actual effects or changes brought about by the fall may be grouped into four basic categories: guilt, separation, death, and distortion.

Guilt

The full awareness and self-consciousness of the couple's guilt, loss of innocence, and feelings of vulnerability are manifested in the shame of their nakedness. In the Old Testament, nakedness is always connected with some form of humiliation, and is commonly employed as a symbol of guilt.[24] In an attempt to hide this guilt, Adam and Eve cover themselves. This 'solution,' however, is simply an ineffective attempt at self-atonement. Their fig-leaf coverings could not restore their innocence nor could they undo their rebellion. The relationship with their Creator had been permanently broken. No longer would God walk with them in the garden. They and their offspring are now guilty before God, and this guilt is true moral guilt, not just guilt feelings.

Given that Adam and Eve were the only human beings in existence at this time, how does one reconcile the fact that Scripture teaches all humanity is sinful? How does one account for the transmission or imputation of original sin from the first couple to the rest of humanity? The answer to this question is linked to the propagation of mankind.

If the human race as body, soul, and spirit was created in Adam and Eve and was propagated from them through natural generation, then it follows that their offspring inherited the same spiritual status and physical limitations. The first couple's relationship with their Creator was broken and they now stand in a state of rebellion. Thus, when their children are born they too have no relationship or communion with their Creator. They too are born with a sinful nature that is naturally rebellious against God, as the Scriptures teach.[25] They too are in need of salvation.

Separation

The fall of mankind resulted in separation — separation which affected every aspect of creation.

---

24 Hamilton, *Genesis 1 – 17*, 181. He cites Gen. 2:25; Isa. 20:4, 47:3; Mic. 1:11; Nahum 3:5.

25 Ps. 51:5; Eph. 2:1–3; Rom. 5:12–14. Forster and Marston (*Reason, Science and Faith*, 443), on the other hand, adopt a 'Federal Head' approach and think of 'the man' and 'the woman' as 'real individuals located around the late Natufian period … and "the man" was to "cultivate" (or "serve") and "guard" the garden. The verb to "serve" seems to indicate an intended ecological role, whilst the word "guard" means to "exercise great care over to the point if necessary of guarding." The fall into sin is also a failure to rise to the task of serving and guarding the environment. The breaking of God's moral law is associated, of course, with a breakdown in human relationships — typified by that deepest of relationships the marriage bond. This progresses to the nuclear family — and the violence is exacerbated by the move to farming and settlement typified by Cain.' The 'Federal Head' approach, however, is heretical theology — how can one person be guilty of another person's sin?

(1) God and man: Because of the fall, mankind is now separated from his Creator. This is not simply a case where communion has ceased, but rather the relationship has now turned adversarial. God has become mankind's enemy.[26]

(2) Man and himself: Man is now separated from himself. Humans now experience psychological problems, practice self-deception, and are often confused about their purpose, identity, and sexuality. Indeed, the greatest separation of mankind from himself occurs at death when the spirit is separated from the body.

(3) Man and his fellow man: There is also a social separation — man is separated from his fellow man. This is first exhibited when Adam tried to blame Eve (Genesis 3:12). The criminal — Adam — has the audacity to claim to be the victim! Likewise, when Cain murders Abel, brother is separated from brother. As a result, Cain is also separated from the rest of mankind and forced to be 'a restless wanderer on the earth' (Genesis 4:12).[27] The irony is that the guilty sinner becomes the victim of his own sin: Adam became an exile, and Cain a restless wanderer who feared for his own life. In addition, there is also a separation between those who follow God, such as Enoch, and those who do not, and a separation as a result of mankind's activities at Babel (Genesis 11:1–9).

(4) Man and nature: The metaphysical separations lead to physical separations — man is separated from nature. Rather than having full dominion over the natural world (Genesis 1:26–29), humans increasingly have to fight against nature. Crops fail due to drought or flooding. Fruit and vegetables get infected with disease. Natural disasters cause death and destruction, and nature is often the means of judgment. Human beings can no longer eat all green plants (cf. Genesis 1:29) — many are now indigestible or poisonous — nor can they venture into the water or wilderness without fear of being attacked by wild creatures.

(5) Man and his inheritance: Humans have also been separated from their idyllic environment and their inheritance — the Garden of Eden and the Tree

---

26 Rom. 5:10, 11:28; Phil. 3:18; Col. 1:21; James 4:4.

27 Regarding Cain's punishment, Forster and Marston (*Reason, Science and Faith*, 293) ask: 'Were Adam and Eve the sole humans on earth in Genesis 4:1? If so then Cain's fears in Gen 4:14 would seem a bit bizarre: "Whoever finds me will kill me." If, at this point, his mum and dad were the only other humans on the planet and he was already full-grown, he must have been of a very nervous disposition to be worrying about such distant future eventualities. Then, in verse 17, Cain "had sex with his wife" – where did she come from? Adam's next son Seth and other offspring are mentioned in 5:3–4. But before these are even mentioned, Cain had a son, and built a city named after him. Who lived in it? Wouldn't it have seemed a bit pretentious for just the three of them?' The answer to this 'problem' is straightforward: Gen. 5:3 states that Adam was 130 years old when he fathered Seth. Gen. 5:4 states that Adam also fathered other sons and daughters. It is highly unlikely that Adam had none of his other children before Seth was born. In all probability, he had many children prior to this time. In turn, these children would have married each other and had their own children. Thus, Cain most probably married his sister, was afraid of his siblings and their children, and built a city for his own numerous descendants.

of Life (Genesis 3:23–24). The first couple were not content with their blissful life in the garden. They wanted more — they wanted to be like God Himself. Instead, their covetousness and arrogance only led to their exile.[28]

Note that Adam and Eve were not expelled from the garden because it alone was paradise — the only perfect part of the creation. Rather, their expulsion was to stop them from partaking of the Tree of Life. The inheritance they lost was the life-sustaining power of the fruit from the Tree of Life.

There is some disagreement whether Adam and Eve had already eaten from the Tree of Life at the time of the fall. Robert Starke argues that the use of the perfect tense in Genesis 3:22 indicates 'unique or instantaneous action' and the explicit use of גַם (*găm*, 'also') suggests Adam and Eve had not yet eaten from the Tree of Life.[29] However, the perfect forms to which Starke refers are all *waw*-consecutive perfect verbs that express actions that are logically and temporally consequential to the preceding imperfect verb יִשְׁלַח (*yišlăḥ*, 'stretch out'). The *waw*-consecutive perfect verbs לָקַח (*lāqăḥ*, 'take'), אָכַל (*ăkăl*, 'eat'), and וָחַי (*wāḥăy*, 'live') are not only consequential but take on the same sense as the preceding non-perfective verb. In this case, the preceding imperfect verb *yišlăḥ* ('stretch out') has a futuristic/telic sense.[30] In other words, God had to stop Adam and Eve from accessing the Tree of Life because otherwise they may continue to stretch out their hands for the purpose of taking the fruit, eating it, and thus, as a consequence, go on living.

The fact that God gave Adam and Eve permission to eat 'from any tree in the garden' apart from the Tree of the Knowledge of Good and Evil (Genesis 2:16), strongly suggests they had indeed eaten from the Tree of Life. Starke, however, objects to this line of reasoning: 'Yet, following the Fall, God's establishment of an angelic guardian to prevent man's approach to the Tree of Life clearly contradicts this idea (Gen. 3 :24).'[31] Yet Starke's conclusion would only hold if a one-time eating of the fruit was enough to obtain immortality, but there is nothing in the text that suggests this. Regular eating of the fruit was most likely necessary, and would further illustrate the first couple's complete dependence on their Creator. Therefore, the angelic guardian could simply have been preventing any further access to the tree, thus cutting them off from their only source of life-preserving sustenance.

Munday, however, argues that if this was a literal tree, 'how would dispersed descendants have had access to it?'[32] Although the first couple most probably

---

28 Umberto Cassuto, *A Commentary on the Book of Genesis*, 2 volumes, translated by Israel Adams (Jerusalem, Magnes Press, 1961), 1:114.

29 Robert Starke, 'The Tree of Life: Protological to Eschatological' *Kerux* 11/2 (September 1996), 24.

30 *IBHS* 32.2.1d. Gen. 3:22 is explicitly identified as an example of the consequential *waw*-consecutive perfect with a telic sense.

31 Starke, 'The Tree of Life: Protological to Eschatological,' 23.

32 John C. Munday Jr., 'Creature Mortality: From Creation or the Fall?' *JETS* 35/1 (March 1992), 55.

required repeated serves of the tree's fruit in order to maintain their immortality, there is no indication of how often they needed it. It may have only been once a year, which would have meant an annual journey to the tree. Moreover, there is no reason to think that the Tree of Life was different from a normal fruit tree in any other respect. There is no reason why its seeds could not be have been collected and planted elsewhere so that it reproduced 'according to its own kind' (Genesis 1:12). This would have meant that those who wanted to migrate far from the garden would most probably have taken seeds with them in order to plant and cultivate their own 'local' Tree of Life.

Nevertheless, when Adam and Eve were banished from the garden, they were also separated from the Tree of Life and its life-sustaining fruit, nor could they plant and cultivate another. This tree was unique to the garden and either subsequently became extinct, or was eventually removed.

Death

God had told Adam that the consequence of taking the fruit was certain death (Genesis 2:17). As a result of his disobedience, Adam and Eve embarked on a journey towards death which began when they were expelled from the garden and denied the fruit from the Tree of Life.[33] As the apostle Paul wrote in Romans 5, sin entered the world through one man, and death spread to all humanity through that sin (v. 12).

Yet Forster and Marston view Paul's statements in a very different way:

> In Romans 5 [Paul] speaks of the coming of sin. He tells us that unless a moral law is recognised (either explicitly or in one's conscience), there is no sin (Rom 5:13) ... Paul pictures death first entering through one man (Rom 5:12). This is logical enough, as there must have been a very first individual to recognise the authority of a divinely revealed moral law. In this sense there surely must have been an 'Adam': an individual whose experience first began the experience of Man with sin and death. Paul goes on (5:12) to picture death as spreading to all men, because all men sinned. Neither the spreading of the sin nor the parallel spreading of salvation through Jesus is automatic — both involve choices of the individuals.[34]

Unfortunately, Forster and Marston have failed to see that their interpretation is basically identical to the heretical view known as Pelagianism, which sees all individual souls as just like Adam — immediate creations of God, created innocent capable of choosing to obey or disobey. The effect of Adam's sin on his descendants was merely that of a bad example. In other words, all humanity incurred eternal death by choosing to sin after the example of Adam.[35]

---

33 Bill T. Arnold, *Encountering the Book of Genesis* (Grand Rapids, Michigan, Baker, 1998), 57.

34 Forster and Marston, *Reason, Science and Faith*, 289–290.

35 Henry C. Thiessen, *Lectures in Systematic Theology*, revised edition (Grand Rapids, Michigan, Eerdmans, 1979), 186–187.

How then should Romans 5:12–14 be understood? In verse 12, ἐφ' ᾧ (*eph hō*) is best understood as a conjunction meaning 'because'[36] and ἥμαρτον (*hāmarton*) as a reference to each person's own actual sin as a result of the corrupt nature they inherit from Adam.[37] Verse 13 states that before the law sin was not taken into account. Yet verse 13 also makes it clear that sin was still in the world — indeed death reigned because of it (v. 14). In what sense, then, is sin discounted when there is no law? Cranfield answers: '[I]n comparison with the state of affairs which has obtained since the advent of the law, sin may be said to have been, in the law's absence, "not registered," since it was not the fully apparent, sharply defined thing, which it became in its presence. It is only in the presence of the law … that the full seriousness of sin is visible and the responsibility of the sinner stripped of every extenuating circumstance.'[38]

Thus, the interpretation proposed by Forster and Marston is totally contrary to Scripture, which communicates that every human being inherits a sinful nature.[39] All people are by default under condemnation as a result of the first couple's sin (Ephesians 2:3). In fact, in saying that 'unless a moral law is recognised (either explicitly or in one's conscience), there is no sin,' Forster and Marston appear to have totally misread verses 12–13. Firstly, Paul states in Romans 1 that the existence of moral law is obvious to all even though people suppress it (vv. 18–32). Secondly, contra Forster and Marston, verse 13 does not say that there was no sin before the law was given. Rather, sin did indeed exist, but was not clearly defined and therefore was not directly credited to each person. Nevertheless, as verse 14 states, those who lived before the law still died as a result of their own sin.[40] Note also that Paul is talking about physical death. Why does the sudden awareness of moral law bring about physical death? Forster and Marston's interpretation makes no sense at all of the link between sin and physical death — a link which is highlighted by the small scale chiasmus in verse 12:

> Therefore, just as through one man
> A   *sin* entered the world ,
>   B   and *death* through sin,
>   B′   and in this way *death* came
> A′   to all men, because all *sinned*

Indeed, the definite link between sin and death was most noticeably manifested when Cain murdered his brother Abel (Genesis 4:8). Thus, sin not only leads

---

36 Another example of this rendering can be found in 2 Cor. 5:4.

37 C.E.B. Cranfield, *A Critical and Exegetical Commentary on the Epistle to the Romans*, 2 volumes, ICC (Edinburgh, T & T Clark, 1975). 1:274–275.

38 Ibid., 282.

39 Job 14:4, 15:14; Ps. 51:5; Eph. 2:1–2.

40 Indeed, those in the time of Noah (Gen. 6–7) and those who lived in the towns of Sodom and Gomorrah (Gen. 19) were directly judged by God due to their outrageous wickedness.

to a person's own death but, in many circumstances, to the death of his or her neighbor also.

In sinning against their Creator, Adam and Eve not only brought the curse of death upon themselves and their descendants but also upon the animal kingdom. The harmony of creation was shattered. Not only did animals begin to suffer from disease, some also began to prey upon other species. Moreover, God eventually permitted mankind to hunt and kill any living creature for food (Genesis 9:2–3).[41] Indeed, the fossil record is a vivid display of death, disease, and suffering — none of which is indicated by the Genesis account prior to the fall.

Interpreters, however, who hold the consensus of modern science above the propositions of Scripture reject the idea of no animal death prior to the fall. Indeed, the acceptance of animal suffering and death as normative and as part of God's original plan for creation is typical of *all* 'old-earth' interpretations. Ramm, for example, believes that understanding 'world' in Romans 5:12 as a reference to all of creation, is an imposition on the text: 'Ideal conditions existed only in the Garden. There was disease and death and bloodshed in Nature long before man sinned.'[42] Again, these views are motivated purely by a commitment to modern scientific paradigms, rather than the text of Scripture. Nevertheless, Robert Newman states: 'Nothing is said one way or the other about animal death in the Genesis account.'[43] Yet, as Poythress points out, '[s]traightforward arguments from silence are almost worthless … The amount of omitted information in *any* historical narrative is enormous. It is therefore rash to guess at what could *not* have been honestly omitted.'[44]

Walter Bradley argues that stomach bacteria necessarily involve death.[45] Similarly, Pattle Punn points to the death of plants, insects, and bacteria which would have necessarily occurred before the fall.[46] But this is clearly a misrepresentation of what Scripture means by death. Things that live and die are 'living' creatures (Heb. נֶפֶשׁ, *nĕpĕš*)[47] — creatures that *breath* or have the *breath of life*

---

41   While Gen. 9:3 only mentions mankind's new diet, the same could also be said for animals, which most probably would have began hunting and eating each other long before this time. The reason for the omission of a specific statement regarding the animals' change of diet is probably due to the fact that God's major concern was the conduct of mankind.

42   Bernard Ramm, *The Christian View of Science of Scripture* (London, Paternoster, 1955), 233. See also Hugh N. Ross, *Creation and Time* (Colorado Springs, NavPress, 1994), 61, 70–71.

43   Robert C. Newman, 'Old Earth (Progressive) Creationism' in J.P. Moreland and John Mark Reynolds (editors), *Three Views on Creation and Evolution* (Grand Rapids, Michigan, Zondervan, 1999), 111.

44   Vern Sheridan Poythress, 'Adequacy of Language and Accommodation' in Earl D. Radmacher and Robert D. Preus (editors) *Hermeneutics, Inerrancy and the Bible* (Grand Rapids, Michigan, Zondervan, 1984), 373.

45   Walter Bradley, 'Response to Nelson and Reynolds' in Moreland and Reynolds, 77.

46   Pattle P.T. Punn, 'A Theology of Progressive Creation' *PSCF* 39/1 (March 1987), 12–13, 18.

47   See entry for נֶפֶשׁ in BDB and Holladay; *TWOT* 2:587–588.

(cf. Genesis 1:30; 2:7).[48] Plants, on the other hand, 'wither' and 'pass away' rather than die (cf. Isaiah 40:6–8; James 1:10–11).

Regarding the absence of permission to eat flesh, Punn argues: 'this omission may or may not be construed as an argument for vegetarianism … It seems that there is no compelling reason to justify the claim that animal killing is permitted only after the fall.'[49] Punn adds: 'unless one completely abandons the fossil record of life, one has to acknowledge the presence of carnivorousness long before man's appearance.'[50] And 'The fossil record is replete with carnivores who existed long before the appearance of man.'[51] Again, Punn accepts the standard evolutionary interpretation of the fossil record and ignores the revelation of Scripture in which God declares that animals may only eat vegetation (Genesis 1:30).

Munday, however, attempts to nullify the force of verses 29–30:

> The focus in 1:29–30 is on man's needs, not on those of animals, since otherwise green plants would have been given to the beasts in 1:24. Man is here specifically given seed-plants and seed-fruits, while other creatures are given, in contrast, herbage or grass in general. The prescription taken as a whole recognizes the dependence of the animal kingdom upon the plant kingdom. It is an instruction as to the liberal grant of God's providence, not necessarily a restriction on what may be eaten.[52]

This is pure nonsense. Firstly, if verses 29–30 focus on human needs then why would they contain a prescription diet for animals? Secondly, appealing to the presence of the prescription diet in verse 30 rather than in verse 24 as evidence that the text focuses on human needs, is surely begging the question. Munday is clearly assuming an old-earth scenario, but the whole motivation for accepting animal death before the fall is to justify an old-earth scenario! In any case, Munday himself goes on to state that he believes the text concerns the dependence of the animal kingdom upon the plant kingdom, and a testimony to God's providence.

Similarly, Kidner argues that the vegetarian diet assigned to the animals does not imply that all were once herbivores, any more than the vegetarian diet assigned to mankind implies that all vegetation is equally edible.[53] The problem

---

48 Blocher (*In the Beginning*, 185, fn. 31) argues that interpreting *nĕpĕš* in this way is philologically unacceptable since the smallest marine creatures and insects are explicitly classified as having *nĕpĕš* in Gen.1:20–24. However, Blocher is holding to a much greater linguistic precision than the author of Genesis. Although the terms used to describe the sea creatures and the flying creatures in verses 20–24 are quite generic, they clearly refer to large sea creatures, and the many types of fish and birds. The account is not an exhaustive exposition of God's creative activity and it is highly unlikely that the original readers were aware of the existence of microscopic organisms such as plankton, dust mites, and bacteria.

49 Punn, 'A Theology of Progressive Creation,' 12.

50 Ibid.

51 Ibid., 17.

52 Munday, 'Creature Mortality: From Creation or the Fall?' 65.

53 Derek Kidner, *Genesis*, TOTC (Leicester, IVP, 1967), 52.

with this argument is that Kidner assumes the original state of creation is more or less identical to what we see and experience in the world today. Yet the account of the fall clearly indicates otherwise. All of creation was placed under a curse, human immortality was withdrawn, and our capacities began to decrease. Thus, it is entirely likely that many of the plants which are presently inedible, toxic, or poisonous to human beings were originally fine to eat. Unsuitability for human consumption most probably came about as a result of a reduced capacity of the human digestive system to process such plants. This reduced capacity may have been brought about by genetic deterioration within the human body, or within the plant itself.[54]

Regarding Genesis 1:29–30, Forster and Marston claim that such a statement does not imply that all animals were initially vegetarian since elsewhere in the Old Testament it states that lions, ravens, and eagles receive their food (meat) from *God* (Psalm 104:21; Job 38:39–41; 39:27–30).[55] However, these verses merely affirm God's continuing providence — even after the fall. Such verses do not imply (contrary to Genesis 1:29–30) that it was God's original intention for animals to eat meat.

Forster and Marston also deny that Isaiah 11:6–9 and 65:25 speak of the physical restoration of the animal creation in the kingdom of God, since Isaiah 35:9 states that there will not be any lions there at all, which would imply that the references to the lion are not literal.[56] Yet even on the face of it, this line of reasoning is self-contradictory. In their attempt to prove the non-literalness of the lion in Isaiah 11:6–9 and 65:25, they apparently *accept* the literalness of the lion in Isaiah 35:9! In any case, the context of Isaiah 35:9 reveals that there will actually be no lion on 'The Way of Holiness' — the road which signifies *the path to the kingdom* (Zion). It does not say that there will be no lions in the kingdom itself.[57]

Alan Hayward, on the other hand, in his discussion of animal death, argues that Adam could not possibly have understood God's warning in Genesis 2:17 unless he had seen at least one dead animal.[58] Likewise, Forster and Marston write: 'Indeed, if physical death had not been familiar to Adam, then it is hard to see what meaning at all God's warning could have had to him. We understand the concept of the second or spiritual death only by analogy to the physical one with which we are familiar.'[59] However, this conclusion does not follow. It is not necessary to see or experience something in order to grasp the concepts behind it. For example, a child can understand that he and his siblings came from their mother's body without actually seeing a birth. Almost everyone understands the concept of an atmosphere even though no one can actually see the different

---

54 See Jerry Bergman, 'Understanding Poisons from a Creationist Perspective' *JoC* 11/3 (1997), 353–360.

55 Forster and Marston, *Reason, Science and Faith*, 259.

56 Ibid.

57 Even if Isaiah 35:9 did say what the authors claim, it would actually be a contradiction not a proof of non-literalness.

58 Alan Hayward, *Creation and Evolution* (London, Triangle, 1985), 182.

59 Forster and Marston, *Reason, Science and Faith*, 258.

kinds of gas molecules floating in the air around us. In addition, given that Adam could understand and communicate with his Creator, he clearly had a 'pre-programmed' vocabulary so it is entirely possible that Adam understood the concept of death even without ever seeing a dead animal.

Bradley and Olsen point to the existence of large claws and sharp teeth as indicators that certain animals were designed to be predators and meat eaters rather than vegetarians.[60] But the existence of such things does not necessarily imply carnivorous behavior. Large claws are also needed for climbing, and the Giant Panda, for example, has some of the sharpest teeth in the animal kingdom, yet their diet contains no meat at all. In addition, animals thought to be strictly carnivorous[61] can and do survive on a vegetarian diet.[62]

Another argument raised against the absence of animal death is the existence of the various defense mechanisms and bodily protection and repair systems. These mechanisms appear to be designed for life in a world potentially dangerous and harmful in the physical sense.[63] However, some attack and defense mechanisms may have had other applications. For example, some baby spiders use their webs to trap pollen for food.[64] In the case of poisonous and toxic venoms, our body has a complex means of protecting itself from many of these substances. For those compounds which are harmful or deadly to humans, the problem is most likely a result of the breakdown or degradation of the human immune system after the fall.[65] Alternatively, it is not unreasonable to think that God may have introduced genetic problems as a result of the fall to limit our constitution and regenerative capacity, given that He apparently altered the physical form of the serpent (Genesis 3:14).

Yet another objection comes from Munday, who argues that Scripture allows for the possibility of the death of aquatic life in the original creation:

> When God said in Gen 8:21 that he would not again curse the ground on account of men and would never again destroy all living creatures, marine life was omitted. According to 6:7, 17–20; 7:21–23 the curse of the flood included only terrestrial creatures. In a generally parallel fashion the curse in Genesis 3 mentioned only the ground and its vegetation, not sea life. Note the omission of marine life from both prescriptions, an omission that is both curious and significant … The exclusion of sea life from both curses at least permits the possibility of marine animal death as part of the original created order.[66]

---

60 Walter L. Bradley and Roger Olsen, 'The Trustworthiness of Scripture in Areas Relating to Natural Science' in Radmacher and Preus, 310.

61 e.g. reptiles, canines, bears, and lions.

62 James Stambaugh, 'Creation's Original Diet and the Changes at the Fall' *JoC* 5/2 (1991), 134; David Catchpole, 'The Lion that Wouldn't Eat Meat' *Creation* 22/2 (March–May 2000), 22–23; David Catchpole, 'Piranha' *Creation* 22/4 (September–November 2000), 20–23.

63 Munday, 'Creature Mortality: From Creation or the Fall?' 52.

64 'Pollen-Eating Spiders' *Creation* 22/3 (June 2000–August 2000), 8.

65 In many cases, poisons and toxins are only harmful in certain circumstances while in others they can be life-saving. See Bergman, 'Understanding Poisons.'

66 Munday, 'Creature Mortality: From Creation or the Fall?' 66.

But this line of argument is flawed. Firstly, the curse of the flood was aimed at land-dwelling creatures since they are obviously the ones primarily affected. Given that marine life would be largely unaffected by a flood, sea dwelling creatures were not wiped out.[67] Secondly, as Wenham points out, the two curses are not parallel:

> It is important to note the position of עוד in this sentence, coming after לקלל to 'curse,' not after אסף 'do again' as in the parallel clause 'Never again shall I smite.' This shows that God is not lifting the curse on the ground pronounced in 3:17 for man's disobedience, but promising not to add to it. The flood was a punishment over and above that decreed in 3:17. This is further confirmed by the milder word for 'curse,' קלל 'treat lightly, disdain,' used here as opposed to the graver term ארר, used in 3:17.[68]

Therefore, the unique circumstances pertaining to the flood cannot be projected back to the original state of creation.

Forster and Marston also deny the existence of a link between death and Adam's sin in 1 Corinthians 15:21–22 by arguing that the lack of a definite article before 'man' (v. 21) shows that this is not a reference to a historical individual: 'We already noted that Paul speaks ambiguously, sometimes speaking as though "Adam" is "Man" … The word "man" (15:21) has no definite article and there is no indefinite article in Greek, so it could mean "man" or "a man" (reflecting Romans "one man"). But in verse 22 the tense is present (all *die*), so surely a historical individual cannot be meant?'[69] But again their conclusion is false. Adam is explicitly named in verse 22 (Ἀδάμ, a proper noun, as opposed to ἄνθρωπος, the generic term for 'man') as the individual man who has brought death to all people. Furthermore, the second part of the verse is a contrasting parallel which identifies Christ as the individual who can bring life to all people. This teaching is echoed in Romans 5:12–17[70] making the link between death and the sin of a single historical man undeniable.

---

67 This is not to say that no sea-dwelling creatures were destroyed in the flood. Indeed, most of the well-preserved fossils found are of sea-dwelling creatures. Nevertheless, the various species of aquatic creatures would have survived the flood.

68 Gordon J. Wenham, *Genesis 1–15*, WBC (Dallas, Word, 1987), 190.

69 Forster and Marston, *Reason, Science and Faith*, 289.

70 Rom. 5:12–17: 'Therefore, just as sin entered the world through one man, and death through sin, and in this way death came to all men, because all sinned — for before the law was given, sin was in the world. But sin is not taken into account when there is no law. Nevertheless, death reigned from the time of Adam to the time of Moses, even over those who did not sin by breaking a command, as did Adam, who was a pattern of the one to come. But the gift is not like the trespass. For if the many died by the trespass of the one man, how much more did God's grace and the gift that came by the grace of the one man, Jesus Christ, overflow to the many! Again, the gift of God is not like the result of the one man's sin: The judgment followed one sin and brought condemnation, but the gift followed many trespasses and brought justification. For if, by the trespass of the one man, death reigned through that one man, how much more will those who receive God's abundant provision of grace and of the gift of righteousness reign in life through the one man, Jesus Christ.'

Munday also tries to argue that φθορά (*phthora*) in Romans 8:21 cannot refer to death (of animals)[71] but scriptural usage and the standard lexicons flatly contradict this.[72]

Munday also appeals to the predator–prey relationships mentioned in Psalm 104:21 and Job 38–41, arguing that there is 'no hint that they are a corruption of [God's] original intent,' and that God 'extols them as part of his wisdom.'[73] But only Psalm 104:2–9 specifically refers to creation events[74] while the rest of the psalm focuses on God's providence over creation. Likewise, Job 38–41 also concerns God's providence over His cursed creation. Thus, the references to carnivorous feeding relates to God's continued provision even after the fall. God has cursed creation — He has not abandoned it.

In addition, Munday points out that, unlike Adam, animals — especially those outside the Garden — were not offered access to the Tree of Life. Thus, they had no possible way to achieve immortality, and therefore one may conclude that animals were created mortal by nature.[75] However, this is an argument from silence. Firstly, both the account of creation and the account of the fall focus on humanity and their relationship to their Creator and to the world in which they live. These accounts tell us virtually nothing about the relationship of animals with their Creator. Secondly, while it is true that animals are inherently mortal (only God is immortal [1 Tim 6:16]), this does not mean that they died. God could have sustained them in some other way apart from the Tree of Life. Given that only humans are created in the image of God, it should not be surprising to find that these chapters say very little about the pre-fall nature and attributes of animals.

Again, Munday asks: 'If animals turned predator at the fall, why was Adam not warned of this danger upon banishment from Eden?'[76] Firstly, the change of diet would most probably have been a gradual process rather than a sudden event. Secondly, Genesis 9:2 states that it is actually the animals who have the most to fear since they are the ones who are hunted, killed, and enslaved by mankind — not the other way round.

---

71 Munday, 'Creature Mortality: From Creation or the Fall?' 64. He goes on to state: 'it cannot be proven that "decay" or "corruption" must point unambiguously to death and dissolution of animals. Plants were already subject to death and dissolution before the fall. The passage here does not distinguish plants from animals when speaking of "decay." Creation's "decay" seems to be taken as quite general. If so, how can the passage be forced to focus only on creaturely decay?' However, no-one is claiming that 'decay' refers exclusively to animal death, only that it *includes* animal death.

72 φθορά refers to death of humans in 1 Cor. 15:42 and Col. 2:22, and animal death in 2 Pet. 2:12. See also Louw-Nida 20.38: 'a state of ruin or destruction, with the implication of disintegration … In 2 Pet 2.12 it may be more appropriate in a number of languages to translate "… to be killed".' BAGD states: 'in the world of nature … γενεσις κ. φθορά = coming into being and passing away.'

73 Munday, 'Creature Mortality: From Creation or the Fall?' 66.

74 The creation of light, the stretching out of the heavens, and the appearance of dry land, i.e. days 1–3.

75 Munday, 'Creature Mortality: From Creation or the Fall?' 59.

76 Ibid., 66.

Yet the most bizarre and disturbing objection comes from Hugh Ross who regards death as a 'blessing' which was designed to restrain the spread of evil.[77] Many liberal commentators view death as a release from a hopeless existence.[78] Pattle P.T. Pun, on the other hand, asserts that death in not necessarily a bad thing, and in fact can be a vehicle for blessing!

> God called His creation good. This does not necessarily mean that there was no physical death in the creation before the Fall. I Timothy 4:4–5 states that 'everything God created is good, and nothing is to be rejected if it is received with thanksgiving, because it is consecrated by the word of God and prayer' (NIV). This passage seems to suggest that 'good' is used in contrast with 'evil,' so that we can receive everything God created with thanksgiving because it is not evil. Death in the physical world does not necessarily represent evil. Natural selection is evil only when it is exploited by man. In certain situations, death actually means peace for the righteous when God overrules (Isa. 57: 1–2).[79]

However, these objections all fail. Appealing to 1 Timothy 4:4–5 begs the question, since one must assume that death is a creation of God in the sense that it is an inherent part of the created order. Pun must show this from Scripture rather than merely asserting it. Furthermore, arguing that because God employed death to restrain evil, death is somehow a good thing, simply demonstrates theological confusion concerning God's providence and His plan and purpose for creation. The 'very good' creation was perfect in every aspect, and the absence of sin and the curse meant that there was no requirement to restrain evil, either through death or through any other means. It was not until after the fall that God took the lives of wicked people in order to halt the spread of their wickedness. Therefore, death was never a part of God's original plan for His creation. Death was a response to human rebellion and the propagation of evil.

Again, the reason for holding to interpretations that see the death and suffering of animals as an inherent part of God's plan is purely because a commitment to an 'old-earth' creation scenario demands it. Not only do these interpretations allow scientific speculations to override the revelation of Scripture, but they lead to a belief that death and suffering, and the survival of the fittest, were actually part of God's original creation which he described as 'very good' (Genesis 1:31). As Cameron points out, '[t]he world which God made for man to inhabit was "very good." It had been prepared to receive him as its crown, and the setting was constructed so as to be ideal for the probation to which Adam and Eve were called. The world was not created with the Fall in prospect, still less with the curse already let loose.'[80] Moreover, if Genesis 1–2 not only describes the creation but also the goal of redemption to which the universe and humanity

77 Ross, *Creation and Time*, 62.

78 e.g. Bruce Vawter, Gerhard von Rad, John Skinner, and Claus Westermann.

79 Punn, 'A Theology of Progressive Creation,' 18.

80 Nigel M. de S. Cameron, *Evolution and the Authority of the Bible* (Carlisle, Paternoster, 1983), 66.

will return when the promise of the kingdom is fulfilled,[81] then the possibility of death before the fall (even animal death) is ruled out along with the concept of an old earth. As Stambaugh notes, '[i]f God originally intended death to be an integral part of His creation, then God should allow death to continue into eternity.'[82]

Furthermore, in contrast to the present world, the picture of the future kingdom in Isaiah 11:6–9 describes a world of harmony — a world where animals no longer prey on each other, and a world where humans and wild animals live in peace:

> *The wolf will live with the lamb,*
> > *the leopard will lie down with the goat,*
> *the calf and the lion and the yearling together;*
> > *and a little child will lead them.*
> *The cow will feed with the bear,*
> > *their young will lie down together,*
> > *and the lion will eat straw like the ox.*
> *The infant will play near the hole of the cobra,*
> > *and the young child put his*
> > *hand into the viper's nest.*
> *They will neither harm nor destroy*
> > *on all my holy mountain,*
> *for the earth will be full of the knowledge of the LORD*
> > *as the waters cover the sea.*

No longer will the wolf prey on the lamb, and the lion on the calf. Carnivorous animals will change their diet and begin eating plants instead of meat. And in contrast to the present state of enmity between humans and snakes (Genesis 3:15), children will no longer fear these creatures, and snakes will pose no threat to children.[83]

Isaiah 65:19–25 paints a similar picture, but Munday points out that some of the language used suggests that death will remain a reality (v. 20, 'He who dies at a hundred will be thought a mere youth; he who fails to reach a hundred will be considered accursed'; v. 22, 'For as the days of a tree, so will be the days of my people').[84] It must be remembered, however, that Isaiah 65 is a prophetic oracle regarding the eschatological kingdom, and, as such, employs a great deal of imagery and symbolism. Therefore, it is inappropriate to expect a purely objective report like those found in historical narratives. The point the prophet appears to be making is not that we will still experience death in the kingdom of

---

81 Wenham, *Genesis 1 – 15*, lii.

82 James Stambaugh, 'The Relationship Between Sin and Death in Genesis: Death Before Sin?' *Impact* 191 (May 1989).

83 Munday ('Creature Mortality: From Creation or the Fall?' 60) objects: 'Isaiah 11, however, is entirely forward-looking except for declaring that God will regather the exiles. It does not even hint at a death-free creation.' But Munday fails to recognize that the future kingdom is in part a restoration of the original creation and reflects its purity and perfect harmony.

84 Munday, 'Creature Mortality: From Creation or the Fall?' 60.

God, but that the nature of the kingdom stands in stark contrast to our present experience. Unlike today, in the future kingdom, there will be no sorrow nor suffering. Infants will no longer die, nor will a person's life be prematurely cut short. Indeed, the reason why we can be confident of this is because death itself will be eradicated: 'He will wipe every tear from their eyes. There will be no more death or mourning or crying or pain, for the old order of things has passed away.' (Revelation 21:4).

Because God declared His creative acts to be 'good' and His completed pristine creation to be 'very good' (Genesis 1:31), understanding the death of animals as normative and part of God's original intention is to view death as something inherently 'good' and pleasing to God. Yet Scripture consistently presents death in a negative light. Death is only ever a result of evil actions,[85] punishment for doing evil,[86] the consequence of disobedience,[87] the result of God's judgment,[88] or simply the inevitable fate of all fallen human beings.[89] Indeed, Jesus wept when he heard of Lazarus' death even though He knew He had the power to raise him (John 11:35). In contrast, men like Enoch and Elijah were spared from death as a reward for their service and devotion to God.[90] In fact, Scripture explicitly identifies death as the 'last enemy' (1 Corinthians 15:26). With this in view, understanding death as anything but a blight upon creation is completely untenable.

Interpreters who view death as anything other than a negative consequence of the fall are in essence deflecting the responsibility for sin and its effects back onto God: 'Any theory that somehow sanctions the existence of evil in God's good creation fails to do justice to sin's fundamentally outrageous and blasphemous character, and in some subtle and sophisticated sense lays the blame for sin on the Creator rather than on ourselves in Adam.'[91]

Distortion

The fourth consequence of the fall is distortion. Creation is no longer what God intended it to be. It has degraded in virtually every respect. Fallen humanity now bears a distorted image of God, and we are at odds with the world in which we live.

In Genesis 3, we read that the serpent is cursed 'above all the livestock and all the wild animals' and is made to crawl on his belly and 'eat dust' for the rest of his life (v. 14). Hamilton argues that if verse 14 is taken as a reference to a change in the snake's mode of locomotion, then it would also imply a change in

---

85 e.g. Cain killing Abel (Gen. 4:5–8).

86 e.g. Ananias and Sapphira (Acts 5:1–10).

87 e.g. Achan (Josh. 7:10–25).

88 e.g. The Passover in Egypt (Exod. 12:29).

89 e.g. The family line of Adam (Gen. 5) constantly makes reference to the death of each individual: '… and then he died.'

90 Enoch (Gen. 5:22–24); Elijah (2 Kgs 2:11).

91 A.M. Wolters, *Creation Regained* (Carlisle, Paternoster, 1996), 48–49.

the snake's diet.[92] Therefore, he understands 'eat dust' (Heb. עָפָר תֹּאכַל, *ʿāpār tōʾḵāl*) as an expression of 'humiliation and subjugation.'[93] Wenham agrees and cites Psalm 72:9, Isaiah 49:23 and Micah 7:17 as examples where such expressions clearly refer to humiliation,[94] although the expression used in these verses is actually 'lick the dust' (Heb. עָפָר יְלַחֵכוּ, *ʿāpār yᵉlāḥḵû*). Nevertheless, in Genesis 3:14, 'eat dust' is preceded by 'You will crawl on your belly,' which strongly suggests the serpent also experienced an actual physical transformation. Rather than walking like other animals, he is now made to experience the humiliation of crawling on his belly in the dust.

The phrase 'above all the animals' suggests that the other animals were also cursed but in a less dramatic way. This point has been hotly debated however. E.J. Young argues that 'the thought is not that of comparison, as though the Lord had said that all the beasts would be cursed, but that the serpent would be cursed more than any. Rather, in the curse the serpent is separated from the other beasts. Whereas they are free, he is now in a peculiar bondage. Upon him alone of all the beasts does God pronounce the curse, for he alone had tempted the woman.'[95] At the heart of the matter is whether to understand the preposition מִן (*mîn*) as comparative ('cursed above all the animals') or separative ('cursed [banished] from all the animals'). Hamilton takes *mîn* with a separating force, meaning that the serpent is to be alienated from all other creatures. However, this interpretation appears very weak. In what sense are serpents/snakes alienated from the rest of the animal world? Furthermore, while the separative use of *mîn* can be found in Genesis 4:11, the context makes it very clear that this meaning is intended, but no similar contextual markers can be found in Genesis 3:14–19.

Nevertheless, Munday claims the key conclusion 'is that the curse of Genesis 3 involves the ground's response to man's disobedience to God. Neither this curse nor any other, in context, explicitly involves a fundamental alteration of the law-order of the cosmos or of the life-death cycle of the animal realm. No such changes even seem to be implied.'[96] But Munday's stance is completely unsustainable. The notion that animals, along with the rest of creation, are under God's curse is confirmed in Romans 8:18–30. Verses 19–30 essentially support and expound verse 18: 'our present sufferings are not worth comparing with the glory that will be revealed in us.'[97] Creation has been subjected to 'frustration' (NIV) or 'futility' (NRSV). It groans like a woman in labor, and looks forward to the time when it will be liberated from its bondage to decay.

Note that in verses 19–20 'creation' cannot be referring to mankind, since this would obviously include Adam, who could hardly be described as being

---

92 Hamilton, *Genesis 1 – 17*, 196–197.

93 Ibid.

94 Wenham, *Genesis 1–15*, 79.

95 Young, *Studies in Genesis One*, 97.

96 Munday, 'Creature Mortality: From Creation or the Fall?' 62.

97 Cranfield, *Romans*, 1:410.

subjected 'not by his own choice.' Consequently, Cranfield understands 'creation' as 'the sum-total of sub-human nature both animate and inanimate.'[98] Furthermore, the frustration or futility (Greek, ματαιότης, *mataiotēs*) the creation experiences should be understood as denoting 'the ineffectiveness of that which does not attain its goal.'[99] Thus, Paul is teaching that 'the sub-human creation has been subjected to the frustration of not being able properly to fulfill the purpose of its existence.'[100] Similarly, James D.G. Dunn explains:

> The point Paul is presumably making, through somewhat obscure language, is that God followed the logic of his purposed subjecting of creation to man by subjecting it yet further in consequence of man's fall, so that it might serve as an appropriate context for fallen man; a futile world to engage the futile mind of man. By describing creation's subjection as 'unwilling' Paul maintains the personification of the previous verse. There is an out-of-sortedness, a disjointedness about the created order which makes it a suitable habitation for man at odds with his creator.[101]

Regarding the agent who brought creation into subjection, Adam, man in general, and Satan have all been suggested, but these options are unlikely since they are all incapable of altering the order of creation by themselves. Thus, the general consensus is that God Himself was the One who placed the creation into the futile state of bondage in which we now find it.[102] Indeed, the statement itself appears to be a 'divine' or 'theological' passive — a Jewish method of referring to God without explicitly naming Him.[103]

Note also that φθορά (*phthora*) focuses on a real process of decay that eventually ends in destruction or death.[104] Thus, '[t]here is little doubt that Paul has in mind the judgment related in Gen 3.17–19, which includes (v. 17) the words "cursed is the ground for thy sake."'[105] The good news is that creation will eventually be liberated from its bondage to decay and enter the glorious freedom of the coming kingdom.[106] As Cranfield puts it, creation will be liberated 'from the condition of being slaves of death and decay, of corruption and transitoriness, which is the very opposite of the condition of glory.'[107]

---

98 Ibid., 411–412. Note that the personal language used in no way invalidates this interpretation. Such personification is used frequently in the Old Testament.

99 Ibid., 413.

100 Ibid.

101 James D.G. Dunn, *Romans 1–8*, WBC (Dallas, Word Books, 1988), 487–488.

102 James Stambaugh, 'Creation, Suffering and the Problem of Evil' *JoC* 10/3 (1996), 397.

103 See Zerwick § 236.

104 Louw-Nida (20.38): 'a state of ruin or destruction, with the implication of disintegration,' or (23.205): 'to rot or decay, in reference to organic matter.' BAGD: 'ruin, destruction, dissolution, deterioration, corruption.'

105 Cranfield, *Romans*, 1:413.

106 This will be further discussed in chapter 11.

107 Cranfield, *Romans*, 1:415.

Not surprisingly, Forster and Marston object to the idea of taking Romans 8:21 as a reference to the fall: 'Paul does not say in Romans 8:21 at what time God subjected the creation to a servitude to mortality which he pictures as a state of ineffectuality. It is far from clear that it was the fall and involves moral evil. This could be one possible interpretation, but it is also possible that it was at creation, and that mankind's task was to transform and give it purpose by the introduction of altruism and eternity.'[108] Munday also objects to including animal death in Romans 8:20–21: 'to infer fall-caused creature mortality from Rom 8:20–21 is incorrect.' Like Forster and Marston, he believes 'it is presumptuous to assert that the creation was "subjected" to creature mortality at the fall rather than "subjected" (given that attribute) at the beginning as a feature of man's probationary environment.'[109]

Yet, not only does Genesis 1–2 indicate the opposite (that is, a 'very good' creation not a frustrated one) the explicit reference to God's act of subjection in verse 20 clearly indicates that creation was not like this in the beginning. In fact, this very eccentric interpretation is held by no notable theologian or commentator on Romans, past or present. Again, as Cranfield notes, Paul is clearly alluding to the curse of Genesis 3:17–19.[110] John Murray concurs: 'In relation to this earth this is surely Paul's commentary on Gen. 3:17, 18.'[111]

Thus, the curse resulting from the fall was not limited to Satan, but affected the entire physical creation including the animal kingdom. 'Man's actions will invariably affect creation. When man fell, creation fell as well.'[112] This was necessary so that mankind's authority over creation would be maintained. Goldsworthy adds:

> Within the creation, however, a further vital distinction is made between humanity, which is created in God's image, and the rest of the creation. Human beings are given dominion over the creation while at the same time they are subject to the sovereign God. Sin is the human rejection of this order and involves our rebellion against the sovereign rule of God. Salvation is God's plan to restore all of reality to right relationships. God ruling his people who, in turn, rule over creation is the essence of the kingdom of God. There is no part of the Bible that does not portray this kingdom situation as it was or will be, or which does not project this plan of God into the context of present human fallenness.[113]

The curse also resulted in the instigation of hostility between the serpent and the woman and between her offspring and the serpent's offspring (Genesis

---

108 Forster and Marston, *Reason, Science and Faith*, 261.

109 Munday, 'Creature Mortality: From Creation or the Fall?' 63–64.

110 Cranfield, *Romans*, 1:413.

111 John Murray, *The Epistle to the Romans*, NICNT (Grand Rapids, Michigan, Eerdmans, 1968), 303.

112 Quek Suan Yew and Jeffrey Khoo, 'The Bible and Science: Progressive Creationism examined in the light of Scripture' *The Burning Bush* 8/1 (January 2002), 4.

113 Graeme Goldsworthy, *Preaching the Whole Bible as Christian Scripture* (Leicester, IVP, 2000), 116.

3:15). This text is commonly interpreted as the *protoevangelium* — the first allusion to the gospel. The offspring of the woman is understood as a reference to Christ, who deals a fatal blow to Satan. However, this interpretation is highly problematic. Firstly, when 'offspring' (זֶרַע, *zĕrăʿ*) refers to an individual child, it normally refers to immediate offspring rather than a distant descendant. *zĕrăʿ* does, however, often refer to a collective distant offspring, that is, a person's collective descendants.[114] Some commentators argue that the use of second person, masculine, singular suffixes in the Hebrew ('you', 'your') suggest that this is indeed a reference to Satan because serpents do not continue to exist throughout the generations. However, this argument cannot be sustained based on Hebrew grammar. The same Hebrew suffixes are also used in Genesis 28:14 when God tells Jacob: 'Your descendants will be like the dust of the earth, and you will spread out to the west and to the east, to the north and to the south.' The singular 'you' cannot refer to only Jacob because he obviously cannot spread out in all directions. It was Jacobs's seed that spread out.

Secondly, the same Hebrew verb שׁוּף (*šûp*) lies behind the English verbs 'crush' and 'strike' in the NIV. This verb occurs in only two places apart from Genesis 3:15: in Job 9:17, it refers to the battering of a storm, and in Psalm 139:11 it refers to being enveloped by darkness. The common idea appears to be that of 'attack' or 'assault.'[115] Thirdly, these verbs are both Qal imperfects denoting future iterative action. In other words, the 'crushing' or 'striking' cannot be fatal to the snake since it is repetitive. Indeed, given that the woman's offspring strikes first, the serpent would never have the opportunity to strike back if the blow was fatal. The statement could refer to the ongoing struggle between humans and deadly snakes, which was a grim reality in the ancient world, but this seems to be a trivial point to include in such a theologically significant account. A more likely meaning is that the serpent — rather than just being either the literal creature possessed by Satan, or the form which Satan took to deceive Eve — serves as an anti-God symbol representing sin, death, and the power and craftiness of evil.[116] Therefore, this curse envisages the long war against God and His people undertaken by the serpent and his followers.

Eve also receives a direct curse. She (and her descendants) will experience intense pain when bearing children (Genesis 3:16). Again, this suggests that Eve's body and genetic structure underwent a physical alteration at some level. Note that the reference to the woman's pain 'increasing' does not necessarily mean that the process of childbirth was somewhat painful to begin with. In fact, Eve had not yet given birth. Moreover, pain is, after all, an over-stimulation of particular nerve endings. The same nerve endings which produce pleasure can also produce pain if they are overloaded. God may have initially intended childbirth to be a highly pleasurable experience much like sexual intercourse.

---

114 e.g. Gen. 12:7.

115 See entry for שׁוּף in BDB.

116 Wenham, *Genesis 1–15*, 80. John H. Walton, *Genesis*, NIVAC (Grand Rapids, Michigan, Zondervan, 2001) 226.

Note also that עִצָּבוֹן (*ʿiṣṣebôn*, 'pain,' 'toil') includes more than just physical pain. It also refers to emotional distress, and the same word is used in verse 17 to describe Adam's painful toil in the field.[117]

Eve's relationship with her husband, and consequently their marital relationship, was also changed and distorted from what God had originally intended. Most English translations[118] render תְּשׁוּקָה (*tešûqāh*) as 'desire' but recent research has demonstrated that 'control' is a better choice.[119] Instead of a harmonious union based on mutual love and respect, the woman will always want to control her husband but he will dominate her (compare the New English Translation). This interpretation fits in well with the judgmental tone of the passage.

Adam, on the other hand, does not receive a direct curse but an indirect one. His sin resulted in the ground — which he subsequently had to work — being cursed. It will never regularly and effortlessly yield a bountiful harvest. Much of mankind's toil will be fruitless since it will only produce useless thorns and thistles, which now grow wild. Only after much frustration, back-breaking work, and a great deal of stress, will mankind produce enough to eat. 'Man, who was no longer able to enjoy the fruits of the Garden of Eden, was compelled *to till the ground* …'[120] Moreover, he will continue to toil in this way until he dies.[121]

The human body is also in a state of degradation. Instead of being a perfect, unblemished vessel for the human spirit, it is now a damaged vessel, subject to a vast array of diseases, infections, and injuries (cf. Revelation 21:4), and destined to return to the ground from which it came (Genesis 3:19). Indeed, the human body now needs to be clothed, not only for the sake of modesty, but for protection from exposure. God made garments of animal skin to clothe the first couple (Genesis 3:21), so again, humanity's sin resulted in the death of animals.

The fall and the spread of sin has severely affected humanity in other areas and especially our minds. Romans 1:18–32 points out that there are many godless and wicked people who suppress the truth. Many live futile lives and become foolish in their thinking (v. 22). They abuse and dishonor their bodies (v. 24). They reject truth and would rather believe lies (v. 24). They entertain dishonorable passions and engage in shameless perverse acts, receiving in them the due penalty for their sin (vv. 26–27) — a clear reference to the numerous sexually transmitted diseases and infections which can often be very painful and, in many cases, fatal.

---

117 David T. Tsumura, 'A Note on הרון (3,16)' *Bib* 75 (1994), 398–400.

118 KJV, ASV, NKJV, NASB, NIV, NRSV.

119 Susan T. Foh, 'What is the Woman's Desire?' *WTJ* 37 (1975), 376–383. This nuance can be clearly seen in Gen. 4:7.

120 Cassuto, *Commentary on the Book of Genesis*, 1:102.

121 Note also the repetition of 'to till the ground' in Gen. 3:23 (from 2:5). This reinforces the idea that the reason why there were no such plants in Gen. 2:5 was due to the absence of man in general and the absence of *sinful* man in particular. See chapter 8.

Humans continue to suppress the knowledge of God and His decrees (vv. 28, 31). We have depraved minds with a strong inclination to practice evil. We are filled with every kind of unrighteousness, wickedness, covetousness, and malice. We are rife with envy, murder, strife, deceit, and hostility. We are gossips, slanderers, haters of God, insolent, senseless, heartless, ruthless, arrogant, and boastful. We are disobedient to our parents, we break the law, and we go out of our way to contrive new ways of doing evil (vv. 29–30). Moreover, we encourage others to do likewise (v. 32)

Summary

A.W. Pink rightly notes that Genesis 3 'is one of the most important [texts] in all the Word of God. What has often been said of Genesis as a whole is peculiarly true of this chapter: it is the "seed-plot of the Bible." Here are the foundations upon which rest many of the cardinal doctrines of our faith.'[122]

Contra Arthur Lewis,[123] the fall of mankind caused the physical creation to change in a very real way, and in a direction away from what God originally intended.

> Adam and Eve's fall into sin was not just an isolated act of disobedience but an event of catastrophic significance for creation as a whole. Not only the whole human race but the whole nonhuman world too was caught up in the train of Adam's failure to heed God's explicit commandment and warning. The effects of sin touch all of creation; no created thing is in principle untouched by the corrosive effects of the Fall.[124]

Instead of experiencing bliss, Adam and Eve encounter misery. Rather than living in paradise, they are expelled from the garden. In taking the forbidden fruit, Adam and Eve 'not only fail to gain something they do not presently have; the irony is that they lose what they currently possess.'[125] Schaeffer concurs: 'The simple fact is that in wanting to be what man as a creature could not be, man lost what he could be. In every area and relationship men have lost what finite man could be in his proper place.'[126]

Nevertheless, fallen humans are still human. Our sin has not caused us to cease being human. We are still image bearers of God — even if that image is somewhat distorted. Yet, the presence of sin and the effect it has on creation is repulsive to a holy God, and is the reason why there is a definite need for Christ's propitiatory work on the cross. The restoration of our relationship with God was only made possible through Christ's suffering and death on the cross at the hands of the Jewish leaders and the Romans. Thus, historical sin has historical redemption.

---

122 Arthur W. Pink, *Gleanings in Genesis* (Chicago, Moody Press, 1922), 33.

123 Lewis ('The Localization of the Garden of Eden' *BETS* 11 [1968], 174) writes: 'Nothing in the narrative suggests that the realm of nature has been altered in a fundamental way ... There is no indication that the Lord God added thorns to the roses or sharp teeth to the carnivorous animals.'

124 Wolters, *Creation Regained*, 44.

125 Hamilton, *Genesis 1–17*, 208.

126 Schaeffer, 'Genesis in Space and Time' in *Complete Works*, 2:70.

CHAPTER 10

The Flood and Its Effects

As fallen humans began to procreate and spread throughout the earth, their rebellion against God became more intense and their wickedness increased. In order to restrain the spread of evil, God brought judgment upon His creation, judgment that the world had never seen before and has never seen since — the judgment of a global, catastrophic flood.

The Fallen World

The Wickedness of Humanity

The growth of the earth's population is accompanied by a growth in corruption and evil. Fallen humans produce a fallen society, and Genesis 6 records how great human wickedness had become: 'every inclination of the thoughts of [the human] heart was only evil all the time' (v. 5). Humans were dedicated to doing evil at every opportunity. Every thought and motive was oriented toward doing evil, and the earth had become full of corruption and violence (vv. 11–12).[1] Note that in verse 11 'earth' is a metonym for *all the inhabitants of the earth*.[2] However, verse 12b indicates that both the earth and its inhabitants are in view here. Note also that the corruption referred to is moral corruption (cf. Ezekiel 20:44). This is echoed by the use of דֶּרֶךְ (děrěk, 'way'), which here refers to behavior or moral character.[3]

In addition, the Niphal form of שָׁחַת (šāḥǎt, 'corrupt') in verses 11 and 12a expresses the common notion that the action or state expressed by the verb affects the subject or its interests.[4] Similarly, the Hiphil form in verse 12b indicates the subject ('all the people on earth') caused the object ('the earth') to participate indirectly as a second subject in the notion expressed by the verbal root.[5] Thus, mankind's sin is viewed as having an adverse effect upon the earth.

---

1 Note that 'violence' (Heb. חָמָס, ḥāmās) can refer to various criminal actions, including unjust treatment (Gen. 16:5; Amos 3:10), malicious testimony (Deut. 19:16), deadly assault (Gen. 49:5), murder (Judg. 9:24), and rape (Jer. 13:22). See also entry for חָמָס in BDB and Holladay.

2 A metonym is a word that is used in place of another word or phrase which it suggests.

3 See entry for דֶּרֶךְ in BDB.

4 *IBHS*, 23.1h.

5 GKC § 53.c; *IBHS* 27.1d.

Yet Noah and his family were the sole exceptions. Noah found favor in God's eyes. He was a righteous man who was blameless among the people of that time. He believed in God, honored Him, and enjoyed His communion.

The Promise of Judgment

Because of humanity's spiraling rebellion and escalating wickedness, God was grieved about making mankind and 'his heart was filled with pain' (Genesis 6:6). As a result, God decided to wipe out not just mankind, but all animals from the face of the earth, including every creature that moves along the ground and all the birds of the air.[6] In fact, God vowed to destroy the earth itself (Genesis 6:13). According to Genesis 6:17, this judgment will come about by means of a catastrophic flood, which will destroy 'all life under the heavens, every creature that has the breath of life in it.' Indeed, every living thing on earth would perish.

The expressions 'all people' (6:12, 13) and 'all life' (6:17) are renderings of the Hebrew כָּל־בָּשָׂר (kāl-bāśār, literally, 'all flesh'). This Hebrew expression is used twelve times throughout the flood narrative.[7] Given the context of each specific instance, all but two refer to 'all living creatures, both human and animal.'[8] Indeed, Genesis 7:21 explicitly defines the general meaning of the expression in this context: 'Every living thing that moved on the earth perished — birds, livestock, wild animals, all the creatures that swarm over the earth, and all mankind.' Note that וַיִּגְוַע כָּל־בָּשָׂר הָרֹמֵשׂ עַל־הָאָרֶץ (wăyyigwă' kāl-bāśār hārōmēś ăl-hā'āreṣ, 'Every living thing that moved on the earth perished') is followed by the preposition בְּ (bᵉ, lit. 'in') which in this case is used explicatively, and can be rendered as 'comprising,' 'namely' or 'that is.'[9] Thus, 'Every living thing that moved on the earth' is elaborated as 'birds, livestock, wild animals, all the creatures that swarm over the earth, and all mankind.' Note also that the two instances of kāl-bāśār in Genesis 9:15–16 are preceded by כָּל־נֶפֶשׁ חַיָּה בְּ (kāl-nĕpĕš ḥăyyāh bᵉ, 'every living creature ...'). In these cases, the explicative use of bᵉ strengthens the expression 'every living creature' resulting in 'every living creature of every kind,' which would surely include both humans and animals. It follows, then, that the promise of judgment and destruction refers to both humans and animals. This is supported by Genesis 9:13–17 where God establishes His covenant with 'all life on the earth,' namely, both humans and animals. Nevertheless, some have argued that kāl-bāśār could not refer to all life because the Hebrew term for 'violence' (Hebrew, חָמָס, ḥāmās) in Genesis 6:13 is only used in connection with humans. Yet the general meaning of the word

---

6   מָחָה (māḥĕh, 'wipe out,' 'blot out') is used frequently to describe total destruction or total erasure.

7   Search performed with GRAMCORD on Groves-Wheeler Westminster Morphological Text v. 3.1.

8   Gen. 6:19 and 7:16 refer to animals only. For instances outside of the flood narrative which refer to both animals and humans, see Lev. 17:14; Num. 18:15; Ps. 136:25, 145:21.

9   See *IBHS* 11.2.5e and GKC § 119i. Note that Gen. 7:21 is listed as a specific instance by both grammars.

is 'violence' or 'wrong' and makes reference to wickedness and unrighteousness in general.[10] The verb form means 'do violence' or 'treat violently.'[11] In any case, Jonah 3:8 appears to indicate that both humans and animals may do violence.

Another objection to taking *kāl-bāśār* as a reference to all life including animals is based on the claim that the expression 'corrupted their way' in Genesis 6:12 is only applicable to mankind. However, this objection cannot be sustained. Proverbs 30:19 speaks of 'the way of an eagle' and 'the way of a snake' as well as 'the way of a man with a maiden.' Furthermore, the Hebrew verb translated 'corrupted' is used of both animals and humans. In 1 Samuel 6:5, using the same Hiphil form used in Genesis 6:12, mice are said 'to corrupt the earth.' Thus, 'corrupted their way' is probably a reference to the violent behavior animals have adopted since the fall.

Since the primary function of Genesis 6:12–13 is to highlight the existence of moral corruption, the NIV translators understand the referent to be humans only. But *kāl-bāśār* often refers to any kind of flesh, both human and animal.[12] This understanding makes more sense in the context of the flood, and suggests that the author intends to picture all living creatures, both humans and animals, as guilty of moral failure, and explains why both humans and animals were subsequently destroyed by the flood. Indeed, several Scriptures indicate that animals are morally culpable.[13] Other Scriptures indicate that human sin can contaminate other people as well as animals.[14] Therefore, it appears that the animals were morally contaminated because of their association with sinful humanity.

God's reaction to this moral corruption is to pronounce judgment upon the sinful creation. Human beings, animals, and the earth itself were to be destroyed by a catastrophic global flood, which essentially causes a reversal of creation — a retreat back to the beginning of day three when the earth was covered in water. When God causes the flood waters to retreat and dry ground to appear we are reminded of God's creative acts on day three.[15]

Noah's Ark

Because Noah was a righteous man and had found favor in God's eyes, he and his family were given an opportunity to escape the flood — a way of salvation.

God makes a covenant with Noah and his family, and instructs him to build an ark — a ship big enough not only to accommodate his family but also to

---

10 See entry for חָמָס in BDB and Holladay.

11 See Jer. 22:3; Ezek. 22:26; Zech. 3:4; Prov. 8:36, BDB and Holladay. For use with beings other than humans, see Job 15:33 and Lam. 2:6.

12 A GRAMCORD search on Groves-Wheeler Westminster Morphological Text v. 3.1 reveals that *kāl-bāśār* occurs 37 times, 17 of which clearly refer to both humans and animals. See also entries for בָּשָׂר in BDB and Holladay.

13 Gen. 9:5; Exod. 21:28–29; Jonah 3:7–8.

14 See, for example, the story of Achan (Josh. 7), and King Saul's defeat of Agag, king of the Amalekites (1 Sam. 15).

15 Victor P. Hamilton (*The Book of Genesis: Chapters 1–17*, NICOT [Grand Rapids, Michigan, Eerdmans, 1990], 291), on the other hand, posits that the two sources of water are allusions to the waters above and below in Genesis 1.

accommodate a pair (male and female) of every kind of living creature (6:19–20), and seven of every kind of clean animal and bird (7:2–3), as well as all the different kinds of food required to sustain them all for over a year (6:21).

The ark was the only way of salvation — the only way to be saved from the floodwaters. Only those humans and animals that entered the ark would be saved. Every other living creature would perish.

The ark was 450 feet long, 75 feet wide, and 45 feet high, and made from cypress wood. It was made waterproof by a coating of pitch on both the inside and outside. It was covered by a roof with an 18-inch gap to allow light in, and had a door on one side. Inside, the ark was divided into three decks, each of which contained many rooms.[16]

Bernard Ramm rightly affirms the credibility of the details of the ark and the authenticity of the account itself:

> Suffice it to say, the ark was a reasonable structure. For its specific purpose it was of credible shape, credible size, and credible proportions. It was made from a wood well adapted for such a barge and was divided into stories and staterooms for proper bracing. It apparently had some system of lighting and ventilation. All in all, the record of the ark bears witness to the credibility of the construction of such a ship ...[17]

The ark was a truly remarkable vessel. It remained the largest vessel ever constructed until 1858, when *Great Eastern* (692 by 83 by 30 feet) was built.

The Flood

Seven days after Noah and his family entered the ark, the floodwaters came — apparently from two sources: (1) the springs of the great deep, and (2) the floodgates of the heavens (7:11). In fact, the primary source of water was most probably the 'springs of the great deep' given that even though it rained for forty days and forty nights (7:12), the floodwaters still kept coming for a further 110 days (7:24).

Leupold suggests that the number forty is not accidental and notes that in Scripture this number often indicates a period of trial terminating in the victory of good and destruction of evil.[18]

The floodwaters covered the entire earth including all the high mountains, and the ark floated on the surface of the water and was lifted high above the earth. Again, every living, land-dwelling creature with breath in its nostrils perished — all birds, all livestock, all wild animals, all creatures that swarm over the earth, and all humans (7:21–23). Only Noah and his family survived — just as God had promised.

---

16 Regarding the age of the earth, Davis Young (*Creation and the Flood* [Grand Rapids, Michigan, Baker, 1977], 211–212) argues that the use of pitch on the ark is a problem for those who hold to a young earth, since this pitch is derived from oil and coal (so it is claimed) and oil and coal takes thousands of years to form. But engineer and geologist, Tas Walker, has pointed out that pitch does not need to be made from petroleum. The pitch-making industries in Europe made pitch from pine resin for centuries ('The Pitch for Noah's Ark' *Creation* 7/1 [1984], 20).

17 Bernard Ramm, *The Christian View of Science of Scripture* (London, Paternoster, 1955), 157–158.

18 H.C. Leupold, *Exposition of Genesis* (Grand Rapids, Michigan, Baker, 1942), 1:291. See Num. 14:33; Exod. 24:18; 1 Kgs 19:8; Jonah 3:4; Matt. 4:2; Acts 1:3.

God did not forget Noah and those with him in the ark. He sent a wind over the earth, causing the waters to begin receding, and after 150 days, the floodwaters had gone down to a level where the ark came to rest on the mountains of Ararat.

Although the floodwaters continued to go down, they would not be completely gone until the twenty-seventh day of the second month — more than a year after the flood began. It was at this time when Noah and his family, and all the animals with him, were finally allowed to leave the ark.

Note also the chiastic pattern of the narrative:

A Noah and his family: the only righteous people on earth (6:9–10)

  B God promises to destroy the earth and its inhabitants by a global flood (6:11–22)

    C God instructs Noah, his family and the animals to enter the ark (7:1–10)

      D The floodwaters come upon the earth (7:11–16)

        E The floodwaters rise and cover the earth (7:17–24)

          F God remembers Noah (8:1a)

        E′ The floodwaters recede from the earth (8:1b–5)

      D′ The floodwaters disappear and the earth is dry (8:6–14)

    C′ God instructs Noah, his family and the animals to leave the ark and replenish the earth (8:15–9:7)

  B′ God promises to never again destroy the earth and its inhabitants by a global flood (9:8–17)

A′ Noah and his family: the only people on earth (9:18–19)[19]

Wenham insightfully points out how well-suited such arrangements are to communicating God's message: 'Palinstrophic writing [chiastic arrangement] is particularly suited to telling a flood story: the literary structure closely resembles the real-life situation. Noah enters the ark and later leaves it. The waters rise and then fall. In other words, the story falls into two halves that ought to resemble each other to some extent. The surface structure of the narrative mirrors the deep structure of the event being described.'[20] Wenham goes on to point out that the focus of the chiasmus is *God remembering Noah*. 'It was divine intervention that saved Noah, and the [chiastic] pattern reminds the reader of the fact.'[21]

Although the flood narrative has all the hallmarks of real historical narrative and has the same form as the other historical accounts in Genesis, Cassuto

---

19 Similar patterns have been suggested by B.W. Anderson ('From Analysis to Synthesis: The Interpretation of Gen 1–11' *JBL* 97 [1978], 23–39) and Gordon J. Wenham ('The Coherence of the Flood Narrative' *VT* 28 [1978], 336–348).

20 Gordon J. Wenham, *Genesis 1–15*, WBC (Waco, Texas, Word, 1987), 157.

21 Ibid.

rejects any idea that the flood narrative records a real event, claiming that it is 'poetic in character.'[22] But, for the same reasons outlined in chapter 4, such claims have no basis whatsoever.

Furthermore, there are several historical references to the flood in Matthew 24:37–39 and Luke 17:26–27. Hebrews 11 also affirms the historical nature of the account of Noah and the flood. Forster and Marston, on the other hand, consider the flood account to be truly historical, but imply that the language used in hyperbolic.[23] In other words, the flood was a real historical event but only covered a large region of the Middle East even though the language used suggests it covered the entire globe.

Global or Local?

The author of the flood narrative quite clearly presents the flood as a real historic inundation which covered the entire globe. Nevertheless, although many laymen and commentators understand the flood as significant and catastrophic, it is often reduced to only a localized event. Furthermore, many commentators point to recent archaeological and geological findings which are said to indicate wide-spread flooding in the Middle East in the pre-historic period.

Bill Ryan and Walter Pitman have published evidence for a large local flooding of a huge area around the Black Sea, and linked it to the biblical account of Noah's flood.[24] They claim that the Black Sea was once an isolated freshwater lake 110 to 150 metres below its present level. It was proposed that the sudden rise in water level was brought about by melting ice sheets at the end of the ice age which raised the level of the Mediterranean until it eventually topped the land bridge across the Bosporus. This resulted in massive amounts of water gushing catastrophically into the Black Sea, and the excavation of the channel linking it to the Mediterranean.

A closer look at the biblical account of the flood, however, shows that the 'Black Sea' interpretation cannot be sustained. The biblical flood covered the then highest mountains, but the Black Sea flood simply rose 110 to 150 metres. In this scenario not even the known world was submerged! The water would have needed to rise another 1500 metres to cover the Krymskiye Gory mountains on the adjacent Crimean Peninsula.[25]

In addition, the proposed flood would have caused the water level to rise only fifteen centimetres per day, so why build an ark when people and animals could have easily escaped at a leisurely pace? Birds would also not have been threatened by such a flood — they could have easily flown away. Even if some animals drowned, no species would have been threatened with extinction. Nor

---

22 U. Cassuto, *A Commentary on the Book of Genesis*, 2 volumes, translated by I. Adams (Jerusalem, Magnes Press, 1964), 2:47.

23 Forster and Marston, *Reason, Science and Faith*, 236–237.

24 W.B.F. Ryan et al., 'An Abrupt Drowning of the Black Sea Shelf' *Marine Geology* 138 (1997), 119–126; W.B.F. Ryan and W.C. Pitman, *Noah's Flood: The New Scientific Discoveries About the Event That Changed History* (New York, Simon & Schuster, 1998).

25 Tas Walker, 'The Black Sea Flood: Definitely Not the Flood of Noah' *JoC* 14/1 (2000), 42.

would all people have perished — indeed, even Ryan and Pitman suggest many of the displaced people migrated to Europe.

In the Black Sea flood the water gushed through a localized channel, but the biblical flood has water coming from the 'springs of the great deep' and the 'floodgates of the heavens' (Genesis 7:11). Furthermore, the waters of the Black Sea flood have clearly not receded, whereas the land was completely dry at the end of the biblical flood (Genesis 8:14). The two scenarios have nothing in common. To accept that the Black Sea flood was the biblical flood of Noah is to reject the truth of the Bible, and therefore, the inerrancy of Scripture.

Glenn R. Morton also holds to a local flood scenario but suggests the Mediterranean basin as the setting, rather than the Black Sea.[26] He argues that the entire human population was confined to the once empty Mediterranean basin, which was then catastrophically filled due to the collapse of the Gibraltar dam. Noah and his family were transported in the ark by the rising water and deposited on the mountains of Ararat. Morton offers strong evidence in favor of a flood occurring in this way, but was it Noah's flood? The answer must be 'no' and for similar reasons why the Black Sea flood cannot be Noah's flood. If the Mediterranean has flooded as Morton describes then that flood has not ended and the waters have not subsided as the Bible describes.

In addition, an analysis of the language employed strongly supports a global flood scenario rather than merely extensive but localized flooding. Both the Hebrew Old Testament and Greek New Testament use words to describe the Noahic flood which are different from the words normally used to describe a local flood.[27] Thus, the Noahic flood was pictured as a totally unique event.

Moreover the repetitive use of כֹּל (kōl, 'whole', 'all') throughout Genesis 6–9 also strongly indicates the globality of the flood. Nevertheless, because kōl is occasionally used in a hyperbolic sense, many claim the instances in the flood narrative are also hyperbolic. Yet kōl most often refers to the wholeness, totality or entirety of something,[28] and is only limited when it has the article and when the context necessitates such a limitation.[29] In the case of the flood narrative, neither of these requirements are satisfied. Furthermore, Michael Kruger has pointed

---

26 Glenn R. Morton, 'The Mediterranean Flood' *PSCF* 49/4 (1997), 238–51.

27 In biblical Hebrew, a flood is described in various ways, including: (1) שֶׁטֶף (šĕṭēp, 'flood') in Dan. 9:26; Nahum 1:8, and the verbal form שָׁטַף (šāṭap, 'overflow') in Dan. 11:10; (2) שִׁפְעַת־מַיִם (šip'āt–mayim, lit. 'a multitude of waters') in Job 22:11, 38:34, or just מַיִם (mayim, 'waters') by itself, as in Job 27:20; Ps. 88:18; 124:4; (3) אִשָּׁחֶה ('ăśḥěh, 'make swim') in Ps. 6:6; (4) זֶרֶם מַיִם (zěrěm mayim, lit. 'flooding downpour of waters') in Isa. 28:2; (5) שִׁבֹּלֶת שְׁטָפָתְנִי (šibōlĕṭ š'ṭāpāt'nî, lit. 'the flowing water overflowed me') in Ps. 69:2, 15; and (6) מַבּוּל (mabbûl, 'flood') which exclusively refers to the Noahic flood, i.e. used throughout Gen. 6–9 as well as Gen. 10:1, 32; 11:10 and Ps. 29:10. In New Testament Greek, a normal flood is described using πλήμμυρα (plēmmūra, 'flood') as in Luke 6:48. In 1 Pet. 4:4 ἀνάχυσις (anachusis, 'flood', 'excess') refers to flooding in a figurative sense, but the Noahic flood is always — and exclusively — referenced using κατακλυσμός (kataklysmos, 'flood', 'deluge') as in Matt. 24:38–9 and Luke 17:27.

28 See entry for כֹּל in Holladay.

29 See entry for כֹּל in BDB.

out that *kōl* is used 72 times in the flood narrative (a total of 85 vv.), which is 21 percent of all occurrences in Genesis. Thus, Moses seems to be emphasizing that the flood covered *all* the earth and destroyed *all* life.[30] Indeed, regarding the use of *kōl* to describe the covering of the mountains, Leupold writes: 'One of these expressions alone would almost necessitate the impression that the author intends to convey the idea of the absolute universality of the flood ... Yet since "all" is known to be used in a relative sense, the writer removes all possible ambiguity by adding the phrase "under all the heavens." A double *kōl* cannot allow for so relative a sense. It almost constitutes a Hebrew superlative.'[31]

Hugh Ross, on the other hand, asserts that כָּסָה (*kāsāh*, 'cover') in Genesis 7:19–20 can also mean 'running over' or 'falling on' and appeals to the *Theological Wordbook of the Old Testament* (*TWOT*) and *Gesenius' Hebrew and Chaldee Lexicon*.[32] But neither of these citations offer any real support for Ross's assertions. Gesenius' lexicon is hopelessly outdated and the *TWOT* article by R. Laird Harris says nothing of the sort. Harris writes: 'In Gen 7:19–20 the hills were "covered;" the Hebrew does not specify with what. The NIV specification of water goes beyond the Hebrew. The Hebrew may merely mean that the mountains were hidden from view by the storm.'[33] But the immediate context clearly rules out Harris's alternative interpretation. It would be absurd to claim the mountains 'were covered from view by the storm' when verses 18–20 state: 'The *waters rose* and increased greatly on the earth, and the ark floated on the *surface of the water*. They rose greatly on the earth, and all the high mountains under the entire heavens were covered. The *waters rose* and *covered* the mountains to a depth of more than twenty feet.' Indeed, there is no reference at all to the storm or storm clouds.

In any case, *kāsāh* means 'cover' or 'hide'[34] and in verse 19 it appears in the Pual *waw*-consecutive imperfect form (Heb. וַיְכֻסּוּ, *wǎyᵉkŭssû*), which communicates the idea of causation but in the passive voice: 'and then ... were covered.' In other words, '[t]he waters rose and increased greatly on the earth' (v. 19a) which subsequently caused 'all the high mountains under the entire heavens' to be covered with water (v. 19b).

Ross also claims that the expressions 'under the entire heavens' in Genesis 7:19 is used in a non-global way.[35] This expression *may* be used in a non-global

---

30 Michael J. Kruger, 'Genesis 6–9: Does "All" Always Mean All?' *JoC* 10/2 (1996), 215–216.

31 Leupold, *Exposition of Genesis*, 1:301.

32 Hugh N. Ross, *The Genesis Question* (Colorado Springs, NavPress, 1998), 145.

33 *TWOT* 1:448–449.

34 See entry for כָּסָה in Holladay. Entries in BDB and Holladay also list 'forgive' as a possible rendering. Cf. Ps. 32:1.

35 Ross, *The Genesis Question*, 142–3. Ross appeals to Gen. 41:56 and 1 Kgs 10:24 as examples but neither of these texts contain the same Hebrew expression (תַּחַת כָּל־הַשָּׁמָיִם, *tǎhǎt kāl-hǎššāmāyim*) used in Gen. 7:19. A GRAMCORD search on Groves-Wheeler Westminster Morphological Text v. 3.1 shows that this expression is used 6 times apart from Gen. 7:19 (Deut. 2:25, 4:19; Job 28:24, 37:3, 41:3; Dan. 9:12) none of which demand a non-global sense. Only Deut. 2:25 may be understood in this way.

sense in other passages where the context demands it but, as shown above, the context of Genesis 7:19 leaves no room for such an interpretation.

Similarly, Ross argues that the expression 'the face of the earth' in Genesis 7:21 also refers to something less than a global perspective. He cites Genesis 8:5 and 8:9 as support and argues that 'all the surface of the earth' in verse 9 could not refer to the entire globe because verse 5 states that the water had receded to the point where the tops of the mountains were now showing. But again, Ross's argument is flawed. Firstly, the expression used in Genesis 7:21 is actually עַל־הָאָרֶץ ('āl-hāʾāreṣ, 'on the earth') rather than פְּנֵי כָל־הָאָרֶץ (pᵉnê kāl-hāʾāreṣ, 'all the face/surface of the earth') so the two expressions are not really comparable. In any case, pᵉnê kāl-hāʾāreṣ is used eleven times in the Old Testament and always in reference to habitable land where people and animals live, rather than any land mass such as a mountain top protruding from the water's surface. Therefore, the intention of Genesis 8:9 is to communicate that the dove could not find any land upon which it could make a nest and find food. Indeed, this was precisely the reason why Noah sent it out — to see if there was habitable land upon which they could all disembark from the ark (cf. 8:11ff.).

There are several other factors in this account and other texts which indicate a global rather than local flood. In Genesis 9:9–10, God makes a covenant with the survivors from the ark: 'I now establish my covenant with you and with your descendants after you and with every living creature that was with you — the birds, the livestock and all the wild animals, all those that came out of the ark with you — every living creature on earth.' Note that 'every living creature on earth' stands in apposition to the preceding clause, 'the birds, the livestock and all the wild animals, all those that came out of the ark with you.' Likewise, this clause stands in apposition to the preceding sentence (vv. 9–10a). That is, 'every living creature on earth' encompasses all the birds, livestock, wild animals and humans who came out of the ark, which were the same creatures that were with Noah on the ark. In other words, God made a covenant with 'every living creature on earth' which equates to those humans and animals that came out of the ark. There were no other creatures on the earth apart from those that went into, and came out of, the ark, so the flood must have been global in order to wipe out all other creatures all over the earth.

Another important reference to the Noahic flood is found in 2 Peter 3:4–7: Scoffers will come and say: 'Where is this "coming" he promised? Ever since our fathers died, everything goes on as it has since the beginning of creation.' But, as Peter points out, 'they deliberately forget that long ago by God's word the heavens existed and the earth was formed out of water and by water. By these waters also the world of that time was deluged and destroyed. By the same word the present heavens and earth are reserved for fire, being kept for the day of judgment and destruction of ungodly men.' These scoffers will deny that God judges His creation, arguing that because He has not done so in the past, there is no reason to think He will do so in the future. But, in doing so, they *deliberately* forget that God created this world, and that He judged it by means of a (pᵉ catastrophic flood in the time of Noah. Indeed, God will judge the world again at the second coming. By His word, God formed the earth out of water and by water (v. 5), and by this same water, He judged His creation during the flood of Noah (vv. 6–7). In other words, the same water that God used to form the earth, He also used to destroy it. God brought the heavens and the earth into existence by His word, and He will also judge and destroy them by His word.

Note also the allusions to the creation account. For example, in verse 5 'by God's word the heavens existed …' is an obvious reference to Genesis 1:1. Similarly, the forming of the earth 'out of water and by water' refers to the dividing of the waters and the formation of the land in Genesis 1:7–10.

These parallels in 2 Peter 3 are further emphasized by a chiastic pattern:

A Formation of heavens (sky) by God's word (v. 5a)

B Formation of land by water and out of water (v. 5b)

B′ Destruction of world (land and occupants) by water (v. 6)

A′ Destruction and judgment of heavens and land and ungodly men by God's word (v. 7)

Both A and A′ refer to God's fiat acts, while B and B′ refer to the role of water in both creation and judgment. Note also that both A and B are concerned with creation, while B′ and A′ are both concerned with destruction.

Peter's presentation of destruction caused by the flood as a contrasting parallel to creation is powerful evidence for a global flood. The destruction caused by the floodwaters was a global phenomenon, just as the emergence of dry land from the primeval waters on the third day of creation was a global phenomenon.[36]

Hugh Ross, however, claims that the phrase 'the world of that time' in 2 Peter 3:6 suggests a limited geographical area.[37] Likewise, Douglas Moo argues that the shift from 'the heavens' and 'the earth' to 'the world of that time' in verses 5–6 suggests that only the inhabited and organized human dimension is in view. Thus, Peter is only affirming that the flood destroyed the ungodly human beings of Noah's day. But this interpretation is unsustainable at several points. Firstly, τότε (*tote*, 'then', 'at that time') is a purely *temporal* particle — the emphasis is on the moment of time itself, not on the circumstances of the moment. Secondly, κόσμος (*kosmos*, 'world') always indicates a totality — be it in reference to the physical world, the world order, the realm of existence or mankind.[38] If a limited geographical region was intended then γῆς ('land',

---

36 Forster and Marston (*Reason, Science and Faith* [East Sussex, Monarch, 1999], 298–299) attempt to dismiss 2 Peter 3:5–7 as evidence for a global flood by explaining that γῆ (*gē*) and κόσμος (*kosmos*) never refer to a globe. However, this is a moot point. The point is not whether *gē* or *kosmos* refer to a globe but whether the flood was universal in the sense that it covered the entire surface of the land. The language, context, and logic overwhelmingly supports this notion.

37 Ross, *The Genesis Question*, 143.

38 See Louw-Nida, 1.1, 1.39, 9.23, 41.38, 59.55, and BAGD κόσμος § 2–8. One could argue that the reference is just to mankind who inhabited only a limited area of the earth's surface, but this interpretation is ruled out on other grounds. See previous and following discussion.

'country', 'region') would have been a more appropriate choice. Thirdly, given that Peter is talking about future judgment compared with past judgment, the temporal aspect of the world (that is, the world of *that time*) is in focus here, not its geographical extents. Indeed, this meaning is greatly reinforced by the reference to 'the present heavens and earth' in verse 7, which not only confirms the temporal emphasis but also negates Moo's suggestion of a shift in meaning.

In light of the above, and when one also considers that almost every culture around the world has a flood legend with a high degree of commonality with the Genesis account,[39] it is impossible to conclude that the Noahic flood was anything other than a global catastrophe.

Nevertheless, these observations have not stopped some commentators claiming that the flood is universal in the sense that it covered the entire visible and known region, not that it covered the entire globe. Bernard Ramm, for example, writes 'the deluge was universal *in so far as the area and observation and information of the narrator extended.*'[40]

Again, this line of reasoning cannot be sustained. The Bible is clear that mankind had multiplied upon the face of the earth (Genesis 6:1), and the Mesopotamian region can only support a limited population. There would also have been a natural dispersion effect fueled by the increasing violence and corruption at the time (Genesis 6:11–12). Moreover, given that the flood also destroyed all animals, it would be absurd to argue that they too were confined to the Mesopotamian region!

Note that those who hold to a local flood are almost always committed to an 'old-earth' interpretation of creation, which seeks to integrate the doctrine of creation with the conclusions and consensus of modern (evolutionary) science. Note that the consensus of palaeontologists and archaeologists, who invariably base their conclusions on the same old-earth, uniformitarian assumptions to which local flood advocates hold, is that modern people-groups such as the Australian aborigines were living on the Australian continent from 40,000 to 60,000 years ago. However, local flood advocates cannot date the Noahic flood any earlier than 3000–2000 B.C. This means that local flood advocates must reject biblical inerrancy since Genesis 7:21–23 clearly affirms the total destruction of every living being on the face of the earth, or, if they wish to limit the totality of destruction to mankind, they must reject the humanity of modern people-groups such as Australian aborigines, which is clearly absurd.

Several other objections to a local flood can be raised. If the flood was only local, then why was there any need to build an ark? Noah was given many years of warning, so there was ample time to leave the region and travel anywhere on earth. Why build an ocean-liner sized ark to save eight people when they could have migrated as Lot and his family did after being warned about the

---

39 See the impressive list compiled by Tim LaHaye and John D. Morris in *The Ark on Ararat* (Nashville, Thomas Nelson, 1976), 233–239.

40 Ramm, *Christian View of Science of Scripture*, 163. Original emphasis.

impending destruction of Sodom and Gomorrah. The animals would have lived all over the earth not just in the Mesopotamian region, so why bother to bring them on board? If any kinds were unique to this region then they too could have migrated. Why bring birds on board when they are capable of flying hundreds of miles in a day?

The length of time the waters persisted on the earth is also evidence against a local flood. The springs of the deep burst forth and the floodgates of the heavens opened up on the seventeenth day of the second month (Genesis 7:11). The rain fell continuously for forty days and forty nights (Genesis 7:12), and the springs kept pouring out water for a further 110 days (Genesis 7:24). When God sent the wind which caused the waters to begin receding, it took 150 days for the ark to come to rest on the mountains of Ararat (Genesis 8:3–4), and the waters continued to recede until the twenty-seventh day of the second month — more than a year after the flooding began. It is inconceivable that a local flood would last this long.

Furthermore, the fact that the dove released by Noah could find no place to land because there was water over all the surface of the earth (Genesis 8:9) also stands in contradiction to a local flood — especially since doves are capable of flying hundreds of miles without setting down.

In addition, if the flood was only local, God has repeatedly broken His promise never again to destroy the earth and its inhabitants by a flood (Genesis 8:21, 9:11; Isaiah 54:9) since there have been numerous local floods throughout Mesopotamia which have caused great destruction.

We may also question why God would make an 'everlasting' covenant with all living creatures and their descendants (Genesis 9:8–10) if the flood only affected those in the Mesopotamian region? Why is the symbol of the covenant — the appearance of the rainbow — a global phenomenon if it only concerns those creatures in the Mesopotamian region?

Of course, many objections to a global flood have also been raised. A common objection is that there is apparently not enough water on earth to cover all the highest mountains. There are two things, however, that those who raise this objection fail to consider. Firstly, the account indicates that the main source of the floodwaters was 'all the springs of the great deep.' Moreover, in Genesis 8:3, the verb שׁוּב (šûḇ) 'to return' is employed twice, emphasizing that the waters 'returned' to the respective sources from which they came — the skies above and the subterranean lakes within the earth's crust. In other words, most of the floodwaters are no longer visible on the earth. They came from, and returned to, large subterranean wells.[41]

Furthermore, it is not unreasonable to assume that the earth's geography and topography were quite different to what is observed today. Indeed, it is highly likely that the earth's surface was much flatter before the flood since all mountains are formed as a result of either tectonic and volcanic activity

---

41 See Gerhard F. Hasel, 'Some Issues Regarding the Nature and Universality of the Genesis Flood Narrative' *Origins* 5/2 (1978), 97.

or catastrophic deposition and erosion — all of which would have occurred during, or as a result of, a global catastrophic flood.

Davis Young believes that one of the most compelling arguments standing against a global flood concerns the problem of getting animals to and from the ark.[42] However, this would only be a problem if one *a priori* rules out any divine assistance. Such an assumption is unwarranted. Genesis 6:20 states that the animals will come to Noah and 7:8–9 confirms that this did indeed happen.

Ross claims that the ark could not have accommodated all the various species of animals living at that time since '[a]ccording to the fossil record, at least half a billion to a billion new species of life arose between the Cambrian explosion … and the arrival of human beings…'[43] However, Ross is clearly making these figures up, since the total number of species actually catalogued is only about two million. Moreover, 98 percent of these are invertebrates, which include a variety of organisms such as sponges, worms, jellyfish, mollusks, and insects. The remaining 2 percent are vertebrates and number approximately 40,000 species.[44] Note also that Noah was not required to take every kind of living creature on the ark but only those that move along the ground as well as birds (Genesis 7:8–9). Thus, there was no requirement to bring on-board the 25,000 marine vertebrates currently known to exist.[45]

In fact, assuming that speciation has been an ongoing occurrence since creation, the 15,000 vertebrate species in question would have most likely descended from a much smaller number of proto-species, equivalent to what taxonomists call a *genus*[46] and what the Genesis account calls a 'kind.'[47] Indeed, John Woodmorappe's comprehensive and meticulous discussion of this issue reveals that — even with generous concessions — the ark was only required to hold around 16,000 animals.[48]

Numerous other criticisms regarding the capacity and feasibility of the ark have been raised, including the problem of manpower with respect to feeding and caring for thousands of animals, the problem of storing enough fresh water and preserving enough food for so many animals during a year-long flood, the effect on marine ecology of mixing salt water and fresh water, and the need for special diets and specific environmental conditions for certain types of animals. Yet Woodmorappe's feasibility study answers all these questions and many more, including issues relating to floor space allotments, waste management, heating, ventilation, and illumination, as well as comprehensive discussions

42 Davis A. Young, 'Scripture in the Hands of Geologists (Part Two)' *WTJ* 49 (Fall 1987), 279.

43 Ross, *The Genesis Question*, 150.

44 David Burnie, 'Animal' Microsoft® Encarta® Online Encyclopedia 2002, <http://encarta.msn. com>.

45 James W. Orr, 'Fish' Microsoft® Encarta® Online Encyclopedia 2002, <http://encarta.msn. com>.

46 Or possibly the higher taxonomic order known as a *family*.

47 See Pete J. Williams, 'What does *min* mean?' *JoC* 11/3 (1997). 344–352.

48 John Woodmorappe, *Noah's Ark: A Feasibility Study* (El Cajon, California, ICR, 1996), 3–13.

relating to the recovery of the biosphere and the repopulation of the earth after the flood.[49]

Yet the most popular objection to a global flood is the supposed lack of geological evidence. This objection emanates most powerfully from geologists and other scientists within the church community, and is regurgitated by ill-informed commentators.[50] But as discussed in chapter 2, data does not speak for itself — it must be interpreted within a frame of reference. Unfortunately, presuppositions, the need to interpret scientific data, and the selective inclusion or exclusion of data are rarely acknowledged.

With this in mind, one has to ask what we would expect to find if a global flood did indeed occur. The answer seems quite obvious: all over the earth, one would expect to find billions of fossils buried in rock layers laid down by water. Indeed, this is exactly what we do find — even in the most unlikely places. For example, fossils of seashells have been found at the top of Mount Everest above 8,000 m (26,000 ft) where the mountain consists of sedimentary limestone rock formed from silt deposits.[51] Thus, it would appear that this part of the earth's surface was once completely under water for a significant period of time, and eventually rose up due to tectonic forces.

Marine fossils have also been found in many remote places far from the sea or any other water source. For example, an almost complete plesiosaur has been found near Richmond — halfway between Townsville and Mount Isa in central Queensland in Australia — hundreds of kilometers from the sea.[52]

One would also expect the geography of the post-flood earth to be radically different to that of the pre-flood earth. Given the present existence of the Tigris and Euphrates rivers, Davis Young denies that there is any significant difference.[53] However, as pointed out in chapter 8, the biblical description does not match that of the modern day rivers.[54]

---

49 In the introduction to his study, Woodmorappe, who has formal qualifications in both biology and geology, states (ibid., xi): 'This work is a systematic evaluation of the housing, feeding, watering, and waste-disposal requirements of some 16,000 animals on Noah's Ark. It is also a comprehensive rebuttal to the myriads of arguments that have been made against the Ark over the centuries. It is shown that it was possible for 8 people to care for 16,000 animals, and without miraculous Divine intervention. Proven solutions are offered to the problems of animals with special diets, such as the panda and koala. The bulk of hay poses no problem, and neither do the climatic requirements of animals. The latter part of this work considers the immediate post-Flood world. It answers, among other things, arguments related to salinity tolerances of organisms in floodwater, seed survival and germination through the Flood, and a host of genetics "problems" of post-Flood population bottlenecks.'

50 See, for example, Glen R. Morton ('The Mediterranean Flood' *PSCF* 49 [December 1997], 239); Hugh Ross (*The Genesis Question*, 157); and Bernard Ramm (*Christian View of Science of Scripture*, 165).

51 K. Fukada, 'Chapter 1' in Y. Shirakawa and H.N. Abradale (editors), *Himalayas* (New York, Abrams, 1986).

52 Cathy Mobbs, *Australian Geographic* 20 (October–December 1990) 26–27.

53 Young, *Creation and the Flood*, 210–211.

54 This fact appears to have gone unnoticed by Forster and Marston (*Reason, Science and Faith*, 303).

At this point it is instructive to look at the other physical effects of the flood.

Physical Effects

All living creatures that moved upon the earth — birds, livestock, wild animals, all the creatures that swarm over the earth, as well as all humans — were totally wiped out. Only those in the ark were spared (Genesis 7:21–23).

Note that Genesis 7:22 clearly specifies that it was only those creatures that had 'the breath of life in its nostrils' (Heb. נִשְׁמַת־רוּחַ חַיִּים בְּאַפּוֹ, *nišmāṭ-rûăḥ ḥăyyîm bᵉʾăpān*) that were killed. Therefore, there is no reason to think that the flood resulted in the complete extermination of bugs, slugs, insects, or arachnids. Nor is there any reason to think that all micro-organisms were eradicated.

It goes without saying that a global catastrophic flood would have significantly reshaped the earth, giving it an entirely new geography and topography, especially in light of the major topographical changes which have come about as a result of widespread local flooding, mud slides, volcanic eruptions, and earthquakes.[55]

John C. Munday agrees that the flood would have totally obliterated the earth's geography. However, on the assumption that the biblical description of Eden points to a presently existing landscape, he argues that this results in a contradiction with observational data:

> The geography of the garden of Eden according to the Bible interpreted literally (or critically) under geographic actualism indicates its location was in southern Mesopotamia. Observational data combined with the paradigm known as Flood geology … yields the conclusion that Noah's Flood deposited over 9000 m of sediments in this region. Such deposits obviously would have obliterated the garden geography. Thus Eden's geography and Flood geology, both based on literalism, stand in contradiction.[56]

Again, as shown in chapter 8, the biblical description matches no particular landscape presently in existence on earth, despite the references to the rivers Tigris and Euphrates. These rivers were most likely named after the Edenic rivers by Noah and/or his sons in the same way the River Thames and the River Trent in Ontario, Canada were named by English settlers after the rivers of the same name in England.

Numerous young-earth creationists have appealed to the translation of Psalm 104:8 in the NASB as biblical support for the idea that the catastrophic flooding caused the mountains to rise and the valleys to sink: 'The mountains rose; the valleys sank down to the place which Thou didst establish for them.'[57] However,

---

55 See, for example, Steven A. Austin, 'Mt. St Helens and Catastrophism' *Impact* 157 (July 1986); and Andrew A. Snelling, 'Iceland's recent "Mega-flood"' *Creation* 21/3 (June–August 1999), 46–48.

56 John C. Munday Jr., 'Eden's Geography Erodes Flood Geology' *WTJ* 58/1 (September 1996), 154.

57 e.g. Charles V. Taylor, 'Did mountains really rise according to Psalm 104:8?' *JoC* 12/3 (1998), 312–313.

the grammar and context of this verse strongly mitigate against this translation. Firstly, the rendering results in a breach of grammatical agreement between the verb יֵרְדוּ (yēr'dû, 'descend') which is masculine, and its proposed subject בְּקָעוֹת (b'qā'ôt, 'valley') which is feminine.[58] Secondly, the Psalm clearly alludes to the first three days of creation rather than the flood.[59] Nevertheless, it is still highly likely that the flood did in fact cause the mountains to rise and the valleys to sink even though Psalm 104:8 does not explicitly say so. Indeed, a group of scientists have developed a highly sophisticated model of plate tectonics that would cause a global catastrophic flood resulting in mountain uplift.[60]

The notion that the earth's surface was totally reshaped by the flood is further supported by 2 Peter 3:6–7. Douglas Moo acknowledges that while God's future judgment in verse 7 is directed toward human sin, it would certainly have affected the physical world.[61] Given the parallel drawn with the flood, it follows that the flood also involved the physical destruction of the surface of the earth.

Indeed, the flood resulted in the purge of the initial creation and marks the beginning of a new creation — one which began with Noah and his family and all the animals on board the ark. In essence, Noah and his sons became the forefathers of the new human race. Likewise, the pairs of animals representing each kind became the parents of a new generation of animals.

Note also the change in the human diet which occurred after the flood. In addition to green plants, humans were also given every living, moving creature for food (Genesis 9:3).

When comparing Genesis 8–9 with Genesis 1–2, it is clear the author of the flood account intentionally alludes to the creation account using repeated phrases and ideas. Gary V. Smith observes the following correspondences: (a) as with creation, in the flood account the entire globe is covered by water which eventually subsides, resulting in the appearance of dry land;[62] (b) 'birds and animals and every creeping thing that creeps on the earth' are brought forth to 'swarm upon the earth';[63] (c) God establishes the days and seasons;[64] (d) God's blessing rests upon the animals as he commands them to 'be fruitful and multiply on the earth';[65] (e) mankind is brought forth and receives the

---

58 See Pete J. Williams, 'Did mountains really rise?' Letter to the editor, *JoC* 13/1 (1999), 68–69. This point has been disputed by Taylor (*JoC* 13/1 [1991], 70–71) but his objections are very weak (see Andrew S. Kulikovsky, 'Did mountains really rise?' Letter to the editor, *JoC* 13/2 [1999], 69).

59 While the NET has 'as the mountains rose up, and the valleys went down — to the place you appointed for them,' the text note attached to this verse makes it quite clear that the translators believed vs. 7–8 allude to the third day of creation (Gen. 1:9–10.)

60 Steven. A. Austin, et al., 'Catastrophic Plate Tectonics: A Global Flood Model of Earth History' in R.E. Walsh (editor), *Proceedings of the Third International Conference on Creationism*, Technical Symposium Sessions (Pittsburgh: Creation Science Fellowship, 1994). 609–621.

61 Douglas J. Moo, *2 Peter, Jude*, NIVAC (Grand Rapids, Michigan, Zondervan, 1997), 178.

62 cf. Gen. 1:9–10 and 8:1–13.

63 cf. Gen. 1:20–21, 24–25 and 8:17–19.

64 cf. Gen. 1:14–18 and 8:22

65 cf. Gen. 1:22 and 8:17.

blessing of God ('Be fruitful and multiply and fill the earth') — indeed, Noah and his sons were blessed in the same manner as Adam;[66] (f) mankind is given dominion over the animal kingdom;[67] (g) God provides food for man (this license makes a direct reference back to the creation account when it includes the statement, 'Just as I gave you the green plants');[68] and (h) the writer of the flood account quotes from the creation account concerning the image of God in mankind.[69]

It should be clear from the above that the author is emphatic that the world was to begin again with a fresh start.[70] However, Noah does not return to the paradise of Adam, for the significant difference is that 'the intent of man's heart is evil' (Genesis 8:21).[71]

God's Covenant with Noah and Creation

After the flood, God made a covenant with Noah, his sons and with all their descendants. In fact, the covenant extended to all the living creatures that were with them on the ark — the birds, the livestock and all the wild animals.[72] Moreover, it would be an everlasting covenant for all future generations as well. God declared that He would never again destroy all life by the waters of a flood; never again would the earth be destroyed by a flood. The sign of this covenant was marked by the appearance of the rainbow. Whenever the rainbow appears in the clouds, God promises to remember His covenant with mankind, with all living creatures, and with the earth. Never again will God allow such a flood to occur.

Summary

The global catastrophic flood described in Genesis is the outpouring of God's judgment on humanity as a result of our rebellion and wickedness. This rejection of God's authority and law was not limited to an individual, a family, a community, or a nation, but included all mankind. Thus, the flood was global in extent and destroyed every living thing that moved on the face of the earth. As Blocher rightly notes, 'The universality of the scourge corresponds to the universality of the corruption.'[73]

Yet one righteous man and his family found favor in God's eyes. Noah and his three sons and their wives were spared. Noah and his family obeyed God,

---

66 cf. Gen. 1:28 and 9:1, 7.

67 cf. Gen. 1:28 and 9:2.

68 cf. Gen. 1:29–30 and 9:3.

69 cf. Gen. 1:26–7.

70 David L. Petersen ('The Yahwist on the Flood,' *VT* 26 [1976], 441) understands that 'for P, the flood is a return to the pre-creation state described in Gen. 1 ...; the post-flood state is therefore a new creation ...'

71 Gary V. Smith, 'Structure and Purpose in Genesis 1–11' *JETS* 20/4 (December 1977), 310–311.

72 See Gen. 9:8–17.

73 Henri Blocher, *In the Beginning*, translated by D.G. Preston (Leicester, IVP, 1984), 205–206.

built an ark and entered into it before the floodwaters came and destroyed everyone.

In this regard, the ark was a type of Christ. It points forward to the time when only those who trust in the saving work of Christ will be saved from God's judgment of all ungodliness. Indeed, the entire flood account is salvation history, which looks forward to the final judgment and the restoration of creation through the inauguration of a new heavens and a new earth (2 Peter 3:5–13).

CHAPTER 11

Creation, Preservation, and Dominion

Despite its fallen state, God has not abandoned His creation. He constantly sustains and preserves it through His common grace and providence. Moreover, humanity still has dominion over the earth and our charge to tend and take care of the earth and its resources still stands.

God's Present Work in Creation

Divine Immanence

Erickson defines immanence as 'God's presence and activity within nature, human nature and history.'[1] Scripture makes it clear that the Spirit of God lives among us (Haggai 2:5; John 14–16; Matthew 28:18–20), and, as Job 34:14–15 indicates, humanity would perish if God withdrew His Spirit and breath.[2] His all-pervading presence and power permeates all creation (Ps 139). In fact, God fills the universe (Jeremiah 23:24) and, thus, He is never far away from any one of us — indeed, it is in Him that 'we live and move and have our being' (Acts 17:27–8). This notion is echoed by Paul in Colossians 1:17: 'in him all things hold together.'

Unlike pantheism or panentheism, however, God is separate from, and not a part of, the natural world. God and the world are not 'one,' and neither is God the 'soul' or animating force of the universe.

Therefore, it is clear that God is still actively involved with His creation. He continues to preserve it and interact with it both directly and indirectly.

Creation and Preservation

Preservation may be defined as God sovereignly, and by a continuous agency, maintaining in existence all things He has made, together with all their properties and powers.[3] Note, however, that God's acts of preservation are distinct from His acts of creation. God's creative acts ceased on the seventh day of creation week,

---

1 M.J. Erickson, *Christian Theology*, 2nd edition (Grand Rapids, Michigan, Baker, 1998), 329.

2 See also Psalm 104:29–30.

3 Henry C. Thiessen, *Lectures in Systematic Theology*, rev. edition (Grand Rapids, Michigan, Eerdmans, 1979), 120.

but He continues to preserve what He has created, including both mankind and animals (Colossians 1:17; Hebrews 1:3; Psalm 36:6).

God controls natural processes including cloud formation, rain, and photosynthesis (Psalm 147:8), storms, thunder and lightning, snow, ice (Job 37), and hail (Psalm 147:17). He causes day and night to occur (Amos 5:8), and controls the waves of the sea (Amos 9:6). He provides food for both wild and domesticated animals (Job 38:39–41; Psalms 104:14, 21, 147:9; Matthew 6:26), and physical life, in both humans and animals, is his to give and to take away (Genesis 2:17; 1 Samuel 1:27; Job 1:21, 12:10; Psalms 102:23, 104:29–30; Daniel 5:23). Moreover, His acts of preservation are indiscriminate (Matthew 5:45).

Note that God's preservation of His creation does not necessarily imply that He acts or intervenes directly into the natural world. Although God has performed many miracles throughout history, His normal *modus operandi* is to employ natural laws and use human persons — including non-Christians — to preserve His creation.[4]

Creation and Providence

Thiessen defines providence as 'the continuous activity of God whereby he makes all the events of the physical, mental, and moral realms work out his purpose, and this purpose is nothing short of the original design of God in creation.'[5] In other words, God's providence seeks the eventual establishment of His kingdom on earth and the restoration of his creation.[6] This means that God interacts with His creation in such a way as to ensure that His will is done and His purposes are achieved. As Carl Henry explained, the biblical view of providence 'unqualifiedly affirms … that God works out his purposes not merely in life's generalities but in the details and minutiae of life as well … nothing falls outside God's will and concern.'[7] Before we were born, He saw our unformed bodies, and knows whatever we will do before we do it (Psalm 139:16). Indeed, not even a sparrow shall fall to the ground apart from the will of God (Matthew 10:29).

Ultimately, God has supreme dominion over the entire created universe. God can and will do whatever He pleases with His creation (Psalm 135:6), including subjecting it to frustration, bondage, and decay so that it may serve His purposes (Romans 8:19–21).

Although the regularity of the natural world is dependent upon God's will (Genesis 8:22), Scripture also teaches that miraculous irregularities may still occasionally occur. Indeed, God can do whatever He wills with His creation (cf. Genesis 6–8), and the laws of nature, which He established and set in place, are no barrier to His will (Genesis 18:14). Indeed, God may, on occasion, employ 'coincidence miracles' which constitute a number of events or circumstances, all

---

4 Erickson, *Christian Theology*, 337.

5 Thiessen, *Lectures in Systematic Theology*, 122.

6 This is the subject of the final chapter.

7 Carl F.H. Henry, *God, Revelation and Authority*, 6 volumes (Wheaton, Illinois, Crossway, 1999), 6:459.

of which are perfectly natural and plausible, but occur together or in a certain sequence that lead to an extraordinary result or outcome, and which can only ultimately be explained as an act of divine intervention. Examples of such coincidence miracles include the extraordinary catches of fish in Luke 5:4–7 and John 21:6–11, and the presence of the four-drachma coin in the mouth of the first fish Peter caught (Matthew 17:27). Note that the occurrence of miracles not only demonstrates the power of God over all creation, but also reinforces that He is distinct from the natural world and not a part of it or subject to its laws.

Scripture contains many examples of God's providential interaction with the natural world. For example, Psalm 148:8 states that lightning and hail, snow and clouds, and stormy winds do his bidding, and indeed, we see an example of this in 1 Samuel 7:10 when God used thunder against the Philistines to ensure that they were routed by the Israelites. Similarly, He caused the sun to stand still for a full day in order to secure victory for Israel against the Amorites (Joshua 10:12–14).

Job stated that God 'move mountains without their knowing it and overturns them in his anger' and 'shakes the earth from its place and makes its pillars tremble' (Job 9:5–6) which suggests the occurrence of earthquakes such as those referred to in Ezekiel 38:18–19, Matthew 28:2, and Acts 16:26. Job also stated that God could stop the sun and stars from shining (Job 9:7), which is apparently what occurred in Matthew 27:45 when darkness covered the land from the sixth to the ninth hour.[8]

The account of Jonah, where God provided a great fish to swallow Jonah, and keep him inside for three days and three nights (Jonah 1:17), provides a good example of God employing other creatures to achieve His purposes. God also used a donkey to verbally rebuke Balaam (Numbers 22:21–33).

What role, then, does God play in the occurrence of natural disasters — especially those that have caused so much death and destruction? Are they part of His providential plan? It is clear from Scripture that some natural disasters are instruments of divine judgment. Floods are repeatedly used to judge evil-doers, starting with the global flood at the time of Noah (Genesis 6–9), and elsewhere in the Old Testament (Job 20:28, 22:16; Nahum 1:8). Similarly, most of the plagues that God brought against the Egyptians as a result of their defiant refusal to release the Israelites, were essentially natural disasters (Exodus 5–10). The Israelites were also on the receiving end when their camp became infested with deadly serpents (Numbers 21:4–9). Revelation 18:8 predicts that such disasters will also occur in the future.

Nevertheless, many natural disasters occur for no apparent reason, and directly affect God's people. Yet, it must be remembered that we live in a fallen, distorted world that has been subjected to frustration and decay, and natural disasters are manifestations of this frustration and decay. It must also be noted that natural

---

8 According to the Roman system of reckoning time used here, 'the sixth hour' and 'the ninth hour' refer to midday and three o'clock in the afternoon respectively (Donald A. Hagner, *Matthew 14–28*, WBC [Dallas, Texas: Word, 1995], 843).

disasters are not mere random events. Many natural disasters (such as volcanoes, storms, tornadoes, hurricanes, floods, forest fires, earthquakes, and tsunamis) serve a natural purpose. Indeed, many catastrophic events occur in order to equalize the buildup of potential energy, extreme pressure, or heat imbalance. Moreover, specific kinds of natural disasters only occur under specific natural conditions and circumstances: volcanic eruptions only occur at volcanoes; flooding only occurs on low-lying land near rivers, lakes, or on the coast; earthquakes only occur at fault lines in the earth's crust. In addition, some apparent disasters have beneficial consequences. In ancient Egypt, the agricultural economy was dependent on a natural disaster — the annual flooding of the Nile river.

Humanity's Present Relationship with Creation

God's Order in Creation

In Psalm 103:19, David declares: 'The LORD has established his throne in heaven, and his kingdom rules over all.' The kingdom of God is a central element of biblical theology. As Graeme Goldsworthy notes,

> [t]he kingdom of God is a name which is not used in the Bible until much later, but the idea of it immediately comes to mind as we think of creation…[Genesis 1–2] show mankind as the centre of God's attention and the recipient of a unique relationship with him. Thus the focus of the kingdom of God is on the relationship between God and his people. Man is subject to God, while the rest of creation is subject to man and exists for his benefit. The kingdom means God ruling over his people in the material universe. This basic understanding of the kingdom is never changed in Scripture.[9]

This creative order — God, who rules over mankind, who rules over the rest of creation — is clearly expressed in Psalm 8:

> *O LORD, our Lord,*
> *how majestic is your name in all the earth!*
> *You have set your glory*
> *above the heavens.*
> *From the lips of children and infants*
> *you have ordained praise*
> *because of your enemies,*
> *to silence the foe and the avenger.*
> *When I consider your heavens,*
> *the work of your fingers,*
> *the moon and the stars,*
> *which you have set in place,*
> *what is man that you are mindful of him,*
> *the son of man that you care for him?*
> *You made him a little lower than the heavenly beings*
> *and crowned him with glory and honor.*

---

9 Graeme Goldsworthy, *According to Plan* (Leicester, IVP, 1991), 121–122.

You made him ruler over the works of your hands;
you put everything under his feet:
all flocks and herds,
and the beasts of the field,
the birds of the air,
and the fish of the sea,
all that swim the paths of the seas.
O LORD, our Lord, how majestic is your name in all the earth![10]

Humanity's special relationship with the Creator and position over the rest of creation was set in place at the very beginning: 'Then God said, "Let us make man in our image, in our likeness, and let them rule over the fish of the sea and the birds of the air, over the livestock, over all the earth, and over all the creatures that move along the ground. ... I give you every seed-bearing plant on the face of the whole earth and every tree that has fruit with seed in it. They will be yours for food."' It is clear, then, that not all life is equal. Human life stands above all other life. Human life is more precious to God because it reflects his own image.

Yet, there are many people who believe that *all* life, irrespective of its nature, is intrinsically sacred. Moreover, many Christians deny that human life is superior or more precious to God that non-human life. As Calvin DeWitt writes,

> [I]f we read the Bible with ourselves in mind, we naturally see this blessing as ours. And it is. But it is not ours exclusively. It was given before we came. It was first given thus: 'And God created great whales, and every living creature that moveth ... and every winged fowl after his kind: and God saw that it was good. And God blessed them, saying, Be fruitful, and multiply, and fill the waters in the seas, and let fowl multiply in the earth' (Genesis 1:21–22, KJV). That other creatures are so blessed, and blessed first, is not only humbling for us but also critically important. The populations of creatures – in their wondrous variety of kinds – are expected by their Creator to bear fruit through God-given means of reproduction; they are expected to develop biological and ecological interrelationships; they are expected to bring fulfillment of the Creator's intentions for the good creation.[11]

But there is clearly a substantive and qualitative difference between God's blessing of marine life and birds, and His blessing of mankind. God commanded the marine life He had created to 'fill the waters in the seas.' Similarly, He commanded the birds He had created to 'multiply on the earth.' However, God blessed Adam and Eve and commanded them to '[b]e fruitful and increase in number; fill the earth and subdue it. Rule over the fish of the sea and the birds of the air and over every living creature that moves on the ground.' Thus, DeWitt's

---

10 Although this is taken to be a messianic psalm by various New Testament writers in which the 'son of man' is interpreted as Christ, its original meaning referred to mankind's relationship to God and the rest of creation.

11 Calvin DeWitt in 'Foreword' to Susan Power Bratton, *Six Billion and More* (Louisville, Kentucky, Westminster/John Knox, 1992), 9.

view of mankind's relationship with the rest of creation is explicitly rejected by Scripture. Human beings are not equal with fish, birds, or any other created life forms. Human beings are God's greatest creative achievement because they reflect His own image, and have been given dominion over the rest of creation.

Human Dominion

In Genesis 1:28, God commands Adam and Eve to 'Be fruitful and increase in number, fill the Earth and *subdue* it, [and] *rule* over [every creature].' This implies an active role for mankind to take charge of the resources God has provided us in the natural world, and to use them for their benefit. The Hebrew verb כָּבַשׁ (*kĕbăš*, 'to subdue, to subjugate') stresses the act of dominance by force. In Numbers 32:20–22, 32:29, Joshua 18:1 and 1 Chronicles 22:17–19, *kĕbăš* is used in reference to subduing the Promised Land, including the hostile tribes that were occupying it at that time. In 2 Chronicles 28:9–10, Nehemiah 5:5 and Jeremiah 34:11, 16, it refers to subjugation in the form of slavery. In Esther 7:8, it refers to subduing or forcing a woman, and in Zechariah 9:15, it speaks of subduing enemies in warfare. There is also an overlap in the meaning of *kĕbăš* and of רָדָה (*rāḏāh*, 'to rule, to have dominion'). In Leviticus 25:39, 43, 46, the Israelites are forbidden to rule fellow Israelite bondslaves harshly or ruthlessly. In Numbers 24:19, Psalm 72:8 and 110:2, *rāḏāh* is used in reference to the dominion of the Messiah. In 1 Kings 4:24, it refers to Solomon's dominion over the land and kings from Tiphsah to Azzah. In 1 Kings 5:16, 9:23, and 2 Chronicles 8:10, *rāḏāh* refers to officers ruling over workers. In Isaiah 41:2, God subdues kings before the ruler from the east, and in Ezekiel 34:4, it refers to the shepherds of Israel ruling over the people with cruelty.[12] Thus, Calvin Beisner rightly concludes that the nature of the command to subdue and to rule in Genesis 1:28 involves 'subduing and ruling something whose spontaneous tendency is to resist dominion.'[13]

Note also that there is no reason to think that the fall has diminished or cancelled God's charge 'to fill the earth and subdue it. ... Rule over [every creature].' Rather, the fall simply made humanity's task immensely more difficult. Genesis 3:17–19 implies that in the post-fall world, nature has become even more hostile to humanity's efforts to cultivate and develop it further. Many wild animals now pose a threat to human beings and their cultivating efforts, and the ground is now cursed: 'Cursed is the ground because of you; through painful toil you will eat of it all the days of your life. It will produce thorns and thistles for you, and you will eat the plants of the field. By the sweat of your brow you will eat your food until you return to the ground, since from it you were taken ...' (Genesis 3:17–19).

As noted above, mankind stands above the rest of creation, and it all ultimately exists for the benefit of humanity. Indeed, the Garden of Eden was clearly for the benefit of Adam and Eve and they had total dominion over it,

---

12 See also entries for כָּבַשׁ and רָדָה in *HALOT*.
13 E. Calvin Beisner, '*Imago Dei* and the Population Debate' *TrinJ* 18/2 (Fall 1997), 184–185.

apart from one tree — the Tree of the Knowledge of Good and Evil. The fruit of all the other trees in the garden, as well as the seeded fruit from every other tree on the earth, were theirs for food (Genesis 1:29). Note also that God's command to 'fill the earth and subdue it' stands against the common view that the present rate of population growth is unsustainable and that overpopulation is a serious environmental problem and will ultimately destroy the earth.[14]

Of course, dominion does not mean or imply that humans have a license to do whatever they wish, raping and pillaging the land and sea, to the detriment of God's creation. As Schaeffer pointed out, '[b]y creation man has dominion, but as a fallen creature he has used that dominion wrongly. Because he is fallen, he exploits created things as though they were nothing in themselves, and as though he has an autonomous right to them. ... The Christian is called upon to exhibit this dominion, but exhibit it rightly: treating the thing as having value in itself, exercising dominion without being destructive.'[15] Humanity has dominion over the rest of creation, but with that power also comes the responsibility to use it wisely.

Human Stewardship

Moses proclaimed in Deuteronomy 10:14 that 'the heavens, even the highest heavens' and 'the earth and everything in it' belong to God. Again, these ideas are echoed by David (Psalm 24:1) and Paul (1 Corinthians 10:26). Yet, Psalm 115:16 also states that although the highest heavens belong to God, the earth has been given by God to mankind. Creation still belongs to God, but mankind has been given dominion over it. However, this dominion is not without limitation or constraints. In Genesis 2:15, God placed Adam in the Garden of Eden to work it (Heb. עָבַד, ābăd) and take care of it (Heb. שָׁמַר, šămăr). The Hebrew word ābăd communicates the idea of serving another by doing (usually physical) work,[16] whereas šămăr conveys the general idea of 'paying close attention.' More specifically, šămăr is used to refer to ensuring conformance to a law, code, or covenant, and also to the responsibility one has for another person or thing (cf. Genesis 30:31; 1 Samuel 26:16; Isaiah 21:11).[17] Indeed, the reason why God's 'pleasant field' will be made 'into a desolate wasteland ... parched and desolate' is because 'there is no one who cares' (Jeremiah 12:10–11). Thus, mankind has the active responsibility to care about the world, look after it, and ensure that the natural resources God has supplied us with are not misused or abused, or that they are not used in a way that is detrimental to other humans. In short, God has appointed mankind to act as stewards of His creation.

In the context of the natural world, human stewardship comprises the active management and utilization of the earth's natural resources for the common

---

14 This point will be discussed further in a following section.

15 Francis A. Schaeffer, 'Pollution and the Death of Man' in *The Complete Works of Francis Schaeffer*, 5 volumes (Wheaton, Illinois, Crossway Books, 1982), 5:41–42.

16 See entry for עָבַד in BDB.

17 See entry for שָׁמַר in *HALOT*.

benefit of human society in a sustainable way. Natural resources include land and water resources; fish, livestock, and other animals and animal products; forests and other vegetation that could be used for food, clothing, or building materials; minerals, precious metals, and gems, as well as fossil fuels and any other naturally occurring substances of potential value or use. By 'active management,' we mean human intervention, investment, development, farming, and the application of science and technology. By 'utilization,' we mean the process of determining which of the various possible uses of a resource amount to the best or most efficient application. Utilization of resources should also be directed to the common benefit of human society such that one society or community should not benefit at the expense of another (for example, mining materials for the benefit of one community but polluting or destroying the water resources of another community). Utilization should be sustainable in the sense that it can be maintained over a substantial period of time because the resource is abundant or self-replenishing, and the source of the resource is not destroyed and does not suffer from any lasting detrimental effects. Much of this should be common sense: there is clearly no future in burning your own house down, poisoning the well you drink from, or destroying your own food supply!

Unfortunately, there have been many people and companies who have indeed wrongly exploited natural resources and caused lasting and significant damage to the environment. Jeremiah 12:4 indicates that the animals and birds have perished because the people who live in the land are wicked. Nevertheless, those who do so will not go unpunished. God will judge those who damage and destroy the earth. When Christ returns to judge people for their sin, this includes judging 'those who destroy the earth' (Revelation 11:18). As Ian Hore-Lacy rightly notes, '[stewardship] can never be allowed to mean that we, made in God's image, treat God's creation with any less respect than he does,'[18] but adds that it 'also means that meeting the needs of all humans, made in God's image, must be *a very* high priority.' And that '[e]nvironmental concern must not displace our mediation of God's provision.'[19] As stewards, it is surely our responsibility to ensure that several billion more people — all made in God's image — have better access to food, water, basic materials, and energy.

Overpopulation?

That the earth is overpopulated and that this excess of human beings has caused mass destruction to the environment via overconsumption and pollution is a common view among both Christians and non-Christians. But this is by no means a recent idea. Around A.D. 200, Tertullian wrote:

> Everything has been visited, everything known, everything exploited. Now pleasant estates obliterate the famous wilderness areas of the past. Plowed fields have replaced forests, domesticated animals have dispersed wild life. Beaches are plowed, mountains smoothed and

---

18 Ian Hore-Lacy, *Responsible Dominion: A Christian Approach to Sustainable Development* (Vancouver, Regent College Publishing, 2006), 26.

19 Ibid. Original emphasis.

swamps drained. There are as many cities as, in former years, there were dwellings. Islands do not frighten, nor cliffs deter. Everywhere there are buildings, everywhere people, everywhere communities, everywhere life … Proof [of this crowding] is the density of human beings. We weigh upon the world; its resources hardly suffice to support us. As our needs grow larger, so do our protests, that already nature does not sustain us. In truth, plague, famine, wars and earthquakes must be regarded as a blessing to civilization, since they prune away the luxuriant growth of the human race.[20]

In 1973, Catholic scholar Arthur McCormack wrote that '[t]he population explosion of the second half of the twentieth century gives rise to one of the most serious and crucial problems of our day.'[21] McCormack asserted that many Christians are interested in the 'population explosion,' because they rely on a 'false notion of Providence' and 'think — or perhaps "feel"… — that God will provide, that we should not look too far into the future, that population projections may turn out to be as wrong in the future as they have been in the past.'[22] McCormack was convinced the earth's population would soon become unsustainable and that the introduction of either voluntary or forced population restriction measures was inevitable.[23]

In more recent times, David Francis, columnist with the *Christian Science Monitor*, wrote that unless the soaring population growth is not reversed, it 'will have huge economic, environmental, and political impacts on most people alive today.'[24]

The stimulus behind such visions appears to be an acceptance of the view that human beings are no different to the rest of creation, and that all of creation is equally blessed by God. In other words, human beings have no more rights than any other animal, nor do they have any special relationship with God. Calvin DeWitt's explanation is typical of those who hold to this view:

> God's blessed expectation for the populations of other creatures helps put our human population into context. We, and they, are blessed. We, and they, are to reproduce, develop our kinds, and fulfill the earth to its God-intended completeness … Our own population joins with the populations of the other creatures God has made, participating one with another in the blessed expectation of reproducing and increasing our kinds, biologically and ecologically developing our kinds, and fulfilling the earth to its God-intended completeness, and … our own human kind enjoys this blessed expectation not only ourselves but also for the

20 Tertullian, *Opera monastica*. As cited in Susan Power Bratton, *Six Billion & More: Human Population Regulation and Christian Ethics* (Louisville, Westminster, 1992), 76.

21 Arthur McCormack, *The Population Explosion: A Christian Concern* (New York, Harper & Row, 1973), 1.

22 Ibid.

23 Ibid., 6–7.

24 David Francis, 'Fuse on the "population bomb" has been relit' *Christian Science Monitor* 99 (May 21, 2007), 17.

populations of all God's creatures. It is here that we come to our present profound difficulty. Increasingly we people are occupying the land to the exclusion and extinction of the other creatures. This leads us to ask, 'Does our God-given blessing of stewardship of creation grant us license to deny creatures God's blessing of fruitfulness and fulfillment? May we take this blessing of reflective rule to negate God's blessing to the fish of the sea and the birds of the air?' We have come to a time when the impact of humankind — our exploding number multiplied by the power each wields and the defilement each brings — not only denies the creatures fruitfulness and fulfillment but also extinguishes increasing numbers of them from the face of earth.[25]

Note the very negative view of humanity that DeWitt presents in this passage: human beings wield unchecked power, defile the environment, and cause mass extinction.

But, as Beisner has pointed out, 'to fear population growth and its impact on resources and the environment is [to] think more like Lot than like Abram.' Lot chose the best land, while Abram took what was left (Genesis 13:10–18). 'Lot's eyes focused on material circumstances, Abram's on the ability of God to bless his servant regardless of circumstances. Lot's decision was driven by his thoughts about the capacity of the land; Abram's by his faith in God.'[26] Indeed, Abram and Lot parted ways precisely because they thought the land could not support their households and livestock. After Abram was left with the less fertile land rejected by Lot, God promised him that his offspring would be 'like the dust of the earth' — virtually uncountable. Despite Abram's and Lot's present circumstances, this promise to significantly increase the world's population is explicitly identified by God as a blessing and goes against the belief that unchecked population increases are somehow a violation of God's plan.[27]

Moreover, DeWitt's argument 'commits the fallacy of false choice, treating man's filling up the earth as if it were exclusive of other creatures' doing so.' This does not logically follow. In fact, the idea that human population growth has been detrimental to the flourishing of other creatures is not supported by the empirical evidence. Furthermore, to assume 'that continued human population growth must result in more species extinctions, and then to argue on that basis that continued human population growth is therefore not consistent with God's blessing/command for other creatures to multiply is to assume the conclusion to prove the conclusion — to argue in a circle.'[28] In reality, there is no reason why continued human population growth cannot go hand in hand with the continued growth of other creatures. In fact, history has shown that people have not only been able to preserve various species from extinction, but also multiply their numbers far beyond what would naturally occur.[29] This is the case with

---

25 DeWitt in Bratton, *Six Billion and More*, 10–11.

26 Beisner, '*Imago Dei* and the Population Debate,' 174.

27 Ibid., 174.

28 Ibid., 192

29 Ibid.

any of the animal breeds that humans have chosen to domesticate or to use for commercial purposes. Indeed, no one worries, for example, about chickens going extinct, even though Americans alone now slaughter over six billion of them each year. Therefore, it appears that the best way to ensure the survival of any particular species, is to find a commercial use for it.[30]

In any case, the notion of a population explosion is grossly exaggerated and the earth is nowhere near becoming full. Most countries in the developed world have birth rates well below the replacement rate. As Mark Steyn has pointed out, 'the developed world's population is shrinking faster than any human society not in the grip of war or disease has ever shrunk.'[31] In failing to have enough children they are not only disobeying God's command to 'fill the earth' (Genesis 1:28), they are effectively committing national suicide. According to the 2006 revision of the United Nation's *World Population Prospects*, total world population is predicted to peak in around 2050 at approximately 9–10 billion, before it is expected to decline.[32] Steyn noted that '[b]irth rates in the so-called "overcrowded" parts of the world are already 2.9 and falling. India has a quickly growing middle class and declining fertility.'[33] China, also, will soon have a aging and declining population as it starts to reap the consequences of its 'one child' policy.[34] This led Steyn to conclude that human beings are the real dwindling resource, not oil: 'We're the endangered species, not the spotted owl,'[35] and that 'much of the planet will be uninhabited long before it is uninhabitable.'[36] Indeed, even today, human settlements presently occupy only about 2 per cent of the earth's land mass, excluding the continent of Antarctica.[37]

Ultimately, attitudes to human population growth are determined by a person's worldview. Most environmentalists assume that people are principally consumers and polluters. Feminist environmentalist Riane Eisler explains:

> For behind soil erosion, desertification, air and water pollution, and all the other ecological, social, and political stresses of our time lies the pressure of more and more people on finite land and other resources, of increasing numbers of factories, cars, trucks, and other sources of pollution required to provide all these people with goods, and the worsening tensions that their needs and aspirations fuel.[38]

In other words, human society is fundamentally destructive! Yet a truly biblical worldview sees people as principally intelligent, well-meaning, creative producers

30 Ibid.

31 Mark Steyn, *America Alone* (Washington DC: Regnery, 2006), 9.

32 *World Population Prospects: The 2006 Revision — Highlights* (New York: United Nations, Department of Economic and Social Affairs, 2007), 1. <http://www.un.org/esa/population/publications/wpp2006/WPP2006_Highlights_rev.pdf >

33 Steyn, *America Alone*, 14.

34 Ibid., 5, 30.

35 Ibid., 7.

36 Ibid.

37 Beisner, '*Imago Dei* and the Population Debate,' 197.

38 Ibid., 177.

and stewards, because that is the way God created them, and the way they are being transformed through the redeeming work of Christ.[39]

Similarly, environmentalists believe that human population growth will strip the earth of its natural resources and smother it with pollution. A truly biblical worldview holds that continued population growth will result in the increased abundance of resources, rather than in their depletion, and in a cleaner, more developed environment better suited to human habitation, rather than a polluted and poisoned earth.[40]

Thus, the Christian worldview leads to a very different prediction to that of the modern environmental movement:

> [P]eople, because God made them in his image to be creative and productive, because he gave them creative minds like his, can bring order out of chaos, and higher order out of lower order, actually making more resources than we consume. So the biblical view of human beings and the universe predicts that, as we apply our minds to raw materials, scarcity of resources will decline … And that is precisely what we find when we look at history.[41]

Development and Environmentalism

Many modern environmentalists hold to a highly romanticized, virtually pantheistic view of nature. Images and stories of simple, yet idyllic, tribal life reinforce the 'noble savage' stereotype — mankind living in glorious harmony with nature without pollution or overcrowding. These environmentalists, therefore, oppose any development that involves any alteration to nature. Such alteration is inherently bad, amounting to a moral violation. As Paul wrote to the Romans, such people have 'exchanged the truth of God for a lie, and worshiped and served created things rather than the Creator' (Romans 1:25).

Yet many Christians also appear to have accepted this notion. The Evangelical Environmental Network's 'An Evangelical Declaration on the Care of Creation' points to a number of degradations in creation that they claim are a result of resource consumption and sustained population growth:

> These degradations of creation can be summed up as 1) land degradation; 2) deforestation; 3) species extinction; 4) water degradation; 5) global toxification; 6) the alteration of atmosphere; 7) human and cultural degradation. Many of these degradations are signs that we are pressing against the finite limits God has set for creation. With continued population growth, these degradations will become more severe. Our responsibility is not only to bear and nurture children, but to nurture their home on earth.[42]

---

39 Ibid., 195–196.

40 Ibid., 189–190

41 Ibid., 183.

42 The full declaration can be found at <http://www.creationcare.org/resources/declaration.php>.

For many Christian environmentalists, industrial and agricultural development, and the utilization of resources in the natural world, are viewed as morally equivalent to destroying the Garden of Eden, and a crime not only against God but humanity in general. Such views have no theological support, and proponents seem to have forgotten that the fall has taken place. In fact, such ideas are essentially pagan. As Hore-Lacy explains, '[h]armony with nature becomes the prime virtue, rather than a proper corollary of harmony with the Creator.'[43] Or as Schaeffer put it: 'Man is not to be sacrificed, as pantheism sacrifices him, because after all he was made in the image of God and given dominion.'[44] Therefore, it is the duty of all human beings, as image bearers of God, and as stewards of His creation, to explore, study, and analyze the natural world and then apply that knowledge for the benefit of human society.

Nevertheless, virtually all environmentalists, including some Christian ones, believe that resources are limited and are rapidly running out due to increased demand. The reality, however, is that such claims have been circulating since the time of Tertullian in the second century A.D., and we have as yet not run out of any significant resource, nor are we likely to in the foreseeable future. In truth, we have an abundance of natural resources, which is what one would expect from a generous God who provides. Those who claim that humanity will exhaust fundamental natural resources if population growth continues, and development persists, are ultimately denying God's capacity and ability to provide.

Resisting the Fall and Reversing its Effects

Scripture not only teaches that creation was subjected to bondage and decay as a result of humanity's fall, but also that it will be liberated and restored as a result of humanity's redemption (Romans 8:19–23). The liberation of our bodies from sin is linked with the liberation of the entire fallen subhuman creation. Therefore, at the consummation of the kingdom, not only will our bodies be restored, but so will the whole of the subhuman creation.

Christ proclaimed that the kingdom of God is near (Mark 1:14–15), but also that it will not come immediately (Luke 19:11). Although the kingdom has not yet fully come, we are commanded to resist the reign of sin in our mortal bodies, and offer our bodies as instruments of righteousness (Romans 6:11–14). Therefore, establishing and participating in the kingdom of God and living in anticipation of its consummation, implies not only that we resist the power of sin, but also the effects of the fall. The effects of the fall, like the power of sin, will not be overcome until the kingdom fully comes, but the Christian duty is to resist, and to live in anticipation of what will eventually be. This point was made long ago by Francis Bacon:

> For by the Fall man declined from the state of innocence and from his kingdom over the creatures. Both things can be repaired in this life to

43 Hore-Lacy, *Responsible Dominion*, 30.
44 Schaeffer, 'Pollution and the Death of Man' in *Complete Works* 5:43.

some extent, the former by religion and faith, the latter by the arts and sciences. For the Curse did not make the creation an utter and irrevocable outlaw. In virtue of the sentence, 'In the sweat of thy face shalt thou eat bread' [Genesis 3:19], man, by manifold labours, … compels the creation, in time and in part, to provide him with bread, that is to serve the purposes of human life.[45]

Although the fallen creation is naturally in a state of decay, as creative image bearers of God (Genesis 1:1, 27), mankind is not only capable, but obligated, to find ways to repair any damage we have caused, to heal and to restore, and to improve the overall state of creation, making it serve our needs in more productive and more efficient ways. As Bacon hinted, this is best achieved by the application of scientific knowledge and technological innovation to the abundant natural resources God has given us.

Natural Resources, Science, and Technological Innovation

Natural resources are part of God's provision to humanity, and our very survival depends on us capturing, extracting, and applying these resources for the benefit of human society. Clearly, the capture, extraction, and application of natural resources for use in power generation, water supply, food production, communications, transport, building, and medical treatments require detailed scientific knowledge and innovative uses of various resources. But as Goldsworthy rightly notes: 'The human search for knowledge and technology, and indeed our whole cultural development, are tasks assigned to us by God.'[46]

The benefits to humanity from the application of science and technology in the area of medicine and general health are obvious. The decay caused by the fall has wreaked havoc with our bodies. Yet modern medicine, by intervening in the natural processes and functions of the body, has been able to not only cure once incurable diseases, but to repair serious injuries resulting from accidents, and to reconstruct gross deformities inherited at birth. As John Feinberg explains:

> [M]ost medical procedures involve intervention into the natural order … We live in a fallen world where things do not always work as they should. God has commissioned people to subdue the created order and has given them a certain dominion over it (Gen 1:28). While this does not allow us to harm or exploit the natural order, permission to subdue a natural order that does not always function as God intended because of sin's disruptive influence seems to necessitate our intervention into natural processes.[47]

Indeed, by intervening in the natural process using *in vitro* fertilization (IVF) technology, it is now possible for once infertile couples to conceive and have children.

---

45 Lisa Jardine and Michael Silverthorne, *Francis Bacon: The New Organon* (Cambridge, Cambridge University Press, 2004), 221.

46 Graeme Goldsworthy, *According to Plan*, 125.

47 John S. Feinberg, 'A Baby At Any Cost And By Any Means? The Morality Of In Vitro Fertilization And Frozen Embryos' *TrinJ* 14/2 (Fall 1993), 162.

But when it comes to utilizing the earth's natural resources, the benefits gained appear to be not so clear to most environmentalists, including many Christians. Christian environmentalists fail to recognize the implications of God's provision in creation for people's needs. Because we live in a culture where it is easy to take for granted the benefits that science and technology have given us, many people fail to appreciate the extent to which industrial, agricultural and technological development have improved the duration and quality of life of all people in modern society.

Yet, rather than acknowledging that God is a faithful provider and has abundantly supplied us with all the resources we could ever need, environmentalists seem obsessed with the notion that our natural resources are limited and that we are close to exhausting many of those resources we presently rely on. They regard the existing supply of economically useable natural resources as nature-given, rather than as God-given, and they fail to acknowledge the contribution of human intelligence and innovation. In essence, they deny (1) God as provider, and (2) mankind as a creative bearer of God's image.

Having no conception of the role of human intelligence in the creation of economically useable resources, and failing to distinguish between the present supply of natural resources, and the sum total of those available in nature, environmentalists and conservationists naïvely believe that every act of production that consumes natural resources is an act of impoverishment because it uses up allegedly priceless, irreplaceable treasures of nature.[48] Such notions are nothing new. Cyprian, writing in the third century, stated: 'You must know that the world has grown old, and does not remain in its former vigor. It bears witness to its own decline. The rainfall and the sun's warmth are both diminishing; the metals are nearly exhausted ...'[49]

But, as George Reisman points out,

> the fact is that the world is made out of natural resources — out of solidly packed natural resources, extending from the upper limits of its atmosphere to its very center, four thousand miles down. This is so because the entire mass of the earth is made of nothing but chemical elements, all of which are natural resources ... Even the sands of the Sahara desert are composed of nothing but various compounds of silicon, carbon, oxygen, hydrogen, aluminum, iron, and so on, all of them having who knows what potential uses that science may someday unlock.[50]

Although the form or compounds in which the various elements may be found may change, there is no danger of ever running out of any particular chemical element.

48 George Reisman, *Capitalism: A Treatise on Economics* (Ottawa, Illinois, Jameson Books, 1998), 71.

49 St. Cyprian, *Ad Demetrium*, in W.T. Jones, *A History of Western Philosophy*, 2nd edition, 5 volumes (New York, Harcourt, Brace, and World, 1969), 2:6.

50 Reisman, *Capitalism*, 63. Original emphasis.

Nor is there any real shortage of energy in the world. The law of conservation of energy states that energy can neither be created nor destroyed. More energy is discharged in a single thunderstorm than mankind currently generates in an entire year. Therefore, the task before us is not one of generating energy without consuming exhaustible resources, but one of finding efficient ways to harness and deliver the energy already present in creation. Moreover, heat from the sun provides a constantly renewed supply that is billions of times greater than the amount of energy we presently consume. Therefore, for all practical purposes, the energy available to humans is infinite.

In reality, resources are becoming more abundant, not less. Mined minerals, crops (including wood), livestock, and fish are now more abundantly available to human societies than ever before in the past, despite the fact that human population has grown faster than at any other time in history.[51] This is largely due to human ingenuity, especially in the past two centuries, which has devised increasingly more effective and efficient ways to extract, refine, and use the earth's natural resources. For example, it is now possible to mine at greater depths with less effort, and to gain access to regions of the earth previously inaccessible, or to improve access to regions already accessible.

Developed societies have also found uses for things previously thought to have no uses,[52] and discovered new applications for commonly available resources that may be substituted for less common, less efficient, or more expensive resources, but still provide the same benefits. As a result, the demand for the substituted resources is reduced or eliminated.[53]

In agriculture, the development of chemical fertilizers and more efficient methods of irrigation have enabled farmers to radically improve the productivity of fertile land, and, indeed, to create fertile land from land that was previously infertile. Land that was previously desert or semidesert has been made vastly more productive than the very best lands available to previous generations.[54] In fact, it is even possible to grow many crops in scientifically controlled soils in multistory buildings, in virtual factory conditions. Moreover, the possibilities for food production offered by genetically modified crops are enormous.

Nevertheless, environmentalists and conservationists have argued that industrial and agricultural development has led to senseless deforestation. This has undoubtedly happened in the past, but it is not a necessary consequence of development. Timber is a valuable resource and it makes no sense for a commercial operation to cut down trees without bothering to replant them. They would be destroying their future source of income. In essence, trees are a

---

51 Beisner, 'Imago Dei and the Population Debate,' 192–193.

52 For example, silicon (used in integrated circuits) and quartz (used in high resolution digital timers and clocks).

53 Beisner, 'Imago Dei and the Population Debate,' 193–194. An example of such a resource is whale oil from the blubber of whales, which is no longer commercially available, and has been substituted by other products such as jojoba oil.

54 Israel and California are prime examples.

crop like any other, such as wheat or corn. The only difference is that the time to harvest is much longer.

Note, however, that although the earth has effectively limitless resources, the range of applications for those resources is limited. Agricultural land may be used to produce food, or it may be used to produce biofuels. Governments, commercial operators, and society in general will determine whether biofuel production is more important than food production. Unfortunately, at the present time, due to the supposed threat of 'global warming,' there is a definite shift away from food production toward biofuel production. This will have severe ramifications, especially for the poorest people in the world. United Nations World Food Program officials have pointed out that the use of more land and agricultural produce for biofuels has led to significant increases in food prices.[55] The British Government's Chief Scientific Adviser, Professor John Beddington, has also pointed out that the move toward biofuels poses a serious threat to world food production and the lives of billions of people: 'It's very hard to imagine how we can see the world growing enough crops to produce renewable energy and at the same time meet the enormous demand for food.'[56]

In summary, it should be noted that, in Western developed countries in the twentieth century, life expectancy dramatically increased as a result of the enormous contribution of industrial civilization, which generates an ever improving supply of food, clothing, shelter, medical care, and all the conveniences of modern life. Famine does not exist in such societies because industrial and agricultural development has produced the greatest abundance and variety of food in the history of the world, and has created the storage and transportation systems required to bring it to everyone. Furthermore, developed societies have put an end to famines and plagues, and eliminated once dreaded diseases such as cholera, diphtheria, smallpox, tuberculosis, and typhoid fever, among others.[57] All of these developments are a result of human ingenuity in the areas of science and technology, which are themselves products of the Christian worldview.[58]

Therefore, to be effective stewards of God's creation, our task is to discover how the earth's effectively limitless natural resources may be used, applied or transformed in order to meet the needs of human societies. Mankind, made in the image of God, is creative, and this creativity should be applied to the task of discovering this knowledge through scientific research and technological innovation.

In contrast, implementing environmental and conservationist policies that result in the suffering and death of millions of human beings who are

---

55 'Rising prices eat into UN food aid' *The Australian* (February 27, 2008).

56 Lewis Smith and Francis Elliott, 'Rush for biofuels threatens starvation on a global scale' *The Times* (March 7, 2008).

57 Reisman, *Capitalism*, 76–77.

58 Rodney Stark, *For the Glory of God* (Princeton, New Jersey, Princeton University Press, 2003), 197.

created in God's image, is not God-honoring or good stewardship — it is pagan Gaia worship.

Pollution

Pollution is a serious problem and it is a problem that mankind — as stewards of God's creation — has a duty to address. Human societies cannot operate in such a way that destroys or causes significant long-term damage to the environment. Not only does this imply a disrespect for God's creation, but a person, organization, or society that pollutes the environment is, in effect, not loving their neighbor as themselves (Matthew 22:39), since pollution negatively affects everyone.

The term 'pollution,' however, has been used increasingly to refer to any change in the state of nature caused by humans. The traditional, common understanding of pollution referred to how harmful substances had been introduced into the environment in ways that had significant detrimental effects on other people and other creatures (such as the discharge of human fecal material into drinking water). Now, any kind of industrial or agricultural development, is viewed as just another form of pollution. This is a radically different concept of pollution to the traditional, common understanding. This new understanding of pollution has led to the false implication that all industrial development implicitly involves the emission of harmful by-products that pollute the air and water, poison the fish, and destroy rivers and lakes. Industrialization is also said to be responsible for acid rain, the destruction of the ozone layer, the onset of a new ice age, and the contrary onset of global warming. Environmentalists also claim that pesticides, herbicides, and heavy metals are poisoning the food chain, and that chemical preservatives and radiation from atomic power plants, electric power lines, television sets, microwave ovens, and other electrical appliances cause cancer and other detrimental health problems. This has naturally led the environmental movement toward pathological anti-industrialization and anti-development.

Thus, most environmentalists argue that, regardless of resource availability, the pollution emitted by the growing human population and the resultant economic expansion, threatens life itself — human and non-human alike.[59] They believe that fewer people means a cleaner environment, and suppose that a decline in population would increase the amount of food and other resources available to the poor.

Yet, in developed countries today, the air and water are far cleaner than they were fifty to sixty years ago. Although air quality in large towns and cities is lower than that in rural areas — and always has been — it is still far better today than in the past, precisely because of industrial development. Before the advent of modern industry, the open streets served as sewers. All large towns and cities with a heavy concentration of horses suffered from the enormous pollution problem created by the dropping of vast quantities of animal manure and urine.

---

59 Beisner, '*Imago Dei* and the Population Debate,' 194.

The introduction of sewage systems eliminated this sewage problem, and the development of the automobile industry eliminated the need for horses. In fact, technological innovation and industrialization have not only provided the knowledge of how to build large-scale plumbing and sewage systems, but also enabled us to produce materials such as iron, steel, copper, and PVC with which to build these systems. Central heating, air conditioning, indoor plumbing, and modern ventilation methods also made significant contributions to improving the quality of air in which people live and work.[60] In fact, studies have shown the biggest contributor to air pollution is high density dwellings — a strategy preferred by many environmentalists and conservationists.[61]

Furthermore, technological progress and innovation has led to more efficient and cleaner uses of resources, so that modern cities are no longer choked with smoke from steam engines and wood heaters, and cars and trucks get better mileage and are far less polluting. Similarly, population growth has driven society to find more productive ways to grow food, and because of increased crop yields, per capita food production is higher than ever before despite the fact that the global human population has surpassed six billion. Therefore, there is now more forested land in developed countries because so much less acreage is needed for farmland. Also, commercial realities have motivated loggers to replant.[62] In other words, in learning to make more and more from less and less, we are also learning to do it while creating less and less pollution.

Regarding the quality of drinking water, it is well known that the actual safety of drinking water is in direct proportion to a country's degree of economic advancement. One can safely drink tap water in virtually every modern developed country, because the safety of water supplies is guaranteed by chemical purification plants, and the water is safely distributed by a network of pipelines and pumping stations providing instant access to safe drinking water, hot or cold, every minute of the day.[63] However, drinking the water in south and central America, and most of Asia and Africa, would be a dangerous proposition because there are no purification plants, and no secure distribution systems.

In regard to medical and general health benefits, science and technological innovation has produced the vaccines, anesthetics, antibiotics, and all the other 'wonder drugs' of modern medicine, along with all kinds of new and improved diagnostic and surgical equipment. These developments, along with improved nutrition, clothing, and shelter, radically reduced the incidence of almost every type of disease, and put an end to the plagues that ravished medieval Europe

---

60 Reisman, *Capitalism*, 83.

61 Samuel R. Staley, *The Sprawling of America: In Defence of the Dynamic City*, Policy Study No. 251, Mackinac Center for Public Policy and Reason Public Policy Institute (February, 1999), 39–40. <http://www.reason.org/ps_michigansprawl.pdf>

62 W. Bradford Wilcox, 'Fertility, Faith and the Future of the West: An interview with Phillip Longman' *Christianity Today* 13/3 (May/June 2007), 28.

63 Reisman, *Capitalism*, 83.

and polluted the countryside with rotting, infecting corpses. Indeed, as Beisner points out, one only has to read the accounts of the loathsome effects of famines and epidemics on the lives of all people before the nineteenth century, 'to make us appreciate the healthier environment we enjoy today — an environment made that way largely by the introduction of chemicals that kill pests and germs and protect crops.'[64] Daniel Boorstin makes the same point:

> We sputter against The Polluted Environment — as if it was invented in the age of the automobile. We compare our smoggy air not with the odor of horsedung [sic] and the plague of flies and the smells of garbage and human excrement which filled cities in the past, but with the honey-suckle perfumes of some nonexistent City Beautiful. We forget that even if the water in many cities today is not as spring-pure nor as palatable as we would like, for most of history the water of the cities (and of the countryside) was undrinkable. We reproach ourselves for the ills of disease and malnourishment, and forget that until recently enteritis and measles and whooping cough, diphtheria and typhoid, were killing diseases of childhood, puerperal fever plagued mothers in childbirth, polio was a summer monster.[65]

In addition, the average citizen in a modern Western society generates far less garbage today than at any time in the past. As a result of modern packaging methods, there is much less need to dispose of large quantities of animal and vegetable matter, such as chicken feathers, fish scales, and corn husks. Even the kinds of garbage unique to modern developed societies, such as disposable diapers/nappies, fast-food containers and all plastics, make a relatively small and insignificant contribution to overall garbage generation.[66] In contrast, third world, undeveloped, non-industrialized countries are the epitome of pollution and squalor, with all manner of garbage and pollutants including human excrement and, indeed, human corpses contaminating the water ways.

Extinction

Human beings have also been responsible for causing the extinction of various species.[67] In most cases, this has been to due to overhunting. But many environmentalists and conservationists also blame industrial and agricultural development and urban sprawl because they claim it destroys animal habitats.

Although the reckless destruction of species should be avoided and the impact on animal habitats minimized, there will often be a fundamental and unavoidable conflict between the needs of humans and the needs of a particular variety of plant or animal. Therefore, one may ask: is it critical for every species to survive? Putting it in context, is it acceptable to set aside vast tracts of land for

---

64 Beisner, '*Imago Dei* and the Population Debate,' 195.

65 Daniel Boorstin, 'A Case of Hypochondria' *Newsweek* (July 6, 1970), 28.

66 See Llewellyn H. Rockwell, 'Government Garbage' *Free Market* 8/2 (February 1990), 2, 8. See also Peter Passell, 'The Garbage Problem: It May Be Politics Not Nature' *New York Times*, February 26, 1991, B5, B7.

67 For example, the Tasmanian Tiger, Dodo, and Great Auk.

agriculture and/or housing in order to provide food and shelter for hundreds of thousands of people, in exchange for the loss of a particular species of parrot or lizard? Clearly, the answer depends on the relative value one places on human beings compared to other creatures. It is a question of whose needs should ultimately prevail. Human beings are faced with the choice of fulfilling their own needs or sacrificing themselves (or their fellow human beings) for the sake of some variety of plant or animal. For many environmentalists and conservationists, it is human beings who should submit.

The motivation behind such views are rooted in the philosophy of anti-speciesism — the belief that it is wrong to assign rights to creatures purely on the basis of the species it belongs to.[68] To assert that the rights of human beings are superior to any other species is, on this view, morally equivalent to racism.[69] In fact, environmentalists and conservationists even object to the destruction of animal and vegetable species that are useless or even hostile to mankind. Any extinction is inherently immoral. This brand of nature worship and human self-loathing is best illustrated in the comments of David Graber:

> We are not interested in the utility of a particular species or free-flowing river, or ecosystem, to mankind. They have intrinsic value, more value — to me — than another human body, or a billion of them. Human happiness, and certainly human fecundity, are not as important as a wild and healthy planet ... Somewhere along the line — at about a billion years ago, maybe half that — we quit the contract and became a cancer. We have become a plague upon ourselves and upon the Earth ... Until such time as Homo sapiens should decide to rejoin nature, some of us can only hope for the right virus to come along.[70]

Similar views have been expressed by some theologians. St. Francis of Assisi believed in the equality of all living creatures: man, cattle, birds, fish, and reptiles.[71] Indeed, precisely on the basis of this philosophical affinity, St. Francis was officially declared the patron saint of ecology by the Roman Catholic Church. Likewise, Albert Schweitzer advocated a form of pantheism where every manifestation of life stood in a personal, spiritual relationship with the rest of the universe.[72]

But such views are clearly not compatible with the biblical view that human beings are made in God's image and have been given dominion over the rest of creation. In the biblical view of creation, the needs of human beings surpass the needs of any other creature or plant.

---

68 See, for example, Tom Regan, *The Case for Animal Rights* (Berkeley, California, University of California Press, 2004).

69 See, for example, Paola Cavalieri, *The Animal Question: Why Non-Human Animals Deserve Human Rights* (translated by Catherine Woollard) (Oxford, Oxford University Press, 2001).

70 David M. Graber, *Los Angeles Times Book Review* (October 22, 1989), 113.

71 These sentiments are expressed in his poem *Canticle of the Sun*, <http://www.ncca.org.au/departments/youth/resources_for_peace/canticle_of_the_sun>.

72 See Albert Schweitzer, *The Philosophy of Civilization* (Buffalo, New York, Prometheus, 1987).

Moreover, when environmentalists and conservationists deny the special status of human beings, they do not, as a result, elevate flies, snails, and rats to the level of mankind, but rather, reduce human beings to the level of flies, snails, and rats. If human beings are regarded as no better than flies, then that is exactly how they will be treated. Indeed, this is precisely what has happened in other irrational cultures.[73]

There is also a great deal of inconsistency in the 'equality of rights' position advocated by environmentalists and conservationists. They do not appear realize that their view of nature as a beautiful and harmonious utopia apart from the interference of mankind bears no resemblance to actual reality. As Tennyson described it in his poem *In Memoriam*, nature is 'red in tooth and claw' — a place where one creature tears another apart or eats another alive. If human beings are just another animal species, they would be entitled to act in the same way that many other animal species act — by hunting other species for no other reason than to ensure their own survival. Indeed, if human beings were no better than lions or leopards, then an individual human being would have as much right to the fur of a seal as a lion has to the flesh of a gazelle.

Another inconsistency exists in the way 'equality of rights' advocates actually value human life below the lives of animals. In fact, human life is not only below that of animals whose furs they may wear or whose flesh they may eat, but also below the value that some animals attach to other animals. For example, lions value themselves above zebras, yet animal rights advocates value humans below cattle and as less worthy of eating cattle than lions are of eating zebras.

In any case, the disappearance of species has been going on since the fall. Extinctions appear to be no more frequent now than in the past. Moreover, to what extent have extinctions been caused by human activity? Many extinctions have occurred naturally, due to catastrophic events such as meteorite strikes, large-scale flooding, bush fires, and similar. The fossil record is full of extinct creatures (many of which are marine organisms) that had little or no contact with human beings.

Furthermore, the extinction of some species should be contrasted with the emergence of new species. Speciation[74] is very likely to have occurred quite often and quite rapidly due to genetic drift,[75] or selection pressure.[76] Indeed, an

---

73 Reisman, *Capitalism*, 78.

74 Speciation (the emergence of a new species) is *not* the same as biological evolution. The new species is still of the same kind as the parent species (i.e. if the parent species is a bird, the new species is also a bird), it simply can no longer interbreed with the parent species. Speciation does not occur as a result of the creation or development of *new* genetic information. Rather, it occurs as a result of either a change in the frequencies of existing genes or the total loss of existing genes.

75 Genetic drift is the change in the allele frequencies (or gene frequencies) of a population from one generation to the next resulting in a concentration of particular genetic characteristics.

76 Selection pressure refers to the filtering of various physical characteristics as a result of harsh environmental circumstances.

eighteen-year study by zoologist Peter Grant showed that a new species could arise in only 200 years.[77]

In actual fact, human civilization is responsible for the existence of many species of animals and plants in their present numbers and varieties. Human beings are responsible for the existence of the overwhelming majority of the varieties of cattle, sheep, pigs, chickens, goats, horses, and cats and dogs that are alive today.[78] The populations of all varieties of domesticated animals would be greatly reduced if there were no human beings to feed them, promote their health, and protect them from their natural enemies. In the same way, human beings are responsible for the fact that many grain crops, vegetables, flowers, and grasses grow where they would not naturally grow, and are far less suscep-tible to disease than they normally would be. Furthermore, where forest land is privately owned, human beings are also responsible for the existence of many trees and forests, that have commercial value as long-term crops. Of course, human beings also plant trees for aesthetic purposes in order to enhance their surroundings. Indeed, virtually all of the trees in many portions of Southern California and other arid areas are not native to those areas but were planted and maintained by humans.

Therefore, human beings are not inherently destroyers of species. Mankind has greatly promoted and protected those species that are of benefit to human society. In general, human beings have destroyed only those species that are harmful to human society or harmful to other species that humans desire to promote and protect. Human beings have also destroyed those species that they have judged to be expedient because their destruction would lead to overwhelm-ingly beneficial outcomes for human society.

Environmental Ethics

Ethics is concerned with what a person ought to do in any given situation. What, then, are Christians — as stewards of God's creation — to do in light of the environmental challenges we presently face? Clearly, we are to take care of creation, but that does not mean that industrial and agricultural development should be stopped or severely restricted. Nor does it mean that the needs of human beings should be subjugated to the desire to maintain a pristine environment.

With respect to the environmental challenges mankind now faces, and in our assessment of what is to be done, the following principles should be taken into account:

1. Is the problem empirically and scientifically verified? Is the perceived problem really a problem? Is the scientific and factual basis still in dispute?

2. Is the problem caused directly or indirectly by human action, or is it a result of natural processes?

---

77 P.R. Grant, 'Natural Selection and Darwin's Finches' *Scientific American* 265/4 (October 1991), 60–65.

78 Reisman, *Capitalism*, 83.

3. Is the cost (in money and human life) of fixing the problem greater than the cost of coping with the problem?

4. Is the environmental impact or damage insignificant when compared with the overwhelming benefit it provides to human beings? If we build a power station that services a city of several million people, does it really matter, in the grand scale of things, if we destroy the habitat of some obscure bird or animal?

Note that these principles are somewhat utilitarian, that is, guided by the desire to achieve the greatest benefit for the greatest number of people. However, in a fallen world where human beings still retain their God-given dominion, this is the best we can hope for until the return of Christ and the establishment of His kingdom.

Human beings are finite and fallen creatures. While it is certainly true that we have, on many occasions, abused God's creation and treated it in ways that are inconsistent with our role as God's stewards, our fallen nature has also led us to believe things about the world that are simply not true. In particular, some environmentalists and conservationists — motivated by political and economic concerns — have misled many people into accepting a number of things that are demonstrably false. In their eagerness to protect God's creation, many Christians have also accepted these untruths.

One of the greatest — and most tragic — environmental frauds of all time is the banning of, or restriction of, the use of Dichloro-Diphenyl-Trichloroethane (DDT). This is one of the most effective pesticides ever produced, especially against the malaria-carrying *Anopheles* mosquitoes. The spraying of DDT on the inside walls of homes has proven to be the most cost effective way of preventing the spread of malaria which infects and kills thousands of people every year. In 1970, the U.S. National Academy of Sciences stated: 'To only a few chemicals does man owe as great a debt as to DDT. In little more than two decades DDT has prevented 500 million human deaths, due to malaria, that would otherwise have been inevitable.'[79]

Yet, DDT and its derivatives have been blamed for numerous negative effects including causing various cancers, anti-androgenic symptoms in animals and humans, the poisoning of marine life, the thinning of egg shells, and the near extinction of species such as the bald eagle. These claims have been uncritically accepted by many people including many Christian thinkers such as Francis Schaeffer.[80]

The truth is that DDT has been comprehensively tested and demonstrated to be a safe and effective chemical pesticide. As J. Gordon Edwards pointed out:

Human volunteers in Georgia ingested up to 35 milligrams daily, for nearly two years, and did not experience any difficulties then or

---

79 As cited in J. Gordon Edwards, 'Mosquitoes, DDT, and Human Health' *21st Century Science and Technology* 15/3 (Fall 2002).

80 Schaeffer, 'Pollution and the Death of Man' in *Complete Works*, 5:3–4.

later. Workers in the Montrose Chemical Company had 1,300 man-years of exposure, and there was never any case of cancer during 19 years of continuous exposure to about 17 mg/man/day. Concerns were sometimes raised about possible carcinogenic effects of DDT, but instead its metabolites were often found to be anti-carcinogenic, significantly reducing tumors in rats. DDT ingestion induces hepatic microsomal enzymes, which destroy carcinogenic aflatoxins and thereby inhibit tumors.[81]

Edwards elsewhere notes that '[t]there was never any need to wear masks or protective clothing while doing DDT spraying. No adverse effects were ever experienced by the 130,000 spraymen or the 535 million people living in the sprayed houses.[82]

Nor has DDT killed thousands of birds as some have claimed. The danger to them was tested by feeding caged birds known quantities of DDT, but even extreme amounts of DDT did not seriously poison birds. Moreover, during the years when DDT was in use in the USA, bird counts in a number of affected area actually increased![83] Furthermore, egg shell thinning was found to be caused by calcium deficient diets not DDT.[84] The anti-androgenic symptoms in animals and humans were caused by other sources of pollution.[85]

It has often been said that DDT persists for decades in the ocean. In order to test this claim, researchers at the US Environmental Protection Agency's Gulf Breeze Laboratory in Louisiana added DDT to seawater in huge submerged containers. They reported that 9 percent of the DDT *and* its metabolites, DDD and DDE, disappeared from the seawater in only 38 days.[86]

However, as Donald R. Roberts, has pointed out, DDT effectiveness *is* decreased if it is sprayed indiscriminately everywhere in the environment because it allows mosquitoes to build up resistance.[87] Therefore, the common sense Christian response to DDT should be to restrict or prohibit its use in agriculture, but continue to use it widely for indoor spraying where it acts as

---

81 J. Gordon Edwards, 'DDT: A Case Study in Scientific Fraud' *Journal of American Physicians and Surgeons* 9/3 (Fall 2004), 84. In regard to the alleged cancer-causing effects of DDT, see also S. Takayama et al, 'Effects of long-term oral administration of DDT on nonhuman primates' *Journal of Cancer Research and Clinical Oncology* 125/3–4 (1999), 219–225; D. Baris et al., 'Agricultural use of DDT and risk of non-Hodgkin's lymphoma: pooled analysis of three case-control studies in the United States' *Occupational and Environmental Medicine* 55/8 (1998), 522–527; D.J. Hunter et al., 'Plasma organochlorine levels and the risk of breast cancer;' *New England Journal of Medicine* 337 (1997), 1253–1258; P. van't Veer et al., 'DDT (dicophane) and postmenopausal breast cancer in Europe: case-control study' *British Medical Journal* 315 (July 12, 1997), 81–85.

82 Edwards, 'Mosquitoes, DDT, and Human Health'.

83 Edwards, 'DDT: A Case Study in Scientific Fraud,' 84.

84 Ibid.

85 Ibid., 85.

86 Ibid.

87 Donald R. Roberts, 'To Control Malaria, We Need DDT!' *21ˢᵗ Century Science and Technology* 15/3 (Fall 2002), 66–67.

a powerful repellent. This approach enables us to fulfill our stewardship role by saving millions of our fellow humans, while at the same, having little or no effect on the environment.

The other great environmental challenge is the one currently being widely promulgated and publicized: climate change. Thirty years ago, scientists were certain that the world was rapidly cooling, and the first Earth Day was celebrated on April 22, 1970, amid fears of a new ice age. *Fortune* magazine cited a number of leading climatologists who had concluded that global cooling was 'the root cause of a lot of that unpleasant weather around the world,' and that 'it carries the potential for human disasters of unprecedented magnitude.'[88]

Peter Gwynne wrote that there were ominous signs that the earth's weather patterns had begun to change dramatically and that these changes would result in a 'drastic decline in food production — with serious political implications for just about every nation on Earth.'[89] He added:

> The evidence in support of these predictions has now begun to accumulate so massively that meteorologists are hard-pressed to keep up with it … The central fact is that after three quarters of a century of extraordinarily mild conditions, the earth's climate seems to be cooling down. Meteorologists disagree about the cause and extent of the cooling trend, as well as over its specific impact on local weather conditions. But they are almost unanimous in the view that the trend will reduce agricultural productivity for the rest of the century. If the climatic change is as profound as some of the pessimists fear, the resulting famines could be catastrophic.[90]

At the same time, the National Academy of Sciences declared that '[a] major climatic change would force economic and social adjustments on a worldwide scale because the global patterns of food production and population that have evolved are implicitly dependent on the climate of the present century.'[91] Gwynne noted that climatologists 'are pessimistic that political leaders will take any positive action to compensate for the climatic change, or even to allay its effects … The longer the planners delay, the more difficult will they find it to cope with climatic change once the results become grim reality.'[92]

Today, the very same concerns are again being expressed, but in regard to the exact opposite phenomenon: global warming!

During the 1990s, some scientists and environmentalists suggested that the earth was in fact not cooling but warming, and that this warming was caused by a strengthened greenhouse effect that, in turn, was caused by the massive increases in carbon dioxide emissions from human industry and activity. In 2001, the Intergovernmental Panel on Climate Change (IPCC) released their

---

88 'Ominous Changes in the World's Weather' *Fortune* (February 1974).

89 Peter Gwynne, 'The Cooling World' *Newsweek* (April 28, 1975), 64.

90 Ibid.

91 As cited in ibid.

92 Ibid., 64.

Third Assessment Report. The IPCC Summary for Policymakers included a graph generated by Michael Mann and colleagues that appeared to show that the earth's climate was very stable from 1000 to 1900, but then suddenly began to change, and temperatures in the northern hemisphere began to rise dramatically and continued to rise up until the present time. This graph became known as the 'hockey stick' graph.[93]

The IPCC Summary claimed it is likely 'that the 1990s has been the warmest decade and 1998 the warmest year of the millennium' for the northern hemisphere. As a result, many climate scientists, government officials, and media commentators became convinced that climate change or global warming was a very real and serious threat, and called for drastic reductions in carbon dioxide emissions. Given that modern society, industry, and agriculture all require large amounts of energy generated by carbon dioxide producing processes, making significant cuts in carbon dioxide emissions is not easy. Indeed, it would cause severe economic pain and lower everyone's standard of living.

Stephen McIntyre and Ross McKitrick have now thoroughly debunked the Mann hockey stick,[94] and as a result, the graph was left out of the most recent 2007 IPCC Fourth Assessment Report. Nevertheless, its impact still persists. Moreover, NASA's updated surface temperature records for the USA (where most of the heavy industrialization has occurred) indicate that 1934 was the warmest on record, not 1998. The third hottest year on record was 1921, not 2006, and four of the top ten hottest years on record occurred during the 1940s before the large scale growth in carbon dioxide emissions. Moreover, several recent years (2000, 2002, 2003, 2004) are well down in the rankings and 2004 falls behind even 1900.[95]

Nevertheless, there is still great pressure on governments and public policy makers to make drastic industrial, economic, and structural changes in order to reduce carbon dioxide emissions. The Stern Review on the economics of climate change suggested that climate change threatens to be the greatest and widest-

93 See Michael Mann et al., 'Global-Scale Temperature Patterns and Climate Forcing Over the Past Six Centuries' *Nature* 392 (1998), 779–787; Michael Mann et al., 'Northern Hemisphere Temperatures During the Past Millennium: Inferences, Uncertainties, and Limitations' *Geophysical Research Letters* 26 (1999), 759–762.

94 Stephen McIntyre and Ross McKitrick, 'Corrections to the Mann et. al. (1998) Proxy Data Base and Northern Hemispheric Average Temperature Series' *Energy & Environment* 14/6 (2003) 751–771; Stephen McIntyre and Ross McKitrick, 'Hockey sticks, principal components, and spurious significance' *Geophysical Research Letters* 32 (2005), L03710; Stephen McIntyre and Ross McKitrick, 'The M&M Critique of the MBH98 Northern Hemisphere Climate Index: Update and Implications' *Energy & Environment* 16/1 (2005), 69–100; Stephen McIntyre and Ross McKitrick, 'Reply to comment by von Storch and Zorita on "Hockey sticks, principal components, and spurious significance"' *Geophysical Research Letters* 32 (2005), L20714; Stephen McIntyre and Ross McKitrick, 'Reply to comment by Huybers on "Hockey sticks, principal components, and spurious significance"' *Geophysical Research Letters* 32 (2005), L20713.

95 The data table is available from the NASA GISS site: <http://data.giss.nasa.gov/gistemp/graphs/Fig.D.txt>

ranging threat to the market ever seen. Its main conclusions are that 1 per cent of global gross domestic product (GDP) *per annum* is required to be invested in order to avoid the worst effects of climate change, and that failure to do so could risk global GDP being up to 20 per cent lower than it otherwise might be, and it provides prescriptions, including environmental taxes, to minimize the economic and social disruptions.[96] Moreover, Stern declares that the required changes should be implemented immediately:

> The evidence shows that ignoring climate change will eventually damage economic growth. Our actions over the coming few decades could create risks of major disruption to economic and social activity, later in this century and in the next, on a scale similar to those associated with the great wars and the economic depression of the first half of the 20th century. And it will be difficult or impossible to reverse these changes. Tackling climate change is the pro-growth strategy for the longer term, and it can be done in a way that does not cap the aspirations for growth of rich or poor countries. The earlier effective action is taken, the less costly it will be. At the same time, given that climate change is happening, measures to help people adapt to it are essential. And the less mitigation we do now, the greater the difficulty of continuing to adapt in future.[97]

The Australian Evangelical Alliance has also highlighted the supposed urgency and demanded the Australian government act now:

> But there is still time to avoid the top range of risk — provided that we do the necessary things and act immediately. As far as government policy is concerned that probably means establishing a clear policy framework for significantly reducing emissions by the end of the next parliamentary term. The scientific evidence which connects greenhouse gas emissions with climate change is the same evidence which indicates that the goal for developed nations ought to be in the order of a 60% reduction in greenhouse gas emissions from year 2000 levels by 2050. It makes no sense to accept the conclusions about the reality of climate change and not accept the conclusions about the necessary goals for rectifying it as they are based on the same evidence. Nor does it make sense to hold back from acting on this because of the fear it would have a damaging impact on Australia's GDP. A failure to act will cost even more in the long run and the use of fossil fuels (the major causes of human-induced climate change) is itself distorting the economy as it is highly subsidised through not being required to pay for its effects.[98]

---

96 Nicholas Stern, 'Stern Review: The economics of climate change' (2006) <http://www.hm-treasury.gov.uk/independent_reviews/stern_review_economics_climate_change/stern_review_report.cfm>.

97 Nicholas Stern, 'Stern Review: The economics of climate change — Executive Summary' (2006) <http://www.hm-treasury.gov.uk/media/4/3/Executive_Summary.pdf>

98 'Christians and Climate Change: A Statement from the Australian Evangelical Alliance Inc.' Australian Evangelical Alliance (February, 2007) <http://www.ea.org.au/content/documents/pdf%20files/Climate%20Change.pdf>.

Although most scientists agree that the earth's global average surface temperature has increased (by approximately 0.6 degrees Celsius) during the twentieth century, many disagree that this is caused by human action, especially since much of that warming occurred before the advent of large-scale industrialization (before 1940). Instead, they believe the warming is more likely to be part of a natural cycle. Furthermore, they note that rising temperatures may, in fact, result in far greater benefits to mankind, and that these benefits are rarely considered or taken into account by those who desire to reverse global warming.[99] For example, they note that carbon dioxide (as opposed to particulate carbon) is not a pollutant. Carbon dioxide is a naturally occurring gas that is an essential component of the photosynthetic process that causes vegetation to grow. The presence of additional carbon dioxide will stimulate plant growth, and the warmer weather means a longer growing season, and thus greater agricultural production. In fact, retreating ice and ground thawing would cause more arable land to become available for both residential and agricultural purposes.

In addition, those who argue that global warming will produce greater benefits to mankind point to the fact that the world has previously thrived during past warming periods, and that cold periods have always caused serious survival problems for all creatures including humans. Extreme cold always causes far more deaths than extreme heat. Furthermore, with most roads free from ice and snow, driving would be a lot safer. Rail and air transportation would also be far more efficient due to the reduction of weather-related delays and accidents. There would also be a significant reduction in energy use due to reduced heating requirements and less demand for the manufacturing of cold weather clothing.[100]

In any case, Christians face a choice: to implement the drastic policies currently being advocated by those convinced that global warming poses a very real threat, or to wait and see and make adjustments and adaptions as the need arises. Carbon dioxide reduction policies require revolutionary changes to the way we generate energy. 'Clean' renewable energy sources are inadequate sources of baseload power,[101] so the only options are hydro-electric, nuclear and geothermal — all of which have other significant environmental impacts. Thus, to make any real difference, coal-fired power stations around the world will more or less need to be closed down, and millions of vehicles taken off the roads. This will, of course, have catastrophic effects on human civilization, and

99 See, for example, the Oregon Institute of Science and Medicine's petition which has been signed by over 19,000 American scientists. <http://www.oism.org/pproject/s33p1845.htm>.

100 A comprehensive cost-benefit analysis of global warming has been produced by Mendelsohn and Neumann (Robert Mendelsohn and James E. Neumann [editors], *The Impact of Climate Change on the United States Economy* [Cambridge, Cambridge University Press, 1999]). Mendelsohn, Neumann and the other contributors assume a doubling of CO_2 that would lead to a 2.5 degree Celsius increase in global temperatures.

101 Wind power only works when the wind blows; solar power only works during the day and when the sun is shining. Moreover, the output from these sources is so small it could not sustain any significant industry or transport infrastructure.

will inevitably lead to the suffering and death of millions of people. George Reisman explains the absurdity of such policies:

> If we destroy the energy base needed to produce and operate the construction equipment required to build strong, well-made, comfortable houses for hundreds of millions of people, we shall be safer from the wind and rain, the environmental movement alleges, than if we retain and enlarge that energy base. If we destroy our capacity to produce and operate refrigerators and air conditioners, we shall be better protected from hot weather than if we retain and enlarge that capacity, the environmental movement claims. If we destroy our capacity to produce and operate tractors and harvesters, to can and freeze food, to build and operate hospitals and produce medicines, we shall secure our food supply and our health better than if we retain and enlarge that capacity, the environmental movement asserts.[102]

If global warming is indeed the great threat that many claim, it would make more sense, and be more in line with our role as God's stewards, to take steps to cope with it when the need arises. Again, this would only be possible if human societies retain the ability to produce and to use energy in a way that is not crippled by the environmental movement and by government controls.[103]

It should also be noted that the earth's biosphere has proven in the past to be remarkably resilient. This is an important point in light of the various doomsday scenarios that have been put forward by global warming activists. In the past, the earth has endured both long periods of warming and ice ages. It has endured meteorites strikes and massive earthquakes, yet here it remains with its human, animal, and vegetable life still alive. Indeed, the earth has even recovered from the most catastrophic and devastating environmental disaster imaginable — a global flood lasting approximately one year, that at one point covered the entire surface of the earth, including the highest mountains!

Summary

It appears that most non-Christian environmentalists and conservationists make their claims concerning the expiration of natural resources, the destruction of species, and the problems of air and water pollution, not out of any actual concern for human life and well-being, but instead, based on their belief in the intrinsic value of nature.[104] Instead of acknowledging their Father God, they bow before Mother Nature. They worship creation instead of the Creator.

Of course, the same cannot be said of Christian environmentalists and conservationists. They rightly point out that our God-given role is to act as God's stewards of creation and to take care of it, not abuse it or destroy it. But in many cases, they fail to acknowledge God's order in creation, and that mankind has dominion over all. Christians are neither carrying out their stewardship

---

102 Reisman, *Capitalism*, 88.
103 Ibid., 90.
104 Ibid., 85.

role, nor loving their neighbor, by advocating antidevelopment policies that will lead to the death of millions of people, and ensure that millions more endure lives of poverty and destitution. We are called to usher in the kingdom of God and fight against the fall, including the poverty and death that it brought into world. The best way to do this is to employ our God-given creative abilities to use the many resources that God has provided in the natural world effectively and efficiently, in order to develop our environment in ways that sustain human society. Furthermore, we are to have faith in God and His providential work, having full confidence that He can and will protect His creation and provide all that we need, because it is part of His universal plan of salvation. As Carl Henry explains:

> God preserves the forms and structures of life and being not merely to perpetuate them but also in anticipation of a climactic consummation. God's sustaining of the universe is coordinated with his plan from the foundation of the world to unveil Christ Jesus as the source and Savior of the world. Divine preservation anticipates God's covenant with fallen and redeemed humanity; besides the universal dominion and providence he exercises over all creatures, he exercises in addition a special covenant dominion toward the redeemed. The final consummation of all things will be a climactic demonstration of his sovereign justice and sovereign mercy. Divine preservation will be crowned at last by universal divine judgment and by decisive redemptive grace.[105]

And as Berkouwer stated: 'the sustaining of the world ... is also related to His purposes for the future.'[106] To this, the future, we now turn.

---

105 Henry, *God, Revelation and Authority*, 6:457.

106 G.C. Berkouwer, *The Providence of God* (Grand Rapids, Michigan: Eerdmans, 1952) 83.

CHAPTER 12

Creation Restored

Despite humanity's alienation from their Creator because of their sinfulness, and despite the physical world being under a curse, God has not abandoned His creation. Through Christ, the creation will be liberated from its bondage to decay. Through Christ, salvation comes to mankind, and He is the agent through which humans may once again commune with their Creator.

The Work of Christ

The New Testament teaches that Christ is intimately involved with His creation. Indeed, He was there in the beginning, and nothing came into being without Him (John 1:2–3). Creation is for Him, and He holds everything together (Colossians 1:16–17). Thus, it should not be surprising to read that Christ is also the One who will free creation from the curse, bring righteousness and justification, and free the world from its bondage to death and decay (Romans 5:15–19, 8:20–23). Through Christ, all things on earth and in heaven will be reconciled to God (Colossians 1:20). 'The vision is vast. The claim mind-blowing … [The first Christians] see in Christ's death and resurrection quite literally the key to resolving the disharmonies of nature and the inhumanities of humankind, that the character of God's creation and God's concern for the universe in its fullest expression could be so caught and encapsulated for them in the cross of Christ.'[1]

Christ continually works out His plan for the world and particularly for His people.[2] As T.F. Torrance writes:

> In Christian Theology that redemption of the universe is precisely the bearing of the cross upon the way things actually are in our universe of space and time. It represents the refusal of God to remain aloof from the disintegration of order in what he has made, or merely to act upon it 'at a distance.' It is his decisive personal intervention in the world through the incarnation of his Word and love in Jesus Christ. In his life and passion he who is the ultimate source and power of all order has penetrated into the untouchable core of our contingent existence in

---

1 James D.G. Dunn, *The Epistles to the Colossians and to Philemon*, NIGTC (Grand Rapids, Michigan, Eerdmans, 1996), 104.

2 Willem A. VanGemeren, *The Progress of Redemption* (Grand Rapids, Zondervan, 1988), 61.

such a way as to deal with the twisted force of evil entrenched in it, and
thereby to bring about an atoning reordering of creation.[3]

The salvation brought about through Christ's death and resurrection has given
humanity the opportunity to be released from the bondage of death and
disease. Although all humans are condemned to death as a result of Adam's sin,
people can be justified and have eternal life if they receive God's gracious gift of
righteousness in the work of Christ (Romans 5:17–19; 1 Corinthians 15:21–
22).[4] In fact, the work of Christ will result in the restoration of all of creation.[5]
As Paul points out in Colossians 1:20, through Christ, God has sought to
reconcile 'all things' (τὰ πάντα, *ta panta*) to Himself, 'whether things on earth
or things in heaven.'[6] If the whole of creation is affected by the fall, then the
whole of creation is restored in Christ (see Fig 11.1).[7]

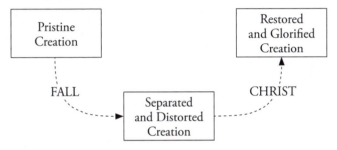

Figure 11.1: The work of Christ in creation's restoration

The New Creation

Many of the apocalyptic portions of Scripture refer to or describe the new
creation. These references can be found in Isaiah 65–66, 2 Peter 3, and Revelation
21–22. However, before examining the nature of the newly restored creation, it
is important first to examine the fate of this present creation.

The Passing Away of the Heavens and the Earth

Several New Testament texts refer to the passing away of the heavens and the
earth.[8] In addition, 2 Peter 3:10–11 predicts the disappearance of the heavens
and the destruction of the earth.[9] Old Testament eschatological texts such

---

3 Thomas F. Torrance, *The Christian Frame of Mind: Reason, Order, and Openness in Theology and
Natural Science* (Colarado Springs, Helmers and Howard, 1989), 103.

4 Such New Testament texts which compare and contrast Christ with Adam present problems
for those who view the creation story as mythical or anything other than history (e.g., Alan
Hayward, Roger Forster and Paul Marston). An unhistorical cause could not bring about a
historical effect.

5 A.M. Wolters, *Creation Regained* (Carlisle, Paternoster, 1996), 57.

6 See also Matt. 19:28.

7 Wolters, *Creation Regained*, 59–60.

8 Matt. 24:35; Mark 13:31; Luke 21:33; Rev. 21:1.

9 See also Matt. 5:18.

as Psalm 102:25–26, Isaiah 34:4, and Isaiah 51:6 allude to similar notions of perishing, dissolving, withering, vanishing, and wearing out. Yet Romans 8:19–21 indicates that, rather than being destroyed, the earth will be liberated and restored. Moreover, the total destruction of the present creation appears to be incompatible with numerous other Scriptures. For example, the meek are to inherit the earth (Matthew 5:5) but this would not be possible if the earth is destined to be destroyed. In fact, God made an everlasting promise to Abraham that he and his descendants would possess the whole land of Canaan forever (Genesis 17:7). Similarly, God made a promise to David that one of his descendants would reign over Israel, and that his house and throne would last forever (2 Samuel 7:11b–16). Yet neither of these covenants could be fulfilled if the earth is to be destroyed.

What, then, is the meaning of texts which appear to present a pessimistic future for the earth? What did Isaiah mean when he proclaimed that the sky will dissipate and the earth will wear out (Isaiah 51:6)? The meaning of this text is revealed in the contrasting parallelism in which it is framed. The permanence of God's deliverance and vindication stand in stark contrast to the transitory nature of this present world.

Similarly, the references to the 'perishing' and 'wearing out' of the heavens and the earth in Psalm 102:25–26 stand in contrast to the God who will remain forever.

Furthermore, the references to the rotting (NRSV) or dissolving (NIV) of the host of heaven in Isaiah 34:4 indicates that 'even the mysterious, unchanging stars, the seeming guarantors of the universe's perpetuity, are in the hands of the God of Jerusalem.'[10]

Regarding the references to the passing away of heaven and earth, the verb used in the synoptic gospels is παρέρχομαι (*parerchomai*) while Revelation 21:1 uses ἀπέρχομαι (*aperchomai*). Both words denote a disappearance or a ceasing to exist.[11] In the synoptics, παρέρχομαι refers to the passing away of the heavens and the earth in their present form only,[12] and in Revelation ἀπέρχομαι merely indicates that the first heaven and earth had disappeared from John's sight.

2 Peter 3:10 also employs παρέρχομαι to describe the disappearance of the heavens. The writer adds that 'the elements will be destroyed by fire' and the earth will be 'laid bare.' But what exactly are these elements (στοιχεῖα, *stoicheia*)? They could be (1) the fundamental principles (of this world), (2) the basic building blocks of the universe, (3) spiritual beings, or (4) the heavenly bodies.[13] Options (3) and (4) clearly do not fit here, and neither does option (1) given that these elements will 'melt in the heat' (v. 12). Most commentators understand

---

10 John N. Oswalt, *The Book of Isaiah, Chapters 40–66*, NICOT (Grand Rapids, Michigan, Eerdmans, 1998), 609.

11 See BAGD 1b and Louw-Nida 13.93.

12 Donald A. Hagner, *Matthew 14–28*, WBC (Dallas, Texas, Word, 1995), 715.

13 BAGD.

stoicheia as the basic building blocks of the world such as rocks, pebbles, sand, water, wood, and similar. It is unlikely that *stoicheia* is a reference to the ancient understanding of the four elements of earth, air, fire, and water, given that one of these 'elements' — fire — is the means by which they are destroyed!

One could argue that the concept of basic building blocks also does not fit. How can the earth's basic building blocks be destroyed, when the earth itself is not destroyed but merely 'laid bare.' However, the word translated 'laid bare' in the NIV is the Greek verb εὑρίσκω (*heuriskō*) meaning 'found.' The usual nuance of this verb appears to make little sense in the present context.[14] However, A.M. Wolters suggests it should be taken as a reference to the smelting and casting of metal.[15] This rendering actually makes good sense of the text and the context. The message here is that the earth will be purified and reformed,[16] and the passing away of the heavens and the earth is not a reference to their total destruction, but rather an indication that God's judgment of His creation will have a climax and an end, and then He will begin again. This is illustrated in apocalyptic prophecy in Jeremiah 4:23–28:

> *I looked at the earth,*
>> *and it was formless and empty;*
> *and at the heavens,*
>> *and their light was gone.*
> *I looked at the mountains,*
>> *and they were quaking;*
>> *all the hills were swaying.*
> *I looked, and there were no people;*
>> *every bird in the sky had flown away.*
> *I looked, and the fruitful land was a desert;*
>> *all its towns lay in ruins*
>> *before the LORD, before his fierce anger.*
> *This is what the LORD says:*
> *'The whole land will be ruined,*
>> *though I will not destroy it completely.*
> *Therefore the earth will mourn*
>> *and the heavens above grow dark,*
> *because I have spoken and will not relent,*
>> *I have decided and will not turn back.'*

As Feinberg points out, this 'is the story of Genesis 1 in reverse' and 'may be taken to describe the coming Day of the Lord.'[17]

---

14 Bruce Metzger (*A Textual Commentary on the Greek New Testament*, 2nd edition [UBS, 1994], 636) remarks: '… εὑρεθήσεται, though the oldest of the extant readings, seems to be devoid of meaning in the context …'

15 A.M. Wolters, 'Worldview and Textual Criticism in 2 Peter 3:10' *WTJ* 49/2 (Fall 1987), 411–412.

16 This understanding will be discussed in more detail below.

17 Charles L. Feinberg, *Jeremiah*, in Frank E. Gaebelein (editor), *Isaiah–Ezekiel*, EBC (Grand Rapids, Michigan, Zondervan, 1987).

A New Heaven and a New Earth

Given that the present creation will not be totally destroyed, how should those biblical texts which refer to the creation of a new heaven and a new earth be understood?[18]

The new heavens and the new earth are not new in the sense of being totally 'brand new,' but in the sense of being repaired and refurbished. Indeed, the word 'new' (καινός, *kainos*) used in these verses, indicates a newness in terms of quality, in contrast to νέος (*neos*), which normally indicates newness with respect to time.[19] Indeed, the New Testament employs *kainos* predominantly as a reference to a change in quality or essence, and especially in texts which relate to eschatological or redemptive-historical transitions.[20]

The present world will be restored and replenished, not replaced. In other words, God is not making a totally new creation, but rather, restoring the present creation to its unspoiled, pristine condition. As Isaiah (51:3) writes: 'The LORD will surely comfort Zion and will look with compassion on all her ruins; he will make her deserts like Eden, her wastelands like the garden of the LORD.' Douglas Moo concurs: 'Restoration suggests not destruction, but transformation. And Peter's claim [Acts 3:19–21] that this restoration will fulfil the promises of the prophets also points in this direction, since the Old Testament typically envisages the last days in terms of a transformed earth.'[21] Jewish writings on Isaiah 65 also considered the new creation to be a renewal or transformation of the present creation.[22]

Regarding the reference to the new heavens and the new earth in Isaiah 66:22, Oswalt notes that the reader is taken back to 65:17, which describes the rejoicing in the messianic kingdom. Oswalt concludes:

> Thus the final segment begins and ends on the theme of joyous re-creation. God has re-created his world, and sin can never stain it again. The tragedies of the old world, which called into question the very faithfulness of God, are gone. God has promised to Abraham a name and seed, children, but the sin of Israel and the rapacity of the world rulers made it seem as if even God could not keep his promises. Nonetheless, God is greater than human sin and human pride and is able to keep his promises. The old heavens and earth had been called to witness the justice of God in punishing his people (1:2); they had also been called to burst into song over the redemption of those people made possible by the work of the Servant (44:23; 49:13). Now the eternity of the new heavens and earth stands as a testimony to the eternity of God's promises.[23]

---

18 See Isa. 65:17, 66:22; 2 Pet. 3:13; Rev. 21:1.

19 These two words can, on occasion, be synonymous.

20 Gregory K. Beale, *The Book of Revelation*, NIGTC (Grand Rapids, Michigan, Eerdmans, 1998), 1040.

21 Douglas J. Moo, *2 Peter, Jude*, NIVAC (Grand Rapids, Michigan, Zondervan, 1997), 201.

22 See the references listed in Beale (*Book of Revelation*, 1043).

23 Oswalt, *Book of Isaiah, Chapters 40–66*, 691.

In Revelation, John regularly reuses material from the Old Testament since he is giving witness to the end times described by many of the prophets before him. In 21:5, he draws on Isaiah 43:19 but changes Isaiah's words from 'I am doing a new thing' to 'I am making everything new!' This addition indicates that the new creation, which was only begun in part, will eventually be completed, including the transformation of the people of God. As Paul writes in 2 Corinthians 5:17, 'if anyone is in Christ, he is a new creation; the old has gone, the new has come!' Thus, Beale concludes: 'All the people of God *together with* the heavens and earth will be transformed into a new creation. The present tense ... does not refer to the present time of the church age but enforces the certainty that the future new creation will occur. It is a "prophetic present"...'[24]

Thus, '[t]he new heaven and the new earth are not alien to the old heaven and the old earth but a fulfillment of it, a continuation and fulfillment of God's original purpose in creation.'[25] The new creation does not merely supersede the old creation. Rather, the new is the result of a heightening and perfecting of the old.[26]

The Disappearance of the Sea

Revelation 21:1 goes on to state that 'the sea existed no more' (NET). On the surface this statement appears to say that one or more of the earth's major bodies of water will cease to exist in the restored creation. But given that this passage is part of an apocalyptic vision, it would be a mistake to equate this sea with the Mediterranean, or the Pacific, Atlantic, or Indian oceans.

Beale notes that elsewhere in Revelation, 'sea' refers to (1) origin of cosmic evil, (2) pagan nations which persecute God's people, (3) the place of the dead, (4) the primary location of idolatrous trade activity, or (5) a literal body of water, and suggests that the reference in 21:1 encompasses to some extent all of these meanings. In other words, when the creation is restored, Satan will no longer be a threat, nor will pagan nations. Neither will there be any death, nor idolatrous trade activity.

Note that this figurative use of 'sea' does not necessarily mean there will be no physical seas in the new creation. Such an interpretation is a possibility given that the sea is often perilous and separates nation from nation, but the allusion to Isaiah 65 and the immediate context suggests that persecution from other nations is primarily in view.[27]

Therefore, to say that 'the sea is no longer' simply means that the corrupt order of things and the power of evil have been removed from John's sight. Indeed, this statement serves to reinforce the passing away of the heavens and

---

24 Beale, *Book of Revelation*, 1052–1053. Original emphasis.

25 Thomas C. Oden, *The Living God: Systematic Theology*, vol. 1 (San Francisco, Harper, 1987), 243.

26 H. Wayne House, 'Creation and Redemption: A Study of Kingdom Interplay' *JETS* 35/1 (March 1992), 5.

27 Beale, *Book of Revelation*, 1042.

the earth.[28] They are no longer a part of John's vision for God's people. As 2 Peter 3:13 states, the new creation will be the home of righteousness.

Purification and Refinement

As noted above, the use of *heuriskō* in 2 Peter 3:10 is most likely an allusion to the smelting of metal ore. A.M. Wolters writes:

> It is striking that for the two occurrences of the absolute use in the letters of Peter [1 Peter 1:7; 2 Peter 3:10] the context in both cases evokes the image of a metal's purification in a melting pot or crucible. Could it be that the common Greek verb *heuriskesthai* has a precise technical sense in the vocabulary of the smelter and refiner? Its meaning would then be something like 'emerge purified (from the crucible),' with the connotation of having stood the test, of being tried and true.

Wolters also points out that this understanding of *heuriskō* is supported by extra-biblical Greek authors.[29]

It appears, then, that the use of *heuriskō* in this text is Peter's method of describing the process of purification and refinement which is destined to occur at the inauguration of the new creation.[30] Peter's statements refer to the purification of the physical world, not the total destruction or annihilation of matter.

This concept of purification and refinement through divine judgment is emphasized by 2 Peter 3:6–7. In this text, there is a clear comparison between the 'destruction' of the present heaven and earth by fire, and the destruction of the world by the global flood in the time of Noah. Note that the flood did not completely destroy the world. Instead, the earth was purged of all wickedness and unrighteousness. Yet, despite the catastrophic nature of the judgment, which totally destroyed everything upon the land, plants from the original creation apparently grew back (Genesis 8:11), and all the various 'kinds' of animals were preserved in the ark along with those few faithful humans (8:13–19).

In the same way that the flood purged the whole earth of wickedness and unrighteousness, the future judgment by fire will also bring about the destruction of all ungodly men, and the purging of all unrighteousness.

In fact, purification and refinement by fire is a common theme in the Old Testament. In Jeremiah 9:7, the Lord proclaims: 'See, I will refine and test them, for what else can I do because of the sin of my people?' In Zechariah 13:9, one third of the people will be brought 'into the fire' and refined like silver and gold. In Ezekiel 22:20–2, the Lord declares: 'As men gather silver, copper, iron, lead and tin into a furnace to melt it with a fiery blast, so will I gather you in

---

28 Ibid, 1041.

29 See the references cited in Wolters, 'Worldview and Textual Criticism in 2 Peter 3:10,' 412 fn. 33.

30 The editors of the UBSGNT recommend the translation 'the earth and its works will be discovered' (i.e. 'found' or 'laid bare'). Even if this translation is taken, the judgment is still one of cleansing or purging rather than a destructive elimination of all that exists. Moo (191) offers the translation 'will be manifest (before God).'

my anger and my wrath and put you inside the city and melt you. I will gather you and I will blow on you with my fiery wrath, and you will be melted inside her. As silver is melted in a furnace, so you will be melted inside her, and you will know that I the LORD have poured out my wrath upon you.' The refiner's fire is also mentioned in Malachi 3:2–3: 'But who can endure the day of his coming? Who can stand when he appears? For he will be like a refiner's fire or a launderer's soap. He will sit as a refiner and purifier of silver; he will purify the Levites and refine them like gold and silver.'

The Curse Removed

Revelation 22:3 declares: 'No longer will there be any curse.' In the new creation, the curse of physical death and suffering, and spiritual separation from God which was unleashed on the human race as a result of Adam's sin in the garden, will be permanently removed.[31] Beale comments:

> Even all the various physical sufferings and sorrows associated with the fallen condition of humanity, to which the redeemed were susceptible, will be entirely removed and will no longer pose a threat in the new order. This means not only that the saints will be free from the danger of separation from God but also that they will be secure from the *entire range* (πᾶν) of persecutions and afflictions threatening them in the former world. Therefore, the removal of the curse includes elimination of both physical and spiritual evils.[32]

Thus, the removal of the curse naturally leads to the elimination of all the adverse effects it has on the physical creation, including suffering and death. These truths are specifically emphasized in the eschatological prophecies of Isaiah 25 and 65:17–25, and John's vision in Revelation 21–22.

Elimination of Suffering and Death

Isaiah prophesies that the Lord will swallow up death forever (25:8). Indeed, He will 'wipe away the tears from all faces.' This sentiment is echoed in Revelation 21:4: 'He will wipe every tear from their eyes. There will be no more death or mourning or crying or pain, for the old order of things has passed away' and 1 Corinthians 15:54–55: 'When the perishable has been clothed with the imperishable, and the mortal with immortality, then the saying that is written will come true: "Death has been swallowed up in victory." Where, O death, is your victory? Where, O death, is your sting?' No longer will humanity experience the futility of death. Neither will there be any need to mourn the death of a loved one. These things are part of the 'old order of things' not a part of the renewed creation in the coming kingdom. The curse of death and its associated sufferings, which were introduced in the first Eden, will be removed in the last Eden.[33]

---

31 Beale, *Book of Revelation*, 1112.

32 Beale, *Book of Revelation*, 1112–1113. Original emphasis.

33 Ibid., 1049.

However, in Isaiah 65:19–22 the prophet appears to be declaring that only *premature death* will be removed. Infants will no longer die and all people will live out their full years. Indeed, anyone who does not live for a hundred years will be judged as being under a curse, and even those who do make it to this age will still be considered a youth. The days of God's people are intended to be as long as the days of a tree. But even if a person lives to a ripe old age, they are still mourned by friends and loved ones. Understanding this text as teaching that death will only come to those who have lived a long time would essentially undermine the central message of the oracle — that death and sorrow will not be part of the coming kingdom. Thus, the picture presented in this prophecy simply refers to the common experience of all humanity in order to stress that these things will not occur in the renewed creation. Rather than denying the complete removal of all death, the prophecy merely declares that all the things which cause sorrow will no longer exist in the restored creation. No one will weep over the untimely death of a loved one since death will not occur at all.[34]

Neither will the new creation experience the futility and frustration characterized by the original creation due to the effects of the fall (65:23). The futility of working the ground, and the scandal of experiencing great pain and even death in child bearing — only to see one's children die before their time — will be cancelled in the coming kingdom of God.[35]

Moreover, there will be no animosity between mankind and the animal world (Isaiah 65:25). The effects of the fall have made nature a potentially dangerous place for mankind. The wolf, lion, and snake symbolize the sheer brutality of the predatorial relationships in the natural world, and all those creatures that are dangerous both to humans and to non-carnivorous animals. But in the new creation, peace and harmony will be restored. Carnivorous activity will cease. Former predators now feed on vegetation alongside their former prey. Humans and animals will have no need to fear each other: 'Nature will no longer be our enemy, nor we its.'[36]

Transformation of the Human Body

In 1 Corinthians 15:39–53, Paul elaborates on the nature of the transformation which God's people will experience when the kingdom is fully established. In this most remarkable passage of Scripture Paul explains that our frail and perishable bodies will be transformed into glorious, imperishable, and immortal vessels:

> All flesh is not the same: Men have one kind of flesh, animals have another, birds another and fish another. There are also heavenly bodies and there are earthly bodies; but the splendor of the heavenly bodies is one kind, and the splendor of the earthly bodies is another. The sun has one kind of splendor, the moon another and the stars another; and star differs from star in splendor.

---

34 Oswalt, *Book of Isaiah, Chapters 40–66*, 658.

35 Ibid., 660.

36 Ibid., 662.

So will it be with the resurrection of the dead. The body that is sown is perishable, it is raised imperishable; it is sown in dishonor, it is raised in glory; it is sown in weakness, it is raised in power; it is sown a natural body, it is raised a spiritual body.

If there is a natural body, there is also a spiritual body. So it is written: 'The first man Adam became a living being;' the last Adam, a life-giving spirit. The spiritual did not come first, but the natural, and after that the spiritual. The first man was of the dust of the earth, the second man from heaven. As was the earthly man, so are those who are of the earth; and as is the man from heaven, so also are those who are of heaven. And just as we have borne the likeness of the earthly man, so shall we bear the likeness of the man from heaven.

I declare to you, brothers, that flesh and blood cannot inherit the kingdom of God, nor does the perishable inherit the imperishable. Listen, I tell you a mystery: We will not all sleep, but we will all be changed — in a flash, in the twinkling of an eye, at the last trumpet. For the trumpet will sound, the dead will be raised imperishable, and we will be changed. For the perishable must clothe itself with the imperishable, and the mortal with immortality.

In Philippians 3:20–21, Paul notes that it is Christ Himself who conducts the transformation of our bodies in order that they become just like His glorious body.[37] In Romans 8:19, he adds that the rest of creation is eagerly awaiting this transformation.

Christ's work on the cross has paved the way for the full restoration of human beings, who will once again serve as full and undistorted image-bearers of God (cf. Genesis 1:26–27). At present, though, God's people only have a foretaste or partial realization of this restoration. Nevertheless, as humans acknowledge Christ as Lord and Savior and become committed to serving him, this restoration progresses. As H. Wayne House put it: 'Heaven gradually comes to earth, though certainly one day this will be so in fullness and glory.'[38]

Liberation and Transformation of the Subhuman World

The transformation at the time of the establishment of the kingdom of God is not limited to human beings, but includes all aspects of creation affected by the fall. Like the transformation of the human body, an actual physical change is in view.

This physical transformation of the natural world is hinted at in Romans 8:19–22: 'The creation waits in eager expectation for the sons of God to be revealed. For the creation was subjected to frustration, not by its own choice, but by the will of the one who subjected it, in hope that the creation itself will be liberated from its bondage to decay and brought into the glorious freedom of the children of God. We know that the whole creation has been groaning as

---

37 cf. Luke 24:36–43 regarding the nature of Christ's resurrection body.
38 House, 'Creation and Redemption,' 11.

in the pains of childbirth right up to the present time.' As George Eldon Ladd comments,

> Creation itself awaits the disclosure of the sons of God when they shall experience the redemption of their bodies, for creation shall be freed from the bondage to decay and shall experience freedom from the burden of evil to which it has been subjected (Rom. 8:19–23). While Paul does not develop this truth of the redemption of nature, there is profound biblical theology underlying it. The redemption of the natural world from evil and decay is the corollary of the redemption of the body. The prophets constantly described the establishment of God's Kingdom in terms of a redeemed world (Isa. 11:6–9; 65:17–25); and the New Testament shares the same theology. Creation is never viewed as something evil that must be escaped. Man as body is a creature of God.[39]

Indeed, God Himself declares that He is 'making *everything* new' (Revelation 21:5, emphasis mine).

Beale explains that the first heaven and earth were 'impermanent and temporary' while the second will be 'permanent and enduring.'[40] There is a figurative depiction of a radically changed cosmos involving not just moral and ethical renovation but 'transformation of the fundamental cosmic structure (including physical elements).'[41]

Although the new creation will be quite distinct from the one that now exists, it will still bear a strong resemblance to the original, in the same way the resurrection body will be different from its former mortal image, yet still resemble a human being.[42]

The restoration of creation effectively reverses the cursed and fallen state. The people of God will no longer toil in vain. A woman's pain in childbirth will be eased, and her children will no longer be doomed to misfortune. The animals will no longer prey upon each other. Instead they will now eat vegetation together (Isaiah 65:23, 25).

Restoration of Paradise

The eschatological vision in Revelation 21–22 presents the Holy City, the new Jerusalem, as the eschatological fulfilment of the Garden of Eden. The garden of peace, beauty, and tranquillity, where God and man walked in harmonious fellowship, now takes the shape of a beautiful, glowing, walled city with twelve gates.

Yet the city has no temple nor does it need light from the sun and moon, for the Lord God and the Lamb are its temple and provide it with light (Revelation

---

39 George Eldon Ladd, *A Theology of the New Testament* (Grand Rapids, Eerdmans, 1974), 567.

40 Ibid.

41 Ibid.

42 Consider, for example, the glorified nature of Christ's post-resurrection body (Luke 24:30–31, 36–43).

21:23).[43] In fact, 'there will be no night there' (Revelation 21:25).[44] In biblical times, the city gates were always closed at sundown for security reasons. But if nightfall never came, the city gates would always remain open. Thus, the point of this vision is not to describe the lighting arrangements in the city but to emphasize that the city gates will always be open, and that God's people will have unlimited access to His glorious presence. Indeed, God's divine glory will be completely manifested because the new creation will contain no more 'darkness' or evil.[45]

A similar point is made in Revelation 22:14, where entering the city through the gates implies free access to the Tree of Life. Therefore, Beale adds '[t]hough direct entrance by humans to the tree of life was blocked by angelic beings throughout history (Gen. 3:24), at the end of history angels stand guard to ensure that they remain open (cf. Rev. 21:12–13).'[46]

Revelation 22:1 also refers to a river of living water which has its origin in God — a clear allusion to the rivers of Eden. Moreover, Trees of Life are lined up on both sides of the river (Ezekiel 47:7, 12; Revelation 22:2).[47] Note that these waters are not just intended to renovate the natural world, but to refresh and to heal the people of God[48] in the same way that the original Tree of Life was able to sustain Adam and Eve. Indeed, the healing effect of the fruit is figurative for the redemption accomplished by Christ which will be consummated at His return.[49]

Thus, it is clear that John understood Ezekiel 47:1–12 as the eternal re-establishment of the Garden of Eden,[50] and both Ezekiel and John envision a time and state where God will openly fellowship with His people as He did with Adam and Eve before the fall.

Note, however, that although these passages promise the restoration of paradise, this involves much more than a mere return to the garden. As Beale points out, there is a certain amount of 'escalation.'[51] In the new creation there will be many Trees of Life, not just a single tree. Furthermore, unlike the original

---

43 The declaration of the absence of the sun and moon is most probably figurative language in accordance with the rest of the vision. As Beale (*Book of Revelation*, 1093) puts it '[t]here may or may not be a literal sun and moon in the new cosmos, but the point here is that God's glory is incomparable in relation to any source of light of either the old or the new creation.'

44 The connecting γὰρ (*gar*) is better translated as an emphatic 'indeed.' See Beale, *Book of Revelation*, 1096.

45 Beale, *Book of Revelation*, 1096.

46 Ibid., 1099.

47 Although Rev. 22:2 has the singular ξύλον (*xulon*, 'tree') Ezek. 47:12 suggests the singular tree is collective for 'trees,' as does logic since a single tree cannot grow on both sides of river. The single Tree of Life in Eden becomes many Trees of Life in the eschatological city-temple, and since all these trees are of the same type they are referred to in the singular.

48 Ezek. 47:12, cf. Isa. 41:17–20, 43:18–20.

49 Beale, *Book of Revelation*, 1108.

50 Ibid., 1107.

51 Ibid., 1106.

garden paradise, which was a limited geographical area, the restored city-temple paradise includes the whole earth. As Beale explains:

> This cosmic reflection of the temple implicitly suggested that its purpose was to point to a future time when it would encompass the whole world ... Since the OT temple was the dwelling of God's presence on earth, the temple's correspondence with the cosmos pointed to an eschatological goal of God's presence tabernacling throughout the earth, an eschatological goal that Rev. 21:1–22:5 appears to be developing ... The Edenic imagery beginning in Rev. 22:1 reflects an intention to show that the building of the temple, which began in Genesis 2, will be completed in Christ and his people and will encompass the whole new creation.[52]

This global extension of the restored city-temple is also suggested by Isaiah 54:2–3, and implied in the parallelism between the new heaven and new earth in Revelation 21:1, 21:2 and the temple-city paradise of 21:9–22:5.[53]

Fellowship with the Creator

The Garden of Eden was the archetypical temple.[54] When Adam and Eve were banished from the garden as a result of their sin, they were not only denied access to the Tree of Life, their rebellion broke their relationship with God. As Beale puts it, 'God's salvific presence does not fully dwell in the fallen creation because of the presence of evil.'[55] No longer were they able to walk in the garden in the presence of their Creator and enjoy His company. Just as Adam and Eve worshiped God and fellowshiped with Him in the original garden paradise, the high priest entered the temple to worship God and experience His presence. Just as cherubim were charged with protecting the entrance to the garden when the first couple were expelled, cherubim also stood on the lid of the Ark of the Covenant, and were embroidered on the curtains separating the Most Holy Place (Exodus 26:31–33). As Starke points out, '[t]he effects of the Fall are thus dramatically revealed in the architecture and furnishings of the earthly tabernacle.'[56]

Yet, the death and resurrection of Christ brought about the reversal of the curse. This began immediately when the curtain separating the Most Holy Place was torn in two (Matthew 27:51), signifying the end of the sacrificial system and the beginning of a new epoch of unrestricted, personal access to God.[57] But when the earth is fully restored and the kingdom fully comes, the curse will be removed altogether (Revelation 22:3). As in the garden, God will then be present

---

52 Ibid., 1110–1111.

53 cf. Isa. 65:17–18.

54 Gordon J. Wenham, *Genesis 1–15* , WBC (Dallas, Word, 1987), 86. Note also the correspondences between Rev. 22:1–2 and Gen. 2:10–15.

55 Beale, *Book of Revelation*, 1096.

56 R. Starke, 'The Tree of Life: Protological to Eschatological' *Kerux* 11/2 (September 1996), 26.

57 See Hagner, 848–849.

with His people (Revelation 21:3). The 'great, high wall' of the heavenly Zion (Revelation 21:12), which is now an unapproachable obstacle, will eventually become a comfort, and the angels guarding the twelve city gates will no longer bar the way with flaming swords, but will welcome weary sojourners as they enter the eschatological rest (cf. Hebrews 4: 1).[58]

Moreover, as Beale points out, the removal of the curse and the ceasing of 'night' (Revelation 22:5) indicates that 'none of the evils and threats of the old world can hinder the saints from fully enjoying the consummate presence of God.'[59]

Creation and Eschatology

Clearly, there is a direct link between the original creation '[i]n the beginning' (Genesis 1:1), and 'the new heavens and the new earth' (Isaiah 65:17; 2 Peter 3:13; Revelation 21:1) of the coming kingdom. As Sailhamer explains: 'The fundamental principle reflected in Genesis 1:1 and the prophetic vision of the times of the end in the rest of Scripture is that the "last things will be like the first things.".... The allusions to Genesis 1 and 2 in Revelation 22 illustrate the role these early chapters of Genesis played in shaping the form and content of the scriptural vision of the future.'[60] He adds: 'The final shape of the Pentateuch reflects an interest in reading the historical narratives both typologically and eschatologically. The events of the past are read as pointers to the future. The future is portrayed as "like" the past.'[61]

Indeed, there are many correspondences and allusions between the Genesis narratives and the eschatological visions in Revelation:

Original Creation	New/Restored Creation
God created the heavens and the earth (Gen. 1:1; 2:1).	A new heavens and a new earth appear (Rev. 21:1).
God created two great lights — one to rule the day, one to rule the night (Gen. 1:16).	There will be no more sun and moon — for God's glory will be its light (Rev. 21:23–24).
The Lord God brought the woman to the man (Gen. 2:22).	The city is prepared as a bride and comes down from God for her husband who is the second Man (Rev. 19:7; 21:2,10).
God walked in the garden with mankind (Gen. 3:8).	God will dwell with mankind (Rev. 21:3).

58 Starke, 30.
59 Beale, *Book of Revelation*, 1049.
60 John H. Sailhamer, *Genesis*, EBC (Grand Rapids, Zondervan, 1976), 20–21.
61 Ibid.

Original Creation	New/Restored Creation
There is good gold, aromatic resin and onyx stone (Gen. 2:12).	The city is made of pure gold, the walls of jasper, and the foundations of the walls are decorated with precious stones (Rev. 21:18–19).
There is a river watering the garden which divides into four rivers (Gen. 2:10).	There is a river of living water (Rev. 22:1).
There is a Tree of Life in the middle of the garden (Gen. 2:9, 3:22).	There are many Trees of Life along both sides of the river (Rev. 22:2).
Anyone who eats the fruit of the Tree of the Knowledge of Good and Evil will surely die (Gen. 2:17).	There will be no more death or mourning (Rev. 21:4).
The pains of child-bearing are increased (Gen. 3:16).	There will be no more crying or pain (Rev. 21:4).
The serpent is cursed and made to crawl on his belly and eat dirt (Gen. 3:14).	The serpent is Satan (Rev. 12:9). He is bound (Rev. 20:2) and thrown into the lake of fire (Rev. 20:10).
Both animals and the ground are cursed (Gen. 2:14, 2:17).	There will be no more curse (Rev. 22:3).

But the most important and theologically significant point is that, despite humanity's rebellion, despite the separation and distortion resulting from the curse, God has not abandoned his creation. There is hope. Christ's death and resurrection have paved the way for God's people to be healed, and for the rest of creation to be released from its bondage to decay. As Figure 11.2 shows, the salvation brought about through Christ's death and resurrection not only enables a person to be justified, by taking away their moral guilt, but also leads to the eventual transformation of nature back into the perfect state of the original creation.

	Humanity	Nature
Creation	Innocent	Perfect
FALL	Adam and Eve sin	
Separation	Guilty	Distorted
SALVATION	Christ's death and resurrection	
Restoration	Justified	Perfect

Figure 11.2: The status of creation throughout salvation history.

Summary

'In the beginning God created the heavens and the earth.' It is no coincidence that this simple proposition is the opening verse of the Bible. This is the key proposition upon which the Christian faith is based. God created the world and everything in it. All humanity is the product of God's creative power, and we all reflect His image. One aspect of God's image is the ability to choose. All humanity has the ability to choose to obey their Creator or to disobey Him. Adam and Eve, however, rejected their Creator's instructions and sinned against God. The ramifications of their rebellion were truly universal. The first couple were expelled from God's presence, and the created world came under a curse which resulted in the great separations and distortions visible in this present world. Creation was never meant to be this way.

It is for this reason that God sent His Son, Jesus Christ, to be a propitiation for humanity's sin. Not only did Christ provide a means of salvation, He began to usher in the kingdom of God where sin and evil will be eradicated. The world is not simply restored to its pre-fall state. It will become something even better — a place of peace, of great pleasure and of unimaginable beauty, where we may dwell forever in communion with our Creator and Savior. This is the 'new creation.' As J.F. Johnson explains:

> A new creation means not simply the reception of certain spiritual gifts, but participation in a new existence, in the new world that has come in Christ. The word 'creation' does not refer primarily to the act of creation, but to the new state which has come in Christ. But this presupposes an act of creation … The same power of God that was active in the creation had now been at work in and through Christ. Thus, the new creation is not entirely discontinuous with the old. It is a restoration of the old to its proper destiny by the unchanging creative Word of God. Creation is thus seen in a christological context, both because Christ is the incarnate Logos in New Testament theology, and because He is the ground of the new humanity. [62]

---

62 As cited by House, 'Creation and Redemption,' 10.

Bibliography

Achtemier, Paul (editor), *Harper's Bible Dictionary*, Harper and Row, San Francisco, 1985.

Albright, William F. 'The Predeuteronomic Primeval' *JBL* 58 (1939).

Amaya, I.E. 'The Bible and God's Revelation in History' *JETS* 14 (Spring 1971).

Anon., 'Pollen-Eating Spiders' *Creation Ex Nihilo* 22/3 (June–August 2000).

Anderson, B.W. 'From Analysis to Synthesis: The Interpretation of Gen 1 – 11' *JBL* 97 (1978).

Aquinas, Thomas, *Summa Theologica*, 1265 – 1273.

Archer, Gleason L. *Encyclopedia of Bible Difficulties*, Zondervan, Grand Rapids, Michigan, 1982.

_____, *Survey of Old Testament Introduction*, Moody Press, Chicago, 1996.

Arnold, Bill T. *Encountering the Book of Genesis*, Baker, Grand Rapids, Michigan, 1998.

Austin, Steven A. 'Mt. St Helens and Catastrophism' *Impact* 157 (July 1986).

Aviezer, N. *In the Beginning: Biblical Creation and Science*, KTAV, Hoboken, 1990.

Baker, Leigh, 'Rising Fears for Academic Freedom' *ANU Reporter* 32/7 (May 11, 2001).

Barber, B. 'Resistance of Scientists to Scientific Discovery' *Science* 134 (1961).

Barentsen, Jack, 'The Validity of Human Language: A Vehicle for Divine Truth' *GTJ* 9 (Spring 1988).

Barlow, Nora (editor), *The Autobiography of Charles Darwin 180–1882*, Collins, London, 1958.

Baris, D., et al., 'Agricultural use of DDT and Risk of non-Hodgkin's Lymphoma: Pooled Analysis of Three Case-control Studies in the United States' *Occupational and Environmental Medicine* 55/8 (1998).

Barr, James, *The Semantics of Biblical Language*, Oxford University Press, Oxford, 1961.

Batten, Donald A. 'Ligers and wolphins? What next?' *Creation Ex Nihilo* 22/3 (June–August 2000).

Bauman, Michael, 'Between Jerusalem and the Laboratory: A Theologian Looks at Science' *JoC* 11/2 (1997).

Beale, Gregory K. *The Book of Revelation*, NIGTC, Eerdmans, Grand Rapids, Michigan, 1998.

Behe, Michael J. *Darwin's Black Box*, Simon & Schuster, New York, 1998.

Beisner, E. Calvin, '*Imago Dei* and the Population Debate' *TrinJ* 18/2 (Fall 1997).

Bergman, Jerry, 'Understanding Poisons from a Creationist Perspective' *JoC* 11/3 (1997).

_____, 'Evolutionary Naturalism: An Ancient Idea' *JoC* 15/2 (2001).

Berkouwer, G.C., *The Providence of God*, Eerdmans, Grand Rapids, Michigan, 1952.

Blackmore, Vernon and Page, Andrew, *Evolution: The Great Debate*, Lion, Oxford, 1989.

Blocher, Henri, *In the Beginning*, translated by D.G. Preston, IVP, Leicester, 1984.

Blum, E. *2 Peter*, EBC, Zondervan, Grand Rapids, Michigan, 1981.

Boice, James Montgomery, *Genesis: An Expositional Commentary 1:1–11:32*, Zondervan, Grand Rapids, Michigan, 1982.

Boorstin, Daniel, 'A Case of Hypochondria' *Newsweek* (July 6, 1970).

Bratton, Susan Power, *Six Billion and More*, Westminster/John Knox, Louisville, Kentucky, 1992

Broderick, R.C. (editor), *The Catholic Encyclopedia*, Thomas Nelson, 1990.

Bruce, F.F. (editor), *The International Bible Commentary*, Zondervan, Grand Rapids, 1979.

Burns, D.E. 'Dream Form in Genesis 2.4b–3.24: Asleep in the Garden,' *JSOT* 37 (1987).

Bush, George, *Notes on the Book of Genesis*, Ivison, Phinney, New York, 1860.

Buswell, J. Oliver, Jr. *A Systemic Theology of the Christian Religion*, Zondervan, Grand Rapids, 1962.

Calvin, John, *Institutes of the Christian Religion*, James Clark, London, 1951.

_____, *Commentaries on the First Book of Moses, Called Genesis*, Eerdmans, Grand Rapids, 1948.

Cameron, Nigel M. de S. *Evolution and the Authority of the Bible*, Paternoster, Exeter, 1983.

Candlish, R.S. *Commentary on Genesis*, Zondervan, Grand Rapids, repr.

Capron, F. Hugh, *The Conflict of Truth*, Jennings and Pye, Cincinnati, 1903.

Carlson, Richard F. (editor), *Science and Christianity: Four Views*, IVP, Leicester, 2000.

Carson, D.A. and Woodbridge, J.D. (editors), *Scripture and Truth*, 2nd edition, Baker, Grand Rapids, Michigan, 1992.

_____, *Hermeneutics, Authority and Canon*, Baker, Grand Rapids, Michigan, 1995.

Cassuto, Umberto, *A Commentary on the Book of Genesis, Part One*, translated by I. Adams, Magness Press, Jerusalem, 1961.

Catchpole, David, 'The Lion that Wouldn't Eat Meat' *Creation Ex Nihilo* 22/2 (March–May 2000).

——————, 'Piranha' *Creation Ex Nihilo* 22/4 (September–November 2000)

Catherwood, C. *Five Evangelical Leaders*, Christian Focus Publications, Fearn, Scotland, 1994.

Cavalieri, Paola, *The Animal Question: Why Non-Human Animals Deserve Human Rights* (translated by Catherine Woollard), Oxford University Press, Oxford, 2001.

Clark, W.M. 'A Legal Background to the Yahwist's Use of "Good and Evil" in Genesis 2–3' *JBL* 88 (1969).

Clarke, A. *The Old Testament*, Hunt and Eaton, New York, n.d.

Cohen, Abraham, *Everyman's Talmud*, Schocken, New York, 1995.

Collins, C. John., *Science and Faith: Friends or Foes?*, Crossway, Wheaton, Illinois, 2003.

Craig, William Lane, 'Evangelicals And Evolution: An Analysis Of The Debate Between The Creation Research Society And The American Scientific Affiliation' *JETS* 17/3 (Summer 1974).

——————————, 'God and Real Time' *RelS* 26 (1990).

Cranfield, C.E.B. *A Critical and Exegetical Commentary on the Epistle to the Romans* vol. 1, ICC, T & T Clark, Edinburgh, 1975.

Cuffey, R.J. 'Bible-Science Symposium' *JASA* 21/4 (1969).

Custance, Arthur C. *Science and Faith: The Doorway Papers* VIII, Zondervan, Grand Rapids, Michigan, 1984 repr.

Davis, John J., *Paradise to Prison*, Sheffield Publishing, Salem, Wisconsin, 1998 repr.

Dabney, R.L. *Lectures in Systematic Theology*, Zondervan, Grand Rapid, Michigan, 1972.

Dahood, M. 'Eblaite ì-du and Hebrew ʾed, "Rain Cloud"' *CBQ* 43 (1981).

Deinhardt, C.L. 'General Revelation as an Important Theological Consideration for Christian Counselling and Therapy' διδασκαλια (Fall 1995).

Demarest, Bruce A. *General Revelation: Historical Views and Contemporary Issues*, Zondervan, Grand Rapids, Michigan, 1982.

Demarest, Bruce A. and Lewis, Gordon R. *Integrative Theology: Knowing Ultimate Reality, the Living God*, 3 vols., Zondervan, Grand Rapids, Michigan, 1987.

Decker, Rodney J. 'Realistic or Historical Narrative?' *JMT* 4/1 (Spring 2000).

Desmond, A. and Moore, J. *Darwin: The Life of a Tormented Evolutionist*, W. W. Norton, New York, 1994.

Diehi, David W. 'Evangelicalism and General Revelation: An Unfinished Agenda' *JETS* 30 (December 1987).

Dillenberger, John, *Protestant Thought and Natural Science*, Doubleday, New York, 1960.

Dockery, David S. (editor), *The Challenge of Postmodernism*, Victor, Wheaton, Illinois, 1995.

Drake, Stillman (editor and translator), *Discoveries and Opinions of Galileo*, Doubleday, New York, 1957.

Dunn, James D.G. *Romans 1–8*, WBC, Word, Dallas, 1988.

_____, *The Epistles to the Collosians and to Philemon*, NIGTC, Eerdmans, Grand Rapids, Michigan, 1996.

Dyrness, William A. 'The *Imago Dei* And Christian Aesthetics' *JETS* 15/3 (Summer 1972).

Edersheim, Alfred, *Bible History: Old Testament*, Hendrickson, Peabody, Massachussets, 1995.

Edwards, J. Gordon, 'Mosquitoes, DDT, and Human Health' *21ˢᵗ Century Science and Technology* 15/3 (Fall 2002).

_____, 'DDT: A Case Study in Scientific Fraud' *Joournal of American Physicians and Surgeons* 9/3 (Fall 2004).

Eichhorst, W.R. 'The Issue of Biblical Inerrancy in Definition and Defense' *GJ* 10 (Winter 1969).

Elbert, Paul, 'Biblical Creation and Science: A Review Article' *JETS* 39 (Jun 1996).

Ellingworth, Paul, *The Epistle to the Hebrews*, NIGTC, Eerdmans, Grand Rapids, Michigan, 1993.

Elton, G.R., *Return to Essentials: Some Reflections on the Present State of Historical Study*, Cambridge University Press, Cambridge, 2002.

Erickson, Millard J. *Christian Theology*, Baker, Grand Rapids, Michigan, 1998.

Fausset, A.R. and Brown, D. *A Commentary on the Old and New Testaments*, Eerdmans, Grand Rapids, 1948.

Fee, Gordon D. and Stuart, Douglas, *How to Read the Bible for All its Worth*, 2ⁿᵈ edition, Zondervan, Grand Rapids, Michigan, 1993.

Feinberg, Charles L. 'The Image of God' *BSac* 129 (July 1972).

_____, *Jeremiah*, in Frank E. Gaebelein (editor), *Isaiah–Ezekiel*, EBC, Zondervan, Grand Rapids, Michigan, 1987.

Feinberg, John S., 'A Baby At Any Cost And By Any Means? The Morality Of In Vitro Fertilization And Frozen Embryos' *TrinJ* 14/2 (Fall 1993).

Finocchiaro, Maurice A. (editor and translator), *The Galileo Affair: A Documentary History*, University of California Press, Berkeley, 1989.

Foh, Susan T. 'What is the Woman's Desire?' *WTJ* 37 (1975).

Forster, Roger and Marston, Paul, *Reason and Faith*, Monarch, Eastborne, 1989.

_____, *Reason, Science and Faith*, Monarch, Crowborough, East Sussex, 1999.

Fouts, David M. 'How Short an Evening and Morning?', *JoC* 11/3 (1997).

_____, 'Selected Lexical and Grammatical Studies in Genesis One' Paper presented at annual meeting of the Evangelical Theological Society, Colardo Springs, 2001.

Francis, David, 'Fuse on the "Population Bomb" has been Relit' *Christian Science Monitor* 99 (May 21, 2007).

Futato, Mark D. 'Because It Had Rained: A Study Of Gen 2:5–7 With Implications For Gen 2:4–25 And Gen 1:1–2:3' *WTJ* 60/1 (Spring 1998).

Geisler, Norman L. (editor), *Innerrancy*, Zondervan, Grand Rapids, Michigan, 1980.

_____, 'The Concept of Truth in the Inerrancy Debate' *BSac* 137 (October–December 1980).

_____, 'The Relation of Purpose and Meaning in Interpreting Scripture' *GTJ* 5 (Fall 1984).

Giberson, Karl, 'Editorial Guidelines: Prejudice or Stewardship?' *Research News & Opportunities in Science and Theology* 2/1112 (July/August 2002).

Goldsworthy, Graeme, *Gospel and Kingdom*, Paternoster, Carlisle, 1981.

_____, *According to Plan*, IVP, Leicester, 1991.

_____, 'Is Biblical Theology Viable?' in R.J. Gibson (editor), *Interpreting God's Plan*, Paternoster, Carlisle, 1998.

_____, *Preaching the Whole Bible as Christian Scripture*, IVP, Leicester, 2000

Goodman, Marvin L. 'Non-literal Interpretations of Genesis Creation' *GJ* 14/1 (Winter 1973).

Grant, P.R., 'Natural Selection and Darwin's Finches' *Scientific American* 265/4 (October 1991).

Grudem, Wayne A. *Systematic Theology*, Zondervan, Grand Rapids, Michigan, 1994.

_____, 'Do We Act as if We Really Believe that "The Bible alone, and the Bible in its entirety, is the Word of God written"?' *JETS* 43/1 (March 2000).

Gwynne, Peter, 'The Cooling World' *Newsweek* (April 28, 1975).

Hagner, Donald A. *Matthew 14–28*, WBC, Word, Dallas, Texas, 1995.

Hagopian, D.G. (editor), *The Genesis Debate*, Crux Press, Mission Viejo, California, 2001.

Hallam, A. *Great Geological Controversies*, 2nd edition, Oxford University Press, New York, 1989.

Ham, Ken A. 'The Relevance of Creation,' *Ex Nihilo* (Casebook II).

Hamilton, Victor P. *The Book of Genesis 1–17*, NICOT, Eerdmans, Grand Rapids, Michigan, 1990.

Hannah, John D. 'Bibliotheca Sacra and Darwinism: An Analysis of the Nineteenth-Century Conflict Between Science and Theology' *GTJ* 4/1 (September 1983).

Harbin, Michael A. 'Theistic Evolution: Deism Revisited?' *JETS* 40/4 (December 1997).

Harris, R. Laird, 'Bible and Cosmology' *BETS* 5 (1962).

_____, 'The Mist, the Canopy and the Rivers of Eden' *BETS* 11 (1968).

Harrison, R.K. *Introduction to the Old Testament*, Eerdmans, Grand Rapids, Michigan, 1969.

Hasel, Gerhard F. *Old Testament Theology: Basic Issues in the Current Debate*, 3rd edition, Eerdmans, Grand Rapids, 1972.

_____, 'The Polemic Nature of the Genesis Cosmology' *EvQ* 46 (1974) 81–102.

_____, 'Some Issues Regarding the Nature and Universality of the Genesis Flood Narrative' *Origins* 5/2 (1978).

_____, 'The Days of Creation in Genesis 1: Literal "Days" or Figurative "Periods/Epochs" of Time?' *Origins* 21/1 (1994).

Hayward, Alan, *Creation and Evolution*, Triangle, London, 1985.

Heilbron, John L. *The Sun in the Church: Cathedrals as Solar Observatories*, Harvard University Press, Cambridge, Massachussets, 1999.

Helweg, Otto J. 'How Long an Evening and Morning?' *JoC* 11/3 (1997).

Henry, Carl F.H. *God, Revelation and Authority*, 6 vols, Word, Waco, Texas, 1976–1983.

Hess, Richard S. 'Genesis 1–2 in its Literary Context' *TynB* 41 (1990).

Hess, Richard S. and Tsumura, David T. (editors), *I Studied Inscriptions from Before the Flood*, Eisenbrauns, Winona Lake, Indiana, 1994.

Hodge, Charles, *What is Darwinism?*, Scribners, New York, 1874.

Hoeksema, Herman, *Reformed Dogmatics*, Reformed Free Publishing, Grand Rapids, Michigan, 1966.

Holmes, A.A. *Principles of Physical Geology*, 2nd edition, John Wiley, London, 1965.

Holmes, Arthur, *All Truth Is God's Truth*, Eerdmans, Grand Rapids, 1977.

Hore-Lacy, Ian, *Responsible Dominion: A Christian Approach to Sustainable Development*, Regent College Publishing, Vancouver, 2006.

House, H. Wayne, 'Creation and Redemption: A Study of Kingdom Interplay' *JETS* 35/1 (March 1992).

Howe, Frederic R. 'The Age of the Earth Part 1: An Appraisal of Some Current Evangelical Positions' *BSac* 142 (January–March 1985).

Humphreys, D. Russell, *Starlight and Time*, Master Books, Green Forest, Arkansas, 1994.

Hunter, D.J., et al., 'Plasma organochlorine levels and the risk of breast cancer' *New England Journal of Medicine* 337 (1997).

ICBI, 'The Chicago Statement on Biblical Inerrancy' *JETS* 21/4 (December 1978).

_____, 'The Chicago Statement on Biblical Hermeneutics' *JETS* 25/4 (December 1982).

James, E.O. *The Tree of Life: An Archaeological Study*, E.J. Brill, Leiden, 1966.

Jardine, Lisa, and Silverthorne, Michael, *Francis Bacon: The New Organon*, Cambridge University Press, Cambridge, 2004.

Jones, T. 'Science and the Bible: Guidelines for Harmonization' *TMC* 4 (Fall 1997).

Jones, W.T., *A History of Western Philosophy*, 2nd edition, 5 volumes, Harcourt, Brace, and World, New York, 1969.

Kaiser, Christopher B. 'Calvin, Copernicus, and Castellio,' *CTJ* 21 (1985).

Kaiser, Walter C. *More Hard Sayings of the Old Testament*, IVP, Downers Grove, Illinois, 1992.

_____, *The Old Testament Documents*, IVP, Downers Grove, Illinois, 2001.

Keil, Carl F. and Delitzsch, Franz, *Biblical Commentary on the Old Testament, The Pentateuch*, Eerdmans, Grand Rapids, 1949.

Kelly, Douglas F. *Creation and Change*, Christian Focus Publications, Fearn, Scotland, 1997.

Kidner, Derek, *Genesis*, TOTC, Tyndale, London, 1967.

Klein, William M., Blomberg, Craig L. and Hubbard, Robbert L. *Introduction to Biblical Interpretation*, Word, Dallas, Texas, 1993.

Kline, Meredith G. 'Because It Had Not Rained' *WTJ* 20 (1958) .

_____, 'Space and Time in the Genesis Cosmogony' *PSCF* 48/1 (March 1996).

Klotz, J.W. *Modern Science in the Christian Life*, Concordia, St. Louis, 1961.

Koestler, Arthur, *The Sleepwalkers*, Hutchinson, London, 1959.

Kruger, Michael J. 'Genesis 6–9: Does "All" Always Mean All?' *JoC* 10/2 (1996).

_____, 'An Understanding of Genesis 2:5' *JoC* 11/1 (1997).

Kuhn, Thomas S. *The Structure of Scientific Revolutions*, University of Chicago Press, Chicago, 1996.

Kulikovsky, Andrew S. 'God's Rest in Hebrew 4:1–11' *JoC* 13/2 (1999).

_____, 'Did mountains really rise?' Letter to the editor, *JoC* 13/2 (1999).

_____, 'A Critique of the Literary Framework View of the Days of Creation' *CRSQ* 37/4 (March 2001).

_____, 'Creation and Genesis: A Historical Survey' *CRSQ* 43/4 (March 2007) 206–219.

——————————, 'Creationism, Science and Peer Review' *JoC* 22/1 (2008).

Kurtz, J.H. *Bible and Astronomy*, 3rd German edition, 1857.

Ladd, George Eldon, *A Theology of the New Testament*, Eerdmans, Grand Rapids, 1974.

LaHaye, Tim and Morris, John D. *The Ark on Ararat*, Thomas Nelson, Nashville, 1976.

Lane, David H. 'Special Creation or Evolution: No Middle Ground' *BSac* 151 (January 1994).

——————————, 'Theological Problems With Theistic Evolution' *BSac* 151 (April 1994).

LaSor, William Sanford, Hubbard, David Allan and Bush, Frederic W. *Old Testament Survey*, 2nd edition, Eerdmans, Grand Rapids, Michigan, 1996.

Lavallee, Louis, 'Augustine on the Creation Days' *JETS* 32/4 (December 1989).

——————————, 'Creeds and the Six Creation Days' *Impact 235* (January 1993).

Leupold, H.C. *Exposition of Genesis*, 2 vols., Baker, Grand Rapids, Michigan, 1949.

Levene, A. *The Early Syrian Fathers on Genesis*, Taylor's Foreign, London, 1951.

Lewis, Arthur, 'The Localization of the Garden of Eden' *BETS* 11 (1968).

Lewis, Jack P. 'The Days of Creation: An Historical Survey of Interpretation' *JETS* 32/4 (December 1989).

Lindberg, David C. and Numbers, Ronald L. (editors), *God and Nature*, University of California Press, Berkeley, 1986.

——————————————————, 'Beyond War and Peace: A Reappraisal of the Encounter Between Christianity and Science' *PSCF* 39/3 (September 1987).

Livingston, George Herbert, *Genesis*, BBC, Beacon Hill Press, Kansas City, Missouri, 1969.

Livingstone, David N. 'Science and Religion: Towards a New Cartography' *CSR* 26/3 (Spring 1997).

Long, V. Philips, *The Art of Biblical History*, Zondervan, Grand Rapids, Michigan, 1994 .

Lubenow, Marvin L. *Bones of Contention*, Baker, Grand Rapids, Michigan, 1992.

——————————, 'Pre-Adamites, Sin, Death and the Human Fossils' *JoC* 12/2 (1998).

Lund, Nils W. *Chiasmus in the New Testament*, Hendrickson, Peabody, Massachusetts, 1992.

MacRae, Allan A. 'The Scientific Approach to the Old Testament Part 1' *BSac* 110 (January 1953).

_____, 'The Scientific Approach to the Old Testament Part 2' *BSac* 110 (April 1953).

_____, 'The Scientific Approach to the Old Testament, Part 3' *BSac* 110 (July 1953).

_____, 'The Principles of Interpreting Genesis 1 and 2' *BETS* 2/4 (1959).

Mann, Michael, et al., 'Global-Scale Temperature Patterns and Climate Forcing Over the Past Six Centuries' *Nature* 392 (1998).

_____, 'Northern Hemisphere Temperatures During the Past Millennium: Inferences, Uncertainties, and Limitations' *Geophysical Research Letters* 26 (1999).

Marshall, I.H., Millard, A.R., Packer, J.I., and Wiseman, D.J. (editors) *The New Bible Dictionary*, Tyndale House, Wheaton, Illinois, 1962.

May, R.M. 'How Many Species Are There on Earth?' *Science* 241 (1988).

McCabe, Rovert V. 'A Critique of the Framework Interpretation of the Creation Account (Part 1)' *DBSJ* 10 (2005) 19–67.

_____, 'A Critique of the Framework Interpretation of the Creation Account (Part 2)' *DBSJ* 11 (2006) 63–133.

McCormack, Arthur, *The Population Explosion: A Christian Concern*, Harper & Row, New York, 1973.

McCune, Rolland D. 'The Formation of the New Evangelicalism (Part One): Historical and Theological Antecedents' *DBSJ* 3/1 (Fall 1998).

McGrath, Alister E. *A Scientific Theology, Volume 1, Nature*, Eerdmans, Grand Rapids, Michigan, 2001.

McIntyre, Stephen and Ross McKitrick, 'Correction the Mann et. al. (1998) Proxy Data Base and Northern Hemispheric Average Temperature Series' *Energy & Environment* 14/6 (2003).

_____, 'Hockey Sticks, Principal Components, and Spurious Significance' *Geophysical Research Letters* 32 (2005).

_____, 'The M&M Critique of the MBH98 Northern Hemisphere Climate Index: Update and Implications' *Energy & Environment* 16/1 (2005).

_____, 'Reply to Comment by von Storch and Zorita on "Hockey Sticks, Principal Components, and Spurious Significance"' *Geophysical Research Letters* 32 (2005).

_____, 'Reply to comment by Huybers on "Hockey sticks, principal components, and spurious significance"' *Geophysical Research Letters* 32 (2005).

McKenzie, J.L. 'The Literary Characteristics of Genesis 2–3' *TS* 15 (1954).

Mcquilkin, Robertson and Mullen, Bradford, 'The Impact of Postmodern Thinking On Evangelical Hermeneutics' *JETS* 40/1 (March 1997).

Mendelsohn, Robert and Neumann, James E. (editors), *The Impact of Climate Change on the United States Economy*, Cambridge University Press, Cambridge, 1999.

Metzger, Bruce M. *A Textual Commentary on the Greek New Testament*, 2nd edition, United Bible Societies, New York, 1994.

Miles, Sara Joan, 'From Being to Becoming: Science and Theology in the Eighteenth Century' *PSCF* 43/4 (December 1991).

Moo, Douglas J. *2 Peter, Jude*, NIVAC, Zondervan, Grand Rapids, Michigan, 1997.

Moore, J.R. *The Post-Darwinian Controversies*, Cambridge University Press, Cambridge, 1979.

Moran, Bruce T. 'The Universe of Philip Melanchthon: Criticism and Use of the Copernican Theory' *Comitatus* 4 (1973).

Moreland, J.P. and Reynolds, J.M. (editors), *Three Views on Creation and Evolution*, Zondervan, Grand Rapids, Michigan, 1999.

Morris, Herbert W. *Science and the Bible*, Ziegler and McCurdy, Philadelphia, 1871.

Morris, Leon and Burdick, D.W. *Hebrews and James*, EBC, Zondervan, Grand Rapids, Michigan, 1996.

Mortenson, Terry, 'British Scriptural Geologists in the First Half of the Nineteenth Century' Unpublished Ph.D. dissertation, University of Coventry, 1996.

_____, 'British Scriptural Geologists in the First Half of the Nineteenth Century: Part 1, Historical Setting' *JoC* 11/2 (1997).

_____, 'British Scriptural Geologists in the First Half of the Nineteenth Century: Part 2, Granville Penn (1761–1844)' *JoC* 11/3 (1997).

_____, 'British Scriptural Geologists in the First Half of the Nineteenth Century: Part 3, George Bugg (1769–1851) *JoC* 12/2 (1998).

_____, 'British Scriptural Geologists in the First Half of the Nineteenth Century: Part 4, Andrew Ure (1778–1857) *JoC* 12/3 (1998).

_____, 'British Scriptural Geologists in the First Half of the Nineteenth Century: Part 5, Henry Cole (1792?–1858) *JoC* 13/1 (1999).

_____, 'British Scriptural Geologists in the First Half of the Nineteenth Century: Part 6, Thomas Gisborne (1758–1846) *JoC* 14/1 (2000).

Morton, Glenn R. 'The Mediterranean Flood' *PSCF* 49/4 (1997).

Muller, Richard A. *Dictionary of Latin and Greek Theological Terms*, Baker, Grand Rapids, Michigan, 1985.

Munday, John C. Jr., 'Creature Mortality: From Creation or the Fall?' *JETS* 35/1 (March 1992)

_____, 'Eden's Geography Erodes Flood Geology' *WTJ* 58/1 (Spring 1996).

Murphy, James G. *A Commentary on the Book of Genesis*, Draper, Andover, 1887.

Murray, John, *The Epistle to the Romans*, NICNT, Eerdmans, Grand Rapids, Michigan, 1968.

Newman, Robert C. and Eckelmann, Herman J. Jr., *Genesis One and the Origin of the Earth*, IVP, Downers Grove, Illinois, 1977.

Niessen, Richard 'Theistic Evolution and the Day-Age Theory' *Impact* 81 (March 1980).

Noegel, Scott B. *Puns and Pundits: Word Play in the Hebrew Bible and Ancient Near Eastern Literature*, CDL Press, Bethesda, Maryland, 2001.

Noll, Mark A. 'Traditional Christianity and the Possibility of Historical Knowledge' *CSR* 19/4 (June 1990).

_____, *The Scandal of the Evangelical Mind*, Eerdmans, Grand Rapids, Michigan, 1994.

Numbers, Ronald L. *The Creationists*, University of California Press, Berkeley, 1993.

Oden, Thomas C. *The Living God: Systematic Theology*, vol. 1, Harper, San Francisco, 1987.

_____, 'Response to Hugh Ross on General Revelation' *PC* 21/1 (Summer 1998).

Orr, James, *The Christian View of God and the World as Centering in the Incarnation*, Eerdmans, Grand Rapids, Michigan, 1960.

Osborne, Grant R. *The Hermeneutical Spiral*, IVP, Downers Grove, Illinois, 1991.

Oswalt, John N. *The Book of Isaiah, Chapters 40–66*, NICOT, Eerdmans, Grand Rapids, Michigan, 1998.

Ouro, Robert 'The Earth of Genesis 1:2: Abiotic or Chaotic? Part 1' *AUSS* 35/2 (1998).

Parker, Don, *Using Biblical Hebrew in Ministry*, University Press of America, Lanham, Maryland, 1995.

Payne, David F. *Genesis One Reconsidered*, Tyndale, London, 1964.

Pearson, Paul N. 'In retrospect: Setting the Evolutionary Record Straight On Darwin and Hutton' *Nature* 425 (16 October 2003).

Pelikan, J.P. and Lehmann, H. (editors), *Luther's Works*, vol. 1, US edition, Concordia, St. Louis, 1955.

Pennant, David F. 'Alliteration in Some Texts of Genesis' *Bib* 68/3 (1987).

Petersen, David L. 'The Yahwist on the Flood,' *VT* 26 (1976).

Phillips, Perry G. 'Are the Days of Genesis Longer Than 24 Hours? The Bible Says, "Yes!"' *IBRIRep* 40 (1990).

Pink, Arthur W. *Gleanings in Genesis*, Moody Press, Chicago, 1922.

Pipa, Joseph A. and Hall, David W. (editors), *Did God Create in Six Days?* Southern Presbyterian Press, Taylors, SC, 1999.

Pitman, John R. (editor), *The Whole Works of the Rev. John Lightfoot D.D.*, 13 vols, J. F. Dove, London, 1822–1825.

Porter, R. *The Making of Geology*, Cambridge University Press, Cambridge, 1977.

Pratt, Richard L. *He Gave Us Stories*, P & R Publishing, Phillipsburg, New Jersey, 1990.

Pritchard, James B. *The Ancient Near East vol. 1: An Anthology of Texts and Pictures*, Princeton University Press, Princeton, 1958.

Pun, Pattle P.T. 'A Theology of Progressive Creation' *PSCF* 39/1 (March 1987).

Radday, Y.T. 'The Four Rivers of Paradise,' *HS* 23 (1982).

Radmacher, Earl D. and Preus, Robert D. (editors), *Hermeneutics, Inerrancy and the Bible*, Zondervan, Grand Rapids, Michigan, 1984.

Ramm, Bernard, *The Christian View of Science of Scripture*, Paternoster, London 1955.

Regan, Tom, *The Case for Animal Rights*, University of California Press, Berkeley, California, 2004.

Reisman, George, *Capitalism: A Treatise on Economics*, Jameson Books, Ottawa, Illinois, 1998.

Remine, Walter J. *The Biotic Message*, Saint Paul, 1993.

Roberts, Donald R., 'To Control Malaria, We Need DDT!' *21st Century Science and Technology* 15/3 (Fall 2002).

Rockwell, Llewellyn H., 'Government Garbage' *Free Market* 8/2 (February 1990).

Ronan, Colin, *Galileo*, Putnam's Sons, New York, 1974.

Rooker, Mark F. 'Genesis 1:1–3: Creation or Re-creation? Part I' *BSac* 149 (July 1992).

——————————, 'Genesis 1:1–3: Creation or Re-creation? Part II' *BSac* 149 (October 1992).

Ross, Allen P. *Creation and Blessing*, Baker, Grand Rapids, Michigan, 1996.

Ross, Hugh N. *Genesis One: A Scientific Perspective*, Wisemen Productions, Sierra Madre, California, 1983.

——————————, *Creation and Time*, NavPress, Colorado Springs, 1994.

——————————, 'General Revelation: Nature's Testament' *PC* 21/1 (Summer 1998).

——————————, *The Genesis Question*, NavPress, Colorado Springs, 1998.

Roth, David L. 'Genesis and the Real World' *Kerux* 9/2 (September 1994).

Roth, W.M.W. 'The Numerical Sequence x/x+1 in the Old Testament,' *VT* 12 (1962).

Runia, David T. *Exegesis and Philosophy: Studies on Philo of Alexandria*, Variorum, Aldershot, 1990.

Rupke, N.A. *The Great Chain of History: William Buckland and the English School of Geology 1814–1849*, Clarendon Press, Oxford, 1983.

Russell, Jeffrey Burton, *Inventing the Flat Earth*, Praeger, London, 1997.

———————, 'The Myth of the Flat Earth,' Unpublished paper presented at the American Scientific Affiliation Conference, Westmont College, August 4, 1997.

Ryan, W.B.F., Pitman, W.C., Major, C.O., Shimkus, K., Moskalenko, V., Jones, G.A., Dimitrov, P., Gorur, N., Sakinc, M. and Yuce, H. 'An Abrupt Drowning of the Black Sea Shelf' *Marine Geology* 138 (1997).

Ryan, W.B.F. and Pitman, W.C. *Noah's Flood: The New Scientific Discoveries About the Event That Changed History*, Simon & Schuster, New York, 1998.

Ryle, H.E. *The Book of Genesis*, Cambridge University Press, Cambridge, 1921.

Ryrie, Charles C. 'The Bible and Evolution' *BSac* 124 (January 1967).

Sailhamer, John H. *Genesis*, EBC, Zondervan, Grand Rapids, Michigan, 1976.

———————, *The Pentateuch As Narrative*, Zondervan, Grand Rapids, Michigan, 1992.

———————, *Genesis Unbound*, Multnomah, Sisters, Oregon, 1996.

de Santillana, Giorgie, *The Crime of Galileo*, University of Chicago Press, Chicago, 1955.

Sarfati, Jonathan, 'A Review of The Genesis Question' *JoC* 13/2 (1999).

Sawyer, M. James, *The Survivor's Guide to Theology*, Zondervan, Grand Rapids, Michigan, 2002.

Schaeffer, Francis A., *Complete Works of Francis A. Schaeffer*, 2nd edition, 5 vols, Crossway, Wheaton, Illinois, 1985.

Schirrmacher, Thomas, 'The Galileo Affair: History or Heroic Hagiography?' *JoC* 14/1 (2000).

Schweitzer, Albert, *The Philosophy of Civilization*, Prometheus, Buffalo, New York, 1987.

Sedgwick, Adam, 'Anniversary Address of the President, 1831' *Proceedings of the Geological Society of London* 1 (1831).

Seely, Paul H. 'The Three Storied Universe' *JASA* 21/1 (1969).

———————, 'Adam and Anthropology: A Proposed Solution' *JASA* 22/3 (September 1970).

———————, 'The Firmament and the Water Above. Part I: The Meaning of raqiya' in Gen. 1:6–8' *WTJ* 53/2 (1991).

———————, 'The Firmament and the Water Above. Part II: The Meaning of "the water above the firmament" in Gen. 1:6–8' *WTJ* 54/1 (1992).

———————, 'The Geographical Meaning of "Earth" and "Seas" in Genesis 1:10' *WTJ* 59/2 (1997).

———————, 'The First Four Days of Genesis in Concordist Theory and Biblical Context' *PSCF* 49/2 (1997).

Shedd, W.G.T. *Dogmatic Theology*, Zondervan, Grand Rapids, Michigan, 1971.

Skinner, John, *A Critical and Exegetical Commentary on Genesis*, ICC, T & T Clark, Edinburgh, 1910.

Smith, Gary V. 'Structure and Purpose in Genesis 1–11' *JETS* 20/4 (December 1977).

Snelling, Andrew A. 'Iceland's recent "Mega-flood"' *Creation* 21/3 (June–August 1999).

Speiser, E.A. *Genesis*, ICC, Doubleday, New York, 1964.

Spetner, Lee R. *Not By Chance*, Judaica Press, 1998.

Staley, Samuel R., *The Sprawling of America: In Defence of the Dynamic City*, Policy Study No. 251, Mackinac Center for Public Policy and Reason Public Policy Institute (February, 1999).

Stallard, Michael, 'Literal Interpretation: The Key to Understanding the Bible' *JMT* 4/1 (Spring 2000).

Stambaugh, James, 'The Meaning of "Day" in Genesis' *Impact* 184 (October 1988).

——————, 'The Relationship Between Sin and Death in Genesis: Death Before Sin?' *Impact* 191 (May 1989).

——————, 'Creation's Original Diet and the Changes at the Fall' *JoC* 5/2 (1991).

——————, 'Creation, Suffering and the Problem of Evil' *JoC* 10/3 (1996).

Stark, Rodney, *For the Glory of God*, Princeton University Press, Princeton, New Jersey, 2003.

Starke, R. 'The Tree of Life: Protological to Eschatological' *Kerux* 11/2 (September 1996).

Steinman, Andrew, 'אחד as an Ordinal Number and the Meaning of Genesis 1:5' *JETS* 45/4 (December 2002).

Sterchi, David A. 'Does Genesis 1 Provide a Chronological Sequence?' *JETS* 39/4 (December 1996).

Steyn, Mark, *America Alone*, Regnery, Washington DC, 2006.

Stigers, Harold G. *A Commentary on Genesis*, Zondervan, Grand Rapids, 1976.

Stoner, Don, *A New Look at an Old Earth*, Harvest House, Eugene, Oregon, 1997.

Stott, John R.W. *Understanding the Bible*, Regal, Glendale, California, 1972.

Strong, Augustus H. *Systematic Theology*, Judson Press, Philadelphia, 1956.

Takayama, S., et al, 'Effects of Long-term Oral Administration of DDT on Nonhuman Primates' *Journal of Cancer Research and Clinical Oncology* 125/3–4 (1999).

Tappert, Theodore G. (editor and translator), 'Table Talk,' *Luther's Works,* Vol. 54, general ed. Helmut T. Lehmann, Fortress Press, Philadelphia, 1967.

Taylor, Charles V. 'Who Wrote Genesis? Are the *Toledoth* Colophons' *JoC* 8/2 (1994).

_____, 'Did mountains really rise according to Psalm 104:8?' *JoC* 12/3 (1998).

Tenney, Merrill C. 'The Bible and History' *JETS* 14 (Spring 1971).

Terry, Milton S. *Biblical Hermeneutics,* 2nd edition, Zondervan, Grand Rapids, 1974.

Thaxton, Charles B., Bradley, Walter L. and Olsen, Roger L. *The Mystery of Life's Origin,* Lewis and Stanley, Dallas, 1984.

Thiessen, Henry C. *Lectures in Systematic Theology,* rev. Vernon D. Doerksen, Eerdmans, Grand Rapids, Michigan, 1979.

Thomas, Robert L. 'General Revelation and Biblical Hermeneutics,' *TMSJ* 9 (Spring 1998).

Torrance, Thomas F. *The Christian Frame of Mind: Reason, Order, and Openness in Theology and Natural Science,* Helmers and Howard, Colarado Springs, 1989.

Torrey, R.A. et. al. (editors), *The Fundamentals,* vol. 1, Baker, Grand Rapids, Michigan, 1972.

Trefil, James, *The Dark Side of the Universe,* Macmillan, New York, 1988.

Tsumura, David T. *The Earth and the Waters in Genesis 1–2,* Sheffield Academic Press, Sheffield, 1989.

_____, 'A Note on הרון (3,16)' *Bib* 75 (1994).

Van Bebber, Mark and Taylor, Paul, *Creation and Time: A Report on the Progressive Creationist Book by Hugh Ross,* Eden Communications, Gilbert, Arizona, 1996.

Vandermey, H. Ronald, *Hosea,* Everyman's Bible Commentary, Moody, Chicago, 1981.

VanGemeren, Willem A. *The Progress of Redemption,* Zondervan, Grand Rapids, Michigan, 1988.

_____, *Psalms,* EBC, Zondervan, Grand Rapids, Michigan, 1991.

Van Groningen, G., 'Interpretation of Genesis' *JETS* 13/4 (Fall 1970).

Van Till, Howard J. *Portraits of Creation,* Eerdmans, Grand Rapids, Michigan, 1990.

van't Veer, P., et al., 'DDT (dicophane) and Postmenopausal Breast Cancer in Europe: Case-control Study' *British Medical Journal* 315 (July 12, 1997).

Von Rad, Gerhard, *Old Testament Theology,* vol. 1, Oliver and Boyd, Edinburgh, 1962.

_____, *Genesis: A Commentary,* OTL, rev. ed., Westminster, Philadelphia, 1973.

Vos, Gerhardus, *Biblical Theology*, Banner of Truth, Edinburgh, 1975.

Walker, Tasman B. 'The Pitch for Noah's Ark' *Creation Ex Nihilo* 7/1 (1984).

—————————, 'The Black Sea Flood: Definitely Not the Flood of Noah' *JoC* 14/1 (2000).

Walsh R. E. (editor), *Proceedings of the Third International Conference on Creationism*, Technical Symposium Sessions, Creation Science Fellowship, Pittsburgh, 1994.

Waltke, Bruce K. 'The Creation Account in Genesis 1:1–3 Part I' *BSac* 132 (January 1975).

—————————, 'The Creation Account in Genesis 1:1–3 Part II' *BSac* 132 (April 1975).

—————————, 'The Creation Account in Genesis 1:1–3 Part III' *BSac* 132 (July 1975).

—————————, 'The Creation Account in Genesis 1:1–3 Part IV' *BSac* 132 (October 1975).

—————————, 'The First Seven Days' *CT* 32 (1988).

—————————, *Genesis*, Zondervan, Grand Rapids, Michigan, 2001.

Walton, John H. *Genesis*, NIVAC, Zondervan, Grand Rapids, Michigan, 2001.

Warfield, B.B. *Biblical and Theological Studies*, Presbyterian and Reformed, Philadelphia, 1968.

Wells, Jonathan, *Icons of Evolution*, Regnery, Washington D.C., 2002.

Wenham, Gordon J. 'The Coherence of the Flood Narrative' *VT* 28 (1978).

—————————, *Genesis 1–15*, WBC, Word, Dallas, Texas, 1987.

Whitcomb, John C., 'Biblical Inerrancy and the Double Revelation Theory' *GJ* 4 (Winter 1963).

White, Andrew Dickson, *A History of the Warfare of Science with Theology in Christendom*, 2 vols., New York, 1896.

White, Robert, 'Calvin and Copernicus: The Problem Reconsidered' *CTJ* 15 (1980).

Wieland, Carl W. 'Regenerating Ribs' *Creation* 21/4 (September 1999).

Wilcox, W. Bradford, 'Fertility, Faith and the Future of the West: An interview with Phillip Longman' *Christianity Today* 13/3 (May/June 2007).

Williams, Donald T. 'The Great Divide: The Church and the Post-Modernist Challenge' Paper presented at the annual meeting of the Evangelical Theological Society, Colorado Springs, November 14, 2001.

Williams, Pete J. 'What Does *min* Mean?' *JoC* 11/3 (1997).

—————————, 'Did Mountains Really Rise?' Letter to the editor, *JoC* 13/1 (1999).

Wiseman, P. J. *Creation Revealed in Six days*, Marshall, Morgan and Scott, London, 1948.

Wolters, A.M. *Creation Regained*, Paternoster, Carlisle, 1996.

_____, 'Worldview and Textual Criticism in 2 Peter 3:10' *WTJ* 49/2 (Fall 1987).

Woodbridge, John D. 'Recent Interpretations of Biblical Authority Part 3: Does the Bible Teach Science?' *BSac* 142 (July–September 1985).

Woodmorappe, John, *Noah's Ark: A Feasibility Study*, ICR, El Cajon, California, 1996.

Yew, Quek Suan and Khoo, Jeffrey, 'The Bible and Science: Progressive Creationism examined in the light of Scripture' *The Burning Bush* 8/1 (January 2002).

Young, Davis A. *Creation and the Flood*, Baker, Grand Rapids, Michigan, 1977.

_____, *Christianity and the Age of the Earth*, Zondervan, Grand Rapids, Michigan, 1982.

_____, 'Scripture in the Hands of Geologists (Part One),' *WTJ* 49/1 (Spring 1987).

_____, 'Scripture in the Hands of Geologists (Part Two)' *WTJ* 49/2 (Fall 1987).

Young, E.J. *Studies in Genesis One*, Baker, Grand Rapids, Michigan, 1964.

Young, G. Douglas, 'The Relevance of Scientific Thought to Scriptural Interpretation,' *BETS* 4/4 (1961).

Young, Richard Alan, 'The Knowledge of God in Romans 1:18–23' *JETS* 43 (December 2000).

Youngblood, Ronald F. (editor), *The Genesis Debate*, Thomas Nelson, Nashville, 1986.

_____, *The Book of Genesis*, 2nd edition, Baker, Grand Rapids, Michigan, 1991.

Scripture Index